The Late and Post-dictatorship Cinephilia Boom and Art Houses in South Korea

To Bae Wŏn-ae

The Late and Post-dictatorship Cinephilia Boom and Art Houses in South Korea

Andrew David Jackson

Edinburgh University Press is one of the leading university presses in the UK. We publish academic books and journals in our selected subject areas across the humanities and social sciences, combining cutting-edge scholarship with high editorial and production values to produce academic works of lasting importance. For more information visit our website: edinburghuniversitypress.com

© Andrew David Jackson, 2024, 2025

Grateful acknowledgement is made to the sources listed in the List of Illustrations for permission to reproduce material previously published elsewhere. Every effort has been made to trace the copyright holders, but if any have been inadvertently overlooked, the publisher will be pleased to make the necessary arrangements at the first opportunity.

Edinburgh University Press Ltd
13 Infirmary Street,
Edinburgh, EH1 1LT

First published in hardback by Edinburgh University Press 2024

Typeset in 12/14 Arno and Myriad by
IDSUK (Dataconnection) Ltd

A CIP record for this book is available from the British Library

ISBN 978 1 3995 1420 0 (hardback)
ISBN 978 1 3995 1421 7 (paperback)
ISBN 978 1 3995 1422 4 (webready PDF)
ISBN 978 1 3995 1423 1 (epub)

The right of Andrew David Jackson to be identified as the author of this work has been asserted in accordance with the Copyright, Designs and Patents Act 1988, and the Copyright and Related Rights Regulations 2003 (SI No. 2498).

Contents

List of tables and figures vii
Preface x
Acknowledgements xii
Note on romanisation, names, film titles and currency xiv
Abbreviations xv
Chronology xvi
Map of venues treated in this volume xvii

Introduction 1

Part 1 Rise

1 Late-dictatorship and post-1987 political and cultural influences on the emergence of cinephilia and art film exhibition 31

2 Non-theatrical exhibition and the emergence of an art film audience 54

3 The theatrical exhibition of art film and Korean cinephilia, 1987–95 85

4 *The Sacrifice*, the Dongsung Cinematheque, film media and the shaping of a new audience, 1995–6 113

Part 2 Decline

5 Challenges to art houses and the decline of cinephilia in a period of Korean cinematic expansion 149

Part 3 Legacy

| 6 | The new millennium evolution of state support for art film exhibition | 175 |
| 7 | Maintaining art houses in the new millennium | 200 |

Conclusion	229
References	240
Appendices	255
Index	264

Tables and figures

Tables

3.1	Hoam Art Hall programming schedule, 1987–92	88
4.1	Attendances at the Dongsung Cinematheque, November 1995–October 1996	126
4.2	Average 1996 importation, distribution and exhibition costs for art films at the Dongsung Cinematheque	137
4.3	Selected international film festivals in South Korea, 1995–2000	140
5.1	Annual attendances for art movies (Seoul)	154
5.2	State-led expansion of Korean entries to international film festivals	159
6.1	The number of art (and independent film) theatres in Korea (2005–13)	188
7.1	Art houses included in Chapter 7	203

Figures

I.1	Crowds waiting for the start of the Jean-Luc Godard evening at the Dongsung Cinematheque, 25 April 1997 (courtesy Lee Kwang-mo).	2
P1.1	Images of the Munhwahakkyo Seoul videotheque (R) and its extensive video archive (L) (courtesy Kim Sŏng-uk).	29
1.1	Multi-use commercial buildings. (L) The Cine Core cinema in 2003 (courtesy Roald Maliangkay, 2022). (R) Site of	

	Ewha Art Theatre in Shinch'on that was typical of the location of many cinemas in the 1980s (author's photo).	46
1.2	Hand-painted posters (*kanp'an*) from the 1970s (L) and from 1988 (R) that were a regular feature of Korean cinemas (courtesy Roald Maliangkay, 2022).	46
1.3	Advertising cards for Ewha Art Theatre from late 1980s (Yu 2015).	47
2.1	Copy of a pamphlet produced by the Munhwahakkyo Seoul to accompany screenings (courtesy Kang Kyoung Lae; permission courtesy Kim Sŏng-uk).	73
2.2	Second issue of *Yŏnghwaŏnŏ* carrying articles on independent Korean film *Declaration of Fools* (Pabosŏnŏn, 1983, Lee Chang-ho, ROK), Andrzeh Wajda (photo, author's collection; permission courtesy Jae Jeon).	74
3.1	Hoam Art Hall newspaper advertising for *Cinema Paradiso* in *Chosŏn Ilbo*, 7 July 1990 (source: Park Kyŏng-ae, HMJ Films).	89
3.2	Map of early art houses in Kangnam; created by Elspeth McVey © Openstreetmap contributors.	91
3.3	Newspaper advertising for *Like Water for Chocolate* (L; source unknown, *Chosŏn Ilbo*, 5 June 1993) and the Italian feature *The Raffle* in the *Dong-a Ilbo*, 12 June 1993 (R; courtesy Park Kyŏng-ae, HMJ Films).	96
3.4	The Core Building in Chongno which housed the Core Art Hall, and which still carries the cinema's name (author's photos).	99
3.5	*Cine 21* from 1995 reflecting the cinephilia of the period. No. 26 (L) investigated women filmmakers and pornography, and no. 27 (R) celebrated the latest French art film release by Krzysztof Kieślowski (courtesy *Cine 21*).	104
3.6	Women make up most of the crowds for the Jean-Luc Godard evening at the Dongsung Cinematheque, 25 April 1997 (courtesy Lee Kwang-mo).	105
4.1	Issues of *Kino*: (L) July 1998; (R) May 1998 (courtesy Kim Chong-wŏn).	121
4.2	Headlines of *Han'gyŏrae* newspaper articles in 1996 championing Lee Kwang-mo's Dongsung Cinematheque and reporting on collaboration with *Cine 21* (courtesy Korean Press Foundation).	125

4.3	Dongsung Cinematheque promotional materials. (L) Guide to the 1995 schedule featuring the cinema's motto: 'The cinematic world you have always dreamed of'. (R) Booklet produced to advertise Peter Greenaway's *The Draughtsman's Contract* (1982, UK). Images courtesy Lee Kwang-mo.	129
4.4	Image of pre-screening talk before the Jean-Luc Godard evening at the Dongsung Cinematheque, 25 April 1997 (courtesy Lee Kwang-mo).	133
4.5	Crowds of cinephiles trying to enter the Jean-Luc Godard evening at the Dongsung Cinematheque, 25 April 1997 (courtesy Lee Kwang-mo).	142
P2.1	Former Dongsung Art Centre in Taehangno, location of Hypertheque Nada, from 2021 the Seoul Foundation for Arts and Culture (Seoulmunhwajaedan) (author's image).	147
5.1	Korea Cinema pamphlet produced by the KMPPC to promote special screenings of domestic films at the 1998 Montreal International Film Festival (courtesy Yi Chae-u, KOFIC).	158
5.2	February 1998 issue of *Kino* (courtesy of Kim Chong-wŏn).	160
5.3	Map of art houses in central Seoul, created by Elspeth McVey © Openstreetmap contributors.	167
P3.1	Seoul Art Cinema advertising, Kyŏnghyang Sinmun Building, Seoul (2022; author's photo, courtesy Kim Sŏng-uk).	173
6.1	Features from early editions of KOFIC's art sector publication *Next Plus* (2 and 3) showing features dedicated to art film exhibitors at the Sponge House and Cinecube (courtesy: KOFIC; *Cine 21*).	192
7.1	Ticket to screening of *Green Fish* and post-film talk with Lee Chang-dong (author's image).	205
7.2	Location of DRFA 365 (courtesy Jonathan Yu, author's image).	206
7.3	The Ewha Women's University campus centre in which the Art House Momo is housed (courtesy Lee Kwang-mo).	207
7.4	Film books and posters in the Seoul Art Cinema foyer (author's image).	208
7.5	The Art House Momo box office (courtesy Lee Kwang-mo).	210
7.6	Film posters in the hallway of the Seoul Art Cinema (author's image).	211
7.7	The Cinecube auditorium (courtesy Lee Kwang-mo).	214

Preface

I recall a 1996 trip with friends to see *Land and Freedom* (1995, Ken Loach, UK) at the Dongsung Cinematheque in Seoul. We arrived late, and the auditorium seemed darker on that particular day, and when we managed to find our seats, in the blackness of the theatre, I remember my companions seemed to disappear. My seat was rock hard, and nothing made it more comfortable, no matter how much I moved around in it. After what in my memory seemed a considerable amount of time, but may have been only a minute, my seat appeared to move, then it shuddered, and then it developed a voice and spoke to me. I stood up to discover I had not been sitting on the plush upholstered cinema seat I had expected but on an elderly man who somehow had managed to bear my frame. Apologising, I took my proper seat and the rest of the screening passed without interruption. This auditorium incident highlighted a central issue about the cinematic experience for me. For while the Ken Loach film, the performances, the famous debate sequences, its portrayal of a complex historical tragedy was very memorable, equally memorable was the auditorium encounter that took up no more than a couple of minutes at the very start. I will forever associate *Land and Freedom* with a specific, although unusual experience of spatiality and as such, this film joins many others linked indelibly in my memory with a specific venue: *Seven Samurai* (*Shichinin no Samurai*, 1954, Akira Kurosawa, Japan) at the Hampstead Everyman, *Thief* (1981, Michael Mann, US) at the Cameo, Edinburgh, *Down by Law* (1986, Jim Jarmusch, US) at the Pasqueno, Trastevere, *Parasite* (*Kisaengch'ung*, 2019, Bong Joon-ho, Republic of Korea, hereafter, ROK) at the Palace, Balwyn. These picture houses changed an ordinary movie-watching experience into something that remains timeless. There is something about the cinematic space, the feeling of sitting in the darkened auditorium, its ritualistic quality, an experience that apparently seems so secondary to the overall sensation of movie viewing but that still remains memorable and meaningful to audiences. Cultural scholars like Dudley Andrew (2002 [1986]) and Roland Barthes (1975) have written poetically of the post-theatrical sense of loss – of feeling a different person from the one who had entered the cinema. What is so transformative about a visit to a cinema? Why is it, in an era where motion pictures are readily available at the touch of a button and at a fraction of the cost of a cinema visit, that people still go to watch movies at theatres? In part, to answer these questions – to understand the hold cinemas can have over us – I started this project, which investigates those spaces themselves. I also look at a particular moment of cinephilia (*sinep'illia*)[1] that occurred in the ten-year period from the late 1980s onwards, and that resulted in a transformation of the significance of the cinema space for many young Koreans. By strange coincidence, I was in Korea at the time of the cinephilia described in this study, and it passed me by entirely, even though I was living approximately 500 metres from the Dongsung Cinematheque, the nominal epicentre of this cinematic revolution. This cinephilia was part of my eleven years in Seoul, and the desire to fill in the past gaps and examine events that barely registered with me at the time proved a strong motivating force for research. I was left with an urge to explore what I had missed, things that had been in front of my eyes all the time.

Note

1. Or 'cine-mania' – see Chapter 3 for an analysis of these terms.

Acknowledgements

I dedicate this work to my wife, Bae Won-ae, who has never wavered in her ongoing fight against cancer. Our Sunday matinees in the old Chongno cinemas of the early 1990s were happy moments and the inspiration for this book.

Map courtesy of Elspeth McVey who used the following source to complete her maps: https://en.wikipedia.org/wiki/Module:Adjacent_stations/Seoul_Metropolitan_Subway © Openstreetmap contributors.

There are many people I wish to thank for their help and their contributions to this work: Brother Anthony of Taizé, Ravi Arya, Baek Moon-im, Cho Hye-in, Jinhee Choi, Choi Sang-hee, Chŏn Hyo-jun, Chŏng Sŏng-il, Chung Chong-hwa, Gloria Davies, Russell Edwards, Shuhei Hosokawa, David Hundt, Perry Iles, Jae Jeon, Sam Johnson, Kang Kyoung Lae, Kim Chong-wŏn of *Kino*, Kim Hong-jun (Kim Hong-joon), Kim Hyo-jŏng, Kim Hyo-sin of the Korean Press Foundation, Kyung-hyun Kim, Kim Mi-hyŏn, Kim Nan-suk, Kim Shin Dong, Kim Sŏng-uk, Kim Young-jin, Irene Hee-Seung Lee, Gillian Leslie, Roald Maliangkay, Niall McMahon, Sonia Dueñas Mohedas, Flynn Nauta, Markus Nornes, Oh Sung-ji, Park Ch'an-sik, Park Jai young, Park Kyŏng-ae of HMJ Films, Madeleine Probst (Watershed, Film Hub South West, Europa Cinemas, UK), Peter Rist, Sin A-ho of Art House Momo, Isolde Standish, Carolyn Stevens, Sung Kyoung-suk, Phil Wickham of the Bill Douglas Cinema Museum, University of Exeter, Yi Chae-u of KOFIC, Yi Ha-na, Jonathan Yu (Yu Sang-uk), Yun Sŏng-gŭn, Bev Zalcock, Yvonne Schulz Zinda, the moderators of the site Extreme Movie and the anonymous peer reviewers for their insightful comments. I also owe a huge debt to Lee Kwang-mo (Kwang-mo Lee), who spoke to me when he was extremely ill, and Father

Kevin Kersten SJ, who took the time to answer my questions from his retirement home in the United States. This book could not have been completed without the assistance of Bae Wŏn-ae. Any errors in this work are my own.

This work was supported by the Core University programme for Korean Studies through the Ministry of Education of the Republic of Korea and the Korean Studies Promotion Service of the Academy of Korean Studies (AKS-2017-OLU-2250002).

Note on romanisation, names, film titles and currency

I have used Pinyin without diacritics to romanise Chinese, Hepburn for Japanese and McCune-Reischauer for Korean except in the case of commonly accepted alternative spellings for places like Seoul. I have used the Korean order of names with surname first and given names hyphenated, as in Ch'oe Nam-sŏn, used Park instead of Pak. The exception is well-known names like Park Chung Hee and author names where I have followed the spellings provided. I have divided up Korean words according to Korean spacing rules. As a historian, I am aware of the importance of names in legitimizing political authority and use 'Korea' and 'Korean' to refer to South Korea for the sake of convenience. Film titles are cited by: English title, translation, year of production, director, country of origin, and where identifiable, box office admissions. All admissions are for Seoul cinemas, unless indicated otherwise. I provide all numerical figures in US dollars based on historical exchange rates. For example, in 1996, US$1 was equivalent to 794 Korean won, although there was significant fluctuation during the Asian financial crisis of 1997–8.[1]

Note

1. I found historical exchange rates using FX Top (2022).

Abbreviations

* An asterisk indicates a pseudonym for a respondent who requested anonymity.

Chronology

This chronology includes political leaders featured in this book. South Korean presidents (and dates in office)

1961–79	Park Chung Hee (Park Chŏng-hŭi; 1917–79)
1980–8	Chun Doo Hwan (Chŏn Tu-hwan; 1931–2021)
1988–93	Roh Tae Woo (No T'ae-u; 1932–2021)
1993–8	Kim Young Sam (Kim Yŏng-sam; 1927–2015)
1998–2003	Kim Dae Jung (Kim Tae-jung; 1924–2009)
2003–8	Roh Moo-hyun (No Mu-hyŏn; 1946–2009)
2008–13	Lee Myung-bak (Yi Myŏng-bak; 1941–)
2013–17	Park Geun-hye (Park Kŭn-hye; 1952–)
2017–22	Moon Jae-in (Mun Chae-in; 1953–)

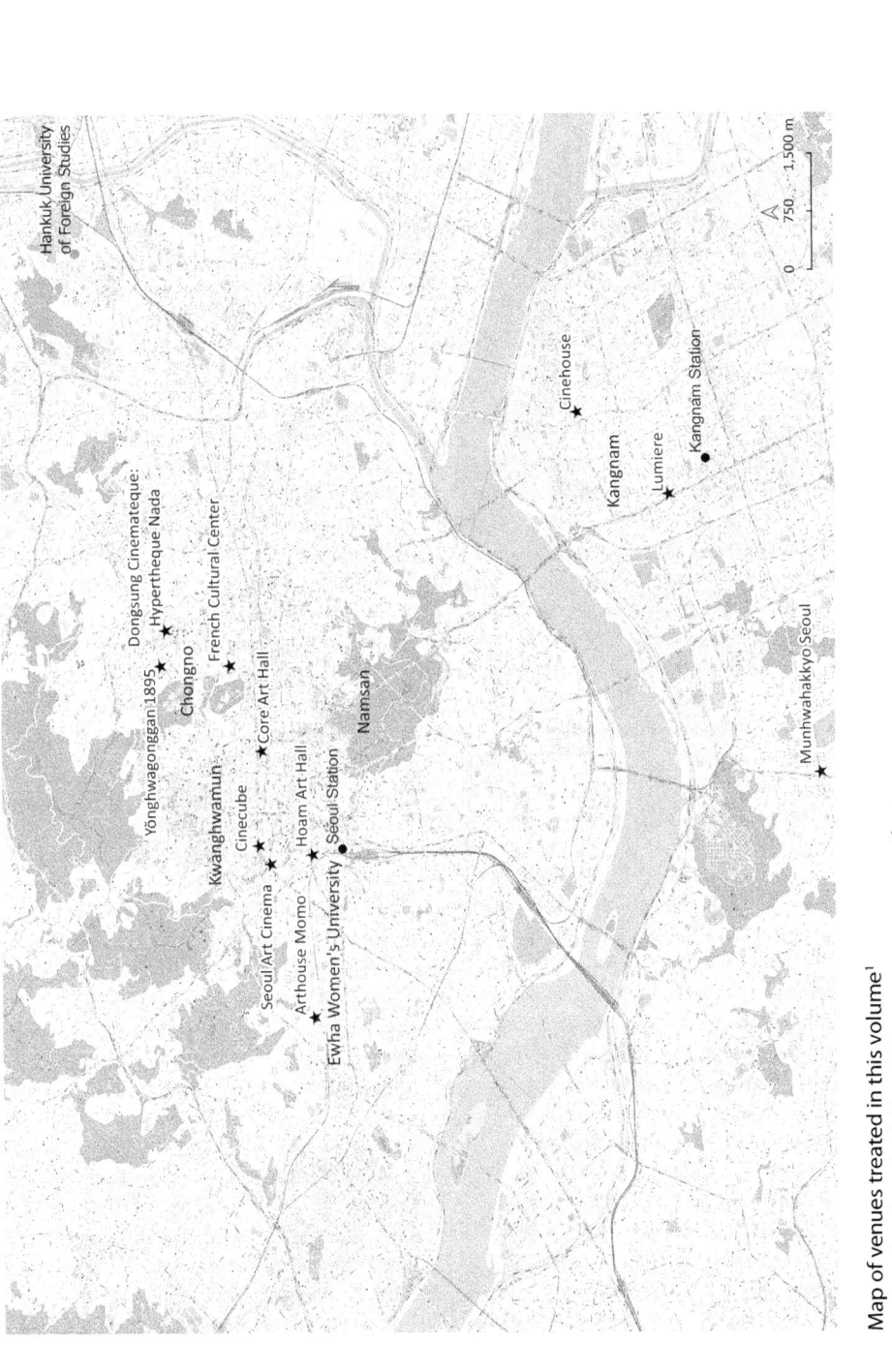

Map of venues treated in this volume[1]
Created by Elspeth McVey, © Openstreetmap contributors.

---

[1] This map shows the historical location of Seoul Art Cinema before it moved to Kwanghwamun in 2021.

Introduction

On 25 February 1996, the eminent scholar of visual and literary arts Susan Sontag published a short essay, 'The Decay of Cinema', in the *New York Times Magazine* to commemorate the centenary of the creation of motion pictures. In her article, Sontag bemoaned the state of commercial film that had become 'bloated (and) derivative ... a brazen combinatory or recombinatory art' (Sontag 1996). Sontag's piece is not just a critique of the decline of cinema; it reflects the passing of the era of the lover of film – the cinephile (a notion discussed in detail below). She argues that with an inferior product, 'predictably, the love of cinema has waned'. This was not any old consumption of movies but 'a certain taste in films (grounded in a vast appetite for seeing and reseeing as much as possible of cinema's glorious past) ... Cinephilia has no role in the era of hyperindustrial films' (Sontag 1996). Filmmaking, she argues, went hand in hand with the love for movies, and only if love for film were resurrected could good filmmaking take place (Sontag 1996).

Sontag's essay is polemical, and many scholars have attacked her dismissal of commercial filmmaking in favour of art film. I discuss this controversial category of movie in depth below, but for our purposes, art film can be understood as motion pictures that play at festivals or art houses, eschew stylistic conventions of mainstream films and have platform releases (Berliner 2018: 68).[1] David Desser criticised Sontag's assertion of the death of cinephilia as simplistic and dismissive of cultures of film consumption in Asia and elsewhere (Desser 2005). Desser's critique is apt because cinephilia certainly had not decayed in South Korea (hereafter, Korea). On the same day Sontag published her essay, audiences packed out the Dongsung Cinematheque – a small 200-seat movie theatre in the Taehangno theatre district of central Seoul – to see *Nostalgia* (*Nostalghia*, 1983, Italy-USSR) by Soviet director Andrei Tarkvosky. A further 11,918 spectators saw the movie that month (Yi Nam 1997). Over the next year, *Nostalgia* would not be the only art film to fill the Dongsung Cinematheque. Abbas Kiarostami's *Where is the Friend's House? (Khane-ye dust kojast*, 1987, Iran) drew 48,209 spectators (outperforming heavily marketed, widely released Hollywood films), while Theo Angelopoulos's *Landscape in the Mist* (*Topio stin Omichili*, 1988, Greece) sold 38,052 tickets. The audience numbers were remarkable considering the subject matter and obscurity of some films shown, but the Dongsung Cinematheque wasn't an exception. Art film flourished in theatres around Seoul and was on the increase in cinemas in the provinces. Korea was in the middle of a wave of cinephilia that grew in tandem with a brief period of intense art film consumption. Cinemas set up libraries and lectures to teach their audiences about movies that had never been screened in Korea before (Figure I.1). Audiences filled art house auditoriums. 'All of cinema is an attempt to perpetuate and to reinvent that sense of wonder', Sontag (1996) argues, and between 1987 and 1998 many audiences embraced that sense of wonder with a passion that is unusual in Korean cultural history. In this period, the activities of Korean cinema fans represented the type of cinephilia that Sontag claimed was dead. Never before – and perhaps never again – would art film be consumed with such intensity in Korea (Rayns 1998).

Figure I.1 Crowds waiting for the start of the Jean-Luc Godard evening at the Dongsung Cinematheque, 25 April 1997 (courtesy Lee Kwang-mo).

Many of the participants saw (and still see) their involvement in this 1990s cinephilia as more than a love for film consumption. 'If you look back at this period from now, this was like our May 1968', claims Kim Sŏng-uk, managing director of the Seoul Art Cinema (author interview, April 2021). Another chief participant in the cinephilia boom, art filmmaker, distributor and exhibitor Lee Kwang-mo says of this end-of-century Korean cinephilia: 'We were carried along by the spirit of the times (*sidaejŏngsin*), we wanted to make a new world through film' (personal correspondence, Lee Kwang-mo, May 2020). Noted film critic Chŏng Sŏng-il said of this period: 'Everything came together at the same time. It was the start of the world we had always dreamt of . . . It was the start of the era of the cinephile' (cited in Paek 2011). For Kim, Lee and Chŏng, the consumption of Tarkovsky, Kiarostami and Angelopoulos films by Korean cinephiles was part of a bottom-up attempt at the cultural reconstruction of a society just recently unshackled from three decades of military rule. Kim, Lee and Chŏng, like many others, saw cinematic transformation as central to the process of democratising socio-political shifts. Freedom did not come with the removal of the pernicious and invasive influence of military rule from the ruling institutions of state, but when the dictatorship was exorcised from the cultural body of the population. This period of artistic renewal was followed by a period of commercial success in Korean film. From late 1998, Korean cinema began one of the most remarkable transformations in fortune in cinematic history, from an industry on the verge of collapse to one of the few places where domestic film captures over 50 per cent market share compared to overseas film.

The intense period of cinematic consumption began with the Korean film industry practically on its knees and ended at precisely the time Korean cinema began its upward trajectory. In cinematic terms, it wasn't just cinephilia that occurred within these few years. In addition to the opening of new exhibition spaces for art film, this period saw an explosion in film print media, the creation of Korea's first international festivals, the rapid establishment of film studies departments in domestic universities, the creation of multiplexes and distribution methods that revolutionised domestic cinematic consumption. The post-1987 period of Korean film saw the emergence of some of the most celebrated directors of the new millennium – Park Chan Wook, Lee Chang-dong, Bong Joon-ho[2] and many others. The mid-to-late 1990s in South Korean cinema – of which this cinephilia was a part – was an intense period of cinematic development.

Questions remain about this brief period of cinephilia and art film exhibition in Korea, particularly relating to the factors that led to it taking place when it did, its character and its significance. Why did this cinephilia emerge at the end of Korean military rule (1961–87), and how did it flourish in post-dictatorship Korea? Who was involved in shaping this moment of widespread art film exhibition and consumption, and what were their motivations? What cinematic cultures formed in exhibition spaces due to this cinephilia and interest in art film and what characterises them? Why and how was the cinephilia of the period so intimately connected to art film viewing? Why did the cinephilia decline when it did? There is also the question of the legacy of this period. How has it been remembered in academic, media and public discourses? What influences did it leave behind on art film exhibition, audiences and the state institutional bodies regulating a diversified cinematic industry? How is it connected to the subsequent success of South Korean film? This book investigates these questions about late-dictatorship and post-1987 cinephilia, art film exhibition and its legacy. It attempts to fill a gap in our understanding of the history of the Korean film industry by looking beyond filmmakers and films and focusing on the links between the culture generated in exhibition spaces and the current state of Korean cinema.

Despite an upsurge of English-language publications on Korean film, there has been little coverage of the 1980s and 1990s rise and fall of art cinema and cinephilia and their impact on the industry. Most previous book-length studies have sought to understand the reasons behind the renaissance of Korean cinema without analysing this specific 1990s cinephilia and art film exhibition in great depth. Much of this research by Shin and Stringer (2005), McHugh and Abelmann (2005), and Kim (2004: 2011) focuses on motion pictures, their stars and directors, with a particular emphasis on textual analysis. Other studies, like Darcy Paquet's 2009 *New Korean Cinema: Breaking the Waves*, Brian Yecies and Aegyung Shim's *The Changing Face of Korean Cinema: 1960 to 2015* (2016) and Min Eunjung, Joo Jinsook and Kwak Han Ju's *Korean Film: History, Resistance, and Democratic Imagination* (2003), also emphasise the shifting cinematic, regulatory, economic and political context when accounting for the transformation of Korean film.

Several recent studies, in particular, have shifted the focus away from texts and onto audiences and important institutions within Korean film that emerged in the 1990s and contributed to the new millennium expansion of the industry. Here 'institution' refers to social and state constructs collectively created and maintained over periods, including academia, media outlets, industries and state regulating agencies (Andrews 2013: 174). Ahn Soo-jeong's *The Pusan International Film Festival, South Korean Cinema and Globalization* (2012) considers the critical role of the Pusan (Busan) International Film Festival (hereafter, BIFF) in globalising the popularity of Korean film and in influencing regional cinematic production. Lee Hyunseon's *Korean Film and Festivals: Global Transcultural Flows* (2022) builds on the ground established by Ahn and investigates the interaction between South Korean directors and domestic and overseas international film festivals. Lee argues that international festivals are locations of transcultural, transnational encounters that have helped establish a 'cultural value' in post-millennium Korean cinema (Lee 2022: 32). In *Unexpected Alliances: Independent Filmmakers, the State, and the Film Industry in Postauthoritarian South Korea* (2015) Park Young-a argues that the Korean independent film movement played an extremely influential role in shaping the current Korean cinema industry. She observes that filmmakers active in both 1980s anti-dictatorship student groups and the independent film movement emerged as influential figures within the main state body administering Korean cinema, the KMPPC (or Korean Motion Picture Promotion Corporation, Han'guk yŏnghwajinhŭnggongsa) and from 1999, KOFIC (the Korean Film Council, Han'guk yŏnghwajinhŭngwiwŏnhoe). Through these steering roles, former activist filmmakers helped control the direction of Korean cinema. These studies investigate vital institutions of Korean cinema that emerged in the 1990s and subsequently influenced later cinematic industrial development.[3] Jimmyn Parc and Patrick Messerlin's 2021 volume *The Untold Story of the Korean Film Industry: A Global Business and Economic Perspective* is an economic analysis of South Korean film's success in comparison with other cinematic industries in Asia, Europe and beyond. Their work is notable because it investigates the impact of state cultural policies and institutions like KOFIC on Korean cinematic development. Another work which takes a different approach from Park and Ahn is nonetheless ground-breaking for its rich ethnographic examination of South Korean audiences and film consumption. In *Campus Cinephilia in Neoliberal South Korea: A Different Kind of Fun*, a monograph based on her 2012 PhD dissertation, Josie Jung Yeon Sohn (2022) argues that the audience tastes that led to the new millennium spike in domestic consumption of Korean film should not simply be characterised as 'consumer nationalism' (2022: 2). Sohn finds evidence of alternative forms of consumption amongst the cosmopolitan cinephilia of Korean university film clubs between 2008 and 2009. Her study is relevant to my book since it analyses the development of the film movement and university film clubs and considers new millennium developments in some of the leading Seoul art houses and their interactions with cinephile fans.

Other essays, book chapters and dissertations (Kim et al. 2004; Kim Soyoung 2005; Kim Sunah 2007b; Paquet 2009; Yi Sŏn-ju 2014; Park 2014; Hwang Ha-yŏp 2017) consider elements of the 1990s cinephilia and art film boom, and of these Kim Soyoung (So-yŏng) (2005), Park (2014) and Hwang (2017) provide the most in-depth analysis of its importance to Korean cinema. Kim (2005) argues that the rise of cinephilia grew in tandem with the 'festival fever' (yŏnghwaje yŏlp'ung) accompanying the establishment of multiple international film festivals by local governments in Korea. She contends that the craze for movies and festivals was a manifestation of post-dictatorship era identity politics.[4] Park A-na (2014) considers the 1990s growth of competing varieties of cinephilia amongst young people in South Korea. In general, however, there has been far less English-language focus from researchers on the history of film exhibition. Apart from Hwang Ha-yŏp's study of the twenty-first-century development of Seoul art houses no research focuses on the historical emergence of commercial exhibition spaces as catalysts for the development of film cultures within South Korea.

There are several reasons for this lack of focus on this late-dictatorship and post-1987 cinephilia and art film exhibition. In accounting for the development of Korean cinema since the 1990s, the phenomenal international success of films like *Parasite* has resulted in an academic focus on stars and directors and the interpretation of cinematic texts rather than anthropological investigation of exhibition practices and contexts. Robert C. Allen has argued that it took several decades to 'dethron(e) the text . . . and textual interpretation' in the study of US film history (Allen 1990: 347). In the Korean case, the focus on film texts is understandable given the highly concentrated period of the cinematic industry's rapid expansion.

Another reason for this general lack of focus on cinephilia and art houses is a critical association of art films exhibited and consumed during this boom period with an 'elitist' form of cinematic production that was 'petrified' because it lacked social relevance during a period when many young filmmakers and film fans argued for the necessity of more politically engaged cinema (Kim Sunah 2007b: 346; Park 2015: 161; Betz 2009).[5]

In addition, there is the apparent insignificance of movie theatres and of the art film sector within Korean cinema as a whole. As critic and scholar Kim Hong-jun has observed of widespread attitudes towards venues: 'Theatres are only a platform to make money for the film industry.' For many looking into Korean film, exhibition spaces have no cultural value (Kim and Lee 2022: 217). Art film consumption in any given year only accounts for a small percentage of the overall cinema market.[6] Interest in art film consumption and cinephilia may also appear to be a diversion from the primary debate about 1990s Korean cinema, which is how the industry managed to survive and flourish. The 1990s increase in art film consumption, after all, happened when many in the industry were uncertain whether direct distribution by Hollywood majors would be the nail in the coffin for the Korean film industry, following a trend that had seen the demise of cinematic industries in Mexico and Taiwan (Yecies 2007: 2; Park 2015: 92). Hollywood majors had direct distribution rights in South Korea from 1987 onwards, giving them a distinct advantage in the domestic film market; a transformation examined in more detail in Chapter 1. Steve Neale argues that Hollywood's international dominance is 'nearly always conceived by the countries whose markets it dominates as a specifically national problem', necessitating a national, cultural and political solution (Neale 1981: 34). According to Neale, critics conceptualise the debate over Hollywood dominance as a binary opposition: them vs us, powerful vs weak, exploiter vs exploited. Framing the remarkable renaissance of Korean film as a victory of domestic culture over the Hollywood behemoth is part of what defines the Korean cinematic success story. Central to this narrative is this sense of opposition that it fought back against Hollywood. Many (but not all) of the movies that helped fuel increased art film consumption and exhibition in the decade of cinephilia were foreign, a fact that may have contributed to the lack of focus. For what role does foreign art film consumption play in this oppositional narrative?[7]

Framing art film exhibition in late-dictatorship and post-1987 South Korea

There are good reasons why art cinema, art houses and this period of cinephilia are worth reconsidering, as I argue in the chapters that lie ahead, but I precis here. First, it is crucial to understand the consumption of art movies within the cinematic market. Although the art film sector in Korea is currently small, art film exhibition still merits analysis. The seat occupancy rates of art film as a percentage of total movie consumption in Korea have been far higher than in other countries historically – occasionally reaching 10–15 per cent of the market (Kim et al. 2004: 27).[8] The people who view art film make up a particularly vocal community of Korean film consumers who help influence the state policy shaping the physical cinematic landscape.

A second reason for understanding art film exhibition is its importance to Korean film's institutional framework. The art film sector occupies a key place within the Korean cinematic industry serving as a defence against commercial domination of the market. The screen quota system (SQS) has been a focus of research for scholars attempting to explain the protection and revival of a Korean film industry opened to unrestricted direct competition from Hollywood majors (Berry 2002: 9–10; Yecies 2007: 1–2; Shim 2011: 225; Parc and Messerlin 2021: 69–72). But there has been little interest in the internal quota system designed to guarantee screening windows for art and independent film and prevent commercial motion pictures from monopolising exhibition. Domination of exhibition by successful commercial narrative film is a contentious issue within Korean film circles, and critics regard both quota systems as a vital means of protecting smaller films (Kim Ji-soo 2020; Howard 2008: 88; Shim 2011: 220–1). Examining the attempts to regulate the art film sector during and after the boom provides an important insight into the state-level understanding of cinema and official involvement in its regulation.

Finally, we should examine the art film boom and its influence in more detail because of the centrality of audiences and exhibition spaces to cinematic development. Many studies have rightly concluded that the filmmakers – the producers, directors, investors – and the films they produce represent the source of the transformation within Korean cinema. However, our understanding of Korean cinematic development is facilitated by inquiry into the role of audiences as agents for change and cinemas as cultural spaces of transformation. The rising interest in art film was consumer-led, shaped by exhibitors and a transformed political and media environment. Exhibitors individually took the financial risk to screen art movies, and audience demands led to the emergence of art houses.

There are also vital historical and socio-political reasons for examining the rise of cinephilia in late-dictatorship and post-1987 South Korea. As evidenced by the statements of Kim Sŏng-uk, Lee Kwang-mo and Chŏng

Sŏng-il that begin this introduction, the 1990s cinephilia and widespread desire to watch art movies represented far more to the participants than film consumption. They believed their cinephilia was linked to socio-political shifts that occurred within post-1987 South Korea. This was a time of institutional transformation between dictatorship and representative government. The military authorities had spent the best part of three decades preventing challenges to their autonomy by restricting the flow of ideas and cultural products into the country. The unravelling of authoritarian structures brought widespread changes amongst younger generations who shifted from political activism to cultural consumption – the shift from the 'era of ideology' (*inyŏmsidae*) to the 'cultural period' (*munhwasidae*) (Yi Sŏn-ju 2017: 432). The belief systems of these younger generations were in a state of considerable flux, moving from a popular and insular ethno-nationalism to a more willing embrace of international cultures. These socio-political shifts occurred throughout post-dictatorship South Korea, but these changes found expression in cinema, especially in the culture of audiences and exhibition spaces.

Finally, there has been a significant focus on texts, textual interpretation and industrial factors such as distribution and investment in relation to the dramatic transformation of Korean cinema; however, there has been less interest in exploring the cinematic practices, experiences and networks that link exhibition with media discourses and state regulating agencies. Exhibition spaces cannot simply be regarded as 'autonomous, neutral, static places' that contain audiences and films randomly thrown together (Allen 2006: 24). I argue that exhibition spaces also have a formative influence on creating a Korean cinematic viewing culture.

Aims, theoretical and historical approaches to art film exhibition

This book is a history of art film exhibition and consumption between late-dictatorship Korea and 2022, focusing on the upsurge in art film-related cinephilia between 1987 and the 1997–8 Asian financial crisis.[9] I examine the links between increased consumption of art film and the development of exhibition practices to cater to the demands of a new group of cinema fans. I consider the political, socio-economic and cultural forces that led to this interest in art film and the motivation of the people who participated in the cinephilia. I investigate the emergence of independent art houses as central locations for this boom, as well as the interactions of exhibitors with cinephile audiences, the media and the state-level administrators responsible for governing the industry. The book also includes an analysis of why cinephilia and art film consumption went into steep decline. The narrative examines the legacy of this *fin de siècle* art film boom and cinephilia – the institutional and physical influences and the links to the present success of Korean film. It concludes by considering the current state of independent art houses and the challenges facing them in the third decade of the new millennium. The book addresses the memorialisation of this art film boom and its place in Korean cinema's personal, scholarly and media histories.

This study is both a chronological history of a period in Korean cinema and an argument about the impact of a moment of cultural renewal on the industry. The stress throughout is on art cinema audiences and exhibitors and I am concerned with the influence of consumption and exhibition practices on a Korean cultural identity emerging from the trauma of military rule. The book offers a snapshot of an industry in flux during a critical period before take-off, it also provides a historical point of reference from which to reflect on the current flourishing cinema. It gives an insight into a time of great cinematic creation, viewed from the frontline by the exhibitors and audiences. My argument draws on two strands: first, theories about cultural production in society from scholars of film, anthropology and cultural studies; second, investigations of the significance of the theatrical space in our understanding of film exhibition and consumption.

To understand how art film exhibitors established a market for their products in late-dictatorship and post-1987 Korea, I use ideas around cultural institutions and power developed by Pierre Bourdieu (1980), refined by film sociologists Andrew Tudor (2006) and Shyon Baumann (2007) and historian Barbara Wilinsky (1996: 2001) to refer specifically to art film exhibition. Bourdieu argues that cultural industries are part of larger fields of power and that they represent sites of constant struggle for economic and cultural dominance (Tudor 2006: 125). Different agents, such as publishers, gallery owners, film exhibitors and distributors, contest this struggle for economic gain and dominance in the market. Some agents consecrate individual products as art to disavow their economic value and promote their cultural worth (Bourdieu 1980: 161; Wilinsky 1996: 143).[10] In so doing, individual agents gain cultural capital by improving their status as experts and help increase the long-term potential for economic gain by extending their product's cultural shelf life (Bourdieu 1980: 289; Tudor 2006: 126).

Bourdieu's conceptualisation of taste also helps us understand what led audiences to embrace foreign forms of culture, particularly European art film in late and post-dictatorship Korea. In *Distinction*, Bourdieu argues that taste is a mechanism that is crucial to naturalising the ranking and structuring of society (Bourdieu 1984: 68; Harbord 2002: 6). Notions of high and low culture are a means people use to create their status in society; these distinctions between what is deemed high or low culture are not objectively determined but socially constructed (Bourdieu 1984: 250). Education plays a vital role in forming particular taste cultures and provides people from outside the traditional realms of high culture opportunities to access these leisure activities (Wilinsky 2001: 83). Bourdieu also argues that central to specific taste preferences is an inherent sense of opposition towards other forms of culture (Bourdieu 1984: 56). Taste preferences thus express opposition and also determine a social identity for the consumer.

A central way art house exhibitors create cultural capital for themselves and help establish their cinemas is through their programming of films. I use concepts of programming developed by Peter Bosma (2015), who distinguishes between schedulers and programmers (or curators). Schedulers, Bosma argues, make selections based on which of the newest releases would attract the biggest audiences and maximise short-term economic profit. At the same time, programmers seek films to consecrate for a particular audience (Bosma 2015: 51). This distinction means that programming is both a 'commercial act' with a monetary function and a 'creative act, expressing an artistic identity' (Bosma 2015: 7: 61). Based on this conclusion, Bosma examines the complex influences that determine the decision-making process of film selection (Bosma 2015: 7). He also sees programming as a 'social phenomenon' as the curator selects films for screening according to a knowledge of the target audience and the institutional and distribution channels determining the availability of movies (Bosma 2015: 7).

The second focus of this volume is the state and non-state institutions that facilitate the circulation of art film. I draw on ideas developed by Jane Harbord (2002) and Shyon Baumann (2007) in their research into art film consumption. Harbord (2002) observes that film cultures like the ones that developed in the art film boom of the 1990s are both 'institutionally and spatially located' (Harbord 2002: 39). Baumann (2007: 3) contends that film became accepted as an art form in the 1960s US through complex interactions of forces, namely, a shifting media environment, developing academic institutions and educational and social changes.[11] In cinematic terms, exhibitors during the 1980s and 1990s acted neither in isolation to the particular tastes of their audiences nor to actions of domestic and international actors helping to regulate the flow of cinematic culture. There was a network of relationships between exhibitors and their audiences and with state agencies controlling domestic cinema and media outlets helping to create discourses surrounding film consumption. To understand this specific historical moment in Korean cinema, we must map out the web of relationships that helped form it, and the impact these networks have on the industry today.

A third area I investigate in this book is the exhibition spaces that influence cinematic consumption. The ideas of Jane Harbord (2002), Robert C. Allen (2006) and Doreen Massey (1994) are pertinent to our understanding of what draws audiences to art houses. Harbord and Allen both emphasise the centrality of spatiality to film viewing:

> The experience of cinema does not exist outside the experience of space, and, as such, it is the product of historically specific, embedded material practices – of performance, of display, of exchange, of architecture, of social interaction, of remembering, as well as of signification and cinematic representation. (Allen 2006: 16)

Allen draws on the geographical theories of Doreen Massey (1994), who argues that spaces are not neutral conveyors of meaning but help to construct (and are constructed by) social relations such as gender and class and that spaces must also be 'conceptualised integrally with time'. Spaces for Massey are 'ever-shifting social geometries of power and signification' (Massey 1994: 2–3). Using these conceptual approaches, Allen contends that the movie theatre is the product of 'interrelationships and interactions extending from the intimate to the global', it is constructed through 'embedded material practices' and is 'always in process' (Allen 2006: 16; see also Massey 1994: 2–4). In other words, the context of exhibition is constantly shaped by interaction with rival exhibitors, global organisations of commercial exchange, state regulating bodies, media and popular and historical discourses.

As I argue in this study, exhibitors explicitly attempted to create a distinctive institutional identity for their art houses to attract audiences. I use 'institutional identity' to refer to particular viewing (or film) cultures created by exhibitors to entice spectators.[12] Exhibitors do this by stressing their specific programming styles, pre- and post-screening activities and theatrical space to distinguish their theatres from competitors. The Korean art house auditoriums, foyers and their associated facilities were (and still are) spaces created or, in some cases, converted for public consumption, their decor and amenities designed to create a certain mystique in contrast to competitors. The films screened at Korean art houses were generally not cast up by chance; programmers organised a 'purposeful arrangement' of motion pictures for audiences (Bosma 2015: 61). Media, state and popular discourses (responses of the public) also helped fashion the institutional identity of specific art houses. These institutional identities are vital because they frame viewers' consumption of film and also help us understand exhibitors' commercial strategies.

A closely linked notion is the 'sociality of moviegoing', a central feature of 'the experience of cinema, and, hence, of its role in identity formation' (Allen 2006: 20). Sociality refers to how audiences consume film communally and interact with other spectators within what Robert C. Allen's terms a 'social site' (Allen 2011: 51). Studies have confirmed that this sociality was often associated with specific cinematic rituals of viewing. In her study of cinema in 1930s Britain, Annette Kuhn argues that the spatiality and sociality of the filmgoing experience were as meaningful for her respondents as the memory of individual movies and stars. For many people, the routines and habits of cinemagoing remained central to the 'fabric of their daily lives' (Kuhn 2002: 17). In other words, exhibition practices and experiences are more than a context or background for understanding the production and consumption of cinematic texts at any specific historical time. As Dudley Andrew observed: 'Films can be studied as isolated texts, but in the life of culture, they play various roles depending on the rituals they appear within' (Andrew 1986: 168). This book seeks to bring to life the significance of these cinematic spaces and experiences for the participants of the art film boom. Research into the sociality and spatiality associated with Korean cinema exhibition and the complex patterns of interactions between state, audiences, media and exhibitors provides insights into the popularity of art film.

Sources

Much of the data has come from interviews, surveys and correspondence I conducted between 2020 and 2022. I have included a diverse range of voices, people who shed light on the 1980s–90s period of intense art film consumption and its legacy. A great deal of information was provided by Lee Kwang-mo (Kwang-mo Lee), whom I interviewed because he was involved in the distribution, exhibition, production and creation of art film during this period, and his perspective offers a unique insight into the boom and its aftermath. Each chapter in the book features Lee's voice, partly because it is difficult to avoid someone so intensely involved in the art scene at the time. Lee's recollections of the vicissitudes of his experience and the political, economic and cultural shifts occurring around him provide valuable, personal insights into the growth of art film in Korea.

Lee's initial involvement in art film began in the late 1980s while studying for an MFA (Master of Fine Arts) in Film and television at the University of California at Los Angeles (UCLA) School of Theatre, Film and Television. The UCLA Film Archive possessed an extensive collection of 35mm movies, and they hosted year-round screenings. In addition to the movies he watched for class, Lee regularly went to the Nuart Art House. These early experiences inspired a lasting passion for art cinema (personal correspondence, Lee Kwang-mo, May 2020). To graduate, UCLA required Lee to turn a script he had written into a movie. His scenario tells of the tragedy that befalls a family during the Korean War, and it would form the basis of his sole feature-length dramatic film, *Spring in My Hometown* (Arŭmdaun sijŏl, 1998, ROK). Lee intended that the film would encapsulate many of the trends of art house that had inspired him during his five years in Los Angeles.[13] In 1991, Lee returned to Seoul to raise sufficient funds to finance his graduation piece (author interview with Lee Kwang-mo, August 2015). Through this roundabout path, his involvement in Korean art film exhibition began. I devote significant space to Lee and the Dongsung Cinematheque because of the central place his experiment in cinematic exhibition occupies in media, scholarly and public recollections of 1990s Korean cinephilia. Lee and the Dongsung Cinematheque are nearly always cast as leading characters in this historical narrative, to the detriment of many others who played important roles, and it is with a view to providing a richer description that, in addition to Lee's input, the chapters that follow also include alternative accounts of the expansion of Korean art houses. I interviewed and corresponded with other exhibitor-distributors of art film such as Kim Sŏng-uk (Munhwahakkyo Seoul; Seoul Art Cinema), Kim Nan-suk (former manager of the Dongsung Cinematheque and Hypertheque

Nada and CEO of the art film company Jinjin Ltd), Jonathan Yu (Yu Sang-uk, DRFA 365 art house) and Yun Sang-jin* (Taegu Dongsung Art Hall). All of my informants were direct participants in the cinephilia boom, and all have maintained an interest in art film that continues to the present. As exhibitor-distributors, they shared a commitment to what they considered the transformative possibilities offered by art film. Each of them saw it as their mission to – in the words of Jonathan Yu – help lift Korean cinema out of the 'dark space' it found itself in during the late 1980s–90s slump in the market (personal correspondence, Jonathan Yu, September 2020). Through art film exhibition, they thought they could change audiences' viewing preferences and transform the artistry of Korean cinema.[14] Despite the phenomenal success of the domestic industry over the past twenty years, all of them still believe in the need to promote art film in Korea.

The book features data collected from Korean art film audiences who responded to my online survey of film memories conducted between December 2020 and February 2021. I questioned art film spectators about their first impressions of attending art film screenings, what kindled their interest, and what has kept that interest from fading (Appendix 3). The book also includes accounts from journalists and scholars such as Choi Sang-hee (Ch'oe Sang-hŭi), Kim Young-jin (Kim Yŏng-jin), Kang Kyoung Lae (Kang Kyŏng-nae) and Irene Hee Seung Lee (Yi Hŭi-sŭng) who were involved in the cinephilia, and because of their ongoing connections to cinema, reflected knowledgeably on events. In seeking the first-hand accounts of direct participants in the cinephilia of the period, I have tried to recreate the quality of individual and collective experiences of cinema exhibition and consumption.

One feature of memories as constituted thoughts in the present to make sense of the past is that they are never linear but iterative in quality and require contextualisation to situate them within the past (O'Brien 2018: 196). The chapters include contemporary media responses to the art boom to ground the experiential data. I consider both newspaper reports from the 1990s and recent articles and fan blogs that reflect retrospectively. Media accounts helped shape public discourses around the function of cinema during the boom and influenced the memorialisation of this period in Korean cultural history. In addition, I have included cinema posters, images and film memorabilia from the 1990s to understand how cinemas promoted themselves and attracted audiences. Where possible, I have also used film schedules, box office statistics and KOFIC reports on the state of Korean cinema to shed light on the fluctuating demand for art film in the period.[15] Officials at the KMPPC and in the nascent KOFIC grappled with ways to support an industry that catered to a diversity of tastes and desires beyond the commercial interests of producers, and they produced copious research to understand audiences and shape policy. By featuring accounts from multiple sources, I have tried to construct a rich history of the period.

Of course, I have written this institutional and cultural history from a personal perspective – that of a foreign outsider to the events. As stated in the preface, I was there at the time, but not as a participant, and the boom in cinephilia was only made known to me through media reports. However, I remember the 1990s in Korea, the atmosphere of social, political and cultural transformation and the urban locations. All of this – the time, atmosphere and places – played a formative part in my youthful development, and as such, it cannot help but cloud my vision of the 1990s cinematic landscape. A peculiar trick of memory tends to make us believe that the past was not only a different country; it was a better country. As we see in the final chapter, for some direct participants in these events – critic Chŏng Sŏng-il, for example – the 1990s cinema boom was a better time than the cinematic present. Susan Sontag, writing her eulogy to the death of cinema and cinephilia, regarded the fifteen years between 1960 and 1975 as the golden age of motion pictures, using it to attack the 1990s era of film (Sontag 1996). With this in mind, and as a distant observer of these events, I have tried to avoid writing the history of a better time. This is not a purer past to hold up as a mirror to the current success of Korean cinema. This period did not produce a superior cinematic product to which Korean film must return. The art film boom brought some critical changes and understanding that time and its transformation adds to our comprehension of the development of Korean cinema as a whole.

Conceptualising art film, art houses and cinephilia in Korea

The term 'art film' may sound outmoded today, especially given the 1960s European associations Sontag identified. Yet 'art film' or '*yesulyŏnghwa*' is the term many 1990s Koreans used to refer to a type of cinema they considered radically different from what they had previously watched. Journalists, fans, historians and film-regulating administrators still employ *yesulyŏnghwa* to refer to much of the cinema consumed in this period of cinephilia and to movies shown in the surviving art houses and I use the term throughout.[16] There are several salient features that help us comprehend what drew young Koreans to art film from the late-dictatorship period onwards and how they conceptualised its difference from other types of cinema. This section aims to introduce some key concepts that help frame the historical analysis of art film consumption and exhibition in late and post-dictatorship Korea. I consider the historical and theoretical scholarship written on the development of art cinema in other contexts that shed some insight into Korean art film consumption and exhibition. I focus first on the association of art films with a 'classical' period of European production and the related concept of art cinema's opposition to Hollywood. Next, I investigate the historical diversity of art cinema, its connections with film festivals, and the salient characteristics that constitute the art house as an institution. These points provide essential background to understanding art films and their exhibition spaces in late and post-dictatorship Korea.

A vital aspect of art film is its association with a particular style of filmmaking that originated in European (and Japanese) cinema between the late 1940s and the early 1970s (Berliner 2018: 66). This was the era of 'classic' art film – a formative moment in the development of its most famous practitioners, including Michelangelo Antonioni, Ingmar Bergman, Federico Fellini, Akira Kurosawa, Jean-Luc Godard and Rainer Werner Fassbinder. Scholars, critics and consumers established a paradigm, a sense of what constituted European art film during this period, seeing it as standing in opposition to Hollywood's commercial cinematic output (Neale 1981: 11–14; Berliner 2018: 55; Bordwell 1986). David Bordwell (1986) argues that while commercial Hollywood cinema featured linear narratives driven by cause and effect, an emphasis on action and continuity editing, art film often emphasised the opposite. Art movies featured episodic narratives held together by more tenuous logic; they stressed character development over action, took more subjective points of view, and espoused a distinct visual style (Bordwell 1986: 206; Neale 1981:13).[17] The aim of such stylistic innovation by filmmakers was to create a more

> personal form that expressed the filmmaker's identity and perception of the world ... it grew out of a radical rejection of the conventions of mainstream culture, reflecting the uncertainties of a world that had lost a clear moral grounding ... not diversion or entertainment ... art films were '*films de cinephile*s,' films of filmmakers ... actively rethinking the possibilities of the cinemas. (Jacobowitz and Lippe 2008: 1)

Implicit in this type of filmmaking was a subversive subtext. As suggested by Jacobowitz and Lippe in their account of this form of cinematic production, art filmmakers rejected what was considered mainstream and rethought conventions. Steve Neale argues critics, scholars, fans and administrators, in their discussions on the defence of art film against the US dominance of domestic markets, frequently depict the opposition between Hollywood and art film as one of 'genre versus personal expression, of (in some extreme instances) trash versus taste, hysteria versus restraint, energy versus decorum and quality . . . ' (Neale 1981: 12). Many filmmakers, critics and fans saw art cinema as a differentiated product and a rebellion against the norms represented by commercial Hollywood motion pictures. This notion of opposition is essential for understanding the lure of European culture for young Koreans at the height of 1980s–90s anti-Americanism.

Also central to the popularisation of art film in South Korea from the late dictatorship is its association with a vital institution of legitimation: the international film festival. Neale observes that festivals are central in reinforcing the idea that certain films oppose and stand above Hollywood cinema, meriting their status as art cinema (1981: 35). Thomas Elsaesser (2005b: 90) argues a Cannes International Film Festival-led transformation resulted in the championing of the auteur director as the creator of art in cinema, further elevating art film above commercial genre cinema. Festivals help establish films as art and act as a vital link in the distribution chain of art films to exhibitors worldwide. Art filmmakers seek distribution deals at film festivals, and art houses also consult film festival programmes to book appropriate films (Berliner 2018: 64–5). The festival connections are essential because they help determine the release and exhibition patterns of art film and the marketing strategies of distributors. Exhibitors and distributors maintain the sense of exclusivity initially created about films shown at festivals by providing platform (rather than wide) releases that deliberately target the niche audiences of art houses (Berliner 2018: 63–8).[18] Posters, pamphlets and other forms of advertising stress festival awards, invitations and screenings to heighten the high art status of individual movies to help exhibitors market their movies. The festival, in short, is art cinema's fundamental support institution in both a commercial and creative sense (Andrews 2013: 182). Festivals became central to the popularisation of pioneering Korean exhibition sites and a primary tool for art film legitimation for local audiences.

While the sense of opposition and association with festivals is vital to our understanding of the popularity of art film, another characteristic that became key to decisions made by South Korean administrators over the regulation of the art film sector was the increasing slipperiness of distinctions between art cinema and commercial Hollywood movies. Todd Berliner and Chris Berry note that since the 1980s, greater overlap has emerged in terms of style, distribution and production between Hollywood and art film (Berliner 2018: 58; Berry 2002: 10–11).[19] This does not mean that art film cannot be distinguished from mainstream cinema – which for our purposes, can be considered as highly marketed, widely released products deliberately aimed at generating rapid incomes at the box office (Ahn 2012: 181 n. 40; Berliner 2018: 64–5). The point is that there has rarely been a clear-cut distinction between all art film and all mainstream film, and this blurring of boundaries became integral to conflict between exhibitors and administrators in the Korean context.

Given the historical complexity surrounding our understanding of what constitutes art film, it is unsurprising that defining an art house is also problematic. Researchers have identified specific physical characteristics – including space, size and physical location – that link art houses across different historical contexts. John Twomey (2002 [1956]: 259) observed that 1950s American art houses were 'small intimate theatres' rather than the picture palaces that dominated commercial exhibition. Many of these 200–300 seaters were located in university towns or urban areas with a higher density of cultural facilities (Andrews 2013: 177). Size and location are features that have remained consistent across different geographical and cultural contexts. In Japan, for example, so-called 'mini-theatres' became the precursor for a 1960s–70s art film boom in the Jinbocho area of central Tokyo (personal correspondence, Shuhei Hosokawa and Markus Nornes, November 2020). This geographical and spatial uniformity reflects the target niche audience of the exhibitors, which was generally a prosperous, urban, professional and educated clientele (Hanson 2007: 183). The small auditoriums, together with a specific decor (often European in style) and facilities (brewed coffee and cakes rather than popcorn), lent a sense of exclusivity to the venue that suited the target market of art film exhibitors (Wilinsky 2001: 145).

Apart from location, size and space, one temptation might be to determine art house status simply by looking at its programming. This is based on the assumption that an art house is a theatre that screens art film as an alternative to cinemas that screen mainstream commercial motion pictures.[20] However, relying wholly on programming to determine whether or not a theatre fits the definition of an art house neglects the complex realities of commercial exhibition. Barbara Wilinsky warns against such an approach, arguing that 1940s American art houses came into being as a result of specific 'industrial pressures', which resulted in the exhibition of film products that proved 'attractive alternatives' at one particular time (Wilinsky 2001: 41). Art house exhibition in the US of the late 1940s and early 1950s, for example, is characterised by the work of European directors such as Vittorio De Sica, Carol Reed and Marcel Pagnol, re-runs of classic US films by Orson Welles or Charlie Chaplin and documentaries (Twomey 2002 [1956]: 259–60). The commercial pressures that led exhibitors to seek out such programming in the first place also resulted in theatre owners altering the emphasis of their programmes just as emphatically, resulting in the screening of very different films and a consequent shift in clientele. Wilinsky observed considerable variation in the programming of art houses in similar timeframes within national borders, for example, between theatres located in urban and rural areas (Wilinsky 2001: 8). Therefore, the fluidity of programming has always been central to the character of art houses.

All these features of art film and its exhibition – the classical period of European cinema with its stylistic divergence, institutional formation and notions of opposition, historical diversity and connections to festivals – are essential to our comprehension of Korean art film exhibition growth and consumption. Above all, art film's historical and conceptual ambiguity is an integral part of Korean art house history. In the 1990s, exhibitors clashed with scholars, film fans, critics, administrators, distributors and fellow exhibitors over what constituted an art film. Disagreements between these parties were not related to any absolute conception of art film but instead based on product differentiation and conflicting interests. These differences of opinion helped form part of the mosaic of a cinematic industry during a period of rapid change.

One important point should be made about the notion of independent film. Berliner proposes that 'independent' is defined in terms of distribution patterns (Berliner 2018: 58–9), although he observes that 'art-house' and 'independent' are often used 'interchangeably'. However, as Park Young-a argues, independent film in Korea is rooted in the politically engaged activist cinema of the anti-dictatorship movement of the late 1980s, which produced films like *Sanggyedong Olympic* (Kim Dong-won, 1988, ROK). As such, the post-dictatorship increase in state and corporate support for filmmaking engendered tensions among independent filmmakers, some of whom saw themselves as continuing the resistance against state and commercial interests, while others saw independent cinema in less politically engaged terms – as a low-budget alternative to Hollywood-style production (Park 2015: 51–3).[21] Therefore, both understandings – independently produced/distributed and politically engaged cinema – are contained within the concept of Korean independent film. By the second decade of the 2000s, 'art' and 'independent' were being used together in KOFIC publications – leading to debate, as we see in Chapter 6.

I end this discussion by considering what cinephilia is. Apart from a love of cinema, several constituent features help us conceptualise the specific Korean cinephilia of the 1990s. The first thing to observe is the connection of cinephilia to art film consumption. David Andrews argues that 'cinephilia has been crucial to the canonical processes that have 'made "art cinema"' (2013: 208). The type of cinephilia referenced by Susan Sontag does not represent love for all film, but enthusiasm for certain types of art film often closely linked to the classical European period (Andrews 2013: 2). Cinephilia also lies at the heart of art film's central institutions – the art house and the film festival (Czach 2010: 140).

To understand its enduring hold over people, Thomas Elsaesser characterises cinephilia as an 'entire attitude toward life' (2005a: 27). The all-consuming nature of cinephilia is in many ways related to cinematic consumption, including how cinephiles construct their lives around the 'rituals and practices of moviegoing' (Keathley 2005: 6). Elsaesser observes that cinephiles often construct such rituals and practices around particular spaces, meaning that film consumption is often 'topographically site-specific, defined by the movie houses, neighbourhoods and cafés one frequented' (Elsaesser 2005a: 30). Christian Keathley argues that the reason for the intensity of experience associated with movie watching is related to a perception of motion pictures as 'events' that '"have happened to us," ones that we revisit in our memory and make up who we are' (Keathley 2005: 21). Keathley also contends that film viewing generates a desire for self-improvement and self-education. Practitioners researched the objects of their desires and demonstrated through their dedication and erudition their membership of a cinephile collective or an 'interpretative community' (Keathley 2005: 15). Such cinephilia also reveals a quasi-religious reverence for certain films and directors and venues forming the sites of weekly pilgrimage (Elsaesser 2005a: 31). As 'events', cinephiles tended to associate the initial experience of a film with a specific time and place. Cinephilia, in which films viewed theatrically are regarded as 'events', is often termed a 'Golden age' that Sontag declared dead by 1996 (Desser 2005: 205; O'Brien 2018: 205). This kind of cinephilia occurred before the use of VCRs (videocassette recorders) and the widespread popularity of television and is probably most closely linked to art film consumption. These were the days when if you missed the screening of a certain film, you might literally never get the chance to see it again (Keathley 2005: 26).

In their analysis of the history of cinephilia, de Valck and Hagener (2005: 13) define the emergence of new technologies as the start of an essential division over various forms of cinephilia, one that focused on the various merits of 'going out' versus 'staying in', or 'big screen' versus 'small screen' (de Valck and Hagener 2005: 13). Some scholars and fans (like Sontag) asserted the superiority of 'classical cinephilia', arguing film could only be appreciated in cinemas. In contrast, others contended that newer technologies represent an equally valid method of viewing. For example, David Desser (2005: 209) observes that the popularity of the VCR in East Asia provided an outlet for a new generation of cinephiles to express their reverence for film not just in the cinema but through small-screen consumption.

The development of this later technology-driven love of film outlined by Desser is clear evidence of what de Valck and Hagener argue is cinephilia's cultural fluidity – its ability to transcend different geographical, cultural and temporal contexts (2005: 12). Cinephilia can regenerate novel meanings for new practitioners in a transformed mechanical age of reproduction. The essential elements of cinephilia – the quasi-religious reverence for film and the need for self-education – survived the transition from theatrical viewing to domestic consumption via VCR and home computer. This is partly due to two intrinsically linked aspects of cinephilia, namely its seditious and generative characteristics. For its practitioners, an essential component of cinephilia is a need to discover new films, images, directors and ways of seeing. Inherent within this desire to discover the new (and often to rediscover older neglected movies) was a concomitant desire to reject the established and the accepted. In the words of Thomas Elsaesser, cinephilia occupies an 'oedipal time' in which practitioners like François Truffaut adopted André Bazin and Alfred Hitchcock to attack *'le cinéma de papa'* (dad's cinema; Elsaesser 2005a: 31). Cinephiles perceive that they are engaged in a 'deviant' behaviour that resists the commonplace, accepted and conventional (Keathley 2005:

19: 26). This perception of rebellion inherent within cinephilia is closely related to the preferred method of cinematic consumption identified by researchers, which is to resist total absorption into the narrative but oscillate between 'immersion and distancing' to retain a 'productive look' (Keathley 2005: 42). The result is a fascination with what is known as the 'excess' or 'slippage' – in other words, those moments in a film that are not meant to be noticed since they generate no meaning in and of themselves and do nothing to drive the narrative.[22] In 'Pausing over Peripheral Detail', Roger Cardinal (1986: 126) argues that these images offer a 'simple yet compelling vision of things in their own right, invested with all the density and "suchness" of real-life objects free of ideas'. These moments of excess focus on incongruous details outside narratives and reflect the viewer's subjectivity, but more importantly, they generate meaning – in other words, they are productive. Such engagement with film is not determined simply by an obtuse desire to be different. Christian Keathley argues that this is the 'cinephiliac moment', a selective preference for specific moments of cinema over others that, in its reconstructive nature, mimics the filmmaking practice itself (Keathley 2005: 42).

Another critical area of our understanding of the Korean situation is the issue of the gendered dimension of cinephilia. Most historical studies traditionally focus on cinephilia as a cultural practice dominated by small groups of elite men, in which women were either absent or played a passive role (Wimmer 2014: 62). Research by Leila Wimmer (2014) into letters to French film journals from their (mainly) female readership has started to redress this imbalance (see Fee n.d.). We should be aware that this gendered dimension also plays a vital role in the story of Korean cinephilia and art house exhibition.

A final and related feature of cinephilia observed by de Valck and Hagener concerns the defining contradictions that lie at the heart of the practice, and which leave it open for attack by politically engaged commentators. De Valck and Hagener (2005: 12) call cinephilia 'Janus faced' because, as a pastime, it is at once democratic by celebrating a popular cultural activity, but it is elitist in that it replaces traditional hierarchies with new taste preferences that are often idiosyncratic and subjective. Movie buffs celebrated cinephilia as a subversive practice in its rejection of films that were perceived to be mainstream, commonplace, generic, contemporary and popular.[23] Yet practitioners of cinephilia (like those in 1960s Paris) often celebrated a rediscovery of mainstream genre cinema. The cinephile's obsession with nostalgia, with reviving and rediscovering older movies, appears to many to be less of a rebellion and more of an elitist attempt to be deliberately contrary (de Valck and Hagener 2005: 14). The contradictory elements of cinephilia made the practice particularly susceptible to criticism from cultural observers, and we see similar attacks on cinephilia emerging in 1990s Korea.

These features of cinephilia: the connections to art cinema, its all-consuming character, the need for self-education, the view of a film as an 'event', the division between classical and technologically driven cinephilia, the associations of alterity, the gendered aspect, the productive engagement of cinephiles with film texts and the popular criticisms of the practice are vital elements that will help us understand the specific fascination for art cinema that arose in late and post-dictatorship Korea.

Organisation of the book

The book is divided into three sections that consider the expansion and decline of art cinema consumption, the character of post-1985 cinephilia and art film exhibition and the development of art houses in new-millennium Korea. I have arranged the events into a chronological and historical narrative between the late dictatorship and the 2020–1 COVID-19 (Coronavirus) pandemic. The opening section, 'Rise', charts the expansion of art film and cinephilia between the mid-1980s and the 1997–8 Asian financial crisis. Chapter 1 provides essential background to the study focusing on the years of transformation between the 1980 Kwangju Uprising and the first civilian government of President Kim Young Sam. It analyses the political, cinematic and socio-cultural factors that contributed to the emergence of art film exhibition and cinephilia in Korea. The second chapter considers the cultural and commercial openings that created an audience for art film and paved the way for art houses. The chapter examines the cultural practices that developed in three non-theatrical exhibition spaces: European cultural centres, university film clubs and private commercial video cinemas or videotheques. These three types of spaces helped shape the institutional identities of art houses that followed during the 1990s and produced influential personnel who dominated new millennium Korean cinema. Chapter 3 examines how art film and cinephilia emerged from underground, non-theatrical spaces and expanded into new commercial art houses. The chapter also looks at the specific character of the late and post-dictatorship cinephilia.

Chapter 4 analyses the critical 1995–6 events that brought cinephilia and art film consumption to the attention of the entire country. I argue the combination of new film media, festivals, education and cinephilic culture was critical in helping to shape an audience that embraced the boundary-pushing domestic cinema of the late 1990s and 2000s.

The book's second section, 'Fall', examines the challenges art film exhibitors faced between 1997 and 1999 and the reasons behind the decline in cinephilia and interest in foreign art film – changes accompanied by the increasing popularity of Korean movies. The book's final part, 'Legacy', concentrates on the vital inheritance bequeathed by the decade-long blossoming of cinephilia and art film consumption. Chapter 6 looks at art houses when art film was no longer a flourishing business but had developed into a commodity that required state protection. This chapter considers the institutionalisation of art film within the industry focusing on KOFIC's creation of an art house network in the early 2000s. This move aimed to guarantee screening opportunities for speciality films and helped shape the Korean cinema industry. The final chapter looks at another important legacy of the art film boom of the 1990s – the continued existence of independent art houses in South Korea. It examines how art houses have survived greater competition from online viewing and multiplexes. The chapter also discusses the memorialisation of the art film boom in media, fan and scholarly discourses, and how journalists, audiences and academics have situated the 1990s cinephilia in the broader success of Korean film.

Notes

1. There are very different ideas of what constitutes art cinema (Wilinsky 2001: 11; Andrews 2013: x). Scholars have defined art cinema from 'every vantage' but still cannot produce an 'acceptable philosophical definition', since the relevant criteria are too 'complex and contested' (Berliner 2018: 54).
2. Bong Joon-ho's film *Parasite* won Best Picture, Best Director, Best Original Screenplay and Best International Feature Film at the 92nd Academy Awards and the Palme d'Or at the 72nd Cannes Film Festival (Pulver 2019; Jung Ji-youn 2008: 10–12). In 1993, Korean films accounted for 15.9 per cent of box office admissions in Korea in comparison to overseas films. Many predicted the imminent collapse of the domestic industry under the pressure of Hollywood product. From 2001 onwards Korean films regularly capture a 50 per cent domestic market share (Berry 2002: 9; Paquet 2009: 82–3).
3. Chi-Yun Shin and Julian Stringer (2005), Frances Gateward (2007) and Jinhee Choi (2010) have defined and categorised the diverse range of movies produced

in Korea to explain the exponential growth of the Korean cinematic industry since the late 1990s. Other studies like Kyung Hyun Kim (2004) take a symptomatic approach to the discussion of unifying tendencies within Korean film reflecting social and political anxieties. Kathleen McHugh and Nancy Abelmann (2005) contextualise the current thriving industry as part of a wider history of cinematic development. David James and Kyung Hyun Kim (2002) and Chung Hye Seung (2012) analyse successful filmmakers on the international festival circuit. Annette Kuhn (2002: 3) refers to such studies stressing textual analysis as a 'humanities-based' approach.

4. Yi Sŏn-ju's 2014 study traces the origins of art houses to the early 1990s videotheques. See also KOFIC studies of art houses (Kim et al. 2004).
5. Mark Betz argues there was a 1980s–90s reaction of US and European academia against art cinema as outmoded and elitist (2009).
6. Art film currently accounts for 2–7 per cent of the Korean market (KOFIC 2019: 286).
7. See Namhee Lee on the 1980s-90s rejection of foreign culture by *minjung* movement activists (2006: 112).
8. In 2014: 10 per cent of movie tickets sold in Seoul were for art film (KOFIC 2019: 286). South Korean art and specialist film attendance is generally higher than for the UK, for example. Between 2002 and 2020, approximately 5–7 per cent of all UK screens were devoted to art or non-mainstream cinema, which gives an idea of consumption rates (Kim et al. 2004: 177; personal correspondence, Madeleine Probst, 2020).
9. Here I take the late-dictatorship period to be Chun Doo Hwan's post-Kwangju 1984–7 rule, characterised by an intensification in resistance against the regime, partial relaxation of overt repression and growing middle-class suspicion of the military government (see Chapter 1).
10. Bourdieu mainly discusses publishers, art dealers, gallery owners (1980: 261).
11. Malte Hagener (2007: 14) argues that 1920s–30s avant-garde film movements developed through a complex node of interconnected social and media relationships.
12. Jane Harbord uses the notion of 'film culture' or 'institutional context' to refer to the features of exhibition – the space, activities, programming and their interrelationship (Harbord 2002: 16: 45).
13. After completing coursework, MFA candidates undertake a final graduation project in which they submit a scenario for approval. If accepted, candidates then turn their script into a film to graduate.
14. See Baekdudaegan (2016).
15. There are limitations to the box office statistics used in this research. Firstly, faced with potential losses in revenue by observing the screen quota regulations, exhibitors often underreported the lengths of runs for lucrative imported films. This explains discrepancies between reports of ticket sales found in the media and in official KOFIC sources; see differences in attendances at the Dongsung Cinematheque between official statistics (Kim et al. 2004: 157–8) and Yi Nam (1996). Kim Hong-Jun questions the value of such figures (personal correspondence, April 2021). However, they provide an approximate idea of trends within Korean film when supplemented with other sources.

16. KOFIC still awards the 'art film' designation to pictures thereby providing them with a special status that determines their distribution and exhibition patterns (see Chapter 6).
17. See also Hyunseon Lee's definition of a festival film (2022: 17).
18. A platform release involves exhibiting a film in selected theatres and later expanding the film to other theatres if it appears to be gaining momentum thanks to reviews, awards or word of mouth recommendations (Berliner 2018: 63).
19. See Berliner (2018: 35) for a discussion of the discrepancies between academic positions on the issue. Berry (2002: 10–11) observed a transition in the late 1990s to early 2000s exhibition practices of European, American and Australasian art cinemas away from showing Korean film that established 'cultural' or 'stylistic' difference from Hollywood product. Instead, art cinemas showed commercial, genre films with clever twists like *Tell Me Something* (1999, Chang Yun-hyŏn, ROK). Some film historians maintain that distinctions between mainstream commercial cinema and art film have seldom been solid (Wilinsky 2001: 12: 28–9). David Andrews argues, what constitutes mainstream, or Hollywood cinema has often been 'an undefined and vaguely imaged Other' (2013: 142). Wilinsky concludes that art film has always been 'if nothing else ... a discursive category' (2001: 11).
20. Several researchers have attempted such a definition (Hanson 2007: 183).
21. Another example of independent film is *Ich'yŏjin Yŏjŏnsa* (Forgotten Warriors, 2005, ROK) (Park 2015: 115).
22. As an example of slippage, Christian Keathley cites his fixation on the colour of Cary Grant's socks during the crop-duster sequence in *North by Northwest* (1959, Alfred Hitchcock, US).
23. According to Elsaesser, cinephiles from the classical period celebrated obscure, well-crafted, original, artistic films (2005a: 31).

Part 1
Rise

Figure P1.1 Images of the Munhwahakkyo Seoul videotheque (R) and its extensive video archive (L) (courtesy Kim Sŏng-uk).

Chapter 1

Late-dictatorship and post-1987 political and cultural influences on the emergence of cinephilia and art film exhibition

On 29 June 1987, Roh Tae Woo, the handpicked successor to dictator Chun Doo Hwan issued the Eight Point Declaration that outlined reforms permitting direct presidential elections, increased press freedom, more local democracy and the restoration of civil rights for political prisoners. These reforms followed the June Uprising, an explosion of mass protest against the continuation of a thirty-year-old military dictatorship. Ordinary citizens joined students and activists, turning smaller protests into nationwide mass demonstrations which severely stretched state forces (Robinson 2007: 144–5). When Chun proposed mobilising the military to quell the unrest, the US threatened to withdraw their support for the administration. As a result, Korea looked likely to lose the Olympic Games scheduled for the following year (Eckert et al. 1991: 383; Robinson 2007: 144–5). The combination of mass popular protest and a lack of international support sounded the death knell for the dictatorship. The June Uprising was an upheaval that signalled a vital shift in Korean society and politics by ending the dictatorship and ushering in an era of greater democratisation. The drama of these events makes it easy to forget that the years of popular struggle prior to June 1987 also significantly influenced Korean society and culture in the decade that followed. This opening section of the book investigates the decade-long rise of Korean cinephilia and art film consumption. In this chapter, I provide vital background to these cultural phenomena focusing on three interrelated areas: (1) the legacy of the protest movement and frustration with politics; (2) economic growth and increased cultural consumption; (3) challenges faced by Korean film and attempts to reform cinema. An examination of the formative experience of the participants of the anti-dictatorship struggle, the 1990s cultural explosion and the problems of the Korean film industry aids our comprehension of why curiosity for art film emerged when it did, how this interest manifested itself amongst audiences and how exhibitors established art houses.

The political struggle, students and post-1987 frustration with politics

The mass protests of the June Uprising represented what Erik Mobrand (2019: 47) calls a 'cacophony of distinct voices clamouring for political change'. These forces are commonly known as the *minjung* (masses) anti-dictatorship movement (*undong*), or 'movement sphere' (*undongkwŏn*; Lee 2006: 96), and they included farmers, workers, church activists, intellectuals and artists (Mobrand 2019: 47).[1] *Minjung* ideology had both nationalistic and politically progressive elements. On one level, it stressed pride in Korean mass culture, everyday life and history, while nationalist elements helped unify the country's citizens against the dictatorship (Mobrand 2019: 48). At the forefront of the *minjung* movement were university students: a vitally important group since many went on to influential positions in society, politics and the cultural industries in 1990s Korea (see Park 2015). Participation in the struggle was all-consuming for many students, and their experience had a vital formative influence on their outlook towards authority, society and culture in subsequent years.

The political motivations of the student vanguard that successfully led the overthrow of the military took their shape from the early days of Chun's rule. Many student activists did not see democratic electoral reform as their principal goal; some stressed unification with North Korea, while others sought major socio-economic restructuring (Mobrand 2019: 49). Carter Eckert argues that during the politically repressive 1972–9 Yushin period of Park Chung Hee dictatorship preceding Chun's rule, the students had primarily embraced social democratic values as guiding principles for resolving Korea's political problems (Eckert et al. 1991: 379).[2] However, one incident in particular radicalised Korean students: the 1980 Kwangju Uprising (5.18 Kwangju minjuhwaundong [Kwangju Democratisation Movement]). Widespread protests against General Chun Doo Hwan's 1979 coup resulted in a massacre in the south-western city of Kwangju, where ROK forces opened fire on demonstrators, killing hundreds – perhaps thousands – of protestors. Kwangju also fuelled widespread anti-Americanism since many students believed the Jimmy Carter (1924– ; in office: 1977–81) administration had sanctioned the ROK military's massacre at Kwangju. In the aftermath of Kwangju, radicals revised previous understandings of the US military presence on the Korean peninsula and saw the USA as a neo-colonialist power propping up the military dictatorship (Cumings 1997: 382–6). The massacre at Kwangju cut deep into the consciousness of an entire generation of students and radicalised anti-dictatorship politics.

With the early 1980s shift to the left, students began organising in a more furtive and underground manner. Not only were they protesting against the government, but they were also now embracing Marxism, an ideology that the South Korean state had virulently suppressed for three decades because of hostility with the North. Student activists developed autonomous, flexible cellular structures to protect the anonymity of leaders and preserve organisational integrity despite the arrests of individuals (Eckert et al. 1991: 380). They infiltrated factories and agricultural workplaces incognito to proselytise and mobilise workers and farmers into anti-government activities. To learn about Marxist political thought, students formed secret self-study groups on university campuses. Active *samizdat*-type circulation of illicit literature and audio-visual materials emerged. Students smuggled Marx's *Das Kapital* and other proscribed political texts from Japan and elsewhere (Cumings 1997: 381; Eckert et al. 1991: 379). Often these works were poorly translated into Korean, and sometimes they had to be read in the original Japanese. The widespread availability of the VCR provided another easy means for students to spread anti-government information. Videotapes of western media coverage revealing the true extent of the massacre in the Kwangju Uprising were smuggled in by students or foreign missionaries and then copied, recopied and circulated furtively amongst student groups (Jackson 2020).

The autonomous cells, self-study groups, secret meetings, *samizdat*-style circulation of contraband, and underground activities strategies were necessary for the continued survival of the student activism against the authorities. The Chun regime created a brutal security and surveillance infrastructure to control society (Cumings 1997: 379). Leaders had also improved organisational techniques after previous failures of the student movement in 1980. Their strategies proved effective in engineering the downfall of the military government in 1987. After the regime had granted electoral reforms and a new government elected, popular support for anti-government protest dissipated and the student-led unified movement for change atomised.

The Eight Point Declaration of reforms signalled the end of the mass struggle and ushered in a new period of democratic politics for Korea. Unfortunately, it did not bring the sort of changes many students demanded. What frustrated them was a failure to achieve real change from dictatorship-era state politics and institutions. For the *minjung* movement and ordinary Koreans, the outcome of the direct presidential elections of 1987 was a primary source of displeasure. After decades of military rule, an opposition politician was hotly tipped to be elected instead of the military-linked contender, former general Roh Tae Woo. However, the two primary candidates, Kim Dae Jung and Kim Young Sam, failed to settle upon a single candidate and stood against each other, splitting the anti-government vote. Roh won with 37 per cent of the vote, an outcome greeted with general public resignation at the self-seeking machinations of opposition politicians (Robinson 2007: 169). Protests led to electoral reforms, but the military was essentially back in power.

This general disgust with democratic party politics continued in many sectors of society long after the reforms. Subsequent moves of opposition politicians seeking power elicited widespread anger at their perceived cynicism. In 1992, Kim Young Sam affiliated his political party with President Roh Tae Woo and the former head of the KCIA, Kim Jong Pil (1926–2018), to win the 1993 election (Robinson 2007: 170–1). Kim Young Sam's presidency was the first peaceful democratic transfer of power and the first civilian administration (Robinson 2007: 171), but Kim had had to ally himself with dictatorship-associated political parties to gain power. Another cause of anger was the lack of closure over Kwangju. That Roh Tae Woo, commonly regarded as an architect of the massacre, was elected in 1987 further devalued Korea's electoral reforms. Radicals felt that democratic changes failed to settle the political problems within Korea and that complete resolution would only come with the punishment of the Kwangju culprits. In the years that followed 1987, Kwangju remained a potent unifying cultural symbol for anti-dictatorship activists and those on the left who associated their political outlook with the legacy of the *minjung* movement (Jackson 2020: 34).

A final area of frustration lay in the continuity of institutions associated with the dictatorship. The military government had close ties to the powerful Korean chaebols (family-owned conglomerates), which had helped engineer the spectacular post-1960 growth of the Korean economy. After 1987, these chaebol conglomerates continued their successful economic expansion despite their links to the dictatorship.

Former political activists believed that the vested interests of elites were too entrenched to allow a genuine transition from military rule. Many argued economic and social structures helped create and nurture the dictatorship. Without changing these structures, the political and economic system would continue to sustain elite interests at the expense of the *minjung*.

An important but seldom defined term that scholars use to refer to the nexus of economic, political, military and other institutional forces is *chedogwŏn* (see Yi Sŏn-ju 2014: 238; Kim et al. 2004: 23; Park 2014).[3] The *chedogwŏn* is similar to a notion of 'the establishment' within South Korea or everything that was state-sanctioned or regulated – including business enterprises such as the chaebols and the security forces, educational institutions and the established system of commercial filmmaking. In other words, the *chedogwŏn* was anything that was *not* underground, illegal, unofficial, engaged, autonomous, autodidactic, student or intellectual-community led, black market-based and actively opposed to the government (Lee 2006: 96).[4] Namhee Lee (2006) argues that the antithesis of the *chedogwŏn* is the movement which characterised itself by its 'oppositional and alternative positions against the dominant culture and value system' (2006: 97).[5] Members of the movement believed they represented the 'moral voice and conscience of their nation and people', which they were responsible for upholding (Lee 2006: 99). During the dictatorship, the notion of both the *chedogwŏn* and *minjung* movement became means for the opponents of the Park and Chun regimes to mobilise support. In the immediate post-1987 period, many *minjung* movement participants regarded the Roh Tae Woo administration as a continuation of military authoritarianism and the Kim Young Sam government as fatally associated with the *ancien régime*. During the early 1990s, the *chedogwŏn* and its antithesis had enduring value as concepts, and the prolonged existence of the movement can be put down to the fact that members believed they were defending a moral position.

For many in the *minjung* movement, the democratic reforms of 1987 represented a 'familiar pattern' in which Korean elites responded to widespread unrest with concessions but refused to let the democratisation movement participate in the actual reforms, only allowing established government and opposition politicians to be involved in the process (Mobrand 2019: 66–7).[6] The result for many Koreans who struggled in the anti-dictatorship *minjung* movement was that the true start of Korea's democracy began with the election of two progressive politicians less tainted by links to the dictatorship, first Kim Dae Jung in 1998 and then Roh Moo Hyun in 2003. Kim Dae Jung had been at the forefront of the democratisation movement; he had been jailed, exiled and threatened with execution for his opposition to successive military dictators. Roh Moo Hyun had been a human rights lawyer who had defended student activists during the dictatorship. The election victories of these two politicians, in particular, represented symbolic moments for many who had struggled against the regime in the 1980s.

Given these ongoing frustrations with party politics, some radicals continued the struggle until the late 1990s, while others drifted away from politics following the loss of popular support in the wake of the 1987 reforms.[7] Most importantly, a group of young people had a shared experience of underground organisation, self-autonomy, suspicion of state institutions and anti-Americanism. This group is part of what is referred to as the 386 (or democratic) generation of Koreans, so-called because they were in their 30s in the 1990s, were born in the 1960s, and had been university students in the 1980s, when many of them had participated in the *minjung* movement protests (Park 2015: 57). This 386 generation played a significant role in the growth of the art film boom and the future expansion of Korean cinema.

The cultural blockade, film censorship and self-censorship

Another political frustration for many Koreans was the maintenance of dictatorship laws and regulations. Erik Mobrand distinguishes between democratisation and 'de-authoritarianisation', stating that a primary challenge faced by post-dictatorship societies is dismantling authoritarian structures (Mobrand 2019: 11). Mobrand's analysis of post-1987 de-authoritarianisation shows some democratic changes liberated the population from an intrusive and assertive state, while others took longer to make themselves felt.[8] In many cases, reforms occurred alongside the re-invigoration of institutions established during the dictatorship (Mobrand 2019: 67). Censorship was one area that was partially reformed but controversially remained in place in the post-1987 period and is directly related to cinema consumption.

Film censorship formed a crucial part of the military authorities' cultural and media blockade of the population, and why censorship in the post-1987 period proved so controversial. The military dictatorship's cultural blockade worked to control the population and aid the regime's drive towards industrialisation and development. The regime used a fervently nationalistic, insular and anti-communist rhetoric to mobilise the population to strive for the sake of the economy (Kim and Sorensen 2011: 11). The dictatorship controlled the media in an attempt to drip-feed information to Koreans. State institutions censored news from official media agencies and restricted both unofficial news sources and, most crucially, international travel. Trips abroad required the approval of state authorities, which vetted and monitored applicants limiting opportunities to bring in information from abroad (Son Min-ho 2014); state operatives scrutinised the activities of diasporic Korean communities (Gillis 2011). The Chun regime's carefully controlled coverage of the Kwangju Uprising is a testament to its desire to suppress information within the country (Jackson 2020: 20). Not only did the state censor news, but it also controlled imports of foreign culture. Severe restrictions on cinematic (and other cultural) imports implemented ostensibly to reduce foreign currency expenditure and protect Korean film also prevented outside ideological contamination (Hwang 2017: 31). These attempts were not always successful, and cracks and fissures allowed news and culture to seep into the country; some Koreans tuned into AFKN (Armed Forces Korea Network), the radio and television broadcasting stations servicing US armed forces garrisoned in the country. This provided people with access to pop music shows, soap operas, first-release movies and network news programmes (Kim Kyung Hyun 2020: 77). The blockade still proved to be a hated feature of the dictatorship (see Jackson 2020: 20).

With the importation of foreign film officially controlled, the military government-enforced restrictions on film production and exhibition ensured no films deemed 'offensive' or 'detrimental' to government interests could be made or screened in state-regulated theatres (Park 2002: 120). Films had to be anti-communist, nationalistic and represent 'wholesome' Korean values (Park 2002: 120). The Public Performance Ethics Committee (PPEC) was accountable to the government's Ministry of Culture, and this body enforced both pre- and post-production censorship, thereby preventing the creation or exhibition of motion pictures deemed contrary to state doctrines (Park 2002: 120–1). The 1988 reforms by the Roh Tae Woo administration brought media liberalisation that permitted greater freedom of expression in Korea, allowing the creation of liberal newspapers like the *Han'gyŏrye* and *Kungmin Ilbo* in 1988, *Segye Ilbo* in 1989 and *Munhwa Ilbo* in 1991 (Park 2015: 90).

The Roh government also removed pre-production censorship in film. However, as Park Seung Hyun (2002) argues, Roh retained pre-production censorship by requiring all filmmakers submit scripts to the PPEC before filming. The PPEC reviewed the content and sent comments about undesirable elements of the script to the producers. The result was that filmmakers voluntarily modified their scenarios before starting the expensive production process to prevent the PPEC from censoring scenes later (Park 2002: 124–5). The liberalising reforms and promises of greater democratic freedoms led to an increase in movies treating hitherto taboo topics like class tensions, social strife, labour problems, poverty, repression and conflict with the DPRK (Park 2002: 121). But, because of the renewed censorship regime enforced by the Roh government, films like *Kuro Arirang* (Park Chong-wŏn, 1989, ROK) and *Resurrection Song* (Puhwalŭi norae, Yi Chŏng-guk, 1990, ROK) covering controversial issues like labour disputes, anti-government protests, brothels servicing US military bases and the Kwangju Uprising were heavily censored (Park 2002: 121, 127; Park 2015: 91). The PPEC's guiding stipulations were broad and ambiguous enough to mock any attempts at free cultural expression in Korea.[9] The content of Park Chong-wŏn's film of the 1980 Kwangju Uprising, *Kuro Arirang*, particularly angered the PPEC, which implemented stringent cuts (Park 2002: 130). The PPEC's decisions were marked by double standards and arbitrariness. On occasions, the PPEC censored Korean films containing violence, nudity, or political oppression while allowing the unexpurgated exhibition of overseas films with less overt political content (Park 2002: 126).[10] At other times, foreign films featuring nudity deemed 'unacceptable' by the committee were heavily cut.[11] Eventually, the Kim Young Sam administration removed script censorship in 1996 (Yecies and Shim 2016: 158). However, the fact that it had survived for nine years after the fall of the dictatorship shows that the authorities believed film could threaten its political authority and, as a result, sought to control cinematic output. Post-1987 cultural censorship was a hated hangover from the military dictatorship that art film exhibitors and consumers worked hard to bypass.[12]

One final irony is that although many anti-dictatorship activists vocally protested Chun's cultural blockade, the *minjung* movement itself restricted the cultural consumption of its members. Namhee Lee argues that in its attempt to construct a new democratic order, like other emancipatory projects, it also 'established "new norms and hierarchies"' (2006: 112). The result was that during the anti-dictatorship struggle leading up to 1987 (and beyond), student activists often took on the role of policing student behaviour by restricting the consumption of fashions, music, films or activities considered 'degenerative', western or decadent and replacing them with more 'wholesome' content reflective of national and working-class values (Lee 2006: 112). The decline of the struggle in the post-1987 period meant the full force of this movement-imposed regime of self-censorship was relaxed for many former activists.

Economic expansion and post-1987 cultural consumption

The slow pace of de-authoritarianisation and the maintenance of dictatorship-era institutions like state censorship were causes of frustration and reasons why many Koreans were deeply suspicious of the authorities. However, post-1987 Korean youth were less actively engaged in politics compared with the older 386 generation, so what replaced the struggle for them? In the post-dictatorship period, we see the start of a period of phenomenal cultural consumption. Leisure instead of work and study became the primary preoccupation of many young people, who developed a significant interest in fashion, travel, sports spectatorship and cultural activities. This was a period when young people flocked to rock cafes (bars playing western and Korean rock music) in major cities and began singing in *noraebang* (private karaoke rooms) (Maliangkay 2014: 304; Lee 2007: 49). In the early 1990s, groups like Seo Taiji and Boys began incorporating rap, reggae, rock and social criticism into their songs in novel ways, helping a diverse popular music industry flourish (Maliangkay 2014: 296).

Several factors facilitated this expansion in cultural consumption. First, there were significant demographic changes, notably the increasing youthfulness of Korean society. People between the ages of fifteen and thirty-nine constituted 46.7 per cent of Korean society in 1995 (Kim 2000: 64). This created a market for cultural producers to tap into. Second, the Korean economy had expanded exponentially under the dictatorship. The late 1980s ushered in a decade-long 'three-low' boom of low dollar rates, low oil prices and low interest. Annual growth rates of 7–8 per cent were the norm and wages rose with the expanding economy (Cho 2020). The 1990s were a golden time of growth, and by 1994, a record 60 per cent of Koreans considered themselves affluent middle-class members (Cho 2020).[13]

Luxury consumer goods proliferated, private cars filled the streets of cities, travel abroad amongst young and old Koreans increased rapidly (Maliangkay 2014: 297; Son Min-ho 2014). The economic growth also meant that in the 1990s, young Koreans had unprecedented amounts of disposable income (Kim 2000: 64). Many young people had relatively affluent parents with high levels of savings. University students – especially those at elite capital colleges – could supplement their allowances with significant earnings from private tutoring of middle and high school students (Kim 2000: 64). In addition, Korean universities rarely fail underperforming students as long as they remain enrolled, so young people often see college as a hedonistic pitstop between the pressure of university entrance exam preparation and a lifetime of dedication to office work in a chaebol (Maliangkay 2014: 304). The result was that many college students, with little pressure from their professors, had opportunities and income to become vital cultural consumers. There are other reasons why cultural consumption amongst the young increased. Kim Seung Guk identifies a growing acceptance of western culture amongst younger people in the early 1990s and a greater desire for overseas travel (Kim 2000: 76; Son Min-ho 2014).[14]

The combination of increased wealth and opportunities for leisure pursuits and relaxed (although not completely liberated) political constraints resulted in a veritable cultural explosion. Many young Koreans felt they could express their pent-up thirst for culture denied them for so long. The result was that by 1990 household levels of leisure expenditure had gone up by 144 per cent compared to 1980 rates (Kim 2000: 69). Spending on pastimes amongst Koreans of all ages doubled Japanese rates and dwarfed consumption figures amongst Europeans and North Americans (Kim 2000: 69). The post-1987 growing acceptance of spending on leisure also brought significant cleavages between children and their parents and amongst the youth themselves. Lee Kee-hyeung argues in the early 1990s, a gap emerged between the so-called New Generation (*sinsedae*) and the older 386 generation. The fissure opened between those just too young to have engaged directly in the democratic struggles and those from the 386 generation with an outlook influenced by the 'deeply ingrained wounds' of the protest years (Lee 2007: 56–7). Michael Robinson evokes Milan Kundera's notion of the 'unbearable lightness of being' to describe the existential dilemma for many former student activists following 1987 (Robinson 2005: 24). This older group was conditioned by the heavy responsibilities of 'national cultural preservation, resistance to authoritarian politics … and the assault of Western popular mass culture' (Robinson 2005: 24–5). The post-1987 liberated cultural consumption of the younger generation looked 'vacuous' to many older former activists. This generational split resurfaced amongst cinephiles during the late 1990s' growth of art film exhibition.

The post-1987 explosion of leisure spending led to a revolution in Korean cultural consumption. However, not all these young people were going to downtown cinemas for reasons that concerned the weakened state of post-dictatorship cinematic production and exhibition.

Challenges within Korean film and institutional changes

The late-dictatorship and post-1987 period witnessed substantial changes to how cinema was financed and produced in Korea, the most significant of which was the opening of the Korean film market. A trade agreement with the US government gave Hollywood companies the freedom to distribute their films directly in Korea from 1987 onwards (Paquet 2009: 50; Berry 2002: 7–8).[15] The deal allowed US film companies to open direct distribution offices in Seoul to service cinemas, TV stations and video rental businesses without restrictions (Yecies 2007: 8). In addition, the US government demanded the removal of protectionist policies designed to protect Korea's cinematic industry. However, to defend the industry, the Chun government retained one central protective measure: a screen quota system requiring the screening of Korean films for a minimum number of days in every cinema (Berry 2002: 8–9). After 1986, Korean cinemas had to screen Korean films for a minimum of 146 days per year (Parc 2017: 622).[16]

Within the established Korean film industry Ch'ungmuro, many opposed the deal, fearing the imminent collapse of weak film producers faced with unbridled competition from Hollywood. The poor showing of domestic films in the immediate post-opening period confirmed these fears. The market share for domestically produced films declined from 34 per cent in 1985 to an all-time low of 16 per cent in 1993 (Cho 2006: 162).[17] The number of Korean movies released annually stood at eighty in 1985, but in 1994 this figure had declined to sixty-five (Paquet 2009: 49; Yecies 2007: 1; Kim Mee-hyun 2007: 415). The enfeebled post-trade deal condition of Korean film was part of an ongoing decline that started in the

1970s (Paquet 2009: 9).[18] Audience numbers had fallen consistently for years; in 1970, 166 million film tickets were sold, compared to 48 million in 1993. In 1970, the average Korean saw 5.1 films annually; by 1993, this had dropped to just 1.1 films every year (Lee Hyang-jin 2000: 55).

The fall in audience numbers was due to several issues: first, the poor shape of domestic film production; second, the existence of other more attractive leisure options; and third, the deteriorated state of theatrical exhibition. Years of under-investment, poor business practices and a lack of innovation undermined domestic filmmaking. During the dictatorship, linking foreign film imports to production resulted in lower-quality Korean movies made by companies seeking lucrative import deals. Another problem that continued after the dictatorship was censorship which hamstrung the creative efforts of filmmakers to express their art and treat political or social issues in the way they desired (Paquet 2009: 9). Chun's early 1980s '3-S' (sex, screen and sports) policy aimed to divert the population's attention away from continued government repression by investing in sports events (like baseball), and partially relaxing film censorship to allow unprecedented erotic imagery, although socio-political content was still heavily censored (Lee Yeon-ho 2007: 277; Yecies and Shim 2016: 148; Min et al. 2003: 63). The result was a plethora of soft-core pornographic melodramas from the early 1980s, such as *Madame Aema* (*Aema puin*, 1982, Chŏng In-yŏb, ROK) and *Mulberry* (*PPong*, 1986, Yi Tu-yŏng, ROK). Making films with more nudity rather than big-budget blockbusters was seen as a cost-effective method of drawing back domestic audiences in an investment-starved industry (Yecies and Shim 2016: 151).[19] However, the production of pornography did little to improve the overall perception that domestic film was inferior in comparison to overseas cinema (Sŏng 2020b).

With one notable exception, the set-up in Ch'ungmuro did not promote the type of innovation that might have helped renew the fortunes of Korea's film industry. Critics attacked Ch'ungmuro as conservative, lacking in creativity, corrupt and governed by vested interests (see Hŏ and Cho 1998). The film industry was dominated by the so-called *tojejedo* (master–apprentice director system), which relegated 'newcomers to the bottom of the ladder in any film production operation' regardless of age, education, experience, or training, thus blocking opportunities for promising young filmmakers (Park 2015: 74). Given such an environment and a system which required producers to apply for government-approved licenses to secure rights to motion picture production, there was a lack of the funds necessary to improve the quality of filmmaking (Paquet 2009: 46).

The exception to the general poor quality Ch'ungmuro films came from a group of directors emerging from the *minjung* anti-dictatorship movement around the mid to late 1980s such as Jang Sun-woo (Chang Sŏn-u), Park Kwang-su and Chung Ji-young (Chŏng Chi-yŏng). Scholars and critics have used different terms including 'New Realism' and 'New Wave' to characterise the post-1987 work of these filmmakers (Standish 1994: 75; Paquet 2009: 21; Lee 2022: 25). This group embraced divergent practices but what was new was their choice of subject matter and protagonists. Jang, Park and Chung made films about social problems and taboo historical issues such as the Korean War. Their main characters were marginal types like activists, striking workers, communist guerrillas and victims of American or state aggression (Lee 2022: 28). This group of directors believed that filmmakers should not just produce entertainment, they should strive to change society (Standish 1994: 112). Films such as Park Kwang-su's *The Black Republic* (*Kŭdŭlto urich'ŏrŏm*, 1990, ROK, 48,851), *A Single Spark* (*Arŭmdaun ch'ŏngnyŏn Chŏn T'ae-il*, 1995, ROK, 235,935), Chung Ji-young's *White Badge* (Hayan chŏnjaeng, 1992, ROK, 151,638), Jang Sun-woo's *A Petal* (*Kkotnip*, 1996, ROK, 213,979) or Im Kwon-taek's *The Surrogate Mother* (Ssibadi, 1986, ROK) often performed well at domestic box offices and were lauded at foreign film festivals.[20] They were important because they attracted considerable critical praise at home and abroad at a time when much of Ch'ungmuro output was believed to be bereft of ideas. They gave the South Korean film industry an essential boost at a low point, allowing it to establish itself abroad when it was neglected at home (Lee 2022: 25). Unlike the independent documentary filmmaker Kim Dong-won who also emerged from an activist background, all of these directors operated within the established Ch'ungmuro system, and although their films were often censored, they still received criticisms for compromising their political ideals by creating films within the *chedogwŏn* and for pursuing 'commercial viability' (Lee 2022: 28).[21] Despite the success of these committed directors, the public largely voted with their feet and the market share of domestic films compared with foreign films continued to decline (Cho Joon-hyeong 2006: 16). Post-1987, Korean cinema was in what film scholar Kang So-wŏn describes as a 'sad' condition (2006: 63). Filmmaker Chung Ji-young reported in a 2020 interview that things had become so bad with Korean pictures that while picketing the screening of Hollywood motion pictures to protest the 1980s market opening, cinemagoers queuing to buy tickets jeered the demonstrators. Chung claimed the crowds shouted: 'Try making better movies!' (Kim Ji-soo 2020; Yu 2007a: 304).

It wasn't just poor domestic film that kept audiences away from cinemas; as in other parts of the world, movie theatres faced stiff competition from different forms of entertainment, notably television. The penetration rate of televisions stood at around 6.6 per cent of all households in 1970, lagging behind North Korea. By 1980, 85 per cent of Korean homes had televisions, and by 1982 – two years after colour broadcasting had begun – almost every family owned a set (Kim 2000: 68; Hwang 2017: 38; Kwon and Kim 2013: 521). In the early 1980s, the three major broadcasters – KBS1, KBS2 and MBC – lacked the necessary technology to produce enough programmes in colour to fill their schedules. Instead, they aired imported foreign films – vintage classics, westerns and recently released movies. Televised film broadcasting dealt a further blow to sales at cinema box offices (Hwang 2017: 38). Intense competition amongst the chaebol in the white goods market resulted in lower prices, and with improved technology, television screen sizes increased, improving the home entertainment experience. The popularity of the videotape became another reason not to go out to the cinema. In 1985, only 10 per cent of Korean households owned a VCR, but by 1994 this had grown to 80 per cent of all families, or 8.29 million VCR systems (Kim Hyae-joon 2007: 325). Virtually every neighbourhood in Korea had a video store where you could rent videos and even borrow VCRs for a nominal cost. In addition to the estimated 30,000 video stores, the mid-1990s saw the appearance of *pideobang* (literally: 'video rooms'), which commonly consisted of multiple booths big enough to fit a video machine, a screen and a two-person sofa (personal correspondence, Lee Kwang-mo, May 2020). They sold refreshments, served alcohol illegally to minors, and allowed people to smoke. Friends or dating couples could spend an evening watching several movies in total privacy for a standard cinema ticket price. These facilities made watching movies on video one of the most popular pastimes of the early to mid-1990s, enticing film audiences away from cinemas. Once VCRs had become a fixture in Korean homes, the video market expanded to the extent that its revenues were twice that of movie theatre revenues by the mid-1990s (Shin Kang-ho 2007a: 307). Like the *pideobang*, the *noraebang* (literally: 'singing rooms') also consisted of private booths, and they sold snacks and alcohol and permitted smoking. They were ideal for courting couples, friends or groups on work nights out as a *samch'a* (a third entertainment destination) following a visit to a restaurant and bar. In early 1990s Korea, *noraebang* became one of the most popular pastimes for a wealthy, hardworking population (Maliangkay 2014: 304; Lee 2007: 49).

Going to the movies in 1980s–90s Korean cinemas

Noraebang, pideobang, television, VCR and other leisure pursuits attracted many young, affluent Koreans away from the big screen. However, there was much in the way film was exhibited in this period that deterred audiences from visiting the cinema in the first place. Watching a movie at a Korean cinema in the post-1987 period was a very different experience from the current era of multiplexes which have spread nationwide across Korea since the new millennium. Between the late 1980s and early to mid-1990s, cinemas in Chongno, the central entertainment district of Seoul, were plush and offered comfortable seating and lounge areas in which customers could relax. But outside the centre and especially in provincial areas, cinemas were often colder venues in varying states of disrepair. Cinemas were frequently situated across the middle and higher floors of multi-use building complexes, which featured a wide range of businesses, including restaurants, billiard halls, travel agencies and private academies (*hagwŏn*; see Figure 1.1). The theatres were easily identifiable thanks to giant hand-painted versions of the official film posters that decorated the front of buildings (Figure 1.2).[22] Inside, uncarpeted marble lobby areas were heated by single paraffin-fuelled 'space' heaters that produced a distinctive odour of kerosene, but which could rapidly heat the largest of halls even in the coldest Seoul winters. In foyers, spectators could purchase salted popcorn, dried and roasted squid with *koch'ujang* (a spicy red pepper sauce), peanuts and soft drinks to take into the auditorium. Often cinemas had separate auditoriums located on different floors from the main foyer, so customers took elevators to reach their theatre. Stairwells were a less pleasant route to the films, since they were frequently used as smoking areas prior to screenings (as were toilets). Seats were assigned, and small maps posted at auditorium entrances helped orientate audiences. Programmes generally consisted of five minutes of local advertising, three or four trailers promoting future screenings, followed by the main feature.

Figure 1.1 Multi-use commercial buildings. (L) The Cine Core cinema in 2003 (courtesy Roald Maliangkay 2022). (R) Site of Ewha Art Theatre in Shinch'on that was typical of the location of many cinemas in the 1980s (author's photo).

Figure 1.2 Hand-painted posters (*kanp'an*) from the 1970s (L) and from 1988 (R) that were a regular feature of Korean cinemas (courtesy Roald Maliangkay, 2022).

As in other parts of the world, weekends were the busiest periods for cinemas, and anyone trying to get tickets would frequently see the term *maejin*, or 'sold out' at box offices about late-afternoon or evening screenings (Paquet 2001). At peak times, demand for tickets to popular films was high, and consequently, theatres often crammed in spectators, making for a challenging viewing experience. In the late 1980s, demand was greatest for Hong Kong action or big-budget Hollywood spectaculars. Many cinema proprietors – even those in Seoul's most famous cinemas – openly flouted health and safety laws by arranging extra foldable chairs and filling up the aisles once the auditorium was at capacity.[23] Reflecting on these cinema-going days, it is a miracle that no serious disaster befell Korean audiences during this period. At busy weekend periods and traditional Korean holidays, theatres organised as many screenings

Political and cultural influences   47

as they could in a single day. It was not unusual for both exhibitors and distributors to illegally cut films to fit more screenings into busy viewing periods (author interview with Lee Kwang-mo, June 2020). In many cases, these cuts were jarring, complicating comprehension of the narrative (Paquet 2001). As soon as the main feature finished, the house lights went on, interrupting the viewing of the end credits (if indeed these were shown at all). As a result, audiences often found themselves filing out past spectators already lined up in front of their seats with the next programme already underway. Getting in and out of busy screenings was a challenge; watching popular films, especially in rural cinemas, could be a noisy affair, with audience members frequently engaging in conversation during screenings.[24]

It was also not uncommon for less popular new releases to be swiftly pulled from the screens if demand was poor. Advertising for cinema showings was frequently done via small cards left in the foyers or handed out in the street with handy calendars on the flip side to encourage continued use (see Figure 1.3). Most people found out about film screenings via full-page adverts in daily newspapers, but since this marketing was arranged in advance, customers might turn up at cinemas to find less popular new releases already pulled and other films playing in their place (MBC 1995). Movies in South Korean cinemas were mainly

Figure 1.3 Advertising cards for Ewha Art Theatre from late 1980s (Yu 2015).

subtitled, and the Korean characters appeared on the right-hand side of the screen with the hangul (Korean alphabet) read from top to bottom and left to right (Paquet 2001). For the non-Korean language films that played, a frequent complaint of consumers was that the subtitles – if they were visible at all – often only had a tenuous relationship with the dialogue they accompanied (MBC 1995). This was the state of exhibition in the early 1990s, one that made cinema a less than comfortable experience for many viewers and a reason why other entertainment options were more attractive. This culture of exhibition practices was also one that many art film exhibitors set out to challenge from the mid-1990s onwards.

The state of film production and theatres and competition from other forms of entertainment help us understand what kept audiences away from post-1987 cinemas, exhibitors interested in art film also faced extreme challenges sourcing movies. Lee Kwang-mo recalled in 2020 that one issue was thirty years of strict controls over foreign film importation meant South Korea lacked some of the developed infrastructure required to source non-Hollywood products:

> The most shocking thing when I came back to Korea in 1991 was that many great movies had never been officially screened or introduced at regular theatres . . . even the Korean Film Archives failed to plan and show foreign films properly.[25] Moreover, the exchange programme with film archives worldwide was not working properly . . . In other countries at the time, art houses could screen various films at a low cost via a rental system.[26] However in Korea there were no archives or rental systems providing such services, so art houses had to go through the formal costly import process to screen a movie. The lengthy censorship process further delayed the pictures. (Personal correspondence, Lee Kwang-mo, June 2020)

According to Lee, therefore, there was no or little financial incentive for companies to risk the importation, distribution and exhibition of 'art films with limited commercial potential' (personal correspondence, Lee Kwang-mo, June 2020). Without established government-run institutions to compensate for the absence of a market for speciality film, the outlook was bleak for those Korean fans who wanted to see art movies on the big screen.

Late-dictatorship and post-1987 reforms and developments in Korean film

Faced with declines in audience numbers, the government had stepped in several times to improve both cinematic production and exhibition, and of these attempts, three, in particular, are vital for our understanding of the development of art houses in the 1990s. The first is the Chun Doo Hwan administration's attempt to invigorate the cinematic industry by reforming exhibition. Until 1981, the government had tightly controlled the construction of movie theatres and the distribution of films. There were hierarchies of first, second and third-run cinemas, a situation determined partly by a policy limiting the number of screening prints of imported movies to save on foreign currency expenditure (Lee Woo-suk 2006: 256). First-run theatres located in larger city centres had priority in screening foreign motion pictures. Second-run cinemas located in industrial and residential areas of suburbs received the prints next (Lee Woo-suk 2006: 257).[27] With declining audiences, many establishments ran into debt, so the government relaxed theatre regulations in 1981, allowing cinemas to divide single large auditoriums into smaller ones to generate more screenings, audience choice and revenue (Shin Kang-ho 2007a: 306). Several large-scale theatres operating at huge losses, including the Far East Theatre (Kŭkdong kŭkjang) and the Pagoda Theatre (P'agoda kŭkjang) divided their auditoriums in this way, predating the multiplex by two decades (Hwang 2017: 40).[28] From 1982, it became possible to establish and operate a small theatre (with 300 seats or fewer) with minimal red tape (Hwang 2017: 40–1). These moves liberalised the operation of cinemas and were financially advantageous for exhibitors, who could now screen multiple films in one cinema or operate smaller auditoriums with lower running costs.

Small theatres were established in the suburbs, operating in low-rent neighbourhoods close to residential areas (Shin Kang-ho 2007a: 306). The next few years saw a large-scale growth of small cinemas across the country, with forty-one opening up in Seoul alone by 1984 (Hwang 2017: 40). The New Core Art Theatre opened in 1982, eventually becoming the Core Art Hall, one of the most influential 1990s art houses (Hwang 2017: 41). The enlargement of municipal public transportation networks into the outlying areas of Seoul and other major cities facilitated this expansion of theatres. The nationwide lifting of the military curfew in 1982 also made it easier for young people to go to cinemas to watch movies (Kang 2006: 51; Hwang 2017: 40–2).

The emergence of these small theatres helped alleviate the dire situation that many cinemas faced at the start of the 1980s and facilitated the 1990s emergence of art houses. These developments did not cure the downward trend in audience numbers, however, and later vital shifts in the market and regulatory changes helped the domestic industry survive.

A critical transformation in the fortunes of Korean cinema from the 1990s onwards came in the form of President Kim Young Sam's 'Creation of the New Korea' or 'Segyehwa' (Globalisation) policy, which aimed to increase Korea's industrial competitiveness, and national image by opening up the country to the global market (Park 2015: 93–5). Kim's Segyehwa also included an important role for the cultural industries as part of this effort to improve Korea's name brand abroad (Park 2015: 93). As far as it concerned domestic film, Segyehwa was partly a continuation of the strategies of the Chun Doo Hwan and Roh Tae Woo administrations. The Chun government encouraged directors to exhibit their works internationally by providing financial support for scenarios that they deemed to be 'quality' and by sponsoring overseas retrospectives such as the 1993 Centre Pompidou celebration of Korean cinema (Lee 2022: 26). However, the incentives to raise Korea's international profile were often undermined by government requirements that films express 'traditional Korean culture' and represent the 'official view of Korean history' to receive financial aid (Min, Joo and Kwak 2003: 64).[29] One key difference was that the Kim Young Sam government's policy was geared towards support rather than control and was more successful in initiating changes. Kim drew up a Five-Year Plan for promoting cultural development that included establishing a cable television system and tax breaks for film production (Park 2015: 99; Paquet 2009: 54).

The moves by Kim encouraged the entry of chaebols into film production. Chaebols also saw financial potential in the rapid growth of the lucrative VCR and home video market. Chaebols such as Samsung, Daewoo, LG and SKC increased their production of VCRs, using their business acumen to expand first into the tape market and then into film production and distribution (Yecies and Shim 2016: 158–60). All these factors – the video market, the introduction of cable television and the tax breaks – helped encourage the chaebols into film. Their impact on the Korean film industry was significant, and by 1994, chaebol investment was behind more than a third of all Korean movies (Cho 2006: 151–2; Park 2015: 61). Chaebols provided vital funding for cash-strapped filmmakers and were open to cooperation with an emerging group of young, media-savvy and adventurous producers such as Shin Chŏl of Shincine Productions. The chaebols' market-driven strategy meant filmmakers no longer needed to rely on the formulaic genres that had been the mainstay of Ch'ungmuro-produced domestic movies for years, and which had provoked widespread public dissatisfaction (Yecies and Shim

2016: 160). Many researchers, including Kim Young-jin (personal correspondence, July 2020), Brian Yecies and Ae-Gyung Shim (2016), have argued these transformations – particularly the entry of the chaebols and the emergence of new producers – were important to changing industrial practices when domestic film was in decline. All these attempts to reform the Korean film industry in the late-dictatorship and post-1987–95 period had significant and diverse impacts on the cinephilia and art film consumption of the mid-1990s.

Conclusion

In the late-dictatorship and post-1987 era, the clash of the shifting plates of two political systems threw up significant social and cultural tensions. On the one hand, the time brought promises of greater possibilities, and on the other, frustration with the speed of de-authoritarianisation. Post-1987, Korea witnessed increased political freedom, economic expansion, cinematic market opening and institutional reforms, which suggested an era of liberated cultural consumption. The opening of the market, however, did not bring in instant access to a diversity of motion pictures, nor to the thirty years of film that had never been screened theatrically in Korea. Throughout the late-dictatorship and post-1987 period, a groundswell of discontent had been bubbling about access to film, and this would find expression in the development of non-theatrical exhibition spaces, a subject we examine in the next chapter.

Notes

1. I use *minjung* movement and *undongkwŏn* synonymously.
2. The 1972 Yushin reforms banned party politics and made Park dictator (Eckert et al. 1991: 359).
3. Yi never explains what she means by *chedogwŏn* but uses it to distinguish between what is and what is not state-sanctioned and approved (see also Kim et al. 2004: 23). Yi's usage also appears to reflect the implicit comprehension of the term by participants at the time.
4. There is also an ethno-nationalistic component to *chedogwŏn*, the implication being that those opposed to the *chedogwŏn* were more representative of true Korean values.
5. Within the *minjung* movement, there was a disparate variety of groups which referred to themselves as 'movements', but were unified by their opposition to the *chedogwŏn*.

6. Mobrand provides the example of elite responses to 1958 and 1960 protests (2019: 66).
7. The reason for the decline of radical student politics is unclear but a series of controversial deaths during violent student protests contributed to the decline of the movement (Sohn 1997).
8. Immediate changes included restrictions on incumbent ruling elites, a less repressive state, legally acceptable civic activism (Son Min-ho 2014).
9. According to Article 18 of the 1986 Sixth Revision to the Motion Picture Laws, the PPEC could make cuts to a film if it impaired the 'spirit of the constitution ... dignity of the state ... social order and morals ... the soundness of people' (Park 2002: 124–5).
10. For example, *Missing* (1982, Costa-Gavras, US), about the disappearance of a US journalist in Pinochet-era Chile, and *Salvador* (1986, Oliver Stone, US) a film criticising the US-backed military of El Salvador (Park 2002: 126).
11. In 1992, for example, the Core Art Hall screened *In Bed with Madonna* (1991, Alek Keshishian, US) that ran at just over one hour when the US running time was considerably longer (thanks to Isolde Standish for this information).
12. The authorities also censored pop music (Maliangkay 2014: 296; Kwon and Kim 2013: 521). When the eponymous Tracy Chapman (1988) album was released in Seoul in the early 1990s, the album cover featured a sticker that stated: 'Featuring the hit single: "Talking 'bout a Revolution"'. The track was removed by the authorities for its leftist connotations.
13. In the 2000s, 50 per cent of Koreans considered themselves to be middle class, and in 2016 only 40 per cent did (Cho 2020).
14. Until January 1989, travel abroad was a privilege accorded citizens by the dictatorship, which could rescind permission. Travel was restricted to people engaged in business, official or academic work, and the government charged hefty sums for travel visas (Son Min-ho 2014).
15. The Sixth Revision to the Motion Picture Law opening the Korean domestic market to foreign competition was enacted in 1987 (Paquet 2009: 47).
16. This was down from an all-time high of 165 days a year (Yecies 2007: 8). The figure of 146 could be reduced by twenty days if Korean films were screened during high season (Yu 2007b: 347); The Roh administration required every cinema to show domestic films for a minimum of 106 days a year (29 per cent of all screening days; Yecies 2007: 9).
17. In 1989, 11 million Koreans saw locally produced films, while 44 million saw imported movies doubling foreign film attendance rates compared with 1983 (Cho 2006: 162).
18. Chun Doo Hwan opened domestic film to secure Korean chaebol access to the lucrative US automobile market (Paquet 2009: 50).
19. Individual films performed well, but the strategy went into decline following the 1987 opening of the cinema market to foreign film (Yecies and Shim 2016: 151).
20. I use Hyunseon Lee's (2022) definition of New Wave directors that includes Im Kwon-taek despite his greater focus on Korean heritage in film.
21. See Standish (1994: 65) for some of these criticisms.

22. See Song Chun's description of the tenth floor Cine Core's 'superior facilities' which were a major draw in the late 1980s (Song 1997).
23. Song Chun claims one noticeable feature of the Cine Core was the emergency exit 'with enough room for eight rows of people to escape simultaneously' (Song 1997).
24. On a trip to Chŏlla province in 1993, I saw a Sunday matinee screening of *Jurassic Park* (1993, dir. Steven Spielberg) at the main cinema in Chŏnju. The seats were ramshackle, and the auditorium was packed with families. Crowds of bored small children ran in a giant circle around the auditorium and the subtitled dialogue was drowned out by the din of constant chatter around the theatre that only abated with the roar of a dinosaur.
25. Park Chung Hee established the first archives in 1974 after North Korea affiliated their collection to the World Federation of Film Archives. The name changed to the Korea Film Archive in 1991 (Sŏng 2020b).
26. Lee claimed that in other countries art film rentals cost a 'few hundred dollars' (personal correspondence, Lee Kwang-mo, June 2020).
27. Theatres attracted different audiences through their screenings – first-run theatres showed Oscar-winning pictures and second-run cinemas specialised in Hong Kong martial arts films. A trip to a first-run theatre was a special treat for suburban families (Lee Woo-suk 2006: 256–7).
28. The Pagoda Theatre's auditorium of 613 seats was divided into a 497- and 299-seat hall (Hwang 2017: 40).
29. For 1980s international film festival award winners see Shin Kang-ho (2007d: 297).

Chapter 2

Non-theatrical exhibition and the emergence of an art film audience

Cinemas were not the only places where Koreans could consume film in the late-dictatorship and post-1987 period. Many young Koreans voted with their feet, given the poor state of theatres and domestic movies. They chose to watch films in alternative sites with other groups of like-minded people, away from first-release cinema-going audiences. The European cultural centres and university film clubs predate the 1987 introduction of direct presidential elections, but both continued to influence cinematic culture well into the 1990s. The small commercial ventures called 'videotheques', run by private associations in major cities, began to open from 1988 onwards and continued until the new millennium. All three spaces offered participants a cinematic means of overcoming the dictatorship's cultural blockade and its continuing post-1987 influence. All were formed in opposition to what was perceived by their devotees as the culture of mainstream theatrical exhibition. These alternative viewing practices and spaces also had an essential influence on 1990s art houses, cinephilia and the Korean cinematic industry in general. They exhibited art film when screening opportunities for movies outside the mainstream were limited, and they helped form a wider audience for the art houses that emerged. In this chapter, I examine the institutional identities of European cultural centres, university film clubs and videotheques focusing on the motivations and desires of the users of these spaces, the type of films consumed there, the sourcing of these motion pictures, and the links with Korean filmmaking and exhibition practices that emerged.

European cultural centres

The European cultural centres were crucial places for film viewing in late-dictatorship era Seoul outside of regular movie theatres.[1] The best known centres that operated film screenings were the German Goethe Institute and the French Cultural Centre (Centre Culturel Français), which opened near Kwangwhamun, central Seoul, in 1968 (Hwang 2017: 31). The activities of the European cultural centres began at the height of the military dictatorship between the 1970s and 1980s, but their influence continued long afterwards.

The dictatorship years

The French Cultural Centre organised screenings from its opening, and film scholar Kim Hong-jun reports attending screenings in 1972 and at the German Cultural Centre as early as 1975 (personal correspondence, Kim Hong-jun, April 2021). In 1977, the French Cultural Centre formed the Cine-Club, where critics, university students and professors gathered to view and discuss cinema (Park 2009: 55). Cine-Club screenings occurred on Thursdays and Saturdays in the small underground Salle de Renoir auditorium, which contained 120 seats. Five to ten previously unscreened films were shipped in from France each month, and the cultural centre charged between six and ten cents for admission (which was roughly one-fifth of the average ticket cost at the time; Hwang 2017: 32). The following year the Goethe Institute started the East-West Cinema Club (Tongsŏyŏnghwa tonguhoe) – another group boasting up to 300 members who engaged in discussions about film theory, translated film scripts, produced films and even ran a small journal (*The East-West Cinema Bulletin*, Tongsŏyŏnghwahoebo) for a short time (Park 2009: 55; Shin Kang-ho 2007b: 259).

When these cultural centres first opened, the Park Chung Hee administration only allowed the importation of one foreign film per film company per year (in 1971; Hwang 2017: 31). Even as late as 1984, only twenty-five imported films were released in Korea (Paquet 2009: 49). The cultural centres were not subject to the strict censorship of the authorities. They were, therefore, venues where audiences could see films that could not be viewed in wider Korean society. One member of the Cine-Club was film critic Chŏng Sŏng-il, who explained that it was through these screenings that he was first introduced to European and especially French cinema. In the Salle de Renoir, he saw films by Luis Buñuel, Jacques Tati and Jean Cocteau as well as films from the French New Wave. Chŏng noted that there were many reasons why he attended the screenings at the French Cultural Centre, not all of which were concerned with cinema:

> In those days, (Korean production companies) made the type of movies the regime approved of, like pro-Saemaŭl (movement)[2] films, anti-communist movies, or literary adaptations. Korean films were totally shredded by censorship. There wasn't any Internet, any DVDs or even videotapes. You could only see movies at the cinemas, or you had to wait until a decent classic film came on TV at the weekends. In my first year of high school, I found out from a radio show that they screened films like *Forbidden Games* (*Jeux interdits*, 1952, René Clément, France) at the French Cultural Centre. I was dying to see these movies, so I gathered all my courage and went to the building opposite the Kyŏngbokgun royal palace. The day I first went, they were screening Jean-Luc Godard's *The Carabineers* (1963, France). I didn't know who Godard was, but from that day onwards, I started to go to 'school' at the French Cultural Centre. There I was without any sense of bearing. I saw Algerian films and African films. During those moments, it was as if I was in a space and time that had absolutely nothing to do with Korea. (Cited in Im In-t'aek 2006)

As Chŏng indicates, going to screenings at the French Cultural Centre was not just a way of accessing unobtainable films. It was an education in itself – a different way of finding out about the world in an atmosphere where the dictatorship restricted information to the population. The relentless ideological indoctrination and the fixation on national reconstruction made visits to the cinema and daily life unremittingly dull for Chŏng and young Koreans at the time. He comments that: 'It was the worst possible time to have been a movie buff in Korea' (Im In-t'aek 2006). One other factor is essential to understand Chŏng's response to his first film experiences in the French Cultural Centre. When the authorities restricted overseas travel, Chŏng's visits to the French Cultural Centre were like trips abroad – an introduction to another world even: 'It was like living in exile – underground!' (Im In-t'aek 2006). This rare glimpse of a world beyond the peninsula provided a crucial practical education for other attendees. Kim Hong-jun reports that many attendees were women in their early twenties who had been granted permission to travel overseas for language study and university education. The screenings offered closer contact with the outside world than what was provided in books (personal correspondence, Kim Hong-jun, April 2021). The Cine-Club attached to the French Cultural Centre was relatively short-lived, and it stopped operating after a year due to declining numbers of student attendees (Park 2009: 55). The East-West Cinema Club lasted longer, although Chŏng claims that the Kwangju Uprising in 1980 signalled the end of the influence of the Cultural centres, as young people became active in anti-dictatorship politics instead (Park 2009: 55; Im In-t'aek 2006).

The post-dictatorship years and the continuing legacy

The end of the Cine-Club and the East-West Cinema Club was not the end of film screenings at the European cultural centres, however; these continued throughout the 1990s. Attendees during the late 1980s and early 1990s revealed multiple motivations for attending. On one level, the screenings still provided many young Koreans with alternative cultural exposure via the type of film they could never see at ordinary cinemas.[3] Film scholar Hana Lee (Yi Ha-na) reports of her visits in the late 1980s and 1990s:

> I didn't really go to the French Cultural Centre to learn about French cinema. There was not much to see except Korean or Hollywood films, and so I had a great deal of curiosity about European cinema. I didn't know what movie was on, it didn't matter; I just went along. (Personal correspondence, Hana Lee, April 2021)

Another occasional attendee in the late 1980s and early 1990s, Na Su-min* reports the same sense of novelty that Chŏng felt at the height of the dictatorship:

> The films were interesting, but more than that, it was the experience. This big French (Korean style) Buddhist monk sat in the audience, reading books and watching the films. He had these piercing blue eyes, and he was speaking Korean. I'd never seen anything like it. (Author interview with Na Su-min*, April 2021)

Thus, even in the immediate post-dictatorship period, young people received an insight into European culture not just through the films but through the experience of the exhibition space itself.

In addition to the educational and experiential side of the screenings, other attendees reported a crucial social function. Park Ch'an-sik recalls his first experiences of European cinema at the French Cultural Centre in the early 1990s: 'It was the type of place where cinephiles got together, watched a film, discussed cinema and then had a drink afterwards.' What Park indicates about his experience is the radically different form of film spectatorship that the European cultural centres provided. These were not random spectators thrown together in an auditorium. Instead, Park and other like-minded film fans regularly gathered to watch movies, talk about them and socialise.

The cultural centres offered young Koreans new ways of consuming European cinematic culture; however, screenings were beset by technical, social and political problems. Na Su-min* reports constant issues with the quality of the screenings, especially the subtitling:

> Of the films I saw, I only really remember *Jeux Interdits* very well, but others I just nodded off. The films were black and white, and the English subtitles were in white letters, so half the time, you couldn't read anything because the background obscured the subtitles. It was as though it was raining on the screen. (Author interview, April 2021)

Another complaint expressed by former attendees concerns the cliquish character of the clientele. Irene Hee Seung Lee reports that: 'I went to the French Cultural Centre once or twice, but I felt quite alienated when I attended this place … I never felt welcome, it felt like a private club' (author interview, March 2021). While most attendees were young women, some of this hostility appears to have been directed by male regulars to first-time female members.

Another criticism of the European cultural centres concerned their lack of connection to the domestic socio-political realities. Notable post-Kwangju splits emerged between those who were *undongjuŭi* (literally 'movement' focused) because they saw film as a tool to radically change society and enthusiasts with a less engaged view of cinema (Sŏng 2020d; Chŏng Hye-yŏn 2008; Sohn 2022: 70). Those who sat in the activist camp saw it as their task to create a 'native' cultural model through film to aid the reconstruction of an egalitarian Korea from the ashes of the dictatorship (Shin Kang-ho 2007b: 260; Park 2015: 41; Sohn 2022: 70). The film as 'art' (*yŏnghwajuŭi*; literally, 'film-centred') camp exemplified by the cultural centre devotees called for an appreciation of film aesthetics (Yi Sŏn-ju 2017: 421). The activist camp frowned upon the Kwanghwamun screenings arguing that watching films in foreign cultural centres was both a 'worship of western culture' and a luxury at a time of hardship for many Koreans (Shin Kang-ho 2007b: 260).[4] Activists also critiqued the film as 'art' adherents' engagement with film as passive, fetishistic and consumption-centred (Yi Sŏn-ju 2017: 422).[5]

Despite these criticisms, the European cultural centres left a significant legacy, as we see in the pages ahead. They provided a vital space for the formation of 1990s cinephilia and impacted cinematic production and film academia in South Korea. They piqued the interest of attendees for European and especially French films. Cultural centre regulars began to attend nascent art houses like the Core Art Hall and Dongsung Cinematheque, which focused on European film from the early 1990s onwards.[6] Many of the early participants of the screenings also formed a central group of film industry personnel in the years that followed. The so-called 'Cultural centre Generation' included critics and academics: Chŏng Sŏng-il, Kim Soyoung, movie directors and producers Kim Ŭi-sŏk (Ui-suk), Shin Chŏl and Korean New Wave filmmaker Chung Ji-young and, amongst many others (Park 2009: 55; Park 2015: 37; Paquet 2009: 15). Another exhibition space that predated the June Uprising of 1987 but continued its influential operations after was the university film clubs, and it is to these groups that we now turn.

Film clubs (cine-clubs)

Most of those in the activist camp formed film study associations, often called 'circles' (*tongari*) or cine-clubs, at universities around the country. The first, Yallasang (Yallyasyŏng), was formed by students in 1979 at Seoul National University, Korea's premier academic institution. However, other groups like Yŏnghwamadang'uri (Our cinema space), which grew out of the East-West Cinema Club or the Seoul Film Collective (Sŏulyŏngsangjiptan) which developed from Yallasang in 1986, were based outside campuses with a membership largely consisting of radical students or recent graduates (Park 2015: 49; Sŏng 2020a).[7] In the three years after Chun Doo Hwan's seizure of power and the Kwangju Uprising, the regime increased its repression against dissent on campuses, but confident that his rule was secure, Chun began to loosen state controls from 1985 onwards, resulting in an intensification of student activism against the regime.[8] The mid-1980s 'Campus Autonomy' school liberalisation policy relaxed regulations on forming small student organisations on campuses, meaning that film clubs could operate more openly (Lee 2006: 111; Shin Kang-ho 2007c: 299). Students spread their film clubs to prominent universities in the capital, including Korea, Yonsei, Sogang and Ewha Women's University (Shin Kang-ho 2007c: 299), and they were influential from this late-dictatorship period onwards.

Film clubs in the late-dictatorship years

Groups like Yallasang and Yŏnghwamadang'uri worked collectively to create and screen films that put into practice the radical ideas of social change that they were preaching (Shin Kang-ho 2007c: 299). There was a robust educational aspect within these groups. The Yallasang Cinema Club showed Italian Neo-Realist films and Third Cinema from Latin America – political films that were often officially proscribed. The club organised festivals and post-screening discussions of film. They made 'discussion manuals' and even produced a theoretical journal, *Yŏllin Yŏnghwa* (Open Cinema), to argue that film should be 'open' to all members of society and that it should assist in democratising society (Min et al. 2003: 76; Sohn 2012: 74; Park 2015: 37, 44). A key event in the development of activist cinema was the 1984 Small Film Festival (*chagŭnyŏnghwajae*) which promoted the creation of politically conscious 8mm or 16mm short films in opposition to the 'big' 35mm commercial format cinema (Park 2008: 46; Sohn 2022: 67). Yŏnghwamadang'uri emphasised production, pioneering short filmmaking courses and training young activist enthusiasts in techniques despite a lack of fully operational equipment (Sŏng 2020a). The names of the film groups provided evidence of their brand of radicalism and nationalism ('collective', 'madang' and 'our'; Park 2015: 51). They believed that the roots of their current travails – the division of the peninsula, dictatorship and poor working conditions – lay not just in capitalism but in western imperialism, meaning a specifically Korean solution to these problems. The Seoul Film Collective produced leftist theoretical books summarising their guiding principles, such as *Towards a New Cinema* (Saeroun yŏnghwa wihayŏ, 1983) (Paquet 2009: 17; Shin Kang-ho 2007c: 299). Most importantly, however, the group went beyond discussing theory; they also produced short films reflecting their ideals. One of the original members, Yi Hyo-in, claims that the group's *raison d'être* was to employ film to both resist the regime and achieve political transformation (Sŏng 2020d; Chŏng Hye-yŏn 2008).

A well-known example of this struggle was the production and exhibition of the 8mm film *Bluebird* (P'arangsae, 1986). The forty-minute film detailed the precarious economic existence of Korean farmers subject to extreme fluctuations in market prices for their goods. The film was proscribed because of its realistic depictions of rural poverty and the manner of its exhibition – since it was not submitted for censorship and was unregistered. The producers took the film on a tour of the country, secretly (and illegally) organising screenings at rural locations for audiences of farmers (Sŏng 2020d; Chung and Diffrient 2021: 22). The security services arrested, interrogated under duress three Seoul Film Collective members Hong Ki-sŏn, Yi Hyo-in and Pyŏn Chae-ran. When the charges of spreading subversive ideas could not be proven, the three were charged with the illegal exhibition and the production of another film, the *Resurrection of Sanha* (Puhwarhanŭn sanha, 1986) made by activists at a Yonsei University film club (Sŏng 2020c). This latter ninety-minute 8mm documentary provided a history of Korean people's struggles against capitalism, dictatorship and foreign imperialism from the 1895 Tonghak Uprising to the 1980 Kwangju Uprising. Like *Bluebird*, the film was then taken on an illegal screening tour of universities nationwide, including Korea and Yonsei universities in Seoul. Equipment was often borrowed or unfit for purpose, so screenings occasionally occurred without sound and with activist-announcers (*pyŏnsa*) providing a commentary for audiences (Sŏng 2020d). The tour prompted the incursion of riot police onto campuses to prevent the screenings leading to pitched battles between activists and security forces (*Chungang Ilbo* 1986; Sŏng 2020d). The production and exhibition of the underground films and the subsequent arrests became known as the *Bluebird* Incident (*P'arangsae sagŏn*), where '*sagŏn*' is a Korean term often used to describe an intensely controversial or shocking event of considerable socio-political significance. The affair caused a minor sensation after it was covered in national newspapers like the *Kyŏnghyang Sinmun*. The confrontation with the authorities and resultant media coverage was seen as a great success by film activists. The incident helped raise the interest of film clubs at universities countrywide and galvanised activists who formed a University Film Collective (Taehagyŏngwayŏnhap) in May 1987. The *Bluebird* Incident was evidence of film activists' commitment to social, political and cultural change within a larger *minjung* movement; it was also proof of what could be achieved in terms of mobilisation and consciousness-raising not just through short film production but most significantly in the way film was exhibited.

Post-1987 film clubs

Convinced that the direct presidential elections had produced a stillborn democracy, many activist film clubs continued after the 1987 June Uprising. Far from believing that the struggle should be wound down, they intensified their efforts for wider social, political, cultural and economic change (Lee Hyang-jin 2000: 148). These groups included Parit'ŏ, which was active between 1989 and 1992, and dedicated itself to promoting female participation in cinematic culture and practice. The group featured women who became prominent in Korean film, including academic, critic and filmmaker Kim Soyoung, and perhaps its most famous member, Byun Young-joo (Pyŏn Yŏng-ju), director of the documentary series on the tragedy of Korean women forced into sexual slavery by the Japanese Imperial Army (Sŏng 2020b; Yecies and Shim 2016: 193; Nam 2007: 167). The group's name is a play on words, with the first two syllables resembling the Korean word '*paridegi*' signifying 'suffering' and the French '*verité*' or 'truth' and the final syllable '*t'ŏ*' meaning 'place' (Yi 2019). The roots of Parit'ŏ are found in the 1970's women's film group – the Kaidu Club – which film critic and director Han Ok-hŭi began at Ewha Women's University (Park 2008: 133). Like the Kaidu Club, Parit'ŏ dedicated itself to promoting the production of short films that sought to undermine the damaging male dominance of Korean cinema. Its founding statement included a strong critique of the structures governing post-dictatorship era domestic film and representations of women in celluloid: 'Now, movies have become commercialised under the guise of art and filmmakers have prostituted themselves through commerce. Women are commodified and stripped off in the name of love and sold. Such a cinema must be transformed' (Sŏng 2020b; Sŏng 2020c). Parit'ŏ's aim was to challenge male-dominated industry structures and create 'a new culture' within Korean film (Sŏng 2020c).

Parit'ŏ faced great resistance against its activities but the impact of this female participation in Korean cinephilia was large. Parit'ŏ like the Kaidu Club before it was instrumental in bringing greater attention to feminist film at a time when female participation in production was blocked by a male-controlled mainstream industry (Sŏng 2020c). However, it was not only commercial filmmaking where male-centred attitudes discriminated against female involvement. Even movement associated male filmmakers strongly resisted institutions that promoted feminist topics. Kim Soyoung observes that some male activists felt so threatened by Parit'ŏ that they ridiculed its name by referring to it as 'PParit'ŏ' or 'place for doing the laundry' (Yi 2019; Sŏng 2020b).

Perhaps the most famous of all the activist film groups was Changsan'gonmae (Changsan-gotmae) formed by members of the University Film Collective including Hong Ki-sŏn and Pyŏn Chae-ran and they produced 16mm films that largely followed the nationalistic, leftist tone of *Bluebird* and the *Resurrection of Sanha*. *Oh, Dream Country!* (O! Kkumŭi nara, 1988, Yi Ŭn, Chang Tong-hong, Chang Yun-hyŏn) tells of a student's disenchantment with the USA following the Kwangju Uprising and *The Night Before the Strike* (P'aŏpchŏnya, 1990, Yi Ŭn, Chang Tong-hong, Chang Yun-hyŏn, Yi Chae-gu) is a story about labour activism in Korean factories. Using exhibition methods pioneered by pre-1987 activists, Changsan'gonmae illegally screened their films on university campuses provoking violent responses from the authorities and creating great publicity for activists. *The Night Before the Strike* drew audiences of over 300,000 students when it was simultaneously released in eleven university campuses (Kim Sunah 2007a: 331; Min et al. 2003: 78). The screenings helped raise public awareness of the continuing struggle of many activists against what they perceived was an unfair and unjust extension of the military's political domination. However, producing and exhibiting film in the manner of Seoul Film Collective and Changsan'gonmae was challenging. Changsan'gonmae only made one more film before disbanding. Many members were wanted by the authorities for their activities, and cases against them were not dropped until 1996, when the courts declared pre-production censorship unconstitutional (Kim Sunah 2007a: 332). Another primary hindrance to the unofficial and independent production of motion pictures – even 8mm or 16mm shorts – was sourcing equipment and finance. The producers of *The Night Before the Strike* had to borrow money and receive anonymous donations of funding and equipment to finish their film. Crews and actors went unpaid (Min et al. 2003: 79).

It should be noted that not all university film clubs were so committed to political change. Several members of less radical cinema groups from the late-dictatorship and immediate post-dictatorship period and who went on to actively participate in the 1990s art film scene, included art film distributor and former Hypertheque Nada Cinema manager Kim Nan-suk. Kim joined a film club in 1986 when she was studying at Hankuk University of Foreign Studies in Seoul. Another film club affiliate was Irene Hee-seung Lee (Yi Hŭi-sŭng). She became a member of the Ewha Women's University Cine-Club and also regularly attended art houses. Then a statistics major, Lee went to the Ewha film club after the transition to civilian government in 1993–5. Kim and Lee's accounts reveal significant commonalities and contrasts in the experiences offered by university film clubs, which is illustrative of the diverse motivations amongst participants.

For Kim, joining the club was about more than watching films; it also provided vital opportunities to participate in filmmaking at school:

> The club had formed the year before I joined, and all my university seniors (sŏnbae)⁹ were mainly Performing Arts majors. At the time, we acted in films and produced them on 8mm and 16mm. But if you didn't show up for one of the screenings, the seniors would tell you off and say do you know how hard we worked to get hold of this (film)? So don't even think about dozing off. I accompanied my seniors to the French or German Cultural Centre. They would write down the timetable, and say on this Saturday, this French director's movie is on at the French Cultural Centre and you lot had better watch this. We had to go back to the club for a debate on Saturday. But if you didn't watch the movie, you couldn't discuss it. It was not the done thing to do to miss turning up for the club. I liked the club, so I went. But the only way you could be eligible for film-production workshops was by attending the club. Back then, it was like that. You were more or less forced into participating. (Author interview with Kim Nan-suk, May 2020)

Kim's account illustrates the diverse motivations for participation in the film clubs. She was committed to the club out of interest and also had a desire to socialise and meet like-minded film buffs. There were also elements of coercion in the hierarchical club relationships (see also Sohn 2012: 71).[10] However, more than anything else it was a longing to take part in production that prompted her involvement. Only by active participation could members enjoy access to production privileges.

This exhibition-consumption-production connection is a vital reason behind the growth of university film clubs in the late 1980s. Sogang University also provided vital access to both the exhibition of rare films and production training and equipment. Throughout the 1980s, Father Kevin Kersten was responsible for Sogang University's Communication Centre (in western Seoul). Kersten was an American Jesuit priest and faculty member who taught media and filmmaking and ran one of the largest collections of overseas cinema in South Korea at the time. Ostensibly, the centre supplied lecturers with audio-visual materials for classes; however, Kersten also organised non-credit-bearing film seminars, including weekly screenings and discussions for students interested in film. Many who participated in these screenings were also taught filmmaking by Kersten, who oversaw the production of one hundred documentaries dedicated to the 'service of faith and the promotion of justice' (author interview with Kevin Kersten, July 2022). The most famous of these documentaries was Kim Dong-won's account of the government's eviction of homeless communities, *Sanggyedong Olympics*. The film was produced with the Communication Centre's equipment, while Kersten facilitated the film's English commentary and its release and promoted it abroad (author interview with Kevin Kersten, July 2022). Sogang became a late-dictatorship focal point for young people interested in cinema, illustrating the lure of production for many film buffs.

Although Kim and Lee's clubs operated during different periods, they had much in common: for example, the poor-quality materials, the desire to screen films that were difficult to source, and the illicit quality of the screenings. Lee recalled that she

> watched incomprehensible materials, like untranslated films that didn't have subtitles or Russian films with Japanese subtitles, but they were attractive because they were forbidden, so no one complained ... We understood that the screenings organised by the Cine-club showed illegal materials ... and we naturally accepted this .... As students, we had seen the first images of the Kwangju Uprising in this manner. We used dark curtains so that no one could see what we were doing. It was just what you did at the time. (Author interview with Irene Hee-seung Lee, April 2021)

Lee's film group had less of the political radicalism of other groups; however, they were still drawn to the subversive connotations of the meetings. Lee and her fellow students saw a direct link between the screening of uncut cinema and the politically seditious activity of watching images about the Kwangju Uprising.

Kim also had to watch films on poorly recorded and subtitled videotapes at screenings that provided the audiences with a less-than-ideal context in which to view films presented as significant artworks. The uncomfortable viewing conditions, like the coercion visited by the seniors upon junior members of Kim's film club, were accepted by club members as an essential part of the experience. The forbidden quality of the gatherings generated an intense sense of excitement that was attractive to club members, as Kim explained:

> We usually watched films on video ... We saw them in the film clubroom, or sometimes we went to a restaurant in front of the university with the video and VCR and got permission from the owner. Normally, it only takes thirty minutes to an hour to eat, and then you are supposed to leave the restaurant, but we were in there watching the films for two or three hours. The seniors sorted it all out in advance (with the restaurant owners). These were films that couldn't be shown in Korea back then, like Stanley Kubrick's *A Clockwork Orange* (1971, UK/US) and Pink Floyd's

> *The Wall* (1982, Alan Parker, Ireland/UK/West Germany), also films by Hou Hsiao-hsien. The most significant film that I saw was *Knife in the Water* (*Nóż w wodzie*, 1962, Poland) by (Roman) Polanski. We didn't really understand them, and the subtitles were shambolic, but we knew they were important. Our seniors got hold of them from the US Army base, or Itaewon, or when on trips to Japan, they used to come back with laserdiscs, and there were several places you could get them copied ... in Chongno. At that time, we loved film so much that we didn't care where we watched them or the poor state they were in. What was important was discussing and watching them together. (Author interview with Kim Nan-suk, May 2020)

Kim's film club saw itself as actively resisting the authorities by screening proscribed films – often in public places – and engaging in the smuggling of illegal videotapes. By seeking alternative forms of cinematic entertainment other than those shown on television and at mainstream cinemas, they deliberately contributed to the cultural undermining of what they saw as an illegitimate regime. Bringing in videotaped films into the country was risky since the luggage of returning Korean travellers was routinely X-rayed and subject to searches by customs officials searching for undeclared high-value goods from abroad. Senior students obtained illegal films in Itaewon, an area of shops, restaurants, markets and bars just outside the main gate of central Seoul's US army base at Yongsan.[11]

Another way unapproved films entered the country and were circulated was through the foreign religious community (author interview with Kim Nan-suk, May 2020; Sŏng 2020b). 1960s European art movies and 1970s American independent films were smuggled in from abroad on videotape by friends and associates of Father Kevin Kersten. Through his regular screenings, Father Kersten screened, copied and helped distribute unapproved and unreleased films (personal correspondence, Brother Anthony, August 2021).[12] This is how Kim's seniors sourced many of their movies, offering a further act of resistance against the authorities.

One additional element of defiance conducted by the film clubs concerned the taboo associations of the movies. Lee's group, for example, sought the uncut version of *Betty Blue* (*37°2 le matin*, Jean-Jacques Beineix, 1986, France), while Kim's club found other sexually explicit films like *In the Realm of the Senses* (*Ai no corrida*, Nagisa Ōshima, 1976, Japan/France). Lee explained that there was an interest in arousing content that was common to many club members despite

> the organisers' strong feminist perspectives ... We were twenty-year-olds, and we were all interested in things related to sex. We were also

attending a women's Presbyterian university, and we were fresh out of girls' high schools, so this was a big thing. People were secretly attending uncut films; for example, the unexpurgated version of *Basic Instinct* (Paul Verhoeven, 1992, US) was screened outside the university, so it was a big selling point of those film club activities. (Author interview with Irene Hee-seung Lee, April 2021)

Even though the Chun administration's 3-S policy had liberalised cinematic depictions of sex in movies several years earlier, the university film clubs had less interest in officially sanctioned pornography.[13] They were enticed by the prospect of having privileged knowledge, of experiencing what could not be felt or seen elsewhere in South Korea at the time. Student audiences making up these groups deliberately sought out forbidden, censored or seditious content.

Overall, there are some important points to note about the film clubs. Kim and Lee's college groupings were clearly not committed to the type of radical political activities espoused by activist camp-associated collectives such as Changsan'gonmae. However, with their furtive, forbidden screenings, illegally sourced films and prohibited sexual content, Kim and Lee's cine-clubs expressed what may be considered anti-*chedogwŏn* politics. As Michael Robinson argues, the late and post-dictatorship was a period when there was little room '*not* to be political' (Robinson 2005: 24–5). The ideological positions of film clubs were never absolute and, in most cases, were fluid, and opposition to the dictatorship and the legacy of authoritarianism united most student film gatherings. The anti-authority attitudes of even moderate film groups are important, and they constitute part of the identity of cinephiles.

Second, as with the foreign cultural centres, many prominent figures in Korean cinema first developed an interest in film via these university clubs, and they were also significant entry points for many of those who participated in the cinephilia of the 1990s. Former Kyungsung University Cine-Club attendees in Pusan helped found the globally recognised BIFF (Ahn 2012: 41). Members of the Seoul Film Collective and Changsan'gonmae such as Park Kwang-su and Jang Sun-woo were instrumental in launching the Korean New Wave of directors, Hong Ki-sŏn became a prominent filmmaker, Pyŏn Chae-ran and Yi Hyo-in became influential critics and academics. Park Chan-wook was a regular at Father Kersten's Communication Centre screenings and classes.

Film clubs like Kim's circle at Hankuk University or radical ones like Yallasang, were more productive than the European cultural centres; members frequently made films and acted. Of course, the university facilities were far more conducive to this type of movie consumption and production than the cultural centres, providing space and equipment. The film clubs mimicked the university class structures with 'senior' members taking the role of educators requiring 'juniors' to attend screenings and engage in post-viewing discussions. There was also a mandatory social and hierarchical element to the clubs – they weren't just watching movies but developing relationships. We also see the emergence of divisions amongst cinephiles, between those interested in consumption or exhibition and those who wanted to produce films, between those movement activists committed to social change through motion pictures and those whose concerns were less politically engaged. These divisions re-emerge as sources of discontent later in the 1990s with a growing audience for art film. From the late 1980s onwards, screenings were also held off university campuses in small commercial ventures commonly known as 'videotheques'. These venues had a significant structural and organisational influence on the cinematic culture that developed in the 1990s.

Videotheques

Often referred to as 'cinematheques', videotheques were private cinemas located in the higher floors or basements of commercial buildings in downtown areas (Kim Sunah 2007b: 345–6). Kim Young-jin contends that 'videotheque' is a more accurate description of what they were since organisers used VCRs rather than projectors to screen films (personal correspondence, July 2020).[14] The first videotheque, the Yŏnghwagonggan 1895 (Film space 1895) opened in 1988 (Sŏng 2020b). Several videotheques then became active in major cities countrywide in the early to mid-1990s, including OFIA, Munhwahakkyo Seoul (the Seoul school of culture, founded in 1991), SA-Sé and Cine Forum in the capital, and Yŏnghwa Kongbang (Film workshop) in Ch'ŏnnan, 1/24 in Pusan and Yŏnghwa Ŏndŏk (Film hill) in Taegu (Yi Sŏn-ju 2014: 224). Yi Ŏn-gyŏng personally funded the establishment of the pioneering videotheque – the Yŏnghwagonggan 1895 – but her original intention had not been film consumption but production. Yi had been a member of the Yŏnghwamadang'uri filmmaking collective, and she had begun to collect films never seen before in Korea to help develop the members' production skills. In a June 1990 interview with the *Han'gyŏrye*, she revealed both a formative and even national motivation behind the creation of the videotheque: 'What was the point of talking about Italian Neo-Realism if you couldn't even see *Rome Open City* (*Roma Città Aperta*, Roberto Rossellini, 1945, Italy)?' Through screenings, discussions and analysis, she argued young filmmakers would 'develop a new language for Korean film' (*Han'gyŏrye* 1990). The only way for Yi to collect the vast number of films she and others like her needed to watch to transform Korean cinema was to pool the collective resources of cinephiles, so she initially set up a video library and study centre (*kongbubang*) at the Yŏnghwamadang'uri's offices in western Seoul (Sŏng 2020b; *Han'gyŏrye* 1990). The twice-weekly themed screenings and video sharing system were such a success that Yi decided to move the study centre into bigger premises to meet demand. Yŏnghwagonggan 1895 was the result.

From 1991 onwards, Yŏnghwagonggan 1895 rented out the second floor of an office building in Hyehwadong (in central Seoul). The videotheque included a library containing over 1500 videos (only 200 of which had subtitles) and rooms that functioned as both private and collective viewing spaces. Videotheques equipped makeshift auditoriums with video machines, chairs and large televisions. Most attendees were students and recent graduates working in offices, and users could attend screenings and rent videotapes (Sŏng 2020b; author interview with Kang Kyoung Lae, April 2021; personal correspondence, Lee Kwang-mo, 2020). The videotheques formed a loosely affiliated network that exchanged film materials with one another (Sŏng 2020b). Better resourced outlets in the capital, like Yŏnghwagonggan 1895, supplied unapproved and unobtainable films to smaller clubs in the provinces. In a way, the circulation of tapes in the videotheque network resembled the underground distribution of proscribed materials during the late 1980s. Attendees referred to themselves as a 'cinematheque' or 'videotheque movement' (*sinemat'ek'ŭ undong*) (Sŏng 2020a), reflecting these anti-dictatorship political associations.

The future director of the Seoul Art Cinema, Kim Sŏng-uk, helped manage the Munhwahakkyo Seoul (located in Sadang in southern Seoul) in the early 1990s and recalled the videotheque held twenty screening days a month, showing three films per day. Screenings at the Yŏnghwagonggan 1895 and Munhwahakkyo Seoul attracted between ten and thirty participants each time. At the height of its popularity in the early to mid-1990s, the Munhwahakkyo Seoul had more than 3,500 regular users[15] (author interview with Kang Kyoung Lae and Kim Sŏng-uk, April 2021; personal correspondence, Lee Kwang-mo, 2020).

One regular user of the videotheques Yŏnghwagonggan 1895 and the Munhwahakkyo Seoul was academic and journalist Kim Young-jin:

> I watched movies and sometimes lectured there as I was a graduate student and a film critic. The films they screened were classic movies, masterpieces; for example, (Italian) Neo-Realism, (French) Nouvelle Vague, New American Cinema, Hitchcock or (Ingmar) Bergman, or something that might be classified as cult, like films by Alejandro Jodorowsky. Because there was no institutional space for screening classics like this regularly (at that time), the space was an oasis for movie buffs (...). (Personal correspondence, Kim Young-jin, July 2020)

As Kim indicated in 2020, these videotheques provided extensive access to film and discussion about cinema. Unlike the European cultural centres, viewers didn't have to watch movies from a single language context; they could see any film from any period. Lee Kwang-mo, for example, recalled borrowing films like *The Travelling Players* (O Thiassos, 1975, Theo Angelopoulos, Greece) and *Red Psalm* (*Még kér a nép*, 1972, Miklós Jancsó, Hungary) (personal correspondence, June 2020). Many screenings were devoted to European art films, especially contemporary international film festival award winners. However, according to Kim Young-jin, various movies were shown, from obscure horrors and cult classics to classical Hollywood. Kim Sŏng-uk remembered that those who operated the videotheques could find out which films to source by reading film magazines like *Roadshow* (from 1989 onwards) or *Screen* (from 1984). These magazines had the latest information about international film festival award winners or classics of cinema:

> Before *Cine 21* and *Film2.0*, it wasn't that we were without information. *Roadshow* and *Screen* weren't cinephile magazines, but they introduced a lot of young people in their teens and twenties to art film; they taught us about the Cannes Film Festival, new films from the US, or New American cinema, they had this kind of information. (Author interview with Kim Sŏng-uk, April 2021)

Between 1993 and 1995, Chŏng Sŏng-il published a column dedicated to cult film in *Roadshow*, and he stated that his articles helped establish a community of like-minded film fans. Although European art film was central to the screenings of videotheques (and film circles and early art houses), some movie fans of the period didn't distinguish between 'art' and other types of cinema they consumed, as Na Su-min* explained when discussing her early experience of watching movies at the French Cultural Centre and at videotheques:

If you ask me ... why we watched art films, I would say we watched everything. We also had 'Bad Film festivals' and cult film screenings. Much later, I thought about it and realised that most of what I watched back then was what we call 'art film'. It wasn't that we didn't distinguish; we did. We had information about festivals. We also went to see mainstream films. And we knew the Hollywood stuff was different from what we watched (at the French Cultural Centre or videotheques). It was more like I wanted to see a film because I'd never seen it before, I had read about it, but it had never been shown. It wasn't that anyone said: 'we have to watch *art film* and only that'. It was more like the films we watched were different – they were films as art, so if anything, we chose films that had to be analysed and understood, and that was the criteria. (Author interview, April 2021)

Na's interest in art film was a conscious decision to consume a particular type of movie that required analysis, explanation and understanding rather than motion pictures that fell under the label of 'art film' (because they had a platform release for a niche audience at a small number of theatres). Na believed that such distinctions were not so important to viewers like her. She was motivated by a desire to maximise consumption of *all* cinema the dictatorship had prohibited during the previous three decades. European art film formed a large part of that repertoire, and with their substantial libraries of tapes, videotheques had the capacity to meet audience demand.

Another prime programming strategy of the videotheques indicated by Na and an important connection to European cinema was the festival (Sŏng 2020a; Sŏng 2020b). Festivals consisted of screenings of films held on single days or over weeks (or even all-night events) dedicated to the celebration of specific aspects of cinema; for example, taboo films or 1970s masterpieces (see Figure 2.1). Between its opening and 1992, the Yŏnghwagonggan 1895 organised Nouvelle Vague (French New Wave), Underground Cinema, Neo-Realism and Erotic film festivals (Sŏng 2020a). In 1993 and 1994, the SA-Sé organised the World's Ten Best Movies festival based on a *Sight and Sound* poll of critics and scholars. It also held a deliberately provocative 'Censorship and Film' festival showing unexpurgated versions of heavily cut films like *My Own Private Idaho* (Gus Van Sant, 1991, US) and *Once Upon a Time in America* (Sergio Leone, 1984, US/Italy (S)). SA-Sé manager Son Chu-yŏn indicated that these festivals proved to be the most popular screenings they held (Sŏng 2020a; Sŏng 2020b). Kang Kyoung Lae also recalls that the Munhwahakkyo Seoul boosted audience numbers by hosting events like the Seoul Special Film

Festival (author interview, 2 April 2021). These occasions served several functions: on the one hand, they satisfied the cravings of audiences for a diverse range of cinema. They created coherence to their programmes by providing a unity of theme and in doing so also generated wider interest by providing a special 'event' status around screenings. But festivals also lent all-important political and cultural capital to the videotheque programmes. Openly advertising festivals of suppressed film was a direct challenge which often provoked an angry response from the authorities, as we see below. The videotheques' festival events helped link the political position of the audiences with their cultural preferences. At the same time, festivals' association with the golden age of European art cinema provided videotheques with important cultural and intellectual kudos.

Educational activities

Videotheques helped consecrate films and film-viewing in different ways. First, as the original French '*thèque*' and many of the names of the videotheques suggest, they had a clear educational function.[16] Videotheques were run on a membership basis, offering different packages depending on how intensively members wanted to study film.[17] A payment of $25 bought a basic six-month membership, preferential entry to popular events, and discounts on all screenings. An investment of $75 purchased all these conditions but also gave members access to study space and resources. This latter membership suited those actively researching film or amateur filmmakers (Hwang 2017: 45).

Videotheques ran a mixture of formal and informal educational sessions to help audiences dissect, analyse and produce films. Kang Kyoung Lae claimed that before 'difficult' movies, a film, or literature student often provided a helpful 5–10 minute, pre-screening explanation. 'They weren't total specialists, they had seen the film before, but it was more like our university seniors helping us a bit' (author interview with Kang Kyoung Lae, April 2021). At other times videotheques ran more formal lecture programmes, to which they invited young lecturers like Kim Young-jin from nearby universities (personal correspondence, Lee Kwang-mo, June 2020; Kim Sunah 2007b: 345–6). Major educational events organised by Yŏnghwagonggan 1895 included the '24-hour Film School' which ran during college vacations and allegedly consisted of twelve two-hour classes taught consecutively. Future directors Lee

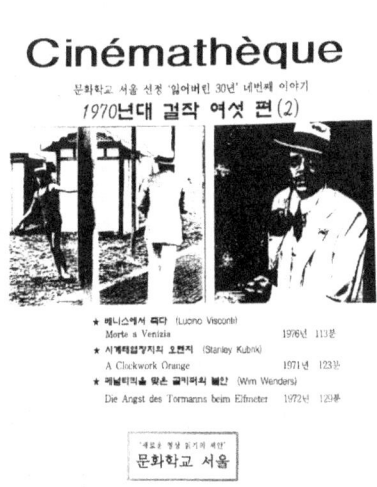

Figure 2.1 Copy of a pamphlet produced by the Munhwahakkyo Seoul to accompany screenings (courtesy Kang Kyoung Lae; permission courtesy Kim Sŏng-uk).

Kwang-mo and Park Hyŏn-ch'ŏl taught direction and production in the 'The Man with a Movie Camera' workshops named after Dziga Vertov's avant-garde Soviet documentary (Sŏng 2020b). SA-Sé also provided classes in directing, screenplay writing and provided other practical filmmaking instruction (Sŏng 2020b).[18] Videotheques (like the cultural centres and university film clubs) had strong ties to university film and literature departments. These academic connections played a critical role in adding to the cultural capital of the users and consecrating art film and its consumption.[19]

Not only did videotheques invite film students and local academics to explain films to other users, but videotheque participants also published film analyses. For example, Munhwahakkyo Seoul produced a fortnightly magazine called *Cinephile* in 1994 but ceased production when *Cine 21* opened (Sŏng 2020b). Members also collectively produced study materials and information pamphlets, which they printed and distributed. For instance, the pictured Munhwahakkyo Seoul pamphlet (Figure 2.1) introduced the 'Six masterpieces of the 1970s' special event, which formed part of a series of film screenings dedicated to 'The thirty lost years'. This corresponds to the three decades of the dictatorship's cultural blockade during which the films listed were made: *Death in Venice* (Morte a Venezia,

Luchino Visconti, 1971, France/Italy), *A Clockwork Orange* (Stanley Kubrick, 1971, UK/US) and *The Goalkeeper's Fear of the Penalty Kick* (Die Angst des Tormanns beim Elfmeter, Wim Wenders, 1972, West Germany/Austria). The rest of the pamphlet consisted of biographies of the directors, synopses and critical analyses. Kang Kyoung Lae said that these pamphlets provided a vitally important function before more widespread access to information on film was available: 'They were well-produced in the days before *Cine 21* had come out . . . and many (of the authors) became critics as a result' (author interview, April 2021). Perhaps the most ambitious of all the publications that were produced as part of this DIY (do-it-yourself) culture was *Yŏnghwaŏnŏ* (Film Language). This publication was linked to attendees of Yŏnghwagonggan 1895, university film clubs, and the European cultural centres, and ran from the late 1980s until 1995. Professionally printed and more polished than the photocopier-printed pamphlets, *Yŏnghwaŏnŏ* was a collaborative effort by Yi Ŏn-gyŏng, along with future filmmaker Kim Yong-t'ae and BIFF chairs Lee (Yi) Yong-kwan and Jeon Yang-joon (Chŏn Yang-jun) (Figure 2.2). The content was the

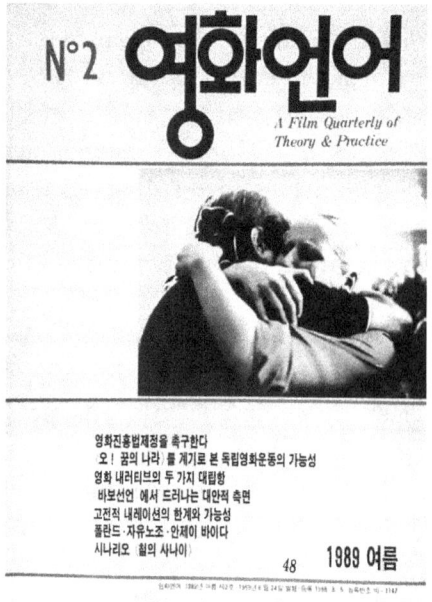

Figure 2.2 Second issue of *Yŏnghwaŏnŏ* carrying articles on independent Korean film *Declaration of Fools* (Pabosŏnŏn, 1983, Lee Chang-ho, ROK), Andrzeh Wajda (photo, author's collection; permission courtesy Jae Jeon).

collaborative result of videotheque workshops and included theoretical features on film style, analyses of independent domestic cinema and translations of complete film scenarios (Sŏng 2020b; *Cine 21* 2003). Yi Sŏn-ju (2017: 421) argues the journal was critical because it featured detailed analyses of movies using Bordwellian Neo-formalism. This academic style was lifted from videotheque lectures and contrasted with journalistic, popular film reviews, which had been prevalent up to that point and influenced later film magazines like *Kino*. These educational activities and publications became defining characteristics of the videotheques.

The self-produced materials and invitational lectures illustrate an autonomous aspect of educational activities. Different videotheques stressed distinct motivations behind this autodidactic impulse. Yi Ŏn-gyŏng regarded films as 'cultural or artistic texts' created by auteurs that had to be analysed and interpreted; it was only through exposure to a wide variety of film that young Koreans could understand cinema and develop filmmaking skills (Hwang 2017: 46; Kim Sunah 2007b: 345–6; *Han'gyŏrye* 1990). The organisers of the Munhwahakkyo Seoul stated that they aimed to create 'self-sufficient, omnipotent' movie audiences (Yi Sŏn-ju 2014: 226). Although these institutions referred to themselves as 'schools' or 'workshops', they were, in fact, unofficial (unrecognised) institutions of learning that consisted of ordinary people organising peer-to-peer cinematic education. The videotheques undercut state-sanctioned learning institutions, and participants received education about film without going through the official state-regulated system or *chedogwŏn* (Yi Sŏn-ju 2014: 238). In so doing, the videotheques provided education with an oppositional cultural value, and their members saw themselves as part of a wider movement which sustained the moral ideals of their dictatorship-era forebears.

Education and cultivation were prime motivations for regular attendees, many of whom attended screenings on their own to study. According to Kang Kyoung Lae, such solitude was unusual when many young people generally spent their free time with others. However, she adds: 'There were also the types of people who came together with their friends as they would when they went to general theatres.' For Kang herself, there was a sense of liberation at being able to see what had been inaccessible for so long: 'Rather than really appreciating these movies, as a cinephile, I think I really wanted to have that feeling of "at long last I'm able to watch a European film or an art movie . . ."' (author interview, April 2021). This was more than entertainment, she was receiving an education, which elevated her status as viewer. As with the European cultural centres, there were diverse reasons for attending videotheque screenings.

The videotape: sourcing and viewing

Not only did videotheques produce instructional materials and organise educational events, but they also self-sourced the movies themselves – often illegally – meaning that organisers frequently fell foul of the law. Kim Sŏng-uk explains how they obtained films:

> Back then, there was a satellite channel broadcasting from Japan called BS2. Satellite TV was broadcast from the Japanese broadcaster NHK's second channel, and they screened classic films throughout the night. In my case, I didn't understand Japanese well, but I watched a lot of classic movies through BS2. My colleague would record it on video and then show it at the videotheque. I was never arrested, but sometimes I was summoned to the police station; they told me the entire enterprise (videotheque) was illegal. (Author interview, April 2021)[20]

However, it was not just because of how films were procured that the authorities attempted to proscribe the videotheque. Many of the films they screened, like Oshima's *In the Realm of the Senses*, had never received official releases and were therefore forbidden from exhibition. Other videotheques also had frequent brushes with the authorities because of infringements of performance laws when they showed films banned by censors (Yi Sŏn-ju 2014: 224). In 1991, the Yŏnghwagonggan 1895 was raided by twenty police officers who confiscated a Korean independent film, *Mother, Your Son* (Ŏmŏni tangsinŭi adŭl, Yi Sang-in, 1991, ROK), scheduled for a premiere that day (Sŏng 2020b). Some videotheques deliberately organised provocative events to attract the attention of the authorities. A 1994 police raid on the SA-Sé 'Censorship and Film' festival led to the arrest of the head of the videotheque, Son Chu-yŏn, after a North Korean film was discovered (Sŏng 2020b).

David Desser (2005) argues that VCD helped revolutionise cinephilia culture amongst Chinese diasporic communities in Hong Kong and East Asia; videotape had a similarly transformative impact on Korean film culture of the late 1980s and early 1990s. The availability and relatively low cost of video and its associated technology was the catalyst for the emergence of a new movie culture 'driven by videos' (author interview with Kim Sŏng-uk, April 2021). 'Suddenly, watching videos became as normal as enjoying television, it became a routine cultural activity, and in the process, young people's cultural desire to see new types of movies exploded' (personal correspondence, Kim Young-jin, July 2020). The prevalence of videos spawned the exhibition culture that emerged in videotheques (and film clubs). On the one hand, videotape was easily transportable and reproducible. Video screenings didn't require the expensive capital investment in auditoriums, seating and projectors of cinemas. Videotheque members could borrow tapes and get them copied cheaply at the time. The process of tape reproduction also had seditious and underground overtones that gained kudos by its association with the *samizdat* culture of the dictatorship era. What videotheques did was to imbue the domestic and often individual video-viewing activity with cultural capital by adding an educational, social and seditious quality.

While the educational materials and atmosphere energised and motivated the participants, the fragility of tape and the DIY ethic that videotape spawned emerged as the significant shortcomings of the videotheques, as Lee Kwang-mo indicated about 1991:

> It was heartbreaking to see only a small number of movie buffs at underground videotheques viewing movies that had been copied so many times that their quality had deteriorated terribly ... The only thing I could do if I wanted to watch non-mainstream movies was go to the French or German cultural centres. However, the screening facilities and conditions at the cultural centres were inadequate compared to the general theatres, and they only showed French or German movies. In many cases, there were no Korean subtitles, so it was difficult for ordinary people to follow them. (Personal correspondence, Lee Kwang-mo, June 2020)

The problem of videotheques, as Lee indicates above, centred on the screening spaces and viewing quality of the films. Videotheques were cramped and uncomfortable and the subtitles and tape quality were poor, making a challenging viewing experience (Park 2015: 150). These exhibition issues undermined the cinematic experience of the videotheques. Kim Sŏng-uk believes that the problems of videotheques ultimately paved the way for the increased popularity of art houses from the early 1990s onwards. 'With videotheques, we were trying to make an environment like we were watching these films at a cinema ... (but couldn't) and that's why something like (Baekdudaegan's) Dongsung Cinematheque ended up being established in 1995' (author interview, April 2021; see also Yi 2010). The videotheques aspired to provide a distinctive cinematic experience but they could not compete with the comfort and polished product offered by the art houses.

Another weakness of the videotheques lay in their operational structure, which meant they struggled to survive long-term. Many were run by cinephiles like Yi Ŏn-gyŏng at Yŏnghwagonggan 1895 and Son Chu-yŏn at SA-Sé with a passion for film and mission to transform Korean cinema that did not transfer to later managers when they left. Both Yŏnghwagonggan 1895 and SA-Sé ceased operating soon after Yi and Son left in the early 1990s. The video collection from Yŏnghwagonggan 1895 was transferred to SA-Sé, which for a time was the pre-eminent videotheque until Son went to work with Lee Kwang-mo at Baekdudaegan (Sŏng 2020b). One videotheque, the Munhwahakkyo Seoul, continued to operate well into the 2000s, eventually becoming the Seoul Art Cinema. The drive and passion of women like Yi and Son were essential in overcoming the problems of increasing rental costs, greater competition with more comfortable art houses and the constant scrutiny of the authorities, all of which wore down the managers of these venues.

Scholars have celebrated the capacity of videotheques like the Munhwahakkyo Seoul to offer non-exclusive access to film education, arguing that such videotheques played a vital role in creating an alternative discourse for film appreciation (Hwang 2017: 45; Yi Sŏn-ju 2014: 238). The videotheques also produced figures who dominated the Korean film industry over the following two decades. Emerging directors such as Ryu Seung-hwan and O Chŏm-gyun received their breaks when videotheques screened their debut films (Sŏng 2020b). Videotheques generated well-known film academics, journalists and senior KOFIC administrators, including Yi Hyo-in, critic and former director of the Korean Film Archives, who lectured at Yŏnghwagonggan 1895. Most significantly, founders of key international film festivals came through the ranks of the videotheques (Chon 2022: 84–5). The taboo festival events hosted by the Yŏnghwagonggan 1895 and SA-Sé served as a training ground for Pusan and Chŏnju. Notable videotheque alumni include organisers of the BIFF like Kyungsung University professor Lee Yong-kwan and critic Chŏn Ch'an-il, and critic and academic Chŏn Yang-jun became a programmer for the Jeonju (Chŏnju) Film Festival (Lee Kwang-mo, June 2020). Kim Hyŏng-sŏk was editor of *Screen* after leaving Munhwahakkyo Seoul and later became the Pyeongchang (Pyŏngch'ang) International Peace Film Festival programmer. More controversially, some current art house managers have noticed the 'paradox' of a crossover of personnel between the early innovative videotheques and the large multiplex firms which dominate domestic distribution:

> If you look at the people who worked in the videotheques, many went on to multiplexes. So, in a short time, interest in film exploded in this way and then suddenly converted directly into multiplex capital. One thing drove it (the multiplex expansion), and one thing alone, and that was the film culture of the time (the cinephilia of the 1990s). (Anon. interview, 2021)

My source did not identify anyone but was arguing that some of the same people who innovated in the videotheques facilitated the rise of multiplexes.

As Christian Keathley observed, all cinephilia has a distinctly 'productive' character. So, it is not surprising that many users of the videotheques (as well as the film clubs) were attracted by the possibility of directing films of their own. Given the logistical and economic barriers to film production and the closed-shop character that was common in Korea then, few would graduate to full-time direction. An example is Yi Ŏn-gyŏng, who never abandoned her dream of becoming a director; she produced several shorts, including *Shattering Moon* (Hŭndŭllinŭn Tal, 1992, ROK) but never broke through into feature-length filmmaking. However, a significant number did. Later prominent filmmakers who received important film education at videotheques include Kim Yong-t'ae, E-J Yong and Bong Joon-ho, who were regulars of Yŏnghwagonggan 1895, with Bong allegedly the 'hardest working student' of a 24-Hour Film School in 1991. Bong also produced his first short films with fellow students and equipment borrowed from the videotheque, while the director of *Thieves* (Todŭkdŭl, 2012, ROK, 12.9 million admissions [ROK]), Choi Dong-hoon, attended SA-Sé and the Munhwahakkyo: 'I went in and out of those places like they were my own home . . . they were where I realised the true value of film', Choi said (Sŏng 2020b). Ultimately, the videotheques helped inspire the art film boom by providing a model for art houses and for the festivals that proliferated from the mid-1990s onwards (Park 2015: 150; Yi Sŏn-ju 2014: 232). They also demonstrated the extent of interest in movies and the need for an infrastructure to provide exhibition and distribution opportunities for non-mainstream film (Yi Sŏn-ju 2014: 227–8).

These three modes of exhibition served as entry points for many of the same people who were influential later in exhibition, production, distribution and creation of commercial, mainstream and art film in Korea. Two things are significant about this entry of a new generation of people who shaped the course of Korean cinema. First, they were not emerging from within the *chedogwŏn*, or established Ch'ungmuro system of filmmaking that had dominated Korean film for many decades and was popularly and critically seen as bereft of new ideas and inextricably linked with the repression and corruption of the dictatorship.[21] Second, what is noticeable is the close circle of human networks or *inmaek* in which many of these influential people moved. These connections formed during a very concentrated period between the late 1980s and mid-1990s in which many of the changes that would transform the fortunes of an entire industry occurred (see Chapter 5). French critic, scholar and editor of *Cahiers du Cinéma* Jean Narboni, speaking of the late 1950s and early 1960s atmosphere in the Paris of Henri Langlois's *Cinémathèque Française* and the rise of the Nouvelle Vague of radical French directors such as François Truffaut, Jean-Luc Godard, Jacques Rivette, Claude Chabrol and Alain Resnais, said: 'it was a concentration of excitement and enthusiasm for film that can't ever be equalled (. . .) because in the 1960s we enjoyed a unique historic compression that won't come again' (Richard 2005: 40:25). In some ways, we see the same 'historic compression' in the Seoul of the late 1980s and early 1990s with the emergence in a short period of a group of people who would be highly influential in the transformed Korean cinema of the 2000s. This factor is encapsulated in the following anecdote about Lee Kwang-mo's early attempt to make his way in the industry:

> In the summer of 1991, when I came back to Korea . . . I decided to set up a production office (called 'Directors Eye') with other directors who like me were trying to make their first films (Kim Sŏng-su, Yi Chae-yong, Park Hŏn-su, Chang Ki-ch'ŏl). I met with Shin Chŏl, head of the independent production company Shincine, who had plans to relocate his office at the same time. We decided to move together into a small five-story building located in a corner of Hyehwadong and we invited the videotheque Yŏnghwagonggan 1895 to move in. We had trouble raising money to pay the rent for our office, so we sub-let a third of our office to Kang U-sŏk, who was about to make the big hit *Mr Mama* (1992, ROK). We rented two desks to the independent production company P'arangsae (Bluebird) and two desks to influential producers of terrestrial broadcasting. There wasn't much room left for us, but day and night, the place was a hangout for young filmmakers. Shincine, of course, had a big hit with *Marriage Story* (*Kyŏrhon Iyagi*, Kim Ŭi-sŏk, 1992, ROK), which kick-started the era of young producers (. . .) The building became a second Ch'ungmuro, and the reason why I talk about it is because it captures all the transformations that occurred in the Korean film industry

of the mid-1990s – in other words, the Korean mainstream commercial film industry, the independent film industry, underground cinema, as well as young professors and critics who mingled and interacted in one building, creating the dynamism and energy of the transformed Korean film industry, something that would be hard to find later. (Personal correspondence, Lee Kwang-mo, 2020)

Lee's account reveals the intimate nature of the film community that existed and the cross-pollination of ideas between alternative exhibition methods such as videotheques, film academia and film producers.

Conclusion

One phrase that consistently features in discussions of the cinematic landscape in the late 1980s and early 1990s is cinematic 'wasteland' (*pulmoji*, Park 2015: 147; Ch'oe 2015; Paek 2009). For many cinephiles, getting hold of and viewing European and American contemporary works or classics of cinema they had read about in film books or magazines was often impossible pre-1987 and post-dictatorship; it remained challenging (Paek 2009; Song 1997; Park 2015: 150).[22] The cultural centres, university film clubs and videotheques compensated for market failings caused by the administration of cinema in Korea. They represented the response of ordinary citizens to the inability of the official state agencies to facilitate the circulation of non-commercial foreign film in Korea.

These three non-theatrical exhibition spaces did not disappear with the emergence of art houses but co-existed contemporaneously. Neither were they mutually exclusive or antagonistic and spectators like Kim Nan-suk, Irene Hee-seung Lee and others alternated between the different viewing spaces according to what was showing. The three spaces also had much in common in terms of programming, showing cinema that required analysis and that had never been shown in Korea. They watched independent films, cult movies, and above all European art cinema from its 1960s-80s heyday that coincided perfectly with the thirty 'lost' years of the dictatorship's cultural blockade. This accounts for the prevalence of European art films at college clubs, cultural centres and videotheques.

All three of these modes of non-cinema exhibition – the cultural centres, university clubs and underground videotheques – provide clear evidence of an emerging interest in the type of film that audiences could not see through state-regulated channels, on network televisions, or at mainstream cinemas. The educational function and DIY spirit link these modes. Young Koreans had an ulterior motive for viewing screenings at these spaces. Ultimately most were driven by a desire to make film and not just the standard fare produced in Ch'ungmuro but a transformed film with a new language as Yi Ŏn-gyŏng argued. There is no doubt that an essential part of the attraction of these three spaces lay in their embrace of taboo, different and forbidden materials. Audiences consumed film in these ways because that was what they were accustomed to doing; some may have seen such consumption of film as a form of defiance against a *chedogwŏn* that had suppressed cultural expression for so long.

In a short period between the mid-1980s and early 1990s, we see the emergence of a small but committed fan base dedicated to art film for whom film meant more than entertainment; it offered a new meaning to their cultural consumption. However, the limitations of video viewing would drive many to view art film in art houses, and it is theatrical exhibition that we explore in the next chapter.

Notes

1. Park (2009), Hwang (2017) and Mun (2011) examine earlier cinephile discussion groups.
2. The Saemaŭl undong (or new village movement) was a government campaign for rural revitalisation (Sorensen 2011: 147).
3. In the 1990s, the Kwanghwamun-based British Council screened Derek Jarman and Peter Greenaway films (personal correspondence, Yvonne Schulz Zinda, November 2020).
4. Yi Hyo-in a member of the Seoul Film Collective, condemned the European cultural centre attendees as reactionary (Yi Hyo-in, cited in Park 2015: 41). Film buffs involved in these European cultural centre cinema clubs would conceal their desire to consume foreign film to avoid social ostracisation (Park 2015: 38, 41). (For further discussion of these splits, see: Park 2015: 41–55; Sohn 2022: 70–1.)
5. Lee Kwang-mo's explanation about how he selected films for exhibition is an example of the attitude that angered activists because of its apparent lack of concern for the social function of cinema. 'We chose modern works that spoke to our lives and masterpieces of total perfection made by directors of world cinema who understand that film is a priceless asset' (cited in An 1995).
6. Kim Hong-jun attended the Dongsung Cinematheque, while Park Ch'an-sik attended the Core Art Hall and other French cultural centre regulars also went to the Cinehouse for example (personal correspondence, Kim Hong-jun, April 2021). Seven per cent of my art film exhibition survey respondents developed an interest in art house film by attending European cultural centres.

7. Yŏnghwamadang'uri was based in Shinch'on near Yonsei University in western Seoul (Sŏng 2020a). Sohn (2022) translates it as 'our open-air cinema', Park (2015) as 'Film community us'. *Madang* is the pure Korean word denoting backyard or garden but also a 'performance space' for traditional cultural dance. The term gained cultural currency after being appropriated by *minjung* activists as a nationalistic tool to mobilise anti-dictatorship support. See Sohn (2022: 66–9) for further information about these university groups.
8. Namhee Lee argues the December 1983 reforms only became effective in 1985 (2006: 111).
9. Someone in a higher year at university than you. An important cultural distinction at universities in Korea or Japan where seniors have social authority over more junior students.
10. Sohn (2022: 65) also argues that in addition to seniors, in the 2000s there was an important role for alumni which helped reinforce hierarchal structures within film clubs.
11. As late as the 1998 financial crisis, the government's official import restrictions to encourage domestic manufacturing resulted in a thriving black market for food, white goods, and cultural products smuggled from Japan and the US Army bases around Korea.
12. Another source was the German Benedictine monk, Father Sebastien in Waegwan (southeastern Korea), who brought in and circulated televised coverage of the Kwangju Uprising and other unapproved film and books (personal correspondence, Brother Anthony, August 2021).
13. As a woman within these film groups, Kim Nan-suk felt uncomfortable watching proscribed films with male seniors like *Pink Floyd's The Wall* and *A Clockwork Orange*, featuring rape sequences (author interview with Kim Nan-suk, May 2020).
14. I use 'videotheque' rather than 'cinematheque' to distinguish between these private video cinemas and the Dongsung Cinematheque and its theatrical exhibition.
15. Approximately 11,000 people visited the Munhwahakkyo Seoul annually (Sŏng 2020b).
16. The French word 'Cinémathèque' is derived from 'cinéma' and 'bibliothèque' meaning library. Examples of names for videotheques were 'school' or 'workshop' (Sŏng 2020b). The pedagogical purpose of videotheques is encapsulated by the slogan of Munhwahakkyo Seoul: 'Let's read film' (Sŏng 2020b).
17. The Munhwahakkyo Seoul videotheque also sold coupons for screenings to attract occasional visitors, which were cheaper than memberships or regular cinema tickets (author interview with Kang Kyoung Lae, April 2021).
18. Dongguk University professor Yu Chi-na provided lectures on filmmaking skills at SA-Sé (Sŏng 2020b).
19. American and European academia played a vital role in the consecration of art film. The arrival of European art film and the dominance of auteur theory that arose to explain it, was the catalyst for the creation of US and UK university Film studies departments (Andrews 2013: 15; Baumann 2007: 74).
20. Yŏnghwagonggan 1895 had members studying in Europe who sent back videos and also travelled to Japan on audio-visual material smuggling trips (Sŏng 2020b).

21. See criticisms of Ch'ungmuro filmmaking from *Cine 21* journalists Hŏ Munyŏng and Cho Chongguk (1998) in their review of *Spring in My Hometown*.
22. The situation for film fans was worse in the provinces, where movie lovers suffered from limited access even to pirated tapes (see Park 2015: 149). These lacks increased the sense of cultural disenfranchisement experienced by cinephiles outside the metropole.

Chapter 3

The theatrical exhibition of art film and Korean cinephilia, 1987–95

There were vital cinematic, economic and social factors in creating what researchers from KOFIC have described as the 1990s 'golden age' of art film cinema in Korea (Kim et al. 2004: 23). It was special because of the 'vibrant film culture' found in pioneering art houses in this period (author interview with Kim Sŏng-uk, April 2021). But this also was a period when art film viewing became a more widely accepted activity. Attendance at cultural centres, film clubs, videotheques and the early art houses occurred in parallel during the late 1980s and early 1990s. Moving into the mid-1990s, the greater acceptance of theatrical art film exhibition provided clear evidence of the pulling power of art houses. This chapter turns its focus onto the cinematic culture that emerged in the pioneering art houses that drew fans in increasing numbers. I investigate the factors that led to the growing popularity of art film viewing in theatres and the strategies of these 1990s art houses to differentiate their exhibition practices from competitors. I also trace the specific character and appeal of the capital's cinephilia that thrived in these new exhibition sites.

Increased art film exhibition in Seoul cinemas

Several key developments facilitated the establishment and spread of art houses between the late 1980s and the mid-1990s. First, the Roh Tae-woo administration organised an 'Exhibition of Superior Foreign Films' (*Usu oegugyŏnghwa sisahoe*) around the time of the 1988 Seoul Olympics showcasing movies from Eastern bloc countries, including the Soviet Union, Poland, Yugoslavia, as well as works from Israel, India and South America. The exhibition focused on international festival award winners, and it was open to the general public (Hwang 2017: 47n.31; Kim et al. 2004: 20). The interest in showing movies from the former Soviet Union and Eastern European countries was partly cultural diplomacy and a post-dictatorship attempt to boost Korean film consumption internationally. The Roh administration implemented a 'Nordpolitik' policy to engage with North Korea's closest allies to reduce tensions on the peninsula (Lee Hyang-jin 2000: 130). Events like these were supposed to signal a new openness from the government towards cultural expression in a democratising Korea and helped introduce people to films from countries other than the US and Hong Kong. Eastern European countries reciprocated the Seoul event with Korean film festivals in Moscow, Tashkent, Alma Ata, Hungary and Romania (KMPPC 1993: 9). The exhibition was a major success, attracting large audiences and providing evidence of the commercial potential for types of films that had rarely been seen in Korea.

A second significant development was the impact of revisions to the Motion Picture Law, which relaxed foreign film importation and introduced a change from a licensing system to a registration system for film companies (Yu 2007a: 303; Kim 2011: 173).[1] Liberalisation meant that companies importing foreign films increased from thirty in 1985 to over a hundred by 1988 (Kim et al. 2004: 20). During the same period, imported films rose from twenty-seven in 1985 to 175 in 1988 and 264 in 1989 (Cho Joon-hyeong 2006: 162). Market reforms also sparked greater competition among these Korean companies for imported films. Thanks to their box office popularity, the prices for Hollywood and Hong Kong films increased exponentially. One result was that importers became more open to importing and distributing other types of foreign films to receive a better return on their investment (Kim et al. 2004: 20). Although the liberalisation of foreign motion picture imports brought initial challenges for exhibitors and distributors (see below), these regulatory changes also opened the door for the importation of foreign movies, which along with the Exhibition of Superior Films whetted the appetite of the Korean public for what was commonly referred to as 'art film'.

What many people understood as 'art' in the late 1980s is what Andrew Tudor classifies as 'respectable cinema' – in other words, literary or stage adaptations, period dramas, previously unscreened classics and films treating 'serious' social or political issues such as racism (2006: 135). Many such films had won awards at international film festivals and performed well at box offices internationally. Films like *Amadeus* (1984, Miloš Forman, US, 475,755 admissions), *A Passage to India* (1984, David Lean, UK/US, 135,032), *Paris Texas* (1984, Wim Wenders, West Germany/France, 98,905), *The Unbearable Lightness of Being* (1988, Philip Kaufman,

US, 66,216), *Empire of the Sun* (1987, Stephen Spielberg, US, 189,300) drew large audiences at capital box offices. While Tudor calls them 'respectable films', KOFIC researchers investigating the emergence of the art film market in Korea referred to these movies variously as a 'third' kind of film, or as 'well-made' or 'art' film in inverted commas to characterise them (Kim et al. 2004: 20).[2] Some were produced partially or wholly in the US, but they are 'third' to distinguish them from Hollywood or Hong Kong pictures. What made them 'quality' or 'art' was the perception by both audiences and administrators that they were different from regular Hollywood or Hong Kong modes of filmmaking practice. Marketing and media discourses shaped these perceptions, showing them as not action-packed, violent, special effects-driven or genre narrative films. Newspaper coverage from the time stressed the literary connections, the emphasis on period and film festival awards to distinguish these movies from first-run cinema programmes (see Figure 3.1). These pictures performed successfully at the box office, providing evidence that art film could represent a viable investment for both importers and exhibitors.

The early art halls

Perceptions of the difference of these films (from other types of cinema) were also shaped by where they were screened, for they were not shown at local or first-run theatres in downtown Seoul. Instead, these films played at chaebol-owned auditoriums founded in the mid-to-late 1980s like the Hoam or Hyundai To Art Halls. All the largest conglomerates established such cultural centres, including art galleries and classical music concert halls, from the late 1960s onwards (Park 2015: 65). This business support shows a convergence of interests; chaebols wanted to be seen as benevolent benefactors of the arts to soften their image as large, ruthless corporations (Park 2015: 70).[3] Chaebol-run art halls promoted what was generally considered high culture, such as fine arts, classical music, or traditional Korean art performances. Perhaps the best known in the period was the Hoam Art Hall, established by Samsung. Between 1987 and 1993, it screened an average of two films each year, many of which were about art – films about composers *Tchaikovsky* (Igor Talankin, 1970, Soviet Union) or cinematic versions of opera (*Dancers*, Herbert Ross, 1987, US) that fit in with its reputation as an arts centre (Table 3.1). The 643-seat auditorium also doubled as a venue for theatrical productions.

Table 3.1 Hoam Art Hall programming schedule, 1987–92.

Year	Film	Attendance
1987	*Platoon* (Oliver Stone, 1987, US)	214,136
	The Mission (Roland Joffé, 1986, UK)	211,724
1988	*Dancers*	205,726
	Modern Times (Charlie Chaplin, 1936, US)	265,590
1989	*Tchaikovsky*	127,879
	Hibiscus Town (Xie Jin, 1986, China)	6,292
1990	*Three Days of the Condor* (Sydney Pollack, 1975, US)	87,995
	Cinema Paradiso (Guiseppe Tornatore, 1988, Italy)	226,956
1991	*My Left Foot* (Jim Sheridan, 1989, UK/Ireland)	155,000
	Field of Dreams (Phil Alden Robinson, 1989, US)	83,245
1992	*Manon Des Sources* (Claude Berri, 1986, France)	190,878
	White Badge (Hayan chŏnjaeng, Chung Ji-young, 1992, ROK)	151,638

Source: KMPPC 1988: 36, 45, 136; KMPPC 1989: 120; KMPPC 1990: 121, 128; KMPPC 1991: 121, 127; KMPPC 1992: 137; KMPPC 1993: 113, 138.

The Hoam marketed itself as a venue that showed the most prestigious and 'serious' films, with images of academy awards or the famous Cannes Palme d'Or featuring prominently in the posters used to advertise its shows (author interview with Irene Hee-seung Lee, April 2021). Two factors were crucial for establishing its success. First, there was a focus on movies with literary, artistic, or adult themes, award-winning motion pictures consecrated by international festivals such as *A Passage to India* in 1985 and *The Mission* and 'classics' unreleased under the dictatorship, for example *Three Days of the Condor*. Second, there was the deliberate strategy of restricting cinematic exhibition and interspersing it with theatrical performances (Park 2015: 70; author interview with Lee Kwang-mo, June 2020). What was the overall impact of this? Steve Neale argues that film distributors maximise box office receipts through specific marketing strategies that give their movies a special 'event' status (Neale 2013: 48).[4] The Hoam Art Hall's marketing also gave 'event' status to films in their programme. They did this through extensive publicity, film selection, the juxtaposition of theatrical and cinematic exhibition and the relative rarity of the screenings; all of which gave the impression the cinema exclusively showed artistically superior works. The attendance statistics of the day

Figure 3.1 Hoam Art Hall newspaper advertising for *Cinema Paradiso* in *Chosŏn Ilbo*, 7 July 1990 (source: Park Kyŏng-ae, HMJ Films).

showed the Hoam's programming strategy was successful, and the theatre attracted great interest from the public at a time when drawing 200,000 spectators over a six-week run was a significant and profitable result. The Hoam Art Hall's drawing power in the early 1990s was so strong that there was significant competition amongst film importers to secure a lucrative exhibition deal with the theatre (personal correspondence, Lee Kwang-mo, May 2020; for import prices and procedures, see Chapter 4).

Mixed programming strategy

While the Hoam Art Hall established a successful formula for maintaining an event status for its exhibition of art films, other theatres adopted a more esoteric approach to programming. In 1989, for example, the Myungbo Art Hall (which opened in 1985) mounted an eclectic eleven-film programme that featured many elements that would characterise much of the programming implemented at Seoul cinemas associated with art film during the 1990s. The mix included mainstream genre films like *Twins* (Ivan Reitman, 1988, US) or the horror movie *The Seventh Sign* (Carl

Schultz, 1988, US) and festival or holiday period family films like *Miracle on 34th Street* (Les Mayfield, 1994, USA). The programme, however, also comprised prominent festival award-winning films and literary adaptations such as *Ghandi* (Richard Attenborough, 1983, UK/India), *The Last Emperor* (L'Ultimo imperatore, Bernardo Bertolucci, 1987, Italy) and *Why Has Boddhi Left for the East?* (Talmaga tongtchokŭro kan kkadalgŭn? Pae Yong-kyun, 1989, ROK). It included the previously unreleased vintage Charlie Chaplin film *Modern Times* and European films such as *Camille Claudel* (Bruno Nuyten, 1988, France). Andrew Tudor (2006: 138) and David Andrews (2013: 152) categorise the likes of *Camille Claudel* as 'mainstream foreign language films'. Such films are intended to reach a mass audience at home and exported through global distribution networks to maximise international returns. According to Tudor, films like *Camille Claudel* are not that different from Hollywood commercial products in terms of style and narrative trajectory that they would alienate audiences.[5] Other films included in this mixed programming strategy were lower budget US or Korean-made features noteworthy for marketing that emphasised their eroticism and suggestive titles, such as *Bocchacchio '92* (Kim Ki-yŏng, 1992, ROK). One early practitioner of this exhibition approach was the Core Art Hall. The Core Art Hall's mantra, displayed in Korean above the box office was: 'Entertainment and Art Together' (*oraksŏnggwa yesulsŏngi hamkkehanŭn*), which effectively summarised the intention of the mixed programming strategy – it aimed to meet the desires of a broad group of cinemagoers (Yi 2004).

Researchers of art film exhibition found that theatre schedulers adopted similar mixed programming strategies in other historical contexts.[6] Barbara Wilinsky argues that film programmes in 1940s and 1950s US art houses were shaped by a need to balance economics with taste and prestige considerations to retain a regular clientele. As a result, exhibitors showed films closer to their theatres' mission but occasionally included more commercial crowd-pullers to make ends meet (Wilinsky 2001: 109). Wilinsky contends that sometimes struggling art houses found themselves unwillingly adopting mixed programming as a pragmatic response to economic realities. Similarly, late 1980s and early 1990s Seoul exhibitors adopted eclectic programming as a practical way to survive in a rapidly fluctuating market. The Chun administration's changes to the Motion Picture Laws meant that the distribution and exhibition system was in a state of comparative flux during this period.

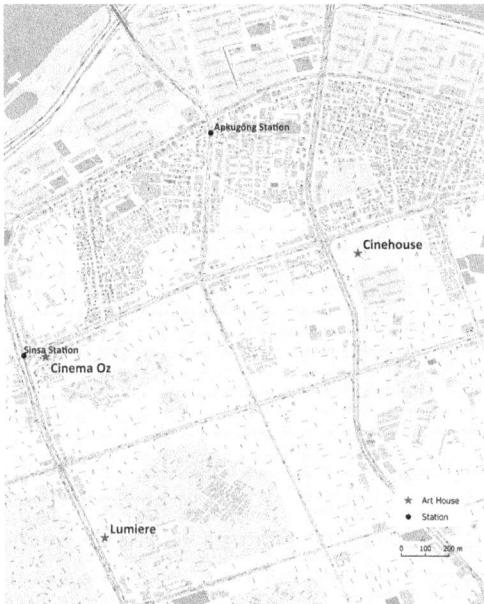

Figure 3.2 Map of early art houses in Kangnam; created by Elspeth McVey © Openstreetmap contributors.

Under the previous distribution system, foreign films could be virtually guaranteed to make a profit, but deregulated imports made it harder to determine which films would succeed (Paquet 2009: 52). In addition to direct distribution by majors, growing numbers of Korean importers resulted in increasing competition for the right to exhibit potentially lucrative Hollywood products. For exhibitors, mixed programming was attractive since the precise ratio of European award winners to mainstream commercial movies could be shifted easily according to availability and costs. Theatre owners adopted mixed programming to remain afloat in an increasingly challenging market.[7]

Many cinemas also attempted mixed programming strategies featuring both art and mainstream commercial product, and some were more effective than others. A successful example was the Cinehouse, one of the country's first multiplexes, which opened in 1989 with six screens in Nonhyŏndong, Kangnam. The cinema had large (600-seater) and small (200-seater) auditoriums, which screened films depending on their commercial potential.[8] Other theatres, like the 700-seater Renaissance Cinema in the Sŏdaemun area of western Seoul, swiftly abandoned their attempt at screening art and mainstream film after a single year in this mode. The mixed programming strategy was more successful at cinemas with smaller auditoriums and lower running costs, where more modest audience numbers could be sustained over longer periods.[9]

When successful, mixed programming provided theatres with a potentially lucrative and flexible way to attract audiences, and the late 1980s to early 1990s saw the opening of a succession of other venues showing art films. In the year it opened, the Cinehouse screened Charlie Chaplin's *Modern Times*, which proved such a success that the cinema had to open the film on an additional screen to meet demand. The film ended up attracting 26,000 spectators and was put on extended-release at the Hoam Art Hall (Kim et al. 2004: 21). Another theatre that adopted a mixed programming strategy was the Dongsung Art Centre (Dongsung Art Hall): a multi-use art space that mounted exhibitions and theatrical performances in Taehangno, close to Chongno. In 1990, to increase its profitability, it started screenings in its 489-seater auditorium (Hwang 2017: 49) and later played a significant part in the art film boom. Another theatre that opened its doors in 1992 south of the river in Kangnam was the Lumiere (Rumierŭ kŭkchang), with an auditorium of 133 seats. All the aforementioned theatres adopted a flexible mixed programming strategy, which shifted according to necessity and availability.[10]

European films, classics and sex

The mixed programming schedule relied on a blend of mainstream Hollywood attractions and European cinema, previously unreleased classics and racy dramas with a strong sexual element. But how did exhibitors promote this mix, and what was the appeal of these latter types of films to fans at this time? A key component of KOFIC's characterisation of third film was cinema that was neither Hollywood nor Hong Kong, and in the early 1990s, this primarily denoted European motion pictures. The programming schedule of the Lumiere cinema in 1993 provides an interesting example. Of the thirty or so films screened over the year, thirteen were produced in the USA, three each from Korea and China, while twelve came from European countries, including Russia, Italy, Germany and most significantly, France (see Appendix 1 for a full list of dates, attendances and opening dates). Like the Hoam Art Hall, the Lumiere marketed non-US films such as *Love at First Sight* (Liebe auf dem ersten blick, Rudolf Thome, 1991, Germany), *Farewell my Concubine*

(Bà Wáng Bié Jī dir; Chen Kaige, 1993, China/Hong Kong) and *Like Water for Chocolate* (Como Agua Para Chocolate, Alfonso Arau, 1992, Mexico) based on their festival success. Intense competition meant non-Hollywood product was more economical, but this is not the only reason for these choices. The schedules in part, met audience expectations and reflected a distinct pro-European bias amongst film fans: 'We were very generous towards European culture (back then)', explains Irene Hee-seung Lee:

> There was definitely a European bias as well as anti-American feeling after decades of US military presence, and it came across in our taste for film ... Film consumption was seen as a form of resistance and was seen as a way of doing it more peacefully. We didn't have that much enmity towards the US. We weren't like our university seniors. Instead, we engaged with world problems and concerns through film. Also not following US film was seen as a sign of intelligence and class; we thought we had a common bond (with Europeans) who went against the Americanised view of capitalism in their own culture. We bought into that idea. (Author interview with Irene Hee-seung Lee, April 2021)

Lee reveals complex political, social and cultural motivations behind her interest in European film in 1990s Korea. On one level, she distinguished herself from audiences at first-run theatres by consuming European film, which added a critical cultural cachet to film viewing for fans like Lee. In many ways, her responses reflect the popularity of 1940s–50s art film consumption in North American and British contexts. For US and UK audiences, the foreignness of European art film added cultural value to cinema-going in a period of post-war social change (Wilinsky 2001: 92, 105; O'Brien 2018: 81). In 1990s Seoul, European film attracted those who aspired to a higher level of refinement and wished to set themselves apart from film consumers at first-run theatres.[11] However, in addition to a desire for greater sophistication, Lee's testimony reveals other political motivations for her preference for European cinema. She saw her cinematic consumption as a rejection of Hollywood film and historic US political links to Korea. At the same time, she also distinguishes herself from the more radical anti-American tendencies of the *minjung* movement generation of her seniors at university. Lee's apparent embrace of what she identifies as an alternative European form of capitalism reveals a critical political shift away from *minjung* radicalism. Viewing European film meant more than simply watching movies; it represented a statement of political and cultural intent.

Another feature of the Lumiere's 1993 schedule common to the mixed programming of other Seoul cinemas was the screening of films that had never been released in Korea. The Lumiere showed *Time of the Gypsies* (Dom za vešanje, Emir Kusturica, 1988, Yugoslavia) five years after its production. Many of the other films shown were from the previous seven decades of cinematic history. These include *Three Days of the Condor* and Charlie Chaplin classics such as *The Gold Rush* (1925, US). Also shown were Soviet-era films like *Come and See* (Idi i smotri, Elem Klimov, 1985, Soviet Union) and *Battleship Potemkin* (Bronenosets Potyomkin, Sergei Eisenstein, 1925, Soviet Union). Classics also provided an education in big-screen history repressed by dictatorship-era regulations. Indeed, the educational aspect is what the distributors and exhibitors stressed in their marketing of these films. Newspaper advertisements for *Battleship Potemkin* claimed that the silent feature was a 'Bible of Film!!' and that 'You can learn the splendour of film art from Eisenstein, and you will come to know the greatness of cinema from *Battleship Potemkin*' (Chŏn 2020). The *Potemkin* advertising also stressed its festival awards and used words like '*myŏnghwa*' or masterpiece –a common feature of European film marketing (Chŏn 2020). Bourdieu (1980: 269) has argued that weaker competitors in a cultural market dominated by stronger forces tend to opt for 'alternative' (or subversive) strategies to differentiate their products to succeed and prosper. Exhibitors and distributors pitched their European and classic films marketing carefully to highlight the differences from first-run theatres. They appealed to the sophistication and intelligence of their target audience, advertising their movies as a cultural and intellectual experience. Not only would these films raise the cultural cachet of the audience, but they would also teach about art.

One feature of scheduling and marketing typical of smaller niche cinemas like the Lumiere was racy films that included – or at least promised audiences – titillating content. Historically, there has always been a close association between European art film and eroticism. Steve Neale (1981: 32) argues that the artistic status of post-war European art films meant that they were accorded greater leeway by audiences, critics and censors than other movies and presented sexual issues more explicitly. David Andrews (2013: 61) observes the association of European art cinema with franker depictions of sex became so intertwined in the consciousness of British and American audiences that explicit sexuality became expected in foreign movies. After that, 'foreign', 'art', 'adult' and 'sex' film were for several years almost synonyms. Significantly, theatres like the

Lumiere, Cinehouse and even the Core Art Hall continued to use the lure of titillation as a marketing tool for their products. The Lumiere screened award-winning films with extensive sexual content, like *Like Water for Chocolate*, and listed the festival accolades next to a suggestive image of the film's two protagonists (Figure 3.3). The Lumiere also screened more lurid films, such as *The Raffle* (La Rifa, Francesco Laudadio, 1991, Italy), which tells of a widow forced to auction herself to rich men to make ends meet. The marketing headline accompanying the image of the semi-clad lead (Figure 3.3) provides titillating details about the narrative: 'Closed bidding. The woman of every man's dreams. But who is going to win her?' However, the Hangul translation retains the original Italian word (*rarip'a*), adding a veneer of refinement to what is, in reality, little more than a cheap sex comedy.[12] The newspaper marketing for European films screened at the Lumiere and elsewhere frequently highlighted sexual imagery even when it was not the main subject. An example is the media marketing image of a scantily clad lead actress from the Soviet film *The Gypsy Camp Vanishes into the Mist* (Tabor Ukhodit v Nebo, 1975, Emil Loteanu) screened at the Cinehouse in 1992.

The juxtaposition of European sophistication, festival consecration and arousing imagery also indicate an attempt to distinguish between the type of American-made and 3-S Policy Korean-made soft-core sex features prominent at the time. In doing so, exhibitors and distributors (consciously or inadvertently) linked their programming with the appeal of viewing sexually explicit movies observed by Irene Hee-seung Lee in the last chapter. Lee identified the viewing of sexually explicit films with a sense of both rebellion and liberation precisely because they were forbidden (Figure 3.3). The marketing strategies of exhibitors and distributors from the period suggest that they understood the appeal this sense of emancipation had for their audiences. The particular combination of European and classic cinema and the more open treatment of sex that made up the mixed programming schedules of theatres like the Lumiere held a specific allure for filmgoers.

Some exhibitors calling themselves 'art theatres' (*yesulkŭkjang*) often appeared to have little interest in showing anything other than mainstream genre and sex films. One example was the Ewha Yesulkŭkjang in western Seoul, which, apart from the odd European film, was 'art' (*yesul*) in name only.[13] Elsewhere, there were enormous fluctuations in programming, and in some years, there was little to distinguish some of the theatres that called themselves 'art halls' from first-run downtown cinemas. Authentic

Figure 3.3 Newspaper advertising for *Like Water for Chocolate* (L; source unknown, *Chosŏn Ilbo*, 5 June 1993) and the Italian feature *The Raffle* in the *Dong-a Ilbo*, 12 June 1993 (R; courtesy Park Kyŏng-ae, HMJ Films).

art house status was established by reputation, and from the late 1980s onwards, some cinemas became known through media reports and word of mouth as places where fans could see art films. For Lee Kwang-mo, the Hoam Art Hall was the venue where you could see big-budget, prominent award-winning films with serious themes like *The Last Emperor* (personal correspondence, Lee Kwang-mo, June 2020). The Cinehouse developed a reputation as a cinema south of the river that showed non-Hollywood international film festival-consecrated foreign movies such as *Ju Dou* (*Jú Dòu*, Zhang Yimou and Yang Fengliang, 1990, China), *Red Sorghum* (Hóng gāoliáng, Zhang Yimou, 1987, China) and *The Double Life of Veronique* (*La double vie de Véronique*, Krzysztof Kieślowski, 1991, France, Poland, Norway) (personal correspondence, Ch'oi So-hŭi*, November 2020).[14] These institutional reputations were established through the programming of art films. However, since scheduling was subject to unpredictable variables – including availability and market fluctuations that impacted the economics of screening film – other spatial and organisational factors became important in shaping institutional identities. One cinema in early 1990s Seoul did more than any other to establish an institutional identity as the vanguard of the booming interest in art film: the Core Art Hall.

The Core Art Hall

The Core Art Hall opened its small (190-seat) auditorium in 1989 in Chongno, the traditional home of cinema exhibition which housed some of the oldest, largest and most prestigious movie theatres in Korea (Figure 3.4).[15] Watching a film at a Chongno cinema carried glamorous associations of traditional movie-going. Film fans who attended the Core Art Hall recalled that the big-screen experience, seating and facilities were superior to the cultural centres, videotheques and film clubs. The Core Art Hall's manager-director, Hwang In-ok, modelled the cinema on the 'leading art film theatre in Japan', the Iwanami Hall, which was established to screen European films in 1967, in Tokyo's Jinbocho district (Shoji 2017; Song 1997).[16] Initially, the Core Art Hall adopted a similar mixed programming strategy to the Cinehouse and other cinemas, but its emphasis shifted during the early 1990s. Changes in the cinema's screening schedules are evident from a comparison of the scheduling between 1990 and 1993 when the number of major Hollywood attractions like *Ghost* (Jerry Zucker, 1990, US), *Backdraft* (Ron Howard, 1991, US) and *Gremlins 2* (Joe Dante, 1990, US) declined considerably (Appendix 1). Compared to the Cinehouse, Lumiere and Dongsung Art Centre, the Core Art Hall consistently showed the fewest number of big-selling, big-budget Hollywood films by mid-decade. Instead, it developed a schedule for which it became well-known, making it attractive to cinephiles.

Academic and critic Kim Young-jin recollected that the Core Art Hall's programming was 'at odds with Hollywood movies' (personal correspondence, Kim Young-jin, July 2020). Irene Hee-seung Lee believed the theatre was 'unique' at the time. While videotheques, film clubs and cultural centres primarily took viewers into cinema's past, the Core Art Hall also stressed the latest releases of art film:

> You could see the pictures you couldn't see in the commercial cinemas . . . contemporary European pictures like *Three colours: Blue* (*Trois couleurs: Bleu*, 1993, Krzysztof Kieślowski, France/Poland/Switzerland), World Cinema and Iranian films like *White Balloon* (Badkonake sefid, Jafar Panahi, 1995, Iran) or the films of Kiarostami, low budget indie movies and films sourced directly from festivals. They also screened older films that had either been banned by or never released under the dictatorship. (Author interview with Irene Hee-seung Lee, April 2021)

Lee referenced newly imported but theatrically unreleased European classics including *The Umbrellas of Cherbourg* (Les Parapluies de Cherbourg,

Jacques Demy, 1964, France), *Jeux Interdits* (Song 1997; personal correspondence, Lee Kwang-mo, June 2020). The Core Art Hall's emphasis on art movies can be seen in its marketing strategies, which highlighted the festival awards of films like *Wings of Desire* (Der Himmel über Berlin, Wim Wenders, 1987, Germany).[17]

For other devotees of the Core Art Hall, like film fan Kim Hyo-jŏng, it was the serious atmosphere that drew them and kept them returning:

> There were lots of people coming alone, and no children or elderly people, it was mainly relatively young people. I remember all the seats were filled, and everyone was concentrating on the film without making a sound. Everyone seemed determined to see the movie. (personal correspondence, Kim Hyo-jŏng, December 2020)

For cinemagoers like Kim and Lee and other attendees, the spaces of the new art houses such as the Core Art Hall and the Lumiere brought a transformation in their viewing habits. Kim and Lee began attending screenings at the Core independently instead of going in groups. They watched differently as well since the films required concentration. This type of solitary, focused consumption was desirable for women like Kim and Lee, as is discussed in more detail below.

The distinct programming style and viewing experience offered by the Core Art Hall proved successful, and between 1991 and 1993, annual audience attendances rose from 110,950 to 525,580. Unlike the Hoam Art Hall, the Core Art Hall provided a year-round schedule almost entirely dedicated to European films and classics. Another part of the Core Art Hall's success came from what journalists called 'Core Culture', which provided a business model for subsequent art houses to emulate (An 1995). According to the manager Hwang In-ok, the Core achieved its early successful expansion by seeking the active participation of cinephiles in its organisation and promotion (Song 1997). The cinema introduced membership schemes encouraging participants to help run the theatre and join groups publicising the movies. Hwang claims advertising for the Core's films was primarily spread by word of mouth in the early days, diffusing further to attract other film lovers. In addition, a circle of volunteer members helped run a library, catalogue film materials and produce brochures for customers (Song 1997). The scheme proved so popular that the number of people signing up grew from seventeen in the first year to 150 in the second and 300 by the third (Song 1997). The use of volunteers in the day-to-day running and advertising of the theatre helped keep running costs low and profits high, providing more capital to reinvest in the purchase of foreign art films. Hwang referred to this as a 'low-cost, high-efficiency strategy', which was so successful that the Core Art Hall opened additional auditoriums seating 178 and 199 spectators in 1988–9, completing its expansion (Song 1997). Participation in the running of the theatre is significant because it helped develop a new kind of fan base for cinema.

In addition, the Core Art Hall's creation of memberships, library and reference materials helped distinguish it from other cinemas. The membership scheme entitled customers to preferential access to popular films, newsletters and other benefits. The inclusion of a library and reference materials added to this atmosphere of distinctiveness for cinemagoers by suggesting that movies were not just there to be watched but also researched by more discriminating filmgoers.

The Core Art Hall also played a crucial role in the distribution of art film. Despite the cutthroat competition and its lack of financial resources, the Core Art Hall soon established itself as the art house in the northern part of Seoul. It was customary for distributors in Seoul to choose one main theatre on the north side of the river and another on the southern part (Kangnam). These would act as the so-called '*nalgae*' (wing) theatres

Figure 3.4 The Core Building in Chongno which housed the Core Art Hall, and which still carries the cinema's name (author's photos).

responsible for distributing films to other parts of the capital and into the provinces. Since the Core Art Hall sales, in general, accounted for more than 70 per cent of art film admissions in this period, it had this role. The Core acted as a principal distribution channel for importers who sourced film from international film festivals such as Cannes, and as a result, it dominated art film exhibition in Seoul between 1989 and 1995 (personal correspondence, Kim Young-jin, July 2020; Lee Kwang-mo, June 2020). The cinema became so well-known that shops in front of the cinema took the 'Core' name to identify the location. Newly released videos featured the note 'Premiered at the Core Art Hall' (*k'oaat'ŭholgaebongjak*) on their sleeves for promotion purposes (Pyŏn 2019). Association with the Core Art Hall consecrated movies.

The financial model developed by the Core Art Hall gained the attention of the wider film business. Suddenly films like *Modern Times* that might have been considered loss-making ventures in previous years demonstrated a commercial appeal. In a late 1990s interview, Hwang explained the financial viability of the model. If distributors marketed a well-known Hollywood film through mass media advertising, they would require audiences of 100,000 to make a profit. The exhibition rights to the films chosen by the Core Art Hall were a fraction of the costs of Hollywood movies, meaning a theatre owner required a much smaller audience to break even. All the Core Art Hall needed to do was find a high-quality and economically priced film (Song 1997). It wasn't just the Core Art Hall; the Lumiere prospered in a niche art film market. In an interview with the *Han'gyŏrye* Newspaper, Ha Myŏng-jung, director of the Lumiere, claimed that 'diversity' in film was helping smaller businesses stay afloat in an intensely competitive market dominated by the direct distribution of Hollywood majors. Ha added that art house successes 'couldn't be ignored any longer' (Hwang 2017: 47n.32).

Hwang In-ok's strategy of mobilising film buff volunteers also fed into a new type of film fan culture. The active and participatory element for the day-to-day running of the Core Art Hall was vital in creating a scene and a new kind of consumer. With its more comfortable facilities and central Chongno location, it was also different from the clandestine, semi-legal and often cramped viewing experiences of film fans in videotheques and film clubs. The participation in the Core Art Hall Theatre in the immediate post-dictatorship period involved fans in running a business venture – one in opposition to mainstream narrative films, but a commercial enterprise nonetheless that depended upon making a profit to ensure its continued survival. The rapid expansion of the membership of the Core Art Hall illustrates the importance the cinema played in the lives of its fan-volunteers (Song 1997). The theatre provided film fans with the physical structures – the auditorium, library, networks and motivation for running the cinema – all of which contributed to increased opportunities to express and develop their interest in cinema.

The Core Art House helped draw attention to the type of film it showed in other ways. Evidence for this connection can be seen in a *Han'gyŏrye* article from the summer of 1994 covering the opening of a cinema expo for film buffs held at the Core Art Hall. This expo displayed and sold posters, film stills, specialist film books and even featured original scripts from films by Jean Cocteau and others (Cho 1994). It was a veritable paradise for film lovers – a space to view, purchase and exchange memorabilia, offer opinions and form new relationships with like-minded fans. Jean Baudrillard famously declared that what we collect defines us because in collecting, 'it is invariably oneself that one collects' (cited in Eisner and Cardinal 1994: 11–12). In other words, gathering objects gives people a place in society and allows them to express their perceived or desired identities through possession. Ownership enables collectors to showcase their lifestyles and their identification with a particular group – in this case, with film lovers. The *Han'gyŏrye*'s account of the 1994 Film Expo provides evidence of the emergence of an intense film fandom and its recognition by the media and society.

Korean cinephilia and the emergence of new fans

The growth of art film consumption is significant because it illustrates the type of cinephilia Sontag claimed was dead in her native USA in 1996 was thriving in Korea. In her 2005 discussion of cinephilia between the early and late 1990s, Kim Soyoung (2005: 82) argues a new term, 'cine-mania', was coined in Korean media discourses to describe a specific type of cinema experience (Hwang 2017: 58). How did this specifically Korean type of cinephilia arise, and what distinguished it?

For Kim, cine-mania connotes 'the swallowing-up of incredible numbers of films ... (it was) a frenzied mode of film consumption' (Kim 2005: 82). The relaxation of authoritarian rule was not the only reason for the sudden intensity of cultural consumption. Kim Soyoung believes that young Koreans replaced the 'quasi-religious energy' of the anti-dictatorship movement with a 'quasi-religious' fervour for film spectatorship (2005: 82). Cinema was attractive to young Koreans because it provided a space in which they could address issues of identity. In particular, sexual and regional identity had never been recognised under the dominant nationalistic discourses of the dictatorship and its opposition movement. The growth of film consumption allowed young Koreans greater freedom to express their identity through cultural engagement activities (Kim 2005: 84–5).[18] Kim's theory of cultural replacement is a compelling explanation for the void left in the lives of many of those in the *minjung* movement when mass resistance against authoritarianism ended in the wake of the introduction of direct presidential elections. For Kim, this specific experience of cultural release as a replacement for *minjung* political activity in the immediate post-dictatorship period made 'cine-mania' a distinct Korean cinephilia.

In contrast to the activism replacement theory, some analysts have offered different explanations to account for the rise and character of cinephilia. Park Young-a associates cinephilia and increased cultural consumption in general with a shift in prosperity markers following the phenomenal growth of the Korean economy between 1960 and 1998. The principal indications of middle-class status changed in the 1990s because of the increasing availability of consumer goods. Instead, the 'demonstrative' effect of cultural consumption became a strong motivation for many Koreans in this period (Park 2015: 161; Kim 2000: 73). Cultural markers – like attending movie festivals or watching non-Hollywood films – were associated with middle-class status (Park 2015: 161). Many Koreans consumed independent movies and attended specific film festivals with 'political legitimacy, moral privilege and authenticity' to demonstrate their cultural capital (Park 2015: 162). Other scholars have further delineated the cinephilia of the period. Park A-na (2014: 60–4: 74: 93) argues the commercialisation of videotheques and art houses caused cinephilia to become institutionalised, thus betraying its original values. Park identifies a more 'resistant' clandestine (or closet) cinephilia that embraced a solitary art cinema consumption.[19] Finally, in her analysis of cosmopolitan cinephilia amongst new millennium university film clubs, Josie Jung Yeon Sohn (2012; 2022: 9) argues the borderless tastes of current university film clubs developed during 1980s–90s cinephilia.

None of these characterisations of cinephilia are mutually exclusive. All point to a post-dictatorship desire by many Koreans to establish their own cultural identity based on film consumption. These theories also clarify the socio-political reasons behind the emergence of cinephilia in this period. However, it is worth identifying other aspects of 1990s cinephilia and how these elements interacted to form a specific form of Korean cinephilia.

One important characteristic is the trajectory of 1990s Korean cinephilia. While de Valck and Hagener (2005) and Desser (2005) observed film lovers in the US, Europe and Hong Kong experienced 'classical' big screen before technologically-driven small screen domestic cinephilia, the situation in Korea during the late 1980s and 1990s was very different. The excessive government controls over film production, importation and distribution during the dictatorship meant pirated videos were the main options for 1980s cinephiles. Film buffs had to source movies, copy, distribute and exhibit illegal materials on small screens. In doing so, film buffs created a do-it-yourself, autonomous and resistant underground cinematic culture. What we see in the film fan volunteers at the Core Art Hall (and more so at the Dongsung Cinematheque later) are attempts to re-introduce the auditorium as a space for film appreciation in the manner Sontag (1996) argued. Korean cinephiles sought an authenticity of experience they associated with the big screen. However, more than this, cinephiles sought to imbue their theatrical experience with some of the spirit that characterised their dictatorship-era consumption of forbidden films. They desired autonomy within this cinema space – they would contribute to its running and be involved in the cultural creation of this cinematic experience.

The second facet of Korean cinephilia is that many of its adherents valued the sociality, ritualistic and symbolic associations of the experience as highly as the film text itself. In cinemas like the Core Art Hall in the 1990s – as in the university film clubs and videotheques – film fans were viewing movies they perceived as different from mainstream cinema and, most importantly, engaging in viewing practices that were distinct from those of ordinary consumers. Several features stand out in the accounts of cinephiles. Kim Nan-suk admits to not understanding the movies, but she watched them because she thought they were 'important' (author interview with Kim Nan-suk, May 2020). Film fans like Kim and Lee also admit to nodding off during screenings. Falling asleep during a motion picture is an understandable response to being in a darkened and heated room, but it contradicts the productive viewing response of the cinephile identified by Christian Keathley (2005). In its place, there was a greater engagement with other aspects of cinema.[20] In the post-dictatorship

Figure 3.5 *Cine 21* from 1995 reflecting the cinephilia of the period. No. 26 (L) investigated women filmmakers and pornography, and no. 27 (R) celebrated the latest French art film release by Krzysztof Kieślowski (courtesy *Cine 21*).

context of the late 1980s to mid-1990s, the film experience, the sociality and solidarity between fans engaged in underground screenings at videotheques or volunteer activities at the Core Art Hall meant that the symbolism of the event and the activity were deeply valued over or equal in importance to the film text itself. Cinephiles created a cultural community which expressed an identity in opposition to other forms of cultural consumption (regulated by the authorities). Far from believing they were coopted into the system, in their social consumption of film cinephiles like Lee and Kim felt they were resisting the *chedogwŏn.*

Another vital point about Korean cinephilia is that it represented a gendered transformation.[21] Women in particular were drawn to art film from the late 1980s onwards (see Figure 3.6). In the mid-1990s, three-quarters of the Dongsung Cinematheque's clientele were women in their twenties (Baekdudaegan 1996: 47). KOFIC's 2003 survey of art film fans found that 64 per cent were female, while my 2020 survey produced similar results. Kim Sŏng-uk believes that the preponderance of female spectators at art houses reflects a general international trend in which women make up most audiences for 'minor, or art or independent movies' (author interview, April 2021). However, the specific Korean character of this gendered cinephilia and its connection with specific socio-cultural

Figure 3.6 Women make up most of the crowds for the Jean-Luc Godard evening at the Dongsung Cinematheque, 25 April 1997 (courtesy Lee Kwang-mo).

structures requires some explanation. Cinephiles from the early to mid-1990s Seoul recall that their participation in cinephilia was closely tied to social expectations of acceptable female behaviour at the time. French Cultural Centre attendee Hana Lee observed that in the 1990s,

> there was little culture for educated women to enjoy. Women had nowhere to go while men went to bars or played billiards. However, European art films had a relatively respectful air for women. Social standing for women was a significant factor in women's admiration for European culture in that period. (Personal correspondence, April 2021)

Irene Lee says of her attendance at the Core Art Hall:

> Back then, it was unusual for young women to go to cinemas alone. I much preferred the Core Art Hall (to the French Cultural Centre). I bought my own ticket. It wasn't a communal space; it was a more individual experience. (Author interview with Irene Hee Seung Lee, April 2021)

Whereas in the late 1980s and early 1990s, attending film screenings as couples or with friends and family may have been the norm, for regulars like Hana Lee and Irene Hee-seung Lee, European art film viewing offered an acceptable form of individual female consumption of cinema. For Irene Hee-seung Lee, attending the Core Art Hall was even more liberating since it provided a space in which she felt free from the restrictive standards of social behaviour she found at European cultural centres.[22] The Core Art Hall was a less scripted and more individualistic experience for her. Irene Hee-seung Lee's solitary film viewing at the Core Art Hall was a liberation from the obligations accompanying socialisation practices within the male-dominated discussion groups. According to Doreen Massey (1994: 2), space is 'tied up with particular social constructions of gender relations'. In other words, spaces like theatres, auditoriums, or makeshift viewing spaces like university classrooms enforce existing gender hierarchies. In the case of the cultural centre, Irene Lee entered a location of social and gender structures to which she was expected to conform. The 1990s art house was a relatively new space upon which such strict relations had yet to be established, and she was allowed to develop her position within that location. Hence, art house attendance liberated her from social practices she associated with other forms of movie consumption. The relative freedom of art film was a major draw for Irene and Hana Lee. Film, in general, and art cinema, in particular, provided young Korean women with an important outlet for individual expression that had not always been available in other situations in Korea up to that point.

It is important to note that this cinephilia was not just passive consumption; it also provided women with greater engagement in the film industry. Yi Ŏn-gyŏng, Son Chu-yŏn and Kwŏn Ŭn-sŏn pioneered the growth of videotheques and played important bridging roles between art film consumption, exhibition and production. Korean women's cinephilia also led to the creation of the first women's film festivals that have become an essential part of the Korean cinematic landscape. After running the videotheque Yŏnghwagonggan 1895, Kwŏn Ŭn-sŏn and Yi Ŏn-gyŏng founded and participated in the women's filmmaking collective Parit'ŏ (Sŏng 2020b). Using their significant experience in film exhibition at videotheques, Yi Ŏn-gyŏng and Son Chu-yŏn helped establish the first Korean festivals dedicated to women's cinema. The Riddle of the Sphinx (Sŭp'ingk'ŭsŭŭi susukkekki) Festival ran over three days in June 1993 at the Yŏn'gang Hall (now Doosan Arts centre) in Chongno. The festival screened women's films from all over the world and organised symposiums on the current state and prospects for women's cinema in Korea (Sŏng 2020c). Yi and Son also organised the Feminist Film Festival in June 1995, and both these events were inspirations for the organisation of the Seoul International Women's Film Festival (SIWFF) by members of Parit'ŏ in 1997.[23]

Kwŏn Ŭn-sŏn eventually became a film critic, academic and executive chair of the SIWFF. Kim Nan-suk took a similar path as Son, from film buff consumption to art film exhibition and distribution, and she opened one of the most famous art houses of the early 2000s, the Hypertheque Nada (see Chapter 7). Other women who actively participated in this cinephilia later became prominent in academia (Kim Mi-hyŏn; Irene Hee-Seung Lee), and film journalism (Yi Eun-jŏng). Ch'ungmuro has traditionally been a male-dominated terrain (Nam 2007: 162), so the high percentage of subsequent female involvement in the art film sector is noteworthy. Participation in cinephilia in this period was more than an expression of identity; it was a participatory and productive activity that liberated women from social and hierarchical codes of behaviour and opened opportunities in an industry that blocked female advancement.

Another feature of 1990s Korean cinephilia is the interest of movie fans in French cinematic culture (Figure 3.5). European film formed a core part of programming at cinemas, but 1990s cinephiles privileged French cinematic culture. French movies were the third most imported and consumed foreign motion pictures after US and Hong Kong films,[24] and references to key elements of French cinema filled media discourses from the time.[25] The name of the videotheque SA-Sé is derived from French terms used in semiotics, signifying 'meaning' or 'expression' (Sŏng 2020b). Yŏnghwagonggan 1895 was named in reference to the year the Lumière Brothers produced their pioneering *Arrival of a Train* (*L'arrivée d'un train en gare de La Ciotat, France*). The primary art house in Kangnam was named the 'Lumiere' in honour of the founders of cinema. The auditorium seating plan of the Dongsung Cinematheque was painted to match the colours of the French tricolour (Figure I.1). *Kino* magazine differentiated itself from competitors by including monthly translated theoretical works of visual culture by Francophone philosophers Roland Barthes, Julia Kristeva, Jacques Derrida and articles from *Cahiers du Cinéma* (Yi Sŏn-ju 2017: 424–5). Journalists, theatre managers, film fans and scholars dropped constant references to the Nouvelle Vague or *Cahiers du Cinéma*, so the discourse of this 1990s period of Korean cinephilia had a strong Gallic flavour.

The reason France was privileged over other European cinemas with prominent cinematic cultures is unclear. However, there is no doubt the influence of the French Cultural Centre was vital, as was the 1990s influx of French art film (Paquet 2009: 38). There were also solid French connections of Korean filmmakers like New Wave director Park

Kwang-su, who travelled to France to attend film school.[26] Knowledge of Gallic cinematic culture became evidence of expertise and standing within the cinephile community – clear markers of distinction.[27] Access to this knowledge helped distinguish cinephile activities from mainstream cinema (see Figure 3.5). Just as 1960s French cinephiles like Truffaut showed their disdain for 'dad's cinema' by embracing US genre film, so 1990s Korean cinephiles expressed their rejection of mainstream and Hollywood film through references to French cinema. Sohn (2022) is right to argue that the roots of new millennium cosmopolitanism were established during this earlier cinephilia. But as she acknowledges, the embrace of French/foreign cinema in this post-dictatorship period had a clear national imperative. Cinephiles saw European and other foreign films as enlightening but believed their consumption of overseas cinema provided opportunities to represent their cultural identities and improve domestic cinematic output.[28] Cinephiles perceived a clear use-value behind the consumption of European culture and, in particular, French cinema.

A final vital characteristic of Korean cinephilia is that it existed with a central tension from which it could never escape; namely, the dichotomy between the acceptance of film as 'art' and film as 'activism' (Sŏng 2020d; Chŏng Hye-yŏn 2008). In the intense political struggles of late and post-dictatorship Korea, this distinction between film as art and film as activism became a powerful weapon of contention between different groups within cinema, even though the distinctions between the two sides were rarely consistent.[29] As we saw with Kim Nan-suk and Irene Hee-seung Lee's less militant college cine-clubs, fans seldom saw themselves as politically unengaged and the sense of antagonism towards what they perceived as the *chedogwŏn* unified the disparate elements that constituted their cinephilia. The celebration of French cinema was a cultural negation of mainstream Hollywood cinema. Women attending art film screenings alone was socially defiant behaviour. Active female involvement in film production was a stand against ossified social hierarchies. Cinephiles' privileging of the community and solidarity of the screening over the film experience reinforced the sense of difference from mainstream cinematic viewing. In this post-dictatorship period, Korean cinephilia was rooted in and marked by a sense of political, social and cultural opposition. However, Korean cinephilia could not easily shed this dichotomy between activism and art, and this contention would lead to increased tensions later in the decade.

Late and post-dictatorship South Korean cinephilia's social and cultural complexity instilled it with a fluid Janus-faced character. The cinephilia had a demonstrative and productive side. It celebrated the new power of youthful consumption of cultural forms that had been off-limits. Yet it retained an activist sensibility – a desire for production as well as a longing for wider political change. Cinephiles embraced foreign film to transform national cinematic culture. Cinephiles celebrated the wider acceptance of art movies but did not always recognise commercialisation as 'selling out'. Korean cinephilia was a site of tension between conflicting forces, which brought an inbuilt fragility into the scene and contributed to its decline, as we see in Chapter 5. In 1995, however, the cinephilia cultural phenomenon was about to achieve greater prominence throughout the country, and it would be aided in this development by the emergence of vital media and cinematic institutions of consecration.

Conclusion

The immediate post-dictatorship period (1985–94) was crucial to the emergence of interest in art film in Korea. Regulatory changes, shifts in the geopolitical context, and the cut-throat economic atmosphere of a cinematic market open to direct distribution by Hollywood majors created a niche for European film exhibition. The opening of the Core Art Hall and the establishment of its 'Core Culture' initiated a new method of screening and consuming art film that generated interest in European film. The Core borrowed generously from the DIY and autodidactic ethos of the videotheques and film clubs. However, the experience provided by the Core Art Hall, Lumiere and Hoam Art Hall was also very different from those offered at campus film clubs, cultural centres and videotheques. With their big screens, superior facilities and prestigious locations, the early art houses provided greater respectability and legitimacy to art film spectatorship. Most importantly, they appealed to a wider audience.

While cinephiles may have existed in small pockets in every era in Korea, as Yi Sŏn-ju (2014: 229) points out, it was only in early-1990s Korea that they gained sufficient socioeconomic and cultural capital to make their presence more widely known in Seoul. This was a Korean cinephilia that was distinct from that of other geographical and temporal contexts. It progressed from small to large screen rather than the other way around because of the economic and social context in which it developed. It emerged with the growing profitability of video and possessed a covert, politically engaged character. It later flourished in the emerging art houses but retained the activist and autodidactic culture that had spawned it. It embraced a Gallic cinematic culture as both liberational and inspirational. It was also born with an inherent tension between film as activism and cinema as art. The culture of cinephilia was at once liberating and empowering for women, many of whom played leading roles in both consumption and exhibition. Non-theatrical exhibition sites shaped these essential features of post-dictatorship Korean cinephilia, and these structures, in turn, moulded the art houses that emerged. In the early 1990s, cinephilia moved from the underground into the light. In the yearlong period between mid-1995 and late 1996, further developments solidified the capital's cinephilic culture. They also publicised cinephilia countrywide, fixing them firmly in the public consciousness, which will be explored in the next chapter.

Notes

1. The 1984 5th Amendment to the Motion Picture Law introduced the registration system, and the 1986 6th Revision to the MPL legalised foreign participation in film production, import and distribution (Yu 2007a: 303).
2. 'Well-made' is an expression that emerged around 2003–4 to describe commercial films that made use of 'defined genres' and stars but that also featured the director's distinct authorial style as well as social commentary (Paquet 2009: 93).
3. Whether a particular chaebol cultural centre included art film in their repertoire depended upon the interests of the management team (Park 2015: 70). See Park's example of the Art Zen* (Park 2015: 69).
4. Steve Neale argues, what defines a blockbuster film is the special status regarding its presence and production generated by publicity – so that the public can anticipate the movie's release as an 'event' (Neale 2013: 48).
5. Andrews argues for the use of the oxymoron 'mainstream art' for films like *Les Diaboliques* (Henri-Georges Clouzot, 1955, France) and *Forbidden Games* produced in the classic French studio system's 'tradition of quality' (Andrews 2013: 15, 140, 152).
6. Margaret O'Brien (2018: 83) calls such an approach a 'mixed economy' of programming, arguing that 1950s British art houses showed racy continental melodramas with Japanese and French films to maximise audience numbers.
7. From 1990 onwards, the Myungbo Art Hall screened fewer European films and instead included more commercial, mainstream US film. By 1995 the Myungbo Art Hall abandoned European or classic film screenings.
8. Small auditoriums dedicated to art films were called: *misulgwan/yesulgwan*.

9. The Renaissance briefly maintained a mixed programming strategy in 1992, showing a series of European films such as *Madame Bovary* (Claude Chabrol, 1991, France) alongside Hong Kong martial arts, sexy thrillers and mainstream comedies (KMPPC 1993: 120–64).
10. For example, in 1990, the Dongsung almost entirely showed mainstream features such as *Honey I Shrunk the Kids* (Joe Johnstone, 1989, US), with only a single European feature: *Elvira Madigan* (Bo Widerberg, 1967, Sweden), but by 1992 its programming stressed European films like: *The Deluge* (Potop, Jerzy Hoffman, 1974, Poland), *High Heels* (Tacones Lejanos, Pedro Almodóvar 1991, Spain) and *Indochine* (Régis Wargnier, 1992, France).
11. Margaret O'Brien's extensive surveys of early consumers of art cinema reveals that for many film fans, European movies offered a glimpse of more cosmopolitan and sophisticated continental societies at a time when the UK population was emerging from a drab period of 1950s austerity and rationing.
12. Instead of the then (common) practice of translating the meaning of the word into Korean.
13. For examples of its programmes see entries for Ewha Yesulkŭkjang in KMPPC (1993,120–64).
14. 10 per cent of my art house memories survey respondents reported that the Cinehouse was where they first discovered art films. Fans considered the Lumiere to be an art house (Chŏng Yu-mi 2008; Kim et al. 2004: 36; Hwang 2017: 47).
15. Like the Seoul *kŭkjang*.
16. One auditorium opened in 1987 and the second in 1989 (Song 1997; Yi Kyu-ch'ang 2004).
17. The theatre also retained occasional 'entertainment' films like *Last of the Mohicans* (Michael Mann, 1992, US).
18. 1990s Korean cinephilia facilitated 'the process of identity and subject formation' for women and underrepresented groups within society (Kim 2005: 87).
19. Park (2014: 60–4) uses the term '*kwangjang*' to characterise the public cinephilia, recalling the *minjung* movement use of the term (see Chapter 4).
20. As exemplified in educational activities and fan-volunteer participation at the Core Art Hall and videotheques. The solidarity between art house audiences is examined in Chapter 7.
21. Paquet (2001) reports that the majority of early 1990s audiences in Seoul cinemas were women.
22. Another example of this socially constrictive viewing culture is evident from Kim Nan-suk's accounts of male-dominated senior–junior relationships in university film clubs in which juniors were obliged to sit through screenings of sexually violent films.
23. Son went onto film distribution, exhibition and production; she pioneered art film screening at the Cinehouse and introduced interactive screenings of the *Rocky Horror Picture Show* (1975, Jim Sharman, UK/US) there. Later she marketed and produced *Harmonium in My Memory* (*Nae Maŭmŭi P'unggŭm*, 1999, Lee Young-jae, ROK), *The Way Home* (*Cibŭro*, 2002, Lee Jeong-hyang, ROK) and *Spring Bears Love* (*Pomnalŭi kom-ŭl choahaseyo?*, 2003, Donald Young-ih, ROK) (Sŏng 2020b).
24. See for example the figures in KOFIC (2000: 79) and KMPPC (1993: 166).

25. See also the frequent newspaper articles on French cinema collated by the KMPPC in 1996 (KMPPC 1997: 239, 242, 248, 256–8, 270–1).
26. In the 1990s, directors Chŏn Su-il, Park Kwang-su and Yim Soon-rye received their film education in Paris, while Kim Ki-duk and Hong Sang-soo directed their own educational activities in the French capital (Chung 2012: 4; Huh 2007: 117).
27. According to Sohn (2022: 167) French cinematic culture was still a vital part of Korean cinephilia discourse in the 2000s.
28. Yi Ŏn-gyŏng, Parit'ŏ and Lee Kwang-mo, for example, claimed their aim in foreign film exhibition was to raise the quality of Korean cinema.
29. 'Selling out' by joining the *chedogwŏn* (*chinip*), was a destructive label. Park (2014) reports that Son Chu-yŏn cried when she left her videotheque SA-Sé to join Baekdudaegan as she worried people would see her as 'selling out'.

Chapter 4

The Sacrifice, the Dongsung Cinematheque, film media and the shaping of a new audience, 1995–6

Perhaps the most important demonstration of the emergence of Korea's young cinephiles and a vital milestone in the art film market's growth came in 1995 with the successful Seoul run of Andrei Tarkovsky's *The Sacrifice* (Offret, 1986, Sweden). The film's release caused a nationwide sensation and was followed in close succession by other milestones in Korean cinema; namely, the rapid expansion of printed media devoted to serious film discussion, the opening of the most well-known of the Seoul art houses, the Dongsung Cinematheque, and the establishment of a significant number of international film festivals including the BIFF. This chapter analyses these 1995–6 events focusing on the significance of the struggle to bring Andrei Tarkovsky's *The Sacrifice* to screen, as well as Lee Kwang-mo's experiment in theatrical film exhibition. I examine the relationship between the new film print media, festivals, academia and the nascent art houses, and I contend that the events of this year would have a vital impact on Korean cinema by helping to transform domestic audience tastes.

The Sacrifice Incident

Several media and scholarly accounts of the art film boom imply the success of *The Sacrifice* was inevitable, given the bubbling cinephilia (see Hong 2018). However, nothing could be further from the truth. What is significant is not so much the film's popularity but the fact that it ever reached the screens in the first place. There was substantial resistance from influential sectors of the film industry to the distribution and exhibition of *The Sacrifice* and the type of art film this movie represented.

The struggle to screen *The Sacrifice* reveals structures that controlled the cinematic industry of the time.

In 1991, Lee Kwang-mo pitched his *Spring in My Hometown* scenario to companies in Ch'ungmuro, hoping to get his project into production. After numerous rejections, in May 1993, Lee started working for a film importer, which agreed to finance his film project if he helped them source European motion pictures. Over six months, Lee toured the international film festival circuit and purchased films from Cannes and the Milan MIFED.[1] When the company backed out of financing *Spring in My Hometown*, Lee took his newfound knowledge of film importation and went into business on his own. In February 1994, with money borrowed from relatives, Lee acquired the rights to twenty classic European art movies at the Berlin International Film Festival. These films included *The Sacrifice* and *Fanny and Alexander* (1982, Ingmar Bergman, Sweden/France/West Germany), and none had ever been screened in Korea.

Lee's new art film import and distribution company, Baekdudaegan recruited a small team, and set up an office in north-western Seoul. In establishing Baekdudaegan, Lee claims he was setting out to 'cleanse' Korean film culture of its 'contamination' by mainstream Hollywood and Hong Kong commercial cinema. Baekdudaegan would do this by introducing Korean audiences to the type of art films that had previously gone unreleased because of a perceived lack of commercial potential (Baekdudaegan 1998: 19). Lee originally named his import company after the Paekdudaegan Mountain range that runs from Chirisan in the south to Paekdusan in North Korea (Baekdudaegan 1998: 19). As a student at Korea University in the 1980s, Lee had actively protested against the dictatorship, and his choice of name reflects the idealistic rhetoric of the late 1980s *minjung* movement with its hopes for reunification and a more powerful Korea. In establishing Baekdudaegan, Lee stressed his aim was patriotic. Cured of its 'provincialism' and strengthened by its contact with the 'masterpieces of world cinema', Korean screen culture would be 'elevated' and Korean film would spread across the world like a 'mountain range' (Baekdudaegan 1998: 1; Baekdudaegan 2016). The critical task for Baekdudaegan was the transformation of exhibition. In importing 35mm prints of classic European art films to Korea, Lee attempted to reverse the viewing trends of videotheques so that classic movies would be shown on the big screen, providing an authentic cinematic experience. Now in possession of twenty such films, Lee looked to start screening them. A chance meeting with the manager of the Dongsung Art Centre led Lee to take his business plan there (personal correspondence, Lee Kwang-mo, June 2020).

From its opening in 1994, the Dongsung Art Centre faced stiff competition from the nearby Core Art Hall, but the cinema identified a potentially beneficial arrangement in Lee's plan to exhibit twenty European and American art films. If Baekdudaegan could use its movies to create an attractive programme, then the Dongsung Art Centre would stand a better chance of competing against its powerful rival (personal correspondence, Lee Kwang-mo, June 2020). The deal was that Baekdudaegan would be in charge of all planning and programming, while the Dongsung Art Centre would rent them the auditorium. With Baekdudaegan's preparations underway for a cinema, the Dongsung Art Centre asked Lee to show them the type of film he proposed to exhibit at the new cinema. Lee showed Tarkovsky's *Nostalgia*. The obscure and slow-moving film tells the story of a writer researching the life of a seventeenth-century Russian composer. The manager of the Dongsung Art Centre was horrified by the film claiming it was too boring to succeed. Lee and his team looked like amateurs in the market in the manager's eyes, especially as Baekdudaegan had never exhibited, publicised or distributed a film before. The manager threatened to pull out of Lee's proposed art house plan altogether unless Lee could prove that this type of film was marketable.

Lee then chose to release another Tarkovsky film, *The Sacrifice*, to demonstrate art film could attract Korean audiences (author interview with Lee Kwang-mo, May 2020). Tarkovsky's tale of an intellectual who bargains with God to prevent nuclear war was his final film, and it won the 1986 Grand Prix at the Cannes Film Festival. *The Sacrifice* is characterised by frequently jarring dissonance between scenes and intensely ambiguous narrative structures (Parkinson 2013). Tarkovsky was one of the main progenitors of 'slow cinema', a form of film production characterised by a preponderance of deep focus, an emphasis on rural lifestyles and the observation of the 'riches of lives, realities and temporalities at odds with, or else at the margins of, dominant economic systems and networks . . . ' (De Luca and Jorge 2016: 14). The film features little action and frequent long takes; the opening shot lasts nine minutes without a cut. There are inexplicable dream-like sequences, one of which is a recurring nightmare of the film's protagonist Alexander, an imaginary flash-forward to the aftermath of a nuclear holocaust. Another scene includes the apparent levitation of Alexander and his housekeeper after lovemaking. Several lengthy monologues by the main characters recount stories with no clear resolution, reflecting the opacity of the film's overall narrative. Disturbing images punctuate the film; Alexander suddenly and inexplicably lashes out at his toddler son, and his wife has a breakdown at the news of the impending nuclear holocaust. One journalist from the *Chungang Ilbo* newspaper described Tarkovsky's film as the kind of work that causes 'the average audience to nod off at least once during the performance' (Yi Nam 1997).

Baekdudaegan set to work pitching the film to Seoul art houses and publicising the movie in the media. They wrote press releases to promote Tarkovsky's film, and eventually, the Dongsung Art Centre, the Core Art Hall, and the Lumiere agreed to exhibit the picture in February 1995. Kim Nan-suk said she deliberately went late to the opening night, thinking that no one else would be there. Instead, she found a queue leading around the block and down to the next street corner (Paek 2011). Despite the limited capacity of art house auditoriums, *The Sacrifice* attracted 25,000 spectators. The *Han'guk Ilbo* (*HanKook Ilbo*) claimed that the film drew 100,000 viewers (Na et al. 2008). Kim Sŏng-uk said of the confusion over the audience numbers: 'Whether it was 25,000 or 100,000 people, it doesn't make any difference, in the mid-1990s, this was an unbelievable number of people going to see an art movie. That was the significance' (author interview, April 2021). *The Sacrifice* became the most popular film at the Seoul box office for a period (Kim et al. 2004: 16). The film shocked many viewers who had never experienced anything like it before. Ecstatic spectators approached Lee post-viewing and confessed that they had indeed fallen asleep but had woken to the most beautiful images they had ever witnessed on the screen. Soon, the film became a must-see event for anyone interested in cinema in Seoul (personal correspondence, Lee Kwang-mo, June 2020). The theatrical release of *The Sacrifice* caused a cinematic sensation. It was evidence of the marketability of even the obscurest European art movies and of the existence of a significant number of dedicated film lovers prepared to watch such motion pictures. The *Han'guk Ilbo* called this '*Hŭisaeng sagŏn*' (*The Sacrifice* Incident). The *Hŭisaeng sagŏn*' was a signal of cultural shift (Na et al. 2008; Hwang 2017: 49n.).

Having proved that the type of art film he had imported could draw significant audiences, Lee turned his attention to consolidating his quest to create a venue dedicated to art film – in direct competition with theatres like the Core Art Hall. The problem was that Baekdudaegan was virtually insolvent by this point. The company had no income, and most of *The Sacrifice*'s profits had gone to promoting the film. To establish their theatre, Baekdudaegan had to recoup the losses through video sales and rentals of *The Sacrifice*.

Video was the primary way many exhibitors and distributors made a profit; if 5,000 videotapes could be sold to the 30,000 video stores, then Baekdudaegan could generate enough profit to offset their losses (Kim et al. 2004: 25; personal correspondence, Lee Kwang-mo, May 2020).[2] In March 1995, Baekdudaegan took *The Sacrifice* to the most extensive video business in Korea, Wooil Film, an affiliate of the Daewoo chaebol, which mainly dealt with genre and erotic films and asked them to manufacture and distribute the tapes. Lee had already received rejections from other video companies because of the obscurity of *The Sacrifice*. The Wooil CEO arranged for company sales staff to attend a preview screening of the film in central Seoul. By halfway through, most of the employees had walked out in horror at the slow-moving film, and by the end credits, only the CEO, the senior sales team and Lee were left. The CEO laughed and said the film would never sell, while the sales officials opposed the distribution, claiming video stores would reject the film. However, the CEO agreed to back the distribution if *The Sacrifice* could receive advance orders exceeding 5,000 copies from video stores. Baekdudaegan's marketing department once again prepared advertising to convince enough retailers to order the film. The following month, *The Sacrifice* received advance orders of 7,000, a success by any calculations. The video was released, its profits saved Baekdudaegan and made its name. Lee opened his art house: 'People in artistic and cultural circles knew who we were. Moviegoers, journalists and critics talked about what we had done. *The Sacrifice* changed everything for us' (personal correspondence, Lee Kwang-mo, June 2020). Lee had proved doubters in the film industry wrong twice. Newspaper reports in the *Han'gyŏrye* from 1995 indicate that Lee's 'persistence' in importing 'controversial art pieces' and his 'reckless risktaking' in promoting the type of cinema he loved had earned him the 'admiration' of many within the film fraternity (An 1995).

Barbara Wilinsky (2001: 27) and Margaret O'Brien (2018: 49) describe the opening of *Rome Open City* in the post-war US and UK as a pivotal moment after which foreign art film rose to prominence and art houses exploded domestically. In this, there are strong parallels to the success of *The Sacrifice* in Korea. *The Sacrifice*'s success was the watershed moment for art film in Korea. There are two distinct eras: before *The Sacrifice* and after, when nothing was quite the same again for the new generation of Korean cinephiles and art cinema exhibitors, distributors, video manufacturers and retailers. A film that could never be marketed, sold or consumed had succeeded. There are, however, significant differences with *Rome Open City*, not least of which is the obscurity of Tarkovsky's film, in terms of subject matter, style and age. *Rome Open City* spoke to British and Americans of recent wartime hardships that they too had known. Barbara Wilinsky (2001: 28) has stated that the film was the most 'stylistically focused of Rossellini's neo-realist films ... It was different from Hollywood but not that different.' *The Sacrifice* was nothing like this. It was obscure, overlong, slow and shown ten years after its Cannes success, but it caused an exhibition sensation in Korea.

A month after *The Sacrifice* Incident, the release of another film – this time Korean – made a second sensation amongst cinephiles. Byun Young-joo had been a founding member of Parit'ŏ, and alongside other members, dedicated herself to producing a film detailing the tragic history of the young Korean women coerced into joining the Comfort Women battalions of sex slaves to service the Japanese Imperial Army during the Second World War. Byun's documentary *The Murmuring* (Chagŭn moksori, 1995), which formed part of a Comfort Women trilogy, was released at the Dongsung Art Centre in late April 1995. What was most remarkable is that Byun had faced even greater obstacles than other activist filmmakers like Changsan'gonmae in raising funds for the production. Byun recalled that she had to sell badges, trinkets and recruit 'celluloid sponsors' to crowd-fund her documentaries. Some of the crew had to walk between locations for the shoots because they couldn't afford transportation, and four bowls of food were occasionally divided up between seven crew members (Sŏng 2020c). Despite the lack of funds, Byun achieved what other activists could not; she had a documentary run at a movie theatre. Word spread amongst film enthusiasts, and its popularity grew. *The Murmuring* was a rare Korean documentary to be given a theatrical release, running for a month and attracting 6,000 admissions (Kim et al 2004: 157; Sŏng 2020c). The successful screenings of *The Sacrifice* and *The Murmuring* were film as event.

New film media

The success of *The Sacrifice* had much to do with Baekdudaegan's marketing and sympathetic journalists, illustrating the powerful reach of the Korean press. The year 1995 saw a rapid expansion of a new film media that dramatically transformed the cinematic environment. In April 1995, the progressive *Han'gyŏrye* newspaper established the weekly *Cine 21* (*Ssinae isipil*) and soon after, the first edition of the monthly *Kino* was published. The Korean edition of the US film magazine *Premiere* followed later (Ch'oe 2015; Kim et al. 2004: 23). These new magazines were different from industry-focused publications like *Pideo/mubi* (Video/movie) but joined established titles like *Roadshow*, *Screen*, the plethora of videotheque-produced pamphlets and journals like *Film Language* dedicated to the serious discussion of cinema for film audiences. In the pre-Internet era, before information about film could be accessed at the touch of a button, this printed literature became a vital vehicle of information about international film festival award-winners, commercial, art and cult movies (author interview with Kim Sŏng-uk, April 2021). The publications facilitated the comprehension and acceptance of hitherto unseen film by a public starved by the dictatorship of foreign culture.

The total reach of the magazines amongst both the cinephile community and Korean public was wide. At $2.60, *Cine 21* swiftly reached a circulation of 30,000 becoming not just the most popular film publication but the biggest selling magazine in Korea (personal correspondence, Lee Kwang-mo, May 2022). Between 1995 and 1998, *Kino* boasted a monthly circulation of 40,000. *Premier* sold approximately 15,000 copies a month, while *Film 2.0* put out 10,000 per week (Paquet 2009: 38; Kim 2005: 90n.6; personal correspondence, Kim Chong-wŏn, May 2022).[3] These are remarkable figures in comparison to the circulations of film publications elsewhere. At its 1960s peak, *Cahiers du Cinéma* had a circulation of 13,000, while *Sight and Sound* had similar sales (Hillier 1986: 23).[4] All the magazines featured information on new releases and, at the same time, championed the work of emerging Korean auteurs. However, they also attempted to target specific audiences by providing different film-related content, and these distinctions provide important insights into the cinematic culture emerging at this time (Paquet 2009: 38; Kim 2005: 90n.6). More than other magazines in this period, *Cine 21* and *Kino* dominated in terms of their influence over cinephilia and patterns of film consumption. *Cine 21*'s coverage included both domestic and foreign commercial genre and festival-oriented film. It positioned itself as an influential proponent for the expansion of Korean cinema (Yi Sŏn-ju 2017: 436), and as we see in the 2001 Waranago Incident

(Chapter 6), *Cine 21* showed itself to be a vocal critic of misguided governmental policy. Its outspoken character and left-wing roots made *Cine 21* especially popular with academics and students.

With its healthy readership, *Kino* saw itself as the vanguard of a cultural movement to reinvigorate film appreciation (Yi Sŏn-ju 2017: 430). Film was more than an entertaining commercial product; it was a serious art form. *Kino* targeted intellectual audiences in several ways. It 'rediscovered' unknown or neglected films; it stressed in-depth theoretical explorations of film. Every edition featured translations of articles from cultural theoreticians and filmmakers, for example, Walter Benjamin, Edward Said, Slavoj Žižek, Paul Virilio, Judith Butler and Pier Paolo Pasolini (Yi Sŏn-ju 2017: 427). The editors attempted to compress thirty years of cultural theory – semiotics, post-colonialism, Marxism, structuralism and psychoanalysis – into its pages, including excerpts reprinted from well-established film magazines *Sight and Sound*, *Positif* and *Cahiers du Cinéma*.[5] The magazine's journalists also readily adopted the challenging linguistic style of French cultural theoreticians such as Jacques Derrida. Kim Nan-suk recalled in a 2020 interview: 'it was a hard read ... but it was like a reference book for ideas on cinema, and I'm reading my way through copies from years ago ... we saw it as our *Cahiers du Cinéma*' (author interview with Kim Nan-suk, May 2020). Such was its intellectual pedigree that *Kino* was the only film magazine stocked in the bookshops and libraries of the elite Seoul National, Yonsei and Korea Universities (personal correspondence, Kim Chong-wŏn, May 2022). *Kino*'s mission was to educate audiences about the actual value of cinema, and film analysis represented a way of achieving a 'critical distance' to film appreciation (Yi Sŏn-ju 2017: 427). *Kino* differentiated itself from competitors and appealed to 'highbrow' readers by offering an exclusive experience (Hwang 2017: 52–4). The magazine has been criticised as fostering an art-for-art's sake outlook on its readership and too readily embracing foreign cinema. However, Yi Sŏn-ju (2017: 434–5) maintains the magazine's political line was more complex since it argued the profit motive was ultimately corrosive to filmmaking. In addition, *Kino* did not just include features on foreign cinematic cultures, but devoted significant coverage to emerging Korean auteurs (Yi Sŏn-ju 2017: 434, see Figure 4.1). The May 1998 *Kino* analysed E-J Yong's *An Affair* (Chŏngsa, 1998, ROK), Chŏng Pyŏng-gak's *17* (1998, ROK) and Pak Ki-hyŏng's horror *Whispering Corridors* (Yŏgogwoedam, 1998, ROK).

Figure 4.1 Issues of *Kino*: (L) July 1998; (R) May 1998 (courtesy Kim Chong-wŏn).

The rise of this new printed film media had important cultural impacts on mid-1990s Korea. The critical reappraisal of Korean cinema in magazines like *Kino* helped invigorate the reception of domestic film over the next few years (see Chapter 5). The magazines also raised awareness of films and a hitherto inaccessible cinematic culture in Korea. Furthermore, the new print media's discussion of theories and revelations about undiscovered films helped elevate the understanding and appreciation of cinema for audiences. For Kim Nan-suk, the publication of film magazines like *Kino* and *Cine 21* represented the start of 'when we really began to talk about movies and film theory, we started taking reviews seriously, and changed how we discussed movies and how we judged films to be good or not good' (author interview with Kim Nan-suk, May 2020). The media opened the eyes of audiences to different ways of conceptualising cinema.

The success of these magazines in this period led to a greater expansion of the literature on film. Demand for more in-depth theoretical examination of film increased, and this is evidenced by first the growing number of cinema-dedicated magazines like *Cinebus* and *Film 2.0* in 2000, and *Movie Week* (2001; Kim Sang-man 2006), and second, the shifting emphasis of cinema-related publications between 1995 and 1998. Studies reveal that most books published before 1997 were basic introductions to film studies, but after 1998, more publications treated film criticism and theory (Hwang 2017: 52–3). These transformations indicate publishers began catering to a more discerning cinema audience demanding a deeper understanding of movies. In 1997, articles also appeared in national newspapers like the *Dong-a Ilbo* (1997) outlining the educational activities of videotheques and art houses. Shyon Baumann (2007: 69, 117) highlights the importance of journals, film-dedicated magazines and books in giving film canonical status and wider acceptance. The greater analytical and theoretical analysis of film in books and magazines and the spread of serious coverage of movies in the Korean press are evidence of the changing consumption of cinema within Korea.

The new film dedicated print media helped solidify the community of Korean cinephiles that had formed around the videotheques, film clubs and new art houses. Film critic, journalist and academic Yi Yŏng-jae claims that *Kino* served as the centre of a community for cinephiles: 'if you saw someone else reading a copy on a subway, you felt an instant sense of solidarity with them' (Hong 2018). The magazines provided an intellectual grounding and justification for the 'alternative' preferences for art and other film adopted by the new cinephiles. This printed literature also played a vital facilitating link between fans and cinemas showing art movies. They promoted the growing interest in cinephilia by providing extensive information about what film-related events were on, where and when. *Cine 21* and *Kino* took a special interest in covering the instructional activities and programmes of the early art houses and videotheques.[6] This had the effect of further publicising the vitality of the new exhibition venues to the rest of the country. New film magazines ran special features on directors and movies playing at the Dongsung Cinematheque and Core Art Hall that appeared to be virtual advertisements. Many contained no news other than details about the movies and when they played.[7] These features on art houses and their screenings appeared in *Cine 21* and its parent publication, the *Han'gyŏrye* newspaper.[8] The media provided essential marketing opportunities for smaller cinemas like the Dongsung Cinematheque, Core Art Hall and the Lumiere, which had limited budgets for publicity (Yi Yŏng-jae 1998; An Chŏng-suk 1995; Chŏng 1996; Yi Sŏng-uk 1996a). *Cine 21*'s May 1996 collaboration with the Dongsung Cinematheque in the 'Unknown Auteurs' (*mijiŭi myŏnggamdokchŏn*) film season is one example (Chŏng 1996). In mounting the event, *Cine 21* aimed to promote directors like Aki Kaurismäki, Stephen Frears and David Lynch, whose work showed the 'richness of life' but had never been screened in Korea before (Chŏng 1996). *Cine 21* was making a statement by championing Lee's programming at the Dongsung Cinematheque. In such collaborations, there appeared to be a quid pro quo aspect to the relationship between the theatre and the publication; *Cine 21* promoted Lee's films and, in doing so, expressed its own cultural identity. The influence of film magazines was critical to the success of art houses and the increased consumption of art film in this period.[9]

Critics played a vital bridging role between the new print media, exhibition spaces and cinephilia. Wilinsky (2001: 92) observes that in post-Second World War USA, 'Film critics gave viewers a means by which to approach and discuss films and provided films with an element of respectability required'. This is true of 1995 South Korea; reviews and articles by scholars and journalists highlighted the significance of directors and theories and gave valuable context for understanding motion pictures. But there was a great intensity of interaction between media, festivals, official and non-official film education, cinephilia, exhibition and film administration. Chŏng Sŏng-il attended the European cultural centre screenings, lectured at the Korean National University of the Arts, programmed film festivals, and served as *Roadshow*, *Kino* and *Film Language* editor. Other critics like Yi Yŏng-jae and Sim Yŏng-sŏp worked both as journalists and lecturers involved in both formal film instruction at universities and informal educational activities at videotheques.

Two points are vital then from the interpersonal and inter-institutional connections of critics of this new print media. One is that the critical tastes of these influencers of public opinion were shaped by the institutions with which they interacted (the art houses, videotheques, intellectual film magazines, European cultural centres). Second, many of these critics straddled influential institutions at the centre of South Korean film during a time of considerable change. Crucially critics were doing more than offering reviews to influence the public's viewing choices; they were not bystanders to change; they were actively participating in this cultural transformation. The exponential growth of print culture and the activities of critics within this new media were central to both the acceptance of serious consideration of film within South Korean society and the future direction of a more prominent cinematic industry. Significantly, many went on to be involved with film festivals and KOFIC, the state body administering film in an official capacity. Chŏn Ch'an-il became a BIFF programmer, Hŏ Mun-yŏng was head of the Pusan Cinematheque and then became BIFF head in 2021, Lee Sang-yong contributes to KOFIC publications. Kwak Yŏng-jin sits on the Video Rating Committee

(Yŏngsangmuldŭngwiwŏnhoe) and Kim Young-jin is the former head of KOFIC. They were shapers of both public discourses at the time and later official policy on cinema. The timing of this explosion of film-centred print media was also fortuitous for the opening of one theatre in particular – the Dongsung Cinematheque – which generated a media sensation (Figure 4.2) and publicised Seoul's art film scene throughout the country.

The establishment of the Dongsung Cinematheque

In November 1995, Lee Kwang-mo's Baekdudaegan took control of the Dongsung Cinematheque, establishing a cinema dedicated to art film.[10] Baekdudaegan set up a library and a small shop selling movie-related merchandise like art film posters and videos in the lobby. Baekdudaegan prepared 200,000 copies of a sixty-page magazine announcing the opening of their art house. Lee's company named the cinema 'Kwangjang', which can be translated as 'plaza' or 'communal place', but according to An Chŏng-suk writing in the *Han'gyŏrye*, has a literal meaning of 'open space' (*yŏllin madang*), recalling the attempts of radical film activists like Yallasang Cinema Club to democratise film (An 1995).[11] The Dongsung Cinematheque was dedicated to the creation of a 'new movie culture', which encouraged 'active audience participation' (*nŭngdongjŏk kwan'gek munhwa*) in cinematic culture and in which the theatre was a 'public space for everyone' (personal correspondence, Lee, June 2020).

The term *Kwangjang* never caught on with most attendees, who continued to refer to the theatre as the Dongsung Cinematheque. Baekdudaegan used custom-made illustrations by well-known cartoonists to demonstrate the transformations the cinema planned to implement. The magazine featured information about screening schedules, the films and their directors, membership and proposed activities (personal correspondence, Lee Kwang-mo, June 2020). It reads like an artistic manifesto, a statement of creative intent, or a proposal to shake up and transform viewing habits and cinematic culture. The Dongsung Cinematheque became one of the most talked-about venues in Seoul. It gained official state-sanctioned status as the first specialist art film theatre; it inspired subsequent Korean art houses and became a future symbol of cinephilia's dynamism. Its status derived from its attempt to transform theatrical exhibition, film education audience tastes and business structures.

Figure 4.2 Headlines of *Han'gyŏrae* newspaper articles in 1996 championing Lee Kwang-mo's Dongsung Cinematheque and reporting on collaboration with *Cine 21* (courtesy Korean Press Foundation).

A new viewing experience and screening culture: exhibition and programming

Baekdudaegan implemented immediate changes to transform the viewing experience of Dongsung Cinematheque audiences. The only way for people to truly experience and appreciate movies was with optimal big-screen viewing conditions (personal correspondence, Lee Kwang-mo, June 2020). The cinema kept the house lights off until the last credit had run so consumers could experience the full emotional impact of films (Paek 2009). So ingrained were old habits that Lee had to repeat his instruction to the projectionist to finish the movies only when the ending credits had played (personal correspondence, Lee Kwang-mo, June 2020). The cinema banned popcorn, roasted squid or soft drinks from the auditorium; it permitted no distractions to the viewing experience (Paek 2009). Baekdudaegan argued the Dongsung Cinematheque laid the foundations for film 'appreciation'; they wanted audiences to consume film as a 'high-level cultural activity' (Paek 2009).

Table 4.1 Attendances at the Dongsung Cinematheque, November 1995–October 1996.

Date of Exhibition	Film	Attendance
November 1995	*Stranger than Paradise* (Jim Jarmusch, 1984, US)	21,162
December 1995	*Sweetie* (Jane Campion, 1989, Australia)	12,144
January 1996	*Boy Meets Girl* (Leos Carax, 1984, France)	17,612
February 1996	*Nostalgia*	11,918
March 1996	*Spider's Stratagem* (*Stratagia del Ragno*, Bernardo Bertolucci, 1970, Italy)	6,747
April 1996	*Red Psalm*	7,175
	My Beautiful Launderette (Stephen Frears, 1985, UK)	16,675
	Eraserhead (David Lynch, 1977, US)	20,402
August 1996	*Where is the Friend's House?*	48,209
September 1996	*Landscape in the Mist*	38,052
October 1996	*Children of Nature* (*Börn náttúrunnar*, Friðrik Þór Friðriksson, 1991, Iceland)	4,217

Source: Kim et al. 2004: 157–8.

Baekdudaegan also attempted to transform standard programming practices at the Dongsung Cinematheque. Before Lee, the Dongsung Cinematheque – like the Lumiere and Cinehouse – had shown a mixed programming schedule with no connecting theme or logical structure and withdrew pictures if they failed to draw audiences.[12] Lee aimed to distinguish his theatre from its competitors through his programming. In an interview at the cinema's official opening in November 1995, journalists asked Lee whether making a theatre dedicated to art film would alienate ordinary people. He disagreed, arguing that the problem lay in prevailing attitudes about the value of movies:

> Art film is stereotyped as something noble (*kosang*) and lofty, but in actual fact, art is connected to our lives and how we think about life. People don't see film as legitimate compared to other cultural forms. It is neglected and looked down upon (*ch'ŏnsi*) in our country, but not in other parts of the world. The problem is the current environment of commercial cinema is excessively stressed. Film is seen as a form of

entertainment and a way of making profits. What we need to do is change the lie of the land (*p'ungt'o t'oyang*). We've got to get our audiences used to this kind of art film, so they enjoy it more. (MBC 1995)

The interview provides indications about the ideas underlying Lee's programming style. Changing the lay of the land meant stressing art over entertainment and profit, and one way Baekdudaegan did this was by creating fixed six-month programmes. The cinema screened movies regardless of their popularity; no one showed up to a screening to find the film had been withdrawn (An 1995). Fixed schedules were crucial to Lee's establishment of a distinct identity and how he renounced profit.

What then constitutes 'art' according to his understanding? How was art in film connected to our lives? A commonality of Baekdudaegan's marketing is 'masterpiece' (*kŏljak*), a notion synonymous with the creative output of particular directors (Paek 2009; personal correspondence, Lee Kwang-mo, May 2020). Baekdudaegan consistently organised screenings focusing on the works of specific directors, opening the Dongsung Cinematheque with a Jim Jarmusch double-bill consisting of *Stranger Than Paradise* after the short *Coffee and Cigarettes* (1993, Jim Jarmusch, USA). Later the theatre screened Jane Campion's short *Peel: An Exercise in Discipline* (1982, Australia) before her full-length feature *Sweetie*. Over the next two years, Baekdudaegan also organised seasons dedicated to the work of specific directors. One, in April 1997, was dedicated to Jean-Luc Godard (Figure 4.4; Baekdudaegan 1998: 1; MBC 1995; An 1995). Using the names of directors as a primary organising principle to construct programmes 'implicitly or explicitly indicates' that the filmmaker has a specific style that identifies them as the 'author' of the movie (Gerstner and Staiger 2003, xi; Bosma 2015: 56). Lee judged masterpieces in terms of the director's innovation and specific style, and this formed one organisational principle for the Dongsung Cinematheque's programme. Such a method was similar to art houses in the United States, the UK and France. However, Lee's idea of showing and hosting so many double features or festivals focusing on specific directors was new to 1990s commercial cinema exhibition in Korea (personal correspondence, Lee Kwang-mo, May 2020).

Peter Bosma argues that in addition to 'craftsmanship or innovative style', one important organisational principle is the screening of films, which are seldom 'seen … unjustly unknown and forgotten' (Bosma 2015: 52). Apart from *Landscape in the Mist*, all the previously unreleased films were shown exclusively at the Dongsung Cinematheque. The rarity of these films lent a certain mystique to the programme and the cinema itself. Another important principle for selection was diversity. Lee programmed films from North America, continental Europe, Iran, Australia and Iceland. The newest was *Children of Nature* (1991), and the oldest was *Spider's Stratagem* (1970). The programme offered a cross-section of art film history featuring directors from the classic era of European art pictures (Bertolucci), American independent movies (*Stranger than Paradise*) and more recent 'waves' of non-European cinema from Iran (*Where is the Friend's House?*) (Ahn 2012: 84). According to Kim Young-jin, this retrospective feature of the programme led film consumers to regard the Dongsung Cinematheque as the place to see art film 'classics' (personal correspondence, Kim Young-jin, July 2020). Lee took Seoul audiences on a journey into a thirty-year cinematic past denied them by censorship, import restrictions, or distributors who feared such films would never turn a profit.

Another characteristic feature of the programme that was alluded to in the MBC interview was the overall tone offered by the films. Peter Bosma argues one possibility for curators is to present either a 'cinema of reassurance' or a 'cinema of disturbance', where the latter 'offers films which confront us with the dark side inside all of us, ranging from films that express existential despair, alienation, a feeling of loneliness, or a pessimistic mood ... ' (Bosma 2015: 63).[13] Lee's choice of films like *Nostalgia*, with its themes of alienation, *Eraserhead*, with its disturbing imagery, *Sweetie*, in its unsettling depiction of mental illness, suggests that his programming closely reflects Bosma's 'cinema of disturbance'.

There was a final factor influencing the selection of movies. Baekdudaegan struggled to import some films simply because they failed to secure copyrights or were prohibitively expensive. Lee eventually had to abandon his novel double-bill policy of screening a short and main feature by the same director because of high importation costs.[14] Instead, he chose a Korean-produced short to screen before each foreign feature, and this became a significant characteristic of his programming style (personal correspondence, Lee Kwang-mo, December 2020).

Those who attended the cinema, such as film journalist Choi Sang-hee, noted the darker tone of the programming and the novelty of the approach Baekdudaegan was taking with the Dongsung Cinematheque.

> The Cinematheque was a fresh idea back then. I was aware that I was watching different types of films unavailable in mainstream cinemas. They were unconventional in subject matter, how they told a story and

cast actors, and even their running time. I think cinemagoers back then were quite excited to see art films. I remember some of those movies I saw at the Dongsung were unusual, but they made me think that stories could be told in diverse ways. (Personal correspondence, Choi Sang-hee, November 2020)

Why was Baekdudaegan taking such an approach to exhibition and programming? Lee claimed in interviews that they took all decisions about exhibition in 'total opposition' to current practice in mainstream theatres (Paek 2009). In the context of post-dictatorship Korea, it was particularly important for exhibitors to distance themselves from outwardly embracing profit since, for many within the 386 generation, the development of South Korean capitalism had been tarnished by its close associations with the dictatorship. Bourdieu (1980: 261) argues entrepreneurs like Lee are not genuinely disinterested in profit but use the 'disavowal of the economy' as a strategy to accrue symbolic capital and increase the 'longer-term potential for economic gain' (Bourdieu 1980: 265–6; Wilinsky 2001: 143). The intensity of Lee's approach suggests Lee believed what he preached, but in expressing his vision, he also competed

Figure 4.3 Dongsung Cinematheque promotional materials. (L) Guide to the 1995 schedule featuring the cinema's motto: 'The cinematic world you have always dreamed of'. (R) Booklet produced to advertise Peter Greenaway's *The Draughtsman's Contract* (1982, UK). Images courtesy Lee Kwang-mo.

successfully against the Core Art Hall and the videotheques. Essentially, in his transformation of space, Lee was doing what had been done by art house exhibitors in many other contexts (Wilinsky 2001: 132, 145; O'Brien 2018: 208). He created an atmosphere that appealed to the taste preferences of discerning audiences seeking a more upmarket cinematic experience. The fixed schedules, bans on popcorn and extended runs of films demonstrate Lee's application of this distinction strategy. Lee was giving his operation the event status vital to commercial film marketing and that he had successfully implemented with *The Sacrifice*. The difference is that Lee was not creating public anticipation about the opening of a specific film but about his new cinema and the change in viewing practices it promised. Part of this transformation was supposed to come via another aspect: public education.

The expansion of film education

Almost exactly a month after the opening of the Dongsung Cinematheque, Lee posted a small advertisement in the entertainment section of the 12 December 1995 *Kyŏnghyang Sinmun*. In it, Lee called for cinephiles to pay $8 to become members of the country's 'one and only cinematheque'. For this nominal amount, members would be supporting a film library and reading room as well as receiving newsletters, discounts and special offers. Lee's call resembles an early form of 'crowd-funding', and it is noteworthy because it is a statement of intent regarding the educational function of the Cinematheque; this would be more than just a commercial enterprise entertaining spectators. The cost, $8 (the equivalent of a film ticket at the time), bought users a regular membership, and around 2000 ordinary members paid these annual fees. A higher yearly payment of $32 provided a premium membership, including entrance to the Kwangjang Academy (Plaza Academy). Non-members could turn up and pay an entrance fee to view any film if tickets were available. Membership of the Kwangjang Academy was restricted to 100 people who signed up on a first-come, first-served basis. Members could participate in regular talks and classes on cinema held at the Cinematheque (Hwang 2017: 51). Baekdudaegan organised pre and post-screening lectures by film scholars and critics who discussed the films with audiences (An 1995; MBC 1995) (Figure 4.4).[15] Professor Ma Kwang-su analysed *That Obscure Object of Desire* (*Cet obscur objet du désir*, Luis Buñuel, 1977, France), Park Chan-wook lectured on *Eraserhead* (Baekdudaegan 1996: 25; personal correspondence, Lee Kwang-mo, June 2020).[16] Including scholars, filmmakers and critics in the theatre's educational activities served several functions. Baekdudaegan promoted the inclusion of academics to help audiences comprehend the significance of the stylistically challenging programme and encourage them to engage in discussion. The pamphlets, newsletters and lectures helped audiences situate films from diverse geographical and temporal origins. This educational input also helped 'propose structures of reflection' to audiences so they could 'construct criteria of judgement' (Bosma 2015: 42). The involvement of intellectuals publicised Baekdudaegan's work, consecrated the cinema's exhibition strategies and established its difference from competitors.

Those who had paid to join the Kwangjang Academy could also participate in other activities as part of their membership. Baekdudaegan provided a training programme aimed at college students or young office workers interested in movies but with no opportunity to receive formal film education. The 'Kwangjang Academy Regular Classes' (*Kwangjang ak'ademi chŏnggi kangjwa*) were pitched at people without prior knowledge of film. Lessons focused on basic film history and theory (An 1995; Figure 4.3). Baekdudaegan also offered a higher-level course at the Dongsung Cinematheque for more knowledgeable participants. These weekly courses were held in two-month blocks and taught by Lee (personal correspondence, Lee Kwang-mo, June 2020). Members were also entitled to borrow cinema-related materials from the Dongsung Cinematheque's small library of books, magazines, DVDs and videotapes. Baekdudaegan purchased the library stock using membership fees, but academics donated books. It was still difficult to find specialist materials about film anywhere other than at university libraries, and these were inaccessible to non-students.

The most ambitious educational project launched by the Dongsung Cinematheque was the 'Guide to Newly-released Films at the Dongsung Cinematheque' (*Yesulyŏnghwa chŏnyonggwan kaebongjak haesŏlsŏ*) (Yi 1997). This booklet contained information about films screened at the Cinematheque and the directors who made them. Typically, the booklet included seventy pages of text and film images. The cinema formed a dedicated commentary team (*Haesŏlsŏ t'im*) of five Kwangjang Academy members to produce these pamphlets. The cinema provided the group with books, videos and photographs to help their research. Members met once a week to coordinate the tasks, and they viewed the films before the public screenings, wrote an analysis in simple-to-understand lay person's terms, and then had the results edited and printed. Typically, they produced 2,000 copies of the guides, and at fifty cents per copy, they usually sold out (Yi 1997). In April 1997, the team consisted of five women in their mid-to-late twenties selected for their enthusiasm and English proficiency. Two studied film at university, while the other three worked in offices, but all were interested in film (Yi 1997). They produced guides to films as diverse as *Leningrad Cowboys Go America* (Aki Kaurismäki, 1989, Finland) and *Trainspotting* (Danny Boyle, 1996, UK). The most challenging aspect of making the booklet was watching the film on video in the original language without subtitles (Baekdudaegan 1998: 1; Yi 1997). Lee attempted to foster an 'active and self-reliant' audience in his cinemas, and the enthusiastic participation of the Kwangjang Academy members – especially those who compiled the booklets – helped bring 'energy' to the theatre (personal correspondence, Lee Kwang-mo, June 2020). The Dongsung Cinematheque provided audiences with an educational and communal experience. Viewers watched the films, listened to lectures and collaborated to produce interpretations of films for other audiences to consume.

How should we interpret these calls for active audience participation and attempts at film education by Baekdudaegan at the Dongsung Cinematheque? The original *Kyŏnghyang Sinmun* advertisement wasn't a call for large-scale corporate sponsorship from one of Korea's many conglomerates or chaebols that had invested heavily in the arts since the 1980s (Kim 2005: 87; Park 2015: 69). For Lee, it was an appeal for an investment that almost anyone could make and one which would provide educational facilities that anyone could access. He promoted his Dongsung Cinematheque as an inclusive rather than an exclusive enterprise. The advertisement and promotional materials clarify that the cinema targeted educational facilities, resources and lectures towards 'ordinary non-specialists' without access to such information or instruction (Baekdudaegan 2016). Lee was disavowing his own desire for economic gain and, in doing so, establishing the reputation of the Dongsung Cinematheque. The call implies this wasn't money going into the profits of film companies. By donating a nominal amount, sponsors were investing something of themselves into the cinema; they were taking ownership of it. Not only that, but they were also contributing to the common good by helping to educate others about cinema. The advertisement was also a very public statement of differentiation from the practices of rivals like the corporate-sponsored Hoam Art Hall. By claiming to be the 'one and only' cinematheque specialising in art film, Lee was engaging in what Bourdieu calls the

> continuous creation of the battle between those who have made their names and... those who cannot make their own names without relegating to the past the established figures ... (this meant) making one's mark ... (and) creating a new position in the avant-garde. (Bourdieu 1980: 289)

Lee's statement suggested a more authentic cinematic experience – where authentic is what Lee believed the experience should be in terms of participatory rather than passive film viewing. He thought it imbued his cinema with a cultural legitimacy that put it ahead of his competitors.

Baekdudaegan's educational drives were also a product of the times. The Dongsung Cinematheque borrowed features of its educational organisation from its competitors. The Core Art Hall, film clubs and videotheques also had a do-it-yourself spirit and membership schemes, film-buff volunteers, libraries, resources and self-produced pamphlets (Hwang 2017: 50; Yi 1997). The repudiation of economic interests reflected the anti-*chedogwŏn* tendency of the *minjung* movement.

Figure 4.4 Image of pre-screening talk before the Jean-Luc Godard evening at the Dongsung Cinematheque, 25 April 1997 (courtesy Lee Kwang-mo).

One significant difference is that the educational activities in Lee's Dongsung Cinematheque did not contain the political agenda of the anti-dictatorship period. In the democratising Korea of the mid-1990s, what needed changing was no longer an authoritarian government but Korean cinema itself – especially one that Hollywood threatened. There are clear historical and socio-cultural reasons behind the desire to educate audiences. The Dongsung Cinematheque shared with these groups the idea that cinema was more than just watching a film; it was about education, discussion, community and sharing experiences with like-minded people.

Another significant influence on Baekdudaegan's activities at the Dongsung Cinematheque, and one that is revealing of the ultimate function of the educational project, was the original Cinémathèque Française established by Henri Langlois in 1950s Paris. In a November 1996 interview with the *Han'gyŏrye*, Lee explained that his inspiration was the 'cradle of the Nouvelle Vague' – the Cinémathèque Française – and he intended Dongsung Cinematheque to have the same educational and 'catalytic effect' as Langlois's '*Cinémathèque*' (Yi Sŏng-uk 1996a). The Cinémathèque Française, through its vibrant atmosphere of screenings and discussion, taught filmmakers such as Jean-Luc Godard and Volker Schlöndorff how to understand the function of cinema (Richard 2005: 33:59; Cowie 2004: 25, 36, 39). It provided networks of human capital to initiate the transformation of French film (see Richard 2005: 22:00; Cowie 2004: 25–39). This is what Lee claimed he was attempting to recreate at the Dongsung Cinematheque.

Lee was not alone in his belief that enlightening Korean audiences would transform the prospects for domestic cinema (Hwang 2017: 52–3). The 1995 opening of the Dongsung Cinematheque coincided with large-scale state expansion in cultural (especially cinematic) instruction through universities and vocational institutes. The number of film schools increased from four to seven by the mid-1990s (Lee 2018).[17] The year 1995 also saw the establishment of the Korean National University of the Arts with filmmaking courses (Park 2015: 100). In the same year, the Korean Academy of Film Arts (KAFA), a two-year school founded in 1984, launched film production courses (Yecies and Shim 2016: 160). Details about this expansion of cinematic education were reported in the national press, spreading awareness of the developments within film. In one month in 1996, for example, the 3 June *Ilgan Sports* newspaper reported the inaugural general meeting of the Korea Film Institute that saw the election of senior academics, including Yu Chi-na, to the board of directors. The 10 June *Korea Economic Daily* (*Han'guk Kyŏngje Sinmun*) revealed the Ministry of Culture's creation of $1.2 million worth of financial support for an animation studies department and nine professors to help develop the animation industry. The 17 June *Dong-a Ilbo* announced the establishment of a new women's culture competition providing awards for outstanding works in theatre, photography and film (KMPPC 1997: 253–4).[18] Media reports from the time indicate that the Korean cinematic industry was at a stage of considerable development and that innovation through education was spearheading this transformation. These new educational institutions were critical to expanding Korean film over the next decade producing prominent filmmakers (Paquet 2009: 66–8).[19] Baekdudaegan's focus on transforming audience tastes through instructional activities also needs to be understood in this context of state-led educational development.

There was, however, a certain intensity behind Lee's drive to develop the educational function of his Dongsung Cinematheque. This can be seen in his passionate desire to recreate the catalytic impact of the Cinémathèque Française on 1960s French cinema through his own cinematheque in 1990s Seoul. This is visible in his urgency for the need to 'transform' audiences, so they recognised the inherent artistry of cinema. In later Baekdudaegan promotional materials, Lee uses religious terms like 'shrine' (*sŏngjiwado kat'ŭn kot*) to describe his art film cinemas (Paek 2009). Lee believed Baekdudaegan's total focus on art film consumption and education set the Dongsung Cinematheque apart from its rivals.[20]

Some of Lee's zeal for film culture was passed on to his audiences. Many years after its opening, the Dongsung Cinematheque regulars recalled that while the theatre space was not particularly comfortable, the audience's single-minded and undistracted focus on the films most distinguished the cinema. Kim Hong-jun recalls that 'it was the atmosphere of the spectators concentrating on the movie much more than the facilities, it was the seriousness that was so different' (personal correspondence, April 2021). Many Dongsung Cinematheque attendees recall an attitudinal shift occurring amongst cinephiles when they attended the Dongsung Cinematheque – an increased intensity of spectatorship. Twenty-five years after first attending the Dongsung Cinematheque, everyone surveyed replied that they were still regularly attending art houses (Appendix 3).

A transformed business: the financial structure of art houses

The impact of Lee's transformation of the Dongsung Cinematheque was phenomenal in terms of ticket sales. In 1994, the year before Lee's involvement, the Dongsung Art Centre's cinema gained 135,039 admissions. However, by 1996 – the first full year that Lee was in charge of the cinematheque – this had increased to 357,119 admissions, representing a tripling of business. In 1997, the cinema drew audiences of 350,000 (Kim et al. 2004: 22). From the very opening of the cinema, the results were, according to all observers, 'astounding' (Kim et al. 2004: 22). The daily seat occupancy rate for the opening film *Stranger than Paradise* was 60 per cent, which was described by KOFIC as 'remarkable' considering that Korean audiences were unused to this type of film (Kim et al. 2004: 22).[21] Baekdudaegan had initially expected 3,000 viewers per film, but average numbers were well over 10,000 (personal correspondence, Lee Kwang-mo, June 2020). Most subsequent releases at the Dongsung Cinematheque remained above the 50 per cent seat occupancy rate targeted by the cinema (Kim et al. 2004: 22). This was impressive given that films ran for an average of a month (An 1995). In November 1996 *Chungang Ilbo* interviews to commemorate its first anniversary, Lee claimed his cinematheque was a commercial success (Yi Sŏng-uk 1996a). *Stranger than Paradise, Where is the Friend's House?, Landscape in the Mist* had all outsold Hollywood competitors in Seoul (Paquet 2009: 38; Yi Nam 1997). After one year of managing the Dongsung Cinematheque, Lee had once again proved his doubters wrong by showing a movie theatre dedicated to art film was a viable commercial proposition.

How did Baekdudaegan's financial model work? Baekdudaegan managed the import, distribution and exhibition of art film, and they required considerable investment to prepare movies for screening.[22] In addition to international travel costs to source movies, Baekdudaegan had to purchase film prints and the rights to screen them. Baekdudaegan then had to import the films, pay Korean customs fees, add subtitles and do the marketing. In 1996, the average cost to get an art film to screen was around US$53,000 (Table 4.2).

The first opportunity to generate an income came through ticket sales, and 15,000 tickets sold for a film would earn roughly US$125,000 based on an $8 admission. The difference between the $125,000 worth of ticket sales and the original investment of $53,000 for the print, subtitles

Table 4.2 Average 1996 importation, distribution and exhibition costs for art films at the Dongsung Cinematheque

Import price	$15,000
Film price	$1,890
Subtitling, translation, censorship	$5,040
Total marketing costs	$31,486
Total costs	**$53,416**

Source: Kim et al. 2004: 25.

and advertising is considerable. However, this model includes the basic costs of getting a movie to the screen but not the daily cinematheque operational charges. There were labour-intensive costs of running the membership. In the era before online banking, easy direct debits and credit card transfers via the net, 2,000 Dongsung Cinematheque ordinary members resulted in 2,000 telephone calls to banks to ensure that individuals had paid their membership fees. It meant regularly sending 2,000 stamped envelopes containing information pamphlets (personal correspondence, Lee Kwang-mo, June 2020). There was also the rent for the cinema, contributions to utilities, repairs and the cost of creating, copying and reproducing materials for members. Baekdudaegan had to pay off debts and share profits with the overseas owners of the film rights. In addition, the income from profitable screenings subsidised less popular films. Finally, they had to purchase other films. The average film importer in Korea shipped in between four and five films a year (Kim et al. 2004: 24), and Lee had bought twenty in one go. Each movie lasted roughly one month, and considering he had sold off some copies, including *The Sacrifice*, for video release, he had approximately one year's worth of films to show. Then, he would have to buy the next lot of films. All of these expenses had to be factored into the profits produced from ticket sales. Margins were tight, and the process required other windows for creating revenue.

Following their exhibition at the Dongsung Cinematheque, Baekdudaegan could rent the print of a film to other cinemas for further screenings. However, the main income opportunities came from selling the film's rights to the television and video markets. Baekdudaegan generated an average profit of around $82,000 by marketing a movie via a video rental company such as Wooil. If Baekdudaegan could agree on further film rights sales with cable TV or terrestrial broadcasting companies, this would generate around $4,400 per movie (Kim et al. 2004: 25). Thanks to these latter sales windows and a robust video market, film importation-distribution-exhibition companies like Baekdudaegan thrived during this period.

Booming art houses

Lee was not the only theatre owner experiencing success. Hwang In-ok, the Core Art Hall managing director, saw impressive demand for art film at his theatre. In the mid-1990s, the cinema was so busy that he could enjoy extended runs of three to six months (Yi 2004). *Before Sunrise* (Richard Linklater, US/Austria, 1995) ran for nearly three months between March and June 1996 and sold 108,375 tickets (KMPPC 1997: 150). Other films also performed well, for instance: *The City of Lost Children (La Cité des Enfants Perdus*, Jean-Pierre Jeunet and Marc Caro, France, 1995: 41,625 tickets), *Landscape in the Mist* (21,798 admissions), *Breaking the Waves* (Lars von Trier, 1996, Denmark/UK, 28,478 admissions) (KMPPC 1997: 160, 171, 185). In November 1996, *Han'gyŏrye* journalists reported film importers were 'queuing up at the doors (of the Core Art Hall) to do business there' (Yi Sŏng-uk 1996b).

Provincial theatres constantly inquired about how they could best open auditoriums dedicated to art film (Song 1997). However, running cinemas outside the metropole posed specific problems for anyone hoping to emulate the success of the Core Art Hall and the Dongsung Cinematheque. A film that ran for a month in Seoul might only last a week in the provinces, meaning that regional theatres had to purchase more movies to keep busy, requiring significant investment (Song 1997). Despite the costs, a 16 November 1996 *Han'gyŏrye* article reported that art houses were 'establishing (their) roots' outside Seoul. The article discussed the Tano Cinema in Suwŏn, south of the capital, which had begun dedicating one of its two auditoriums to art films, showing *The Postman* (*Il Postino*, 1994, Michael Radford, Italy/France/Belgium), *Midnight Express* (Alan Parker, 1978, UK/US) and *Landscape in the Mist*. One student member of a local film appreciation society exclaimed he had an 'intense curiosity for cinema and was delighted he could see films not usually shown outside Seoul' (Yi Sŏng-uk 1996b).

According to Lee Kwang-mo, the successful reception of his theatre's programme completely changed the landscape of the art film market because media, film-fan and public interest shifted from the Core Art Hall to the Dongsung Cinematheque. Suddenly, the Dongsung Cinematheque became the 'in' place to go for film fans (author interview with Lee Kwang-mo, June 2020). However, the popularity of Lee's cinema did not mean that attendance at the Core Art Hall fell; quite the opposite. Kim Nan-suk has argued that theatres thrived in this period because they didn't run the same kind of programmes:

> Each of our theatres had a particular style of movie that we showed. Then (in the 1990s) it wasn't like now (in 2020), where cinemas are like chain stores, like franchises and you have twenty cinemas all showing the same film. (Author interview with Kim Nan-suk, May 2020)

The different approaches to programming between the Core Art Hall and the Dongsung Cinematheque meant they operated successfully despite their overlapping interest in art film and geographical proximity. Individual theatres created an institutional identity and established a devoted following of regulars. In 2004, when asked about the secret of the Core Art Hall's success, Hwang In-ok replied that the weakness of art houses was they catered to a niche market, but their strength lay in the loyalty of return customers. Art fans came from the enormous metropolitan region (comprising Seoul and Kyŏnggi Province) to enjoy the ambience of the Core Art Hall (Yi 2004). Fans went to significant lengths to watch art movies because of the cinemas themselves.

A symbiotic relationship: media, festivals and art houses

While exhibition spaces like the Dongsung Cinematheque, the Core Art Hall and videotheques did much to transform the audience experience of filmgoing and popularise art film, without doubt, they were aided in this goal by the media and also the new festivals that were forming.

The exponential growth of international film festivals caused a massive change to the cinematic infrastructure of the period (see Table 4.3). The establishment of SICAF in 1995 and then the BIFF in 1996 precipitated a period of 'festival fever', resulting in many new film festivals (Park 2015: 4). Before 1995, there had been no major international cinematic event in Korea; the year after the BIFF opened, eight prominent international film festivals emerged; as of 2022, there are eighteen (Lee 2022: 7). The

Table 4.3 Selected international film festivals in South Korea, 1995–2000

Year started	Acronym	Full Name	Location
1995	SICAF	Seoul International Cartoon and Animation Festival	Seoul
1996	BIFF	Busan International Film Festival	Pusan (South Kyŏngsang Province)
1997	SIWAFF	Seoul International Women's Film Festival	Seoul
1997	BiFan/PiFan	Bucheon International Fantastic Film Festival	Puch'ŏn, Kyŏnggi Province
1999	SIYF	Seoul International Youth Festival	Seoul
2000	JIFF	Jeonju International Film Festival	Chŏnju (North Chŏlla Province)
2000	GIFF	Gwangju International Film Festival	Kwangju (South Chŏlla Province)

Source: Paquet 2009: 39; Kim 2005: 80; Kim et al. 2004: 175.

BIFF has become a vital exposition of world cinema and a hub for the East Asian film industry (Park 2015: 7; Paquet 2009: 39).

The expansion of international film festivals in Korea arose partly because of changes in regional political systems enacted around 1995, which allowed local-level legislators greater economic and cultural autonomy from the capital (Park 2015: 138–9). Korea had a proven track record of successfully organising international events showcasing the country's economic growth, including the 1986 Seoul Asian Games, the 1988 Seoul Olympics and the 1993 Taejŏn World Expo. Hosting large-scale international events was a politically popular way of raising a region's profile and investing private and state funds in local infrastructure.[23] Following the creation of the BIFF, other areas of the country and organisations began plans for their own international film festivals (KMPPC 1997: 241, 247, 257, 263).

The establishment of international film festivals outside the capital was a significant economic and cultural change. South Korea has historically been a unipolar country where Seoul dominated national cultural life.

With the introduction of festivals, parts of the country that had felt culturally and economically disenfranchised began holding events that brought local, national and even international attention to the area. Attendances were large, with close to 860,000 people attending screenings at the inaugural BIFF, and over a million attending twenty films at the second (Kim Han-sang 2007: 61–2). Most importantly, regional festivals in the south-east (BIFF) and the south-west (GIFF and JIFF) exposed a diverse range of film to local audiences. Suddenly animation, feminist, art house, and documentary movies that had previously only been seen by small groups of cinephiles in regional videotheques were made widely available. The festivals provided greater access and official approval to a diversity of motion pictures.

The opening of these international film festivals significantly impacted Korean cultural life. The media coverage of the first BIFF, in particular, was intense. The year 1996 saw a steady number of newspaper articles about art and non-mainstream cinema in anticipation of the BIFF and SICAF (KMPPC 1997: 237–83).[24] Articles sought to justify the great expense of the events by the economic and cultural benefits that the festivals brought to the regions. The opening and subsequent success of these festivals also saw the arrival of renowned foreign directors and stars to Korea.[25] Many of those international figures feted in the press were not stars of Hollywood but festival-oriented film. British film critic Tony Rayns, serving as a judge on a festival panel, reported being chased out of Pusan cinemas by autograph-hungry fans. For many years Koreans had been rightly proud of their unprecedented economic expansion and manufacturing exports, but BIFF and the evolution of international film festivals in regional centres represented a cultural achievement. With the opening of these festivals, the world was not just focusing on Korean economic progress but its artistic creativity. In addition to screening and celebrating foreign cinema, the new Korean international film festivals showcased contemporary and classical domestic films, consecrating local directors, as we see in Chapter 5.[26] Most importantly, of all the arts, cinema – an industry that had been in the doldrums – was leading the Korean cultural renewal. The phenomenal expansion of festivals helped change public attitudes toward Korean films and encouraged wider acceptance of a diverse range of movies.

The early Korean film festivals, media outlets and pioneering art houses enjoyed a mutually beneficial relationship. Many of those film fans who dominated the management committees of the inaugural film festivals that emerged in 1995 had their roots in the videotheques, film clubs and cultural centres – it was in these places where they cut their teeth on festival organisation. In addition, 1990s art film exhibition had done much to generate interest in events like the BIFF. Videotheques and art houses created event status to market their venues by organising their own festivals (see Chapter 3). The Dongsung Cinematheque held four festivals in its inaugural year, including one on German expressionism. The Dongsung's mini-festival dedicated to the work of Godard caused a minor sensation with spectators, such was the interest (Figure 4.5). At one event, audiences surged into the auditorium on the opening night, damaging the doors, and fold-up seats were arranged between the stalls to cope with demand (Baekdudaegan 1996: 27–30; personal correspondence, Lee Kwang-mo, June 2020; Chon 2022: 86). Following the opening of the BIFF, theatres tapped into the 'festival fever' by marketing their events as 'must-see' screenings.

The growth of international film festivals impacted the boom in art film, first through the increased media coverage of festivals. Exchange networks between festival organisations and theatres facilitated the art film market. SICAF and the Seoul Short Film Festival supplied notable animations

Figure 4.5 Crowds of cinephiles trying to enter the Jean-Luc Godard evening at the Dongsung Cinematheque, 25 April 1997 (courtesy Lee Kwang-mo).

and shorts to the Dongsung Cinematheque for screenings in 1995–6 (Baekdudaegan 1996: 27–9; An 1996), and Baekdudaegan distributed movies to domestic film festivals.²⁷ Like the sudden increase in print media devoted to film discussion from 1995 onwards, festivals also fed interest in art cinema (Kim 2005: 82; see also Hwang 2017: 52–3). Films that the BIFF showed in its first year were the type of movies screened in Seoul art houses like the Core Art Hall and the Dongsung Cinematheque (Na 2013; Chon 2022: 85). These included: *Dead Man* (1996, US) by Jim Jarmusch; Lars von Trier's *Breaking the Waves*; and films imported by Baekdudaegan, including Theo Angelopoulos's *Landscape in the Mist* and *La Haine* (Mathieu Kassovitz, 1996, France) (BIFF Archive n.d.). Thanks to the international film festivals and the significant media coverage they garnered, art films reached much larger audiences in South Korea than ever before; they were no longer confined to small auditoriums of 150–250 seats; they were attracting national media attention.²⁸

A transformed audience

Art movie exhibition venues, the new film media, academia and domestic film festivals created a circulation of knowledge and consecration, with each institution legitimating others in the cycle and contributing to the overall success of art film. These new cinematic institutions increased the degree to which cinephilia and art film entered the public consciousness – helping to shape tastes as they did so. By late 1996, Korean cinephilia had caught the attention of overseas commentators. Tony Rayns wrote an article extolling the diversity of film consumption in South Korea and the richness of its cinematic culture. On a subsequent visit to the country in September 1997, Rayns used the Lumiere's programme, the new film media and festivals as evidence that the country's cinephilia had intensified and spread since the previous year. The Lumiere was showing Korean New Wave director Jang Sun-woo's *Timeless, Bottomless Bad Movie* (*Nappŭn yŏnghwa*, 1997, ROK), *Anaconda* (Luis Llosa, 1997, US) and Abbas Kiarostami's *Through the Olive Trees* (*Zīr-e Derakhtān-e Zeytūn*, 1994, Iran). Rayns wrote:

> When multiplexes were introduced in western Europe, we were assured that this kind of programming would follow, with space for locally made films, independent and art-house alternatives to Hollywood. These ideals seem so remote that it's a real shock to come across them in reality in downtown Seoul.

It was proof, he claimed, that Korea 'is currently the most cinephile country in the world' (Rayns 1998: 24). What Rayns observed between 1996 and 1997 was exhibition practices meeting the demands of a changing cinema audience prepared to accept the type of obscure film exemplified by *The Sacrifice*, the Dongsung Cinematheque's programming and the new festivals. Rayns wasn't the only observer to notice the transforming tastes of Korean audiences; many other critics noted the same phenomenon.[29] The type of film that had previously been enjoyed by small groups of Korean cinephiles in the capital was now nationwide news, available throughout the country and increasingly consumed.

Rayns ends his article with a caveat: the problem was that Koreans don't always 'understand their own filmmakers', meaning domestic audiences still preferred to watch the consecrated cinema of celebrated foreigners while turning their back on Korean directors who made films with their particular authorial style. Rayns's observations about Korean cinephilia are prescient, but his claims of local hostility to innovative domestic filmmakers in 1996–7 are mistaken. Domestic audiences for innovative Korean films expanded exponentially in 1995–7 (see Appendix 2), and they would continue to do so, transforming Korean cinema.

Conclusion

The creation of Baekdudaegan and importation of art film was not the original intention of Lee Kwang-mo. Rather it was the completion of his film project that was his priority. Neither was the success of *The Sacrifice* certain. Many scholars have discussed Ch'ungmuro's resistance to change as a blockage to the development of Korean film in the last century (Paquet 2009). But it wasn't just in film production, where Korean film was conservative. And this is evidenced in *The Sacrifice* Incident. There was considerable opposition from those who managed film exhibition and distribution for whom nothing in their experience could have prepared them for the movie's reception. The popularity of *The Sacrifice* and the Dongsung Cinematheque was achieved only partly through Lee's determination to transform Korean cinema. Their success came thanks to a complex network of connections within the cinematic world: a symbiotic relationship that the nascent art houses and cinephiles maintained with the new film media and emerging Korean film festival scene. Festival organisers interacted with new art film distributors, academics with exhibitors and all of them with influential film critics.

Most significantly, this moment of interaction and cross-pollination was critical in initiating the transformation of domestic audience tastes. The new media environment had taken the consumption of foreign art film from the small screens of university film clubs and videotheques onto the big screen, helping to shape an audience more open to the type of film they had not tolerated a decade earlier. This would have implications for the future success of Korean filmmakers. The triumphs of *The Sacrifice* and Dongsung Cinematheque proved to be a high-water mark of the art film boom – proof of what was possible. However, by 1997 the bubble was about to burst – not just at the Dongsung Cinematheque, but in art film consumption and the entire Korean economy, and this is explored in detail in the next chapter.

Notes

1. The *Fiero Milano* was an annual international market for audiovisual industries.
2. In 1996, the sale of 5,000 videos generated US$85,000 (Kim et al. 2004: 25).
3. *Kino* managing director Kim Chong-wŏn claims that at the time bookshops, kiosks and the magazines themselves did not keep accurate accounts of circulations or altered them for taxation purposes, so these are his estimates (personal correspondence, May 2022).
4. Based on current sales of *Sight and Sound* (2022).
5. For example, July 1974 *Cahiers du Cinéma* interviews with Michel Foucault were reprinted in the June 1995 *Kino*.
6. *Kino* featured a section dedicated to covering the videotheques from its very first edition.
7. See the features on Lee's *Spring in My Hometown*, which screened at the Dongsung Cinematheque in 1998 in *Kino* (Yi Yŏng-jae 1998).
8. The *Han'gyŏrye* (16 November, 1996) includes an article about Lee Kwang-mo's Dongsung Cinematheque and photographs by *Cine 21* journalists (Yi Sŏng-uk 1996a).
9. Most Dongsung Cinematheque customers attended art film screenings after reading film magazine recommendations (Hwang 2017: 52–3n.47). Two thirds of my survey respondents replied they also regularly read film magazines (December 2020).
10. The Dongsung Art Centre had three auditoriums, and the 200-seater Cinematheque was established in an adjacent building closer to the Taehangno intersection (personal correspondence, Lee Kwang-mo, May 2022).
11. Park A-na (2014: 60) claims that the term '*kwangjang*' originated in Ch'oe In-hun's 1960 novel symbolising public, free and open.
12. Before Baekdudaegan, the Dongsung Cinematheque had been run for a year by the building's owners, the Dongsung Art Centre.
13. A cinema of reassurance includes: 'feel good movies' with a 'positive mood, a happy end and a spirit of optimism or . . . mainstream entertainment . . .' (Bosma 2015: 63).
14. Lee explained that at the time no exhibitors screened a double bill of short and main feature because of the prohibitive costs. Each film had to be individually imported and undergo censorship (personal correspondence, Lee Kwang-mo, May 2020).

15. These talks were held on the evening of the final screening day of a specific film (An 1995; MBC 1995).
16. Other notable discussants included: later BIFF organising committee chair Lee Yong-kwan, critic Chŏn Ch'an-il, and later JIFF programmer Chŏn Yang-jun, and the Dongguk University professor Yu Chi-na (Baekdudaegan 1996: 25; personal correspondence, Lee Kwang-mo, June 2020).
17. By 2000, there were thirty-five film schools in Korea (Lee 2018).
18. Newspaper articles also focused on the emergence of a younger generation of filmmakers challenging Ch'ungmuro, including Park Hŭi-ju, Pyŏn Hŭi-sŏng, Im Sul-lae who represented a 'generational shift' (*sedaegyoch'e*) and 'rebellion' against Ch'ungmuro filmmaking practices (KMPPC 1997: 260, 271).
19. KAFA graduates include Bong Joon-ho, Im Sang-soo and Hur Jin-ho (Paquet 2009: 67).
20. Bourdieu (1980: 268) argues art exhibitors like Lee repudiate their interest in economic profit more aggressively to disparage competitors and establish their own position of power.
21. Jim Jarmusch's debut movie has a minimalist storyline and dialogue and stars non-professional actors John Lurie and Richard Edson. Filmed entirely in black and white, it features scenes without action, dialogue and deadpan humour. The style of the film was very different to movies shown in downtown cinemas at the time.
22. Other cinemas like the Lumiere had a different financial structure because they were mainly involved in exhibition. See Kim et al. (2004) for the different art house models. Todd Berliner (2018: 55) argues: 'For [US] exhibitors, independent art films remain economically viable because they occupy the large territory between highly profitable mainstream cinema and unprofitable experimental cinema.'
23. According to Park Young-a (2015: 139) after the BIFF was launched in 1996, dilapidated theatres were renovated in Pusan.
24. January featured six articles on art (independent, documentary, European, classic or cult) films, three articles on festivals (international and domestic), one on cinephilia; February saw seven on art films and two on festivals; March had seven on art film, one on cinephilia and one on festivals; July had six articles on art film and five on festivals (KMPPC 1997: 237–83).
25. Film director Fruit Chan attended the BIFF in 2009, Willem Dafoe, Juliette Binoche and director Zhang Yimou attended in 2010 (Shackleton 2010).
26. Each of the festivals had a different emphasis, for example, the JIFF stressed independent cinema and short films (Lee 2022: 28).
27. Baekdudaegan (2016) explain that their purpose is to distribute classics of world cinema to supply film festivals.
28. See for example KMPPC (1997: 241, 261, 263–4, 269–72) for a summary of the many daily national newspaper articles devoted to the inaugural BIFF.
29. Scholars such as Kim et al. (2004: 24) and Kang Kyoung Lae believe the formation of an audience prepared to view more challenging films made by these directors was the essential impact of 1990s cinephilia (author interview, April 2021). Parc and Messerlin argue that from the late 1990s onwards a 'market-driven cultural diversity' helped form a Korean audience with broad tastes in cinema (2021: 19).

Part 2
Decline

Figure P2.1 Former Dongsung Art Centre in Taehangno, location of Hypertheque Nada, from 2021 the Seoul Foundation for Arts and Culture (Seoulmunhwajaedan) (author's image).

Chapter 5

Challenges to art houses and the decline of cinephilia in a period of Korean cinematic expansion

Art film was on a roll when in February 1997, just a year after opening its doors to the public, Baekdudaegan's Dongsung Cinematheque applied for and received the official title of 'specialist art film theatre' from the Ministry of Culture and Sports (*Yesulyŏnghwa chŏnyonggwan*) (KMPPC 1998: 224). This was a great accolade for Lee and showed that his efforts at transforming the viewing experience for his audiences had paid off. The designation represented state recognition for his efforts to educate the cinema-going public and introduce a diverse range of movies to Koreans following years of cultural isolation. But the official recognition, which represented perhaps the zenith of Baekdudaegan's Dongsung Cinematheque, coincided with the moment its fortunes began to decline. The challenges for Baekdudaegan occurred alongside a general decrease in the type of art film consumption that had characterised the previous few years of cinema-going. This downswing in the art film sector happened in very different circumstances to the post-1987 cinephilia, when audience interest in art movies represented a beacon of hope for a Korean cinematic industry (considered by some to be) close to collapse. After the Asian Financial Crisis of 1997–8, the situation reversed. The art film sector struggled in competition for audiences with rejuvenated domestic mainstream commercial film. A decline in the type of cinephilia that had characterised cinematic consumption of the previous few years also became apparent as tensions emerged and the shine went out of the scene. In this chapter, I look at the reasons behind the reversal in fortunes for art film consumption and cinephilia. I consider the critical, administrative and economic problems faced by exhibitors like the Dongsung Cinematheque, and how the post-Asian financial crisis rise of domestic mainstream cinema radically impacted the art film exhibition context.

The Dongsung Cinematheque's clashes with government officials and the theatre

The official recognition of its specialist art film theatre status brought the Dongsung Cinematheque great kudos, and it also brought the cinema some significant financial benefits.[1] Changes to the 1995 Film Promotion Law meant that as a specialist art film theatre, the ministry would exempt the Dongsung Cinematheque from paying the Culture and Art Promotion Fund (Munyechinhŭnggigŭm), a 6.6 per cent tax levied on each movie ticket to support the Arts Council of Korea (Han'guk munhwayesulwiwonhoe).[2] While cinemas showing commercial film paid the levy (by passing it on to consumers), the Dongsung Cinematheque was exempt and retained ticket revenues. By 1997, this amounted to a considerable annual total of $78,000 (Yi Nam 1997).

One condition of this support was that 40 per cent of all films screened at the Dongsung Cinematheque had to be Korean to qualify for continued support. This requirement was problematic for Baekdudaegan's theatre since the stipulations determined the cinema could only show domestically produced art films (Yi Nam 1997). Therefore, if the ministry decided the cinema was infringing regulations by not screening a Korean-produced art film, the Dongsung Cinematheque would lose its governmental support. An 11 March 1997 *Chungang Ilbo* article stated that tensions erupted between the ministry and the Dongsung Cinematheque over what constituted an 'art' film. According to the article, Lee initially challenged the ministry, complaining that their definition of art film was vague. The ministry replied that the Dongsung Cinematheque should do what 'Cinematheques did in other countries' and show films that had already been on the market for six months. Lee rejected this proposal, saying he did not want to be a 're-run' cinema because this course of action would be financially unviable (Yi Nam 1997). The ministry proposed establishing a committee of film critics to rule on which films could be considered art, according to objective criteria and the practice of cinematheques overseas. However, Lee again countered that there could be no objective criteria for what constituted an art film and that his exhibition practices differed from the revival houses or repertory cinemas that the ministry appeared to have in mind. Lee stressed that the Dongsung Cinematheque showed a mixture of older classics and first-run pictures he felt worthy of exhibition, such as *Trainspotting* (Yi Nam 1997).

This was not the only time tensions rose between art house managers and state officials over the screen quota. A 1993 *Han'gyŏrye* report shows that the Core Art Hall was also subject to the regulations and forced to exhibit domestic movies. However, the theatre struggled to find enough contemporary Korean films that suited its institutional identity, and therefore resorted to constant re-screenings of classic Korean films from the 1960s such as *Early Rain* (*Ch'ou*, Chŏng Chin-u, 1966, ROK). While the Core Art Hall circumvented the quota by screening 1960s classics, the Dongsung Cinematheque fulfilled its obligations by exhibiting domestically produced independent short films.

The clash reveals the bureaucratic restrictions that hindered Lee's vision and the success of the Dongsung Cinematheque, but that also impacted art film exhibition as a whole. The designation of specialist art film theatre also meant the Dongsung Cinematheque was technically eligible for an exemption from SQS regulations obliging theatres to allocate screentime to Korean film. However, the ministry rejected the Dongsung Cinematheque's application without justifying their decision (Yi Nam 1997). Officials may have been unhappy with the norms and values represented by Baekdudaegan's cinema of disturbance programme. Some scholars believe this decision was related directly to the ministry's unhappiness with the amount of foreign film he was showing – at the expense of domestically produced film (Hwang 2017: 55–6). Whatever the reasons, the government was directly interfering in his scheduling by dictating what he could or could not screen and offering to bring in state-designated film experts to make pronouncements on Lee's programming choices. Such actions went against Baekdudaegan's desire to show 'any film it wanted' to create 'a new viewing experience' (Paek 2009). The *Chungang Ilbo* article's author, Yi Nam, fiercely criticised such state interference. The author also disapproved of ministry officials with only the vaguest notions of what constituted art film and little understanding of the innovations in exhibition culture Lee introduced to his cinematheque. In interviews, Lee argued that in 1997, civil servants essentially saw theatres as tools of cinematic policy:

> At that time, the government didn't pay much attention to foreign art films. They were not very conscious of the meaning, importance, or necessity of classic or foreign art films. They also had no interest in art houses or Cinematheques. They only promoted Korean films and saw no need to support foreign film exhibition. (Personal correspondence, Lee Kwang-mo, June 2020)

The point about the screen quota is that administrators were keen to promote specialist cinemas, but they still wanted significant control over their programming since theatres were a crucial means to protect the domestic film industry. The SQS was also a way for officials – who had recently lost the right to police exhibition through script censorship – to influence cinema programmes. Administrator actions appeared to be governed by an assumption that they had a right to intervene in the scheduling of theatres as a price for state financial support. The mistrust between cultural administrators and film exhibitors was a phenomenon that would return to impact the sector over the evolution of state policy at the start of the next century.

Another issue that Baekdudaegan faced was a deteriorating relationship with the Dongsung Cinematheque's owners, the Dongsung Art Centre. The original arrangement was that the Dongsung Art Centre rented the space to Baekdudaegan, which managed all other aspects of the operation. However, there were misunderstandings between the two bodies from the start. The first arose over the name of the cinema. Baekdudaegan had selected the name 'Kwangjang' for the cinema to differentiate their product clearly from that of the Dongsung Art Centre. Baekdudaegan wanted to demonstrate that its management was ushering in a new culture of programming and exhibition and invested significant funds into marketing materials using 'Kwangjang'. However, the Dongsung Art Centre insisted on retaining the original name. It refused to remove the name on the cinema's exterior, which still showed 'Dongsung Cinematheque'. Despite Baekdudaegan's efforts, the name stuck, and the cinema became popularly known by this name (personal correspondence, Lee Kwang-mo, June 2020).

Naming is a way of establishing control over an institution, and this simple act showed that neither side was prepared to relinquish authority over the cinema. The initial conflict around naming presaged an uneasy partnership between the two companies, which eventually deteriorated. In early 1997, a contract dispute over the division of the ticket receipts broke the already strained relationship between Baekdudaegan and the Dongsung Art Centre.[3] From that moment, Baekdudaegan took a peripheral role in the running of the Dongsung Cinematheque. The two companies still worked together; Baekdudaegan supplied films while the Dongsung Art Centre took over exhibition, programming and educational activities. Baekdudaegan was economically stretched because of its investments, so it remained involved in the Dongsung Cinematheque, but the relationship had become a marriage of convenience.⁴ At the moment it received official state recognition for its activities, Baekdudaegan split with its close collaborators, and Lee Kwang-mo's dream of radically overhauling art film programming, exhibition and education was temporarily over. Baekdudaegan would return to manage other art houses, and for the next few years, the Dongsung Cinematheque continued with most of the structures Lee had introduced intact.⁵ Many regulars continued attending the Dongsung Cinematheque without knowing that Baekdudaegan was no longer in charge (personal correspondence, Lee Kwang-mo, June 2020).

The conflict with the theatre and its brushes with officialdom were not the only reasons for the Dongsung Cinematheque's reversal in fortunes, which was also linked to the post-1997 fall in popularity of art film as a whole.

The end of the 1990s art film boom, 1997–9

The Dongsung Cinematheque saw serious declines in audience numbers from 1998 onwards. The cinema's designation as Korea's first art house appeared to have no positive impact upon its annual attendances, which fell first by 26 per cent, then 16 per cent (Kim et al. 2004: 22). These lower ticket sales were reflected in the statistics for the entire art film sector (see Table 5.1). All theatres – including the Core and the Hoam Art Halls reported falls in ticket sales, which accelerated following the Asian Financial Crisis (Kim et al. 2004: 26). In 1996, a total of fifty-five officially designated art films were shown for the year, and they were watched by 2.4 million spectators, which meant that 12 per cent of all audiences who went to the cinema in Seoul that year saw an art film.⁶ In 1999, art film audiences dropped to 1.5 million and only accounted for 6 per cent of the market, the lowest figures in seven years (Kim et al. 2004: 28). According to KOFIC statistics for 1999, more than half of the sixty films shown failed to sell more than the 10,000 tickets generally considered to be the sign of a successful box office performance for a specialist film (Yi Sŏng-uk 1996a; Yi Sŏng-uk 1996b; Lee 2015: 7–8). The fall in art film attendance between 1998 and 1999 looks worse when compared with the overall performance of the Seoul box office. Until 1996, the mainstream commercial film sector had been in decline while art film consumption had been rising. This situation began changing in 1997, and by 1999 the

Table 5.1 Annual attendances for art movies (Seoul)

Year	Number of art films shown	Total audiences for art film	Audience for Korean cinema as a whole	Share of audiences
1995	44	2,356,418	20,479,681	12%
1996	55	2,406,423	19,925,420	12%
1997	65	2,154,210	22,218,280	10%
1998	60	2,164,498	23,982,179	9%
1999	60	1,526,988	25,270,006	6%
2000	71	4,141,260	28,221,997	15%
2001	71	3,224,537	35,506,030	9%
2002	59	6,323,888	40,355,928	16%

Source: KOFIC, Kim et al. 2004: 28.

situation was reversed: more people were going to the capital's cinemas than in the previous few years, but they weren't going to see art films. By 1999, it appeared that the art film boom was finally over.

One reason for the end of the art film boom was economic, resulting directly from the Asian financial crisis. In the autumn of 1997, a liquidity crisis impacting Thailand began to spread to neighbouring countries, eventually affecting Indonesia, Malaysia, Singapore and Korea. The value of the Korean currency began to fall in early November 1997, and by the end of the month, the government asked for a bailout from the International Monetary Fund. This was the most severe economic challenge the country had faced since the Korean War. The fall in the number of art movies screened resulted from the financial downturn. Core Art Hall Manager Hwang In-ok complained that the film supply for his theatre dried up (Yi 2004). With a currency that had nosedived during the crash, investing in foreign film made importers increasingly concerned about taking risks at the box office that exposed them to significant debt. Since art film tended to be far more dependent upon recouping costs via ticket revenues than through ancillary sales of videos and merchandise, importer-distributors were particularly vulnerable to poor box office performance. A reduced number of films imported and distributed also meant a smaller and perhaps less adventurous selection of movies for consumers. The documentary *The Gate of Heavenly Peace* (1995, Richard Gordon and Carma Hinton, USA) sold just 1,509 tickets, while a run of the cult classic *Easy Rider* (1969, Dennis Hopper, USA) – which at the height of the art film boom might have attracted significant interest – only drew 2,186 spectators in Seoul (Kim et al. 2004: 160–1).

Distributors' unwillingness to take risks with new films was reflected in the consumption patterns of audiences, who became more cautious in their choices, further contributing to the end of the art boom. The only films of 1999 that exceeded 20,000 tickets were works by established directors, such as Akira Kurosawa's *Kagemusha* (1980, Japan, 57,777) and Park Kwang-su's *Les Insurgés* (*Yi Chae-suŭi nan*, 1999, ROK 56,913), or motion pictures awarded prestigious international prizes such as Roberto Benigni's *Life Is Beautiful* (*La vita è bella*, 1997, Italy, 225,291)[7] (Kim et al. 2004: 160–1). Another problem was that art film attendances were dominated by a handful of high-performing films like *Christmas in August* (P'alwŏlŭi k'ŭrisŭmasŭ, Hur Jin-ho [Hŏ Chin-ho], 1998, ROK, 422,930), while other films struggled.

More than anything, the intensity of consumption characterising the art film boom evaporated post-1997. Overall nationwide expenditure on pastime pursuits fell as consumers began to feel the pinch (Kim 2000: 67; Cho 2020).[8] The weaker currency made foreign cultural imports more expensive, and companies began downsizing. Staying in became an attractive option for Koreans with smaller leisure budgets hitting art house attendances. What's more, by 1999, alternative windows for art film consumption were made available. Audiences could view art films on DVD, video and at an increasing number of festivals. The rarity value of art films had become a thing of the past (Kim et al. 2004: 26). More challenging for exhibitors was the competition art houses faced from the late 1990s rise of multiplexes. CGV, a subsidiary of food manufacturing company CJ (Cheil Jedang), expanded into the entertainment sector in the mid-1990s and opened its first multiplex in Kangbyŏn in eastern Seoul in April 1998 (Hwang 2017: 58). From this point onwards, the growth of multiplex chains increased exponentially. Lotte Cinemas, an entertainment division of the giant Korean chaebol, followed with a multiplex in Inch'ŏn in 1999 (Paquet 2009: 101; Hwang 2017: 59). Multiplexes were an attractive proposition to consumers and transformed how Koreans watched movies. CGV and Lotte located their new multiplexes in satellite towns surrounding Seoul – Suwŏn, Pundang and Ilsan – meaning that cinemagoers no longer needed to make long journeys on public transport into the capital's Chongno area to see the latest offerings. They provided consumers with wider choices of films; they were convenient, attractive, modern and family-friendly. In addition to exhibiting big-budget blockbusters, multiplexes also screened the same art films. In 1998, CGV Kangbyŏn, for example, successfully showed Wong Kar-wai's *Happy Together* (1997, Hong Kong), Kim Ki-duk's *Birdcage Inn* (P'aran Taemun, 1998, ROK) and Lee Kwang-mo's *Spring in My Hometown* (KMPPC 1999: 126). Not only were multiplexes competing with art houses, but they were also doing it well,[9] a factor that had implications for art film exhibition as multiplex market dominance increased.

Higher post-Asian financial crisis prices for foreign movies, the greater availability of art film and multiplex competition contributed to the 1997–9 decline in art film exhibition (Kim et al. 2004: 22–30; Hwang 2017). However, there was an additional problem affecting the art film sector's performance: theatres' difficulty in successfully adjusting their exhibition strategies in the context of an increasingly popular domestic cinema.

Art film exhibition in an age of growing Korean cinematic success, 1997–9

From the late 1999s onwards, art films faced stiffer competition for audiences from home-produced mainstream commercial motion pictures. The release of Kang Je-gyu's *Shiri* (ROK, 1999) initiated the phenomenon of record-breaking Korean big-budget spectacular films that drew huge audiences. *Shiri* sold 6.2 million tickets nationwide, and subsequent blockbusters followed up this figure over the next few years. Multiplex chains released Korean blockbuster films simultaneously on screens across the country, receiving blanket media coverage, and as a result, audience numbers skyrocketed (Howard 2008: 94; Hwang 2017: 58; Park 2015: 152). Between 1996 and 1999, there was a 30 per cent increase in overall cinema attendance, but admissions for Korean-made films increased by more than 100 per cent in the same period. By 1999, domestically produced films captured 39 per cent of the market, a figure that advanced dramatically over the next few years (KOFIC 2005: 21; Parc and Messerlin 2021: 38). Scholars have ascribed this box office success to various factors, including the removal of dictatorship-era censorship, improved sources of financing, the collaboration of a talented generation of risk-taking filmmakers and producers, and the innovative coordination of the industry by the government (Paquet 2009: 32–50; Ahn 2012: 67; Yecies and Shim 2016). Two other factors contributed to the revived domestic interest in Korean film: first, the product diversity and, second, the crucial media interest generated by the domestic box office and international festival success. All of these elements helped contribute to a general 'buzz' about Korean film in that period. Changes to the industry did not just herald the era of big-budget blockbuster, action-packed adventures like *Shiri*. They also inspired the widespread popularity of films made by 'commercial auteurs' like Bong Joon-ho, who operated within the generic confines of commercial cinema and produced work featuring their authorial mark (Paquet 2009: 93; Jung Ji-youn 2008: 9; Kim Young-jin 2019: 8). Among the high-performing Korean films for 1998–9, for example, were: *Christmas in August*, *Attack the Gas Station* (*Chuyuso sŭpkyŏksagŏn*, Kim Sang-jin, 1999, ROK, 905,500 [ROK]), *Tell Me Something* (Chang Yun-hyŏn, 1999, ROK, 685,935[ROK]) and *Nowhere to Hide* (*Injŏng sajŏng pol kŏt ŏpta*, Yi Myŏng-se, ROK, 664,861 [ROK]). These films were stylish, inventive productions – often with added touches of social critique.

Directors such as Kim Ki-duk, Hong Sang-soo and Lee Chang-dong also appeared between 1995 and 2000, joining more established Korean New Wave filmmakers like Park Kwang-su and Jang Sun-woo. These directors made formally challenging films treating darker themes or contentious social and political issues in their own characteristic style. Such films include *A Single Spark* (*Arŭmdaun ch'ŏngnyŏn Chŏn T'ae-il*, Park Kwang-su, 1995, ROK, 235,935), Jang Sun-woo's *A Petal* (*Kkotnip*, 1996, ROK, 213,979), *Timeless, Bottomless Bad Movie* (*Nappŭn yŏnghwa*, 1997, ROK, 138,604) and *Lies* (*Kŏjinmal*, 1999, ROK, 303,681), *Crocodile* (*Agŏ*, Kim Ki-duk, 1996, ROK, 3,284), *Three Friends* (*Se ch'in'gu*, Yim Soon-rye, 1996, ROK, 24,758), Hong Sang-soo's *The Day a Pig Fell into the Well* (*Twaejiga umure ppajin nal*, 1996, ROK, 37,103) and *The Power of Kangwon Province* (*Kangwŏndoŭi him*, 1998, ROK, 15,967), Lee Kwang-mo's *Spring in My Hometown*, Lee Chang-dong's *Green Fish* (*Ch'orok mulgogi*, 1997, ROK, 163,655) and *Peppermint Candy* (*Pakha satang*, 1999, ROK, 290,352) (Paquet 2009: 78; Chung 2012: 2–3; Kim et al. 2004: 24). Many of these films, along with those made by commercial auteurs, gained attention at international film festivals. *Timeless, Bottomless Bad Movie* and *Spring in My Hometown*, for example, won major awards at the 1997 and 1998 Tokyo International Film Festival, respectively, *Green Fish* received a 1998 Netpac Prize and *The Day a Pig Fell into the Well* earned the 1997 Best Director Award at the Rotterdam International Film Festival. Peter Rist, who helped organise the 1998 and 1999 Montreal International Film Festivals, recalled that it was the 'incredible range' of late 1990s Korean films that appealed to festival-goers and juries: 'South Korea produced marginal films but also commercial films with a serious subject matter (...) independent filmmakers able to please domestic audiences as well as international festival audiences. It was a winning combination' (author interview with Peter Rist, May 2020). This diversity is exemplified by the Korean offerings at the 1998 Montreal International Film Festival (Figure 5.1).

The triumphs of Korean film at international film festivals occurred for several reasons. First, directors like Hong Sang-soo and Kim Ki-duk actively courted international film festival attention, knowing this to be a means to garner greater awareness of their work (Lee 2022: 3). Second, success was partly due to a state-led drive to increase the global profile of Korean cinema that had been ongoing since the Chun Doo Hwan administration (Kim Millim 2011: 179). Between 1985 and 1999, the number of Korean films entered for international festivals tripled; over the same period, domestic movies entered for prestigious European festivals increased by a factor of five (Table 5.2; Mohedas 2022: 42). While

Figure 5.1 Korea Cinema pamphlet produced by the KMPPC to promote special screenings of domestic films at the 1998 Montreal International Film Festival (courtesy Yi Chae-u, KOFIC).

dictatorship-era restrictions on content hamstrung the success of pre-1987 Korean entries into festivals, the late 1990s commercial, regulatory and creative transformation in the industry meant that Korean film began to garner global attention like never before (Kim 2002: 32; Kim Millim 2011: 179).

The increased global awareness of Korean cinema also helped fuel intense government and domestic media interest in the revived fortunes of the industry. In particular, a media frenzy arose over the phenomenal success of *Shiri*, which had 'defeated' Hollywood rivals at the box office – the so-called 'Shiri syndrome' (Shin and Stringer 2007: 57–8). *Shiri*'s success was popularly seen as a historic moment in Korean cinema – the tipping point after which its fortunes finally changed. In addition, foreign film festival endorsements for Korean movies resulted in extensive coverage in media and official government reports, illustrating the importance of international validation for the industry.[10] International film festival recognition became a vital marketing tool in advertising by exhibitors and distributors of Korean cinema, thus helping to frame domestic consumption of these movies.[11]

As well as international attention, Korean film also achieved greater prominence in this period through its domestic festivals. Ahn Soojeong argues the Pusan International Film Festival played an essential role in increasing the cultural capital of domestic film in important ways (Ahn 2012: 19). By screening *Peppermint Candy* to open the 1999 festival, the BIFF elevated the public standing of local directors and increased domestic acceptance of Korean cinema (Ahn 2012: 67). The festival also staged retrospective programmes of Korean film, like the first BIFF's Korean New Wave programme, creating an identity for

Table 5.2 State-led expansion of Korean entries to international film festivals

Korean Films Entered for International Film Festivals			
Year	1985	1998	1999
No. of films entered	24	68	73
Korean Films Entered for European Film Festivals			
Year	1985	1998	1999
No. of films entered	8	26	38

Source: KOFIC 2000: 29–30.

homegrown cinema in the global film market while legitimising the historical legacy of the domestic industry (Ahn 2012: 79; Lee 2022: 4).[12] The BIFF's programming added to the cultural value of Korean film and generated international interest in an industry that had been in decline. Increased festival interest was accompanied by greater media focus on Korean cinema. Articles in movie magazines and national newspapers on emerging and classic Korean film helped to consecrate local filmmakers (Yi Sŏn-ju 2017: 433). For instance, the February 1998 issue of *Kino* featured an article on the career of Korean cinematographer Yu Yŏng-gil (see Figure 5.2). Art houses closely associated with the screenings of European art films, festival winners and classics were increasingly showing 'alternative' Korean movies. The Dongsung Cinematheque went further than other cinemas and, from 1997, began to hold programmes dedicated to celebrating Korean independent film (*Chungang Ilbo* 1997). In 1998, the Dongsung Cinematheque programmed *Skate* (1998, Cho Ŭn-nyŏng, ROK), *Liver and Potato* (Kan'gwa kamja, 1998, Song Il-gwŏn, ROK) and *Crack of the Halo* (Haetbit charŭnŭn ai, Kim Chin-hwan, ROK) in one eighty-minute show (author interview with Kim Nan-suk, May 2020).[13] Art houses also championed domestic cinema by screening shorts by emerging

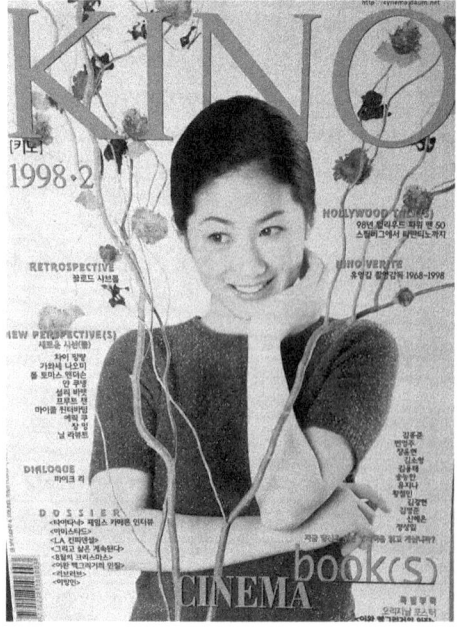

Figure 5.2 February 1998 issue of *Kino* (courtesy of Kim Chong-wŏn).

directors. Bong Joon-ho received his break when the Dongsung Cinematheque screened his short *White Man* (*Paeksaegin*, 1994, ROK) in 1996 (An 1996). In addition, the Dongsung Cinematheque organised retrospectives that re-discovered the work of directors from Korea's cinematic past, such as that of Kim Ki-yŏng (Kim Ki-young; Lee and Ahn 2003). This increased exposure to Korean film in art houses raised the cultural value of locally-produced cinema.

All of these features – the unprecedented diversity and box office success of local movies, international and domestic film festival recognition and the resultant revived media interest –consecrated Korean motion pictures and generated greater public curiosity for domestic cinema.

Exhibition at Seoul art houses, 1997–9

The increased popularity of Korean film that arose in this period had implications for art house programming in the capital. Between the late 1980s and 1996, Seoul exhibitors relied on two art film programming models. One was the mixed programming of commercial, Korean and European art film and classics. The other involved marketing a unique event status for art film programming. Both models stressed foreign (mainly European) art film at its core. Korean film had always featured as part of the mixed programming schedule of art houses, and theatres were legally obliged to screen Korean film under the screen quota regulations. However, Korean film had never been the main focus of theatres like the Core Art Hall, Lumiere or Dongsung Cinematheque. Around 1997, exhibitors recognised the transformed drawing power of domestic film, which can be seen in the increased average attendance for Korean film between 1993 and 1998 in both mainstream cinemas and art houses. Audience numbers for Korean movies at the Dongsung and Cinehouse doubled in this period (Appendix 2). Exhibitors also realised that many of the new domestic features had strong art cinema credentials thanks to directors who often stamped their authorial mark on their works. In addition, KOFIC officially recognised many pictures appearing in 1998 as art films, including *Christmas in August*, *The Power of Kangwon Province* and *Spring in My Hometown* (Kim et al. 2004: 160–1). However, Korean film's new global recognition and box office success challenged Seoul's art house programmers. On the one hand, they had to maintain their clientele by retaining an institutional identity founded on foreign film, and on the other, they had to accommodate the increased drawing power of domestic motion pictures with solid art film characteristics.

Exhibitors responded to the transformed cinematic environment in various ways. Some, like the Core Art Hall, continued to stress foreign art films between 1997 and 1999 (Appendix 2). At the same time, the Classic Cinema Oz, a new theatre established in Kangnam in January 1999, maintained a mixed programme but attempted to differentiate itself with exclusive screenings of Hollywood classics like *Casablanca* (Michael Curtiz, 1942, US), *Imitation of Life* (John M. Stahl, 1934, US), *Rebel Without a Cause* (Nicholas Ray, 1955, US), *Easy Rider and West Side Story* (Robert Wise, Jerome Robbins, 1961, US) (Yi 1998; KOFIC 2000).[14] While the Core and the Classic Cinema Oz stressed foreign art films, other theatres – the Lumiere, Cinehouse and Dongsung Art Centre (including the Dongsung Cinematheque) – dramatically increased the number of Korean movies they showed as part of their programmes.[15] Between 1993 and 1998, the number of Korean films screened by the Lumiere quadrupled and tripled at the Dongsung Art Centre and Cinehouse. Despite the different approaches taken by each theatre, the Dongsung Art Centre, Lumiere and Core Art Hall saw a significant decrease in customers over the period, while attendances at the Cinehouse remained steady. The newly opened Classic Oz saw poor returns and abandoned its attempt at creating a distinct identity as a Hollywood classic theatre by 2000.

There are some crucial points to take away from the experience of these cinemas in late 1990s Seoul. First, art film exhibitors were challenged by the dramatically altered cinematic context in which Korean motion pictures generated significant media interest. The various strategies of different exhibitors to cope in this new environment failed to halt declines in audience numbers. The second vital point is that popular understandings of art film were shifting. International and domestic film festivals as well as significant media attention had consecrated Korean film's quality, variety and creativity, and art film had even been rediscovered in Korea's cinematic past. For many young Korean people, art was no longer the sole preserve of foreign cinema. A KOFIC commissioned survey of art film fans in 2003 discovered that most of those questioned could not identify Jean-Luc Godard, but the same respondents claimed Lee Chang-dong to be an archetypal art filmmaker (Kim et al. 2004: 86). The appearance of innovative Korean filmmakers impacted common understandings of what constituted art film from this late 1990s period onwards. Finally, developments in Korean cinematic production influenced the exhibition practices of some art houses, which transformed from theatres that primarily showed foreign consecrated art films to cinemas that also highlighted domestic pictures.

The decline of post-dictatorship Korean cinephilia

Lower audience numbers did not just occur because of a more challenging economic and programming environment; there was a notable decline in the cinephilia that had characterised the previous decade. It wasn't only the established art houses that saw lower audiences, videotheques depended on membership, and without sources of advertising, they required word-of-mouth recommendations to survive. With fewer film fans signing up, organisers struggled to pay the rents; one by one, the pioneering videotheques closed down, and by the late 1990s, most had disappeared. Memberships declined, audiences grew thinner, and venues shut. One participant explained the fading cinephilia:

> I guess people began to lose interest and drift off (the scene). Gradually from 1998, some of the old faces stopped showing up, and younger people didn't take their place, and that made it less fun. It wasn't that I didn't go to the movies anymore, I carried on going. So, I didn't feel like I was doing anything wrong. I just let my membership lapse. One day, some friends asked me to go and see *Shiri*. I didn't really like that kind of film, but I was curious because I'd heard so much about it. And when I said I couldn't because I had a ticket for another (art) picture, they said: 'you're going to *that*?' So, I went with them (to see *Shiri*). (Na Su-min*, author interview, April 2021)

As Na Su-min* indicates, some of the energy had gone out of the cinephilia. The popularisation of art films led to their evolution from a rarefied, minority, cult-like status to a more mainstream existence. Following the 1996 repeal of pre-production censorship, what had been forbidden before was forbidden no longer. Kim et al. (2004: 23) argue that the popularisation of art film in Korea also caused it to 'enter the system' (*chedogwŏn chinip*).[16] While art film consumption had an underground character, it carried face-validity as an act of resistance, as something rare, obscure and novel. Film fans had struggled to get rare movies screened on video; now, they were more accessible and could be viewed at cinemas and festivals. Cinematic culture that had once only been enjoyed by a few was now nationwide news. Art and obscure film became popularised, and this very success signalled the end of the type of energetic cinephilia that had characterised the previous decade. With decreasing participation, the sense of community that had accompanied the cinephilia dissipated as well.

Evidence of the waning allure of Korean cinephilia can be seen in the declining attendances of the Dongsung Cinematheque's educational activities that had been a cornerstone of its mission. The Dongsung Cinematheque had almost 3,000 members, and initially, fifty or more people had participated in post-screening talks, but by late 1996, this had dwindled to a core group of only ten or so diehards. Lee confessed he felt the Dongsung Cinematheque had failed to challenge the 'general consensus that the cinema is a place where you just watch films' (Yi Sŏng-uk 1996a; Yi Nam 1996). The educational activities represented important facets of the new cinematic culture at other art houses and videotheques, and the decline in audiences, in general, indicates that the attraction of unofficial education had dissipated.

In addition to the declining interest in scholastic activities from fans, the whole notion of cinematic education was singled out for particular criticism by scholars, and these attacks were evidence of wider tensions within Korean cinephilia. Chae Kyung-mun critiqued the obsessive attempts by Korean film fans to educate themselves (and by exhibitors to enlighten their clientele) to acquire sufficient competence to appreciate foreign art film (cited in Park 2015: 151; Kim 2005: 82). These criticisms of viewing habits and autodidactism reflected general unease about young Korean cinephiles' unquestioning embrace of European art films. Other commentators believed the educational drive had lost its way. Chŏng Sŏng-il wrote in 1999 that Korean cinephilia stagnated because it had become 'a competition for knowledge and information, and not a discourse of love'. 'Cinephiles', Chŏng continued, had 'surrendered themselves too easily to bourgeois values' (cited in Yi Sŏn-ju 2017: 441). In other words, cinephiles had lost track of the fact that they were educating themselves to understand better the films they were watching, not to outsmart their peers and prove how cultivated they were. Korean cinephiles had seen education as a liberating means to achieve cultural freedom after decades of authoritarianism, so these criticisms attacked the very core of the enlightening mission of the videotheques and art houses.

Perhaps the most sustained intellectual critiques of the exhibition and education strategies adopted by the art houses came in a 1996 article entitled 'Cinephilia and Necrophilia'. Influential film academic Kim Soyoung reproved cinephile audiences for their lack of social consciousness in their film consumption and singled out the type of 'petrified' European art films championed by *Kino* and screened at the Dongsung Cinematheque for particular condemnation (Kim 1996: 1055; Yi Sŏn-ju 2017: 422). Kim complained motion pictures like *My Beautiful Laundrette*, *Eraserhead* and *The Spider's Stratagem* arrived in Korea after being canonised as art films. The socio-political messages they raised at the time of their creation were irrelevant to current, local (Korean) problems, which deserved greater treatment via documentary or activist film (Kim 1996: 1055–7; Yi Sŏn-ju 2017: 422).

Some researchers have argued there was a resolution of the friction between the film as 'activism' and film as 'art' camps in the late 1980s (see Sohn 2022: 71). However, Kim's 1996 accusations of political ineffectiveness illustrate the ongoing smouldering hostility within Korean cinephilia. Other cinephiles from the period frequently expressed their frustration with destructive infighting. Parit'ŏ members such as Byun Young-joo complained that the mission of the group to produce film by women, for women and from a female perspective, was frequently attacked by other activists as 'bourgeois', 'individualistic' and corrosive of the collective social responsibility of the movement. 'If you look at it, we (Parit'ŏ) were the most left-wing of all the independent filmmakers, but the problem was we constantly had to justify ourselves (as committed)' (cited in Sŏng 2020c).

The tension is also evident in the language used by exhibitors from the period. Lee's interviews with the *Chungang Ilbo* from the same period reveal a defensiveness over the question of the relative economic success of the Dongsung Cinematheque. Lee told journalists that the theatre had made a 'bearable loss' (Yi Nam 1997). Lee's choice of words is noteworthy. He didn't say he had broken even or failed to turn a profit but that he had lost money in an acceptable way.[17] These exchanges indicate an uneasy relationship with commerciality as if turning a profit was not the done thing to admit since it would leave him open to charges of 'selling out' and embracing the values of the *chedogwŏn*.

These attacks on political purity and commercialisation in the charged post-dictatorship period undermined cinephiles' political and cultural sense of self. The criticisms were particularly destructive because they subsumed genuine differences between cinematic cultures; they were a gross simplification of individual identities. Many who embraced art film did not see themselves abrogating their political responsibilities to society. On the contrary, they saw themselves as committed and in opposition to the *chedogwŏn*.[18] Lee Kwang-mo used the terms '*madang*' and 'Kwangjang' to characterise his Dongsung Cinematheque. *Kino* defined its cinematic aims as contrary to commercial cinema. The videotheque organisers called themselves a 'movement'. Those who embraced art film most vigorously defined their aims and framed their philosophies and visions of cinema in the language of film activism and the *minjung* movement. The question is, why? Cultural commentators frequently use one expression about the period: 'spirit of the times'.[19] There was a cross-pollination of ideas and practices between the videotheques, film clubs, cultural centres and early art houses. Exhibitors and consumers operated separately but were influenced by the same spirit of the times that emerged in the anti-dictatorship struggle. Videotheque, film club and early art house consumers and exhibitors often expressed a similar suspicion of the authorities, desire for self-education and autonomous, independent cinematic consumption because, essentially, these different approaches to film were born out of the regime's repression and the aftermath of June 1987. The recurrent political critiques attacked the very terms upon which cinephiles defined themselves and therefore undermined any sense of cinephile community in the late 1990s.[20]

Ultimately, no one reason caused the end of the cinephilia; the evaporation of energy and novelty, the declining interest in educational activities, the tensions over political positions, the perceived loss of purpose all took their toll. Many cinephiles didn't come to a decision one day to quit the scene; as Na Su-min* indicates, they just drifted away.

The start of the new millennium: instability in the performance of art houses

Despite the decline in cinephilia and art house attendances, we see a curious phenomenon between 1999 and 2002 characterised by periods of extreme fluctuations in the performance of art houses. In 1999, audiences for art film dropped to their lowest level in years, while in 2000, Seoul art houses flourished. The following year, art film audience numbers collapsed again, only to recover in 2002 when 16 per cent of all features viewed at Seoul box offices were classified as art movies (see Table 5.1). In this unstable economic environment, two notable theatres opened. In late 2000, Kim Nan-suk's Jinjin, an art film importation and distribution company, established the Hypertheque Nada with 147 seats at the

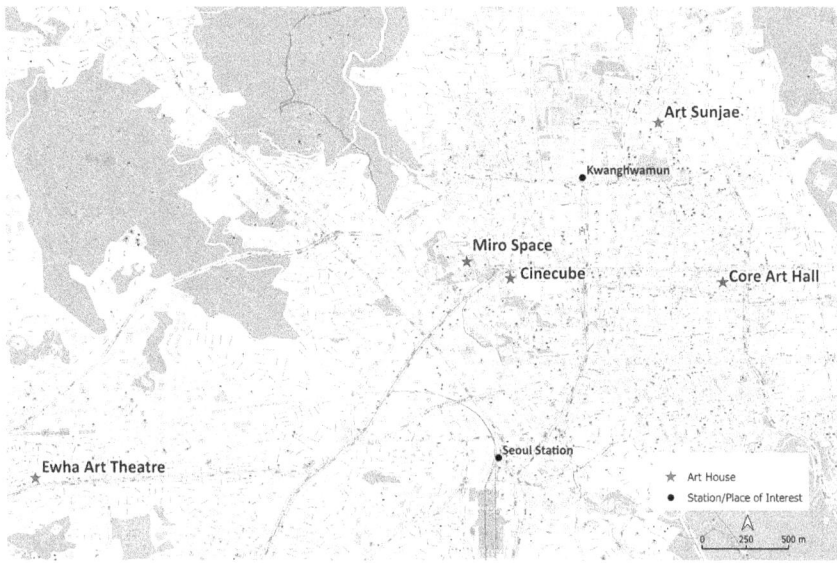

Figure 5.3 Map of art houses in central Seoul, created by Elspeth McVey © Openstreetmap contributors.

premises of the Dongsung Art Centre (Figure P2.1). Kim had taken over operations of the Dongsung Cinematheque after Baekdudaegan had left, but now she was making a theatre with a different character. The same year also saw the return to exhibition of Lee Kwang-mo's Baekdudaegan after a three-year hiatus during which Lee had produced *Spring in My Hometown*. Baekdudaegan based their Cinecube, which had two auditoriums, one with 293 seats and another with seventy-eight seats, at Kwanghwamun in central Seoul.

Media reports highlighted the return of Baekdudaegan and the opening of the Hypertheque Nada. True to form, both Lee and Kim created events in December 2000 to announce the opening of their theatres to the country. Kim held a festival dedicated to classic art films of the 1990s that 'excited and captivated' audiences. Hypertheque Nada's films included Wong Kar-wai's *Chungking Express* (*Chóngqìng sēnlín*, 1994, Hong Kong), *Black Hole* (*Kumŏng*, 1999, Kim Kuk-hyŏng, ROK), *Why has Bodhi-Dharma Left for the East?* (*Talmaga tongtchokŭro kan kkadalgŭn?* 1989, Bae Yong-kyun, ROK) (O 2000). At the same time, Lee Kwang-mo's new cinema, the Cinecube, hosted the 'Adieu Twentieth Century' film festival. Lee showed fifteen films that Baekdudaegan had screened at the Dongsung Cinematheque during the mid-1990s art boom, including *Nostalgia*, *Eraserhead* and *Landscape in the Mist* (O 2000).

When interviewed, Lee shrugged off concerns about declining art film audiences and the local competition his new cinema faced and expressed his hopes for a return to the glory days of the pre-Asian Financial Crisis cinephilia (O 2000).

Despite the openings of the Hypertheque Nada and Cinecube, the general unpredictability of the market continued. Exhibitors lured by the success of the cinephilia boom opened new operations, but several of these cinemas subsequently stopped showing art film or even closed altogether. Baekdudaegan started a second cinema near Kwanghwamun, the Art Cube, which seated eighty (Yi 2001).[21] In 2001, another cinema, the Miro Space, opened near Kwanghwamun (Kim et al. 2004: 29, 36). By 2002, the Classic Cinema Oz had converted into a mainstream theatre after failing to fill its auditoriums with its vintage Hollywood programme. The Miro Space closed outright with spiralling debts resulting from an average 10 per cent seat occupancy rate. The Art Cube also shut, and a KOFIC report from 2004 concluded that there was chronic underperformance in those art houses that managed to survive (Kim et al. 2004: 30).

Several problems impacted art houses in this period, the first of which was increased competition in the market since the first years of the boom. In Seoul, there was overcrowding in a niche sector. Many theatres – the Art Sunjae centre, Cinecube, Art Cube and Miro Space – were located in a small area of central Seoul around Samch'ŏngdong and Kwanghwamun, leading to cinemas selling similar products in a tight geographical area (Figure 5.3). These theatres faced pressure from other art houses and met stiffer challenges from multiplexes, which had significantly expanded. By 2000, Megabox followed CGV and Lotte in opening multiplexes – forming the three major chains dominating Korean exhibition (Hwang 2017: 59; Paquet 2009: 101). CGV, Lotte and Megabox monopolised the Korean cinema market, and by 2007 they owned 48 per cent of the total number of screens nationwide (Howard 2008: 94). All three chains shaped a cinematic environment that drew viewers away from older style single (or double screen) cinemas and to the new multiplexes.

In addition to multiplexes, a second problem facing independent cinemas concerned their source of revenue. The video and rights markets had largely financed many film companies until the late 1990s when sudden changes restricted this income (Kim Young-jin 2007: 7). By the early 2000s, technological shifts resulted in the collapse of the video market, and most people in Korea had begun to download films rather than buy DVDs or tapes. In addition, the rights market collapsed, as

Lee Kwang-mo explained in 2003 to a KOFIC committee analysing the problems faced by art film cinemas over the previous three years:

> The reasons for the current difficulty in running art houses are first, weakening competitiveness in marketing, and second the collapse of the video market. During the Dongsung (Cinematheque as run by Baekdudaegan) period, art film import prices were low, so it was difficult to make a loss. However, with art films today, video rights are not included. If eight movies are imported, none of them include the video rights. At best, you will sell 700 videos. (Cited in Kim et al. 2004: 17)

The loss of the rights market made importer-distributor-exhibitor companies like Baekdudaegan and Jinjin more vulnerable. Theatres that did not source their films had a single opportunity to make a profit, and that was through ticket sales (Yi Hyŏn-ju 2014). For both types of art film operators, the opportunities to turn a profit became far more limited than multiplex cinemas, which generated revenue through ancillary sales, local advertising and selling merchandise in the cinema foyers. The size and scale of art houses meant that advertising revenues were small, and most theatres were prohibited from selling food for the auditoriums (Yi Hyŏn-ju 2014). As a result, all art house owners depended upon box office revenues to make ends meet, and in a competitive environment, when audience numbers fluctuated, theatres faced an ever more precarious existence. Art houses would require other forms of income to survive.

Conclusion

There is no single reason behind the decline in the type of art film consumption and exhibition that had become headline news between 1995 and 1997. There were contingent, economic and cultural factors that resulted in the decline of enthusiasm for art film. The Dongsung Cinematheque was an experiment in film exhibition in Korea, and like many other attempts at radical innovation, it was short-lived. In the end, however, it was not the innovative schedules that caused the end of Baekdudaegan's management of the Dongsung Cinematheque, but a dispute over contracts. Other exhibitors faced serious financial challenges. The economic downturn caused by the Asian financial crisis made imports more expensive and importers less willing to take risks when the sector faced greater competition from multiplexes. A smaller film choice resulted in a declining interest in art movies; while a few pictures dominated box offices, attendances for most others fell. The period also saw increasing local interest in domestic film, exemplified by the box office success of *Shiri*-type blockbusters, works by commercial auteurs and the global critical recognition given to filmmakers like Hong Sang-soo. This fundamental shift proved a significant scheduling challenge for theatres like the Core Art Hall and Dongsung Cinematheque, which struggled with falling attendances. Foreign film had previously formed the central plank of art house programmes, and while many works by Korean commercial auteurs suited the art film label, exhibitors struggled to maintain a clear institutional identity in terms of their programming, and audience numbers fell as a result.

This period also saw a significant decline in cinephilia. If 'thirst' characterised the consumption of cinematic culture by young Korean cinephiles in the late and post-dictatorship period, by 1998, the appetites of some film buffs was sated. The success of art films partly contributed to a waning of interest as the novelty value declined. The scene had lost the excitement of engaging in a form of cultural consumption radically different from what had happened before with its educational activities, police raids and cinema of disturbance. There is evidence of deeper tensions within cinephile communities that made participation less comfortable, along with an overall loss of any sense of purpose. In the new millennium, exhibitors' financial results were inconsistent; they turned a profit in one year and a deficit in the next. Renowned theatres like the Hypertheque Nada and Cinecube opened, but many others ceased operations soon after starting. The ramifications of this unpredictable economic situation were that those exhibitors still attempting to specialise in specific films needed more than box office receipts to survive in the new millennium. Art houses became institutions that required state protection.

Notes

1. Baekdudaegan still prides itself on being the first officially designated specialist art film cinema in promotional materials (Baekdudaegan 2016).
2. The body which promoted arts and culture. Article 15 of the Film Promotion Act enacted in 1995 provided support for 'specialist theatres' (Hwang 2017: 63). Cinemas granted 'specialist' status could show art or independent film (Yi Nam 1997; Shin 2005: 54). Kim (et al 2004: 33) note that since ticket sales are usually divided a ratio of 5:5 (or 6:4) with the film distributor, this amounts to 14.3 per cent extra revenue.

3. In other cinemas, exhibitors and distributors divided ticket receipts by a ratio of 4:6; however, the Dongsung Art Centre allegedly insisted on more profit.
4. Baekdudaegan continued to distribute art films to other cinemas in Seoul including the Dongsung Art Centre.
5. The Dongsung Cinematheque maintained the member-produced information booklets, for example.
6. For a full list of officially designated art films in the 1990s, see Kim et al. (2004: 156–64).
7. *Life is Beautiful* won awards at Cannes and the Academy Award for Best Foreign Language Film.
8. In 1997, the rate of increase in consumption expenditure halved in comparison with the previous three years (Kim 2000: 66). Commentators regard the Asian Financial Crisis as the moment cultural consumption declined (Kim 2000; Cho 2020).
9. Both Kim and Lee drew the largest audiences for their films at the CGV Kangbyŏn. *Birdcage Inn* drew 1,200 of its 5,600 admissions, while *Spring in My Hometown* sold 16,000 of its 98,000 admissions (KMPPC 1999: 125–6).
10. For example, official KOFIC publications include a 'Cinema world diary' [*Yŏnghwagye ilgi*] which lists all the notable events occurring in cinema for the year. Of 115 entries for 1997, 10 per cent listed the awards and plaudits received by Korean film at international festivals (KMPPC 1998: 223–35).
11. International festival participations, invitations and awards featured prominently in the posters for *Spring in My Hometown* and *The Power of Kangwon Province*, for example.
12. Korean retrospective programmes from 1996 to 2005, included: the 'Korean New Wave' (First BIFF, 1996); 'Kim Ki-Young' (Second BIFF, 1997); 'Shin Sang-Ok' (Sixth BIFF, 2001) (Ahn 2012: 79). The 1996 establishment of BIFF, also positively impacted the overseas reception of Korean cinema. Before 1996, the Cannes Film Festival only screened three Korean films; since that time over one hundred Korean made films have been invited. The greater international interest in Korean film, provided further endorsement for domestic audiences of their film (Lee 2022: 4).
13. *Skate* was the first Korean short film to win an award at the Cannes Film Festival.
14. The Classic Cinema Oz opened in Kangnam (Sinsadong) with two 220-seater auditoriums.
15. During this period, the post-Baekdudaegan Dongsung Cinematheque was operating, but I use attendance figures from all the Dongsung Art Centre auditoriums.
16. Lee also claimed Baekdudaegan's exhibition strategies were managed 'with no regard for profit or loss' (Paek 2009; Yi Sŏng-uk 1996a). Park (2015: 7) argues that activist cinema associated with the anti-dictatorship *minjung* movement changed between 1987 and 1994. Films that had previously been produced, circulated, and exhibited illegally and for specific political purposes were subsequently repackaged as 'independent' or 'indie' films (Park 2015: 7). According to Yi Hyo-in, the funding of the Samsung Short Film Festival in 1994 was when the anti-capitalist activist culture of independent filmmaking was 'castrated' and ushered in an 'apolitical' era of indie filmmaking (Yi Hyo-in cited in Park 2015: 51).
17. In this case, Lee was discussing the Cinecube, which he ran from 2000.

18. Sohn (2012: 76) argues that the distinctions between the acceptance of film as art/film as activism were not even that clearly defined amongst members of the most committed 1980s film clubs.
19. See Yi Sŏn-ju (2017: 430–1), for example. Lee Kwang-mo frequently used the term in his interviews with me.
20. Lee Kwang-mo reports that Kim's criticisms impacted his post-Dongsung Cinematheque thinking about film education and programming (personal correspondence, Lee Kwang-mo, June 2020).
21. The Art Cube was in Samch'ŏngdong (Kim et al. 2004: 39).

Part 3
Legacy

Figure P3.1 Seoul Art Cinema advertising, Kyŏnghyang Sinmun Building, Seoul (2022; author's photo, courtesy Kim Sŏng-uk).

Chapter 6

The new millennium evolution of state support for art film exhibition

In 2001, four movies: the *Waikiki Brothers* (2001, Yim Soon-rye, ROK, 82,184 admissions), *Raybang* (2001, Chang Hyŏn-su, ROK, 2,432), *Butterfly* (Nabi, 2001, Mun Sŭng-uk, ROK, 4,878) and *Take Care of My Cat* (Koyangirŭl put'akhae, 2001, Chŏng Chae-ŭn, ROK, 24,182) were released within a few weeks of one another to great media fanfare (Kim et al. 2004: 15; Hwang 2017: 60–4). What linked these movies was that industry observers confidently predicted they would all perform well based on positive critical acclaim. However, after a week, all four films were pulled by multiplexes concerned with slow ticket sales. The movies competed with films like *Hi! Dharma!* (Dalmaya nolja! 2001, Park Chŏl-kwan, ROK, 1,250,875) and *My Wife is a Gangster* (Chop'ok manura, 2001, Cho Chin-kyu, ROK, 1,419,972), which featured a mix of comedy, action and violence with novel twists on the gangster genre – a successful combination that made them domestic and international box office hits (Kim et al. 2004: 15).

The dropping of these four 'Waranago' films – named after the first two letters in their Korean titles – led to widespread uproar. Journalists, fans, filmmakers and citizen's committees protested the multiplexes' cancellation of the Waranago films. Groups banded together to pay for screenings, and distributors leased art houses to exhibit the Waranago films and celebrate motion pictures that eschewed commercial success for artistic endeavour (Kim Hye-ri 2001). In November 2001, *Cine 21* published an influential article that featured representatives of Korean production and distribution companies and KOFIC discussing how to resolve the limited exhibition opportunities for Waranago-type films (Hwang 2017: 60–4).[1] The article was entitled: 'If there is no minor league within the industry, then Korean film has no future', and it argued that there had to be a place within cinema for Waranago films. The representatives agreed it was essential to maintain a 'diverse' range of films in the market and proposed establishing a network of art houses where Waranago films could be guaranteed opportunities for exhibition (*Cine 21* 2001).

The 'Waranago Incident', as it became known, is important because of its catalytic impact. It was evidence of a deeper problem within South Korean cinema and helped change attitudes towards the exhibition of non-mainstream, non-commercial film. The incident had significant implications for Korean art houses in the new millennium. The book's final section shifts the focus from the rise and fall of cinephilia and art film consumption to the legacy of this historical moment on Korean cinema, investigating its impact on Korean film's institutional, physical and symbolic landscape. In this chapter, I consider the transformed cinematic context exemplified by the Waranago Incident that precipitated greater governmental intervention in art film exhibition. I look at structural problems within Korean film and official attempts to resolve them using a countrywide network of art houses. I also investigate the establishment of a systematic state support policy for art film exhibition that began in the early 2000s and formed a small but integral feature of a flourishing Korean cinema. This art house support policy wasn't created overnight but through a trial-and-error process that brought exhibitors into closer cooperation with administrators and sometimes caused conflict. I also analyse the tensions impacting exhibitor/administrator relationships and the resolutions which helped preserve the art house system of support that remains a vital legacy of the cinephilia and art film boom. This chapter, therefore, offers an insight into the place of niche film within Korean cinema and the interaction between policy, administrators and exhibitors.

The legacy of the Waranago Incident

The Waranago Incident raised controversial issues close to the hearts of filmmakers, critics and cinemagoers. The first concerned the nature of the Korean film industry's success. By 1999, domestic cinema was capturing 40 per cent of the market, and between 2001 and 2003, this figure had risen to around 50 per cent (KOFIC 2005: 21). However, the phenomenal performance of hits like *Shiri*, *JSA* (*Kongdonggyŏngbiguyŏk*, Park Chan-wook, 2000, ROK, 5.8 million admissions [ROK]) and *Friend* (*Ch'in'gu*, Kwak Kyŏng-t'aek, 2001, ROK, 8.1 million [ROK]), also gave rise to general anxiety amongst critics, journalists and observers that these impressive figures reflected the mass popularity of a few hits, while the majority of less commercial films made huge box office losses. The Waranago Incident exposed other anxieties about the success of South Korean cinema. Commercial attainment only partially reflected Korean cinema's creative output and potential. As a result, notable films like those that formed the Waranago group were in danger of disappearing from public view. Another issue raised by the controversy lay in the reality that most moneymaking cinematic ventures were produced by male directors, while two of the Waranago films were made by emerging women directors (Yim Soon-rye and Chŏng Chae-ŭn). Waranago highlighted the limited opportunities provided for younger – especially – women filmmakers. These anxieties were expressed by fans, journalists and critics about the Waranago Incident and even by the vice-chairman of KOFIC, Lee Yong-kwan, who in 2000 wrote of his fears of a few companies favouring commercial genre films monopolising cinema distribution (Lee Yong-kwan 2000: 11–13).[2]

In addition to Korean cinema being unbalanced and distorted by a handful of films like *Shiri*, many cultural commentators felt deeply uncomfortable with the values they felt the new home-produced blockbusters represented. For years, one of the primary defences against the opening of the Korean cinema market to direct distribution by foreign (mainly Hollywood) film companies had been the rejection of a film culture that celebrated gratuitous sex and violence for the sake of profit. Many of those who opposed greater openness argued that it would obliterate home-grown films with more wholesome cultural values. For Lee Yong-kwan (2000), the Waranago Incident exemplified a clear-cut case of high-intensity, violent and lightweight cinema replacing culturally and aesthetically substantive films via an exhibition system in which the bottom line was everything. The Waranago phenomenon exposed a central hypocrisy within a revitalised Korean cinematic industry for critics, scholars and film fans. Had Korean cinema now become what it had rejected a few years previously?[3]

The key terms that came to dominate this discussion of balance within the Korean film industry were 'diversity' (*tayangsŏng*) and 'diverse' (*tayanghan*).[4] Diversity is a notion that emerged alongside discourses on the rapidly shifting demographic changes within Korean society. The word had entered dominant state discourses about multiculturalism (*tamunhwa*) to describe the increasing numbers of multicultural families[5] and migrant workers who had taken up residence in the country. Multiculturalism represented an alternative to the ethnocentric notions of a *tanilminjok* (single ethnic nation) dominating state and oppositional discourses until the 1990s. Park Young-a argues that the use of 'diversity' to refer to cinema initially appeared during the 2001 debates among independent filmmakers over the need to retain a screen quota to protect the Korean film industry against domination by Hollywood (2015: 102–3; see also Sohn 2012: 32).[6] However, a shift in usage of the term occurred when activists realised 'cultural imperialism from within is as big a threat as that from without' (Park 2015: 104). In other words, the box office domination of a few Korean-made big-budget blockbuster films led to the disappearance of other forms of cinematic product. From this point onwards, 'diversity' came to indicate different cinemas from within Korea or 'low-budget films, independent films and art films whose styles, narratives, production and distribution systems did not fit the norms of mainstream Korean cinema' – what was also commonly referred to as 'specialist' film (Park 2015: 103). As a definition of films that could or could not be screened at a cinema, 'diversity' is probably no more effective than any of the other terms used in the past (like 'non-mainstream' [*pijuryuyŏnghwa*] or 'non-commercial' [*pisangŏpyŏnghwa*]; Kim et al. 2004: 16). However, as a concept within the dominant state-society narrative of multiculturalism, 'diversity' was a powerful way of presenting a platform of change within cinema. In the wake of the Waranago Incident, the central question KOFIC administrators attempted to resolve was how to help maintain diversity in the market by guaranteeing exhibition windows for Korean specialist films.

The importance of a diversified industry

Turn of the century academic observers noticed that the Korean cinema industry had begun developing as a highly diversified industry in which festivals, archives and different modes of production, including art, independent film, animation and documentary balanced a flourishing mainstream commercial genre film sector (Berry 2002: 7).[7] Thus, South Korea's cinematic development differed from other Asian countries, which either specifically stressed festival-oriented art films (Taiwan) or created commercial genre movies (like Bollywood and Hong Kong) (Berry 2002: 12). Waranago was a stark warning of what can happen when the industry becomes unbalanced in favour of commercially successful films.

Why administrators chose policies that encourage balance and diversification – despite the challenges and the costs involved – is key to our understanding of Korean film. First, in balancing commercial mainstream film with other modes of filmmaking, administrators attempted to cater to different audiences in Korean cinema and influential voices within the industry. Among these significant stakeholders were those within academia and journalism,[8] those who consume and coordinate the numerous Korean film festivals and influential figures in KOFIC (Parc and Messerlin 2021: 194). Park Young-a argues that when the former political dissident Kim Dae Jung came to power, many former activist filmmakers from the anti-dictatorship *minjung* movement became influential within Korean independent filmmaking in Korea and KOFIC (Park 2015: 163). According to Park, many of these figures considered independent film significant precisely because they perceived it to stand in opposition to the values represented by commercial filmmaking. Park contends that KOFIC's embrace of diversity resulted from the influence of these former activists beginning in the late 1990s and early 2000s (Park 2015: 167). Independent filmmaking provided an essential outlet for expressing diverse political and cultural sensibilities, especially for underrepresented groups like women or gay rights advocates (Park 2015: 168; Chung and Diffrient 2021: 24–5). Therefore, the independent filmmaking movement and KOFIC represented two important groups whose voices helped shape and balance the Korean film industry.

Second, a more diversified industry like South Korea's allowed for the significant crossover of personnel and expertise between specialist and commercial filmmaking. Within a multi-sector industry, there was increased potential for cross-fertilisation between specialist and commercial modes that allows filmmakers to move between the two sectors, a feature that many critics, scholars and commentators argued strengthened the entire industry (see Kim Young-jin 2019: 11–12, 15; Paquet 2016: 13). Finally, a diverse industry provided quantifiable evidence of achievement in several different areas. In any given year since 2000, for example, the annual *Korean Cinema* reports have pointed to successes in one part of the industry or another – a high domestic market share compared with Hollywood film, a record-breaking box office success, film festival recognition abroad,[9] the rapid and successful expansion of international film festivals at home, or the emergence of new auteurs, short-film or documentary filmmakers.[10] Commercial and non-commercial cinema offered multiple possibilities for recognition.[11]

Maintaining balance in the domestic industry: the development of Next Plus cinema network

Using ideas similar to those discussed in the *Cine 21* article, KOFIC proposed to support the exhibition of Waranago-type films. KOFIC did this by launching a project to create a nationwide system of art houses called the Art Plus Cinema Network in 2002. KOFIC funded these cinemas, which in turn were supposed to prevent a recurrence of the Waranago Incident by providing screening opportunities to specialist movies. These were 'alternative commercial films, art films and low-budget independent films which had not received screenings following a surge in multiplexes and the spread of wide release strategies' (Kim et al. 2004: 16). By guaranteeing exhibition opportunities through KOFIC-supported art houses, specialist films would have a better chance of receiving investment and going into production and 'thereby protect the health of the market' (Kim et al. 2004: 15–16). Nevermore would filmmakers like Byun Young-joo have to sell trinkets to get their pictures to the screen, and never would Waranago-type films be pulled before they could reach an audience. KOFIC believed the Art Plus network of art houses would balance a diversified Korean film industry.

There are both explicitly stated and implied reasons why KOFIC selected art houses as a frontline defence against the dominance of commercial film. First, administrators believed that subsidising art houses provided an efficient way to develop an alternative screening network supporting Korean art film distribution, exhibition, marketing and production (Kim et al. 2004: 15). Second, art houses were also the natural choice for state support since their regulars were the most likely audiences for specialist cinema. In addition, a legal and administrative framework for subsidising theatres – in the manner of the Dongsung Cinematheque – was already in place. Third, art houses had already actively supported Korean independent, art and classic films, as exemplified by the art house screening of films like *The Murmuring*. Finally, KOFIC administrators, in their plans to protect Waranago-type motion pictures, appeared to draw inspiration from the 1990s art film boom. Kim Mi-hyŏn wrote in her KOFIC-commissioned report on the proposals that the period between the opening night of *The Sacrifice* and the opening of the BIFF was an 'unprecedented heyday' in the art film market, an 'exceptional time' that unleashed a 'fever' amongst cinephiles (Kim et al. 2004: 16). By invoking the spirit of this 'golden age' of art film consumption in Korea, administrators implied that if anything could energise the protection of specialist film, it was the art houses themselves.

KOFIC aimed to expand support for up to forty art houses nationwide by 2007 (Kim et al. 2004: 16). The trial run for the policy started in early 2002 with support for a single cinema in Seoul – the Hypertheque Nada – and a sole cinema in the southwestern provinces – the Kwangju Theatre (Kwangjugŭkjang) (KOFIC 2012: 237). In the second year, KOFIC increased the number of cinemas they supported to include the Cinecube, five others in the capital, and four in the provinces. Furthermore, KOFIC planned to increase the number of theatres they subsidised exponentially. However, the original plan ran into difficulties from the beginning.

Contrary to intentions, the most significant drop in revenue of many art houses came during the period of KOFIC support. The Kwangju Theatre's annual attendance declined by more than 70 per cent between 2000 and 2003 while operating as an official art house (Kim et al. 2004: 44). Before receiving KOFIC subsidies, the Cinecube drew 200,000 people and achieved a seat sales rate of 27.6 per cent, but whilst receiving KOFIC support, sales dropped to 150,000, with a seat occupancy rate of 19.4 per cent (Kim et al. 2004: 39). After a single year (2003) of receiving subsidies from KOFIC, Lee Kwang-mo pulled his Cinecube out of the support process. The Cinecube was, in many ways, the jewel in the crown for the support policy. Lee's Baekdudaegan were pioneers in Korean art film exhibition, and their withdrawal from the network was a setback for KOFIC. As a result of these problems, KOFIC commissioned a second report entitled: 'A study of policy towards supporting specialist art houses' to revise the original plan's perceived shortcomings and develop a new strategy: Next Plus (Kim et al. 2004). A committee of KOFIC researchers led by Kim Mi-hyŏn and Hypertheque Nada manager Kim Nan-suk authored the 2004 report. It helped shape the future of art houses in Korea and KOFIC's attempts to balance the industry. It is also important because it revealed the challenges administrators faced attempting to implement policy, which are outlined below.

Early problems with the Art Plus policy

Although designed to help specialist film and art houses in Korea, the policy opened the door for conflict with the recipients of state largesse: the cinemas. The report's authors used the Cinecube as a case study of three related problems that impacted the Art Plus project. The first complication was that so few Korean films with official art film status were released that theatres like the Cinecube struggled to comply with the 106-day (fifteen-week) annual quota of Korean (art) movies. To resolve the issue, the Cinecube organised re-runs of previously screened Korean art films like *Jealousy is my Middle Name* (*Chilt'unŭn naŭi him*, 2003, Park Chan-ok, ROK), *A Good Lawyer's Wife (Paramnan kajok*, Im Sang-su, 2003, ROK), *Spring, Summer, Fall, Winter and Spring* (*Pom, yŏrŭm, kaŭl, kyŏul kŭrigo pom*, 2003, Kim Ki-duk, ROK) and *The Road Taken* (Sŏnt'aek, 2003, Hong Ki-sŏn, ROK) to fulfil the quota (Kim et al. 2004: 40). As a result, the Cinecube exhibited to near-empty auditoriums.[12]

A second problem resulting from the demands of the quota was that the Cinecube was obliged to show officially designated art movies that Lee Kwang-mo considered 'unsuitable for the direction' of the cinema (cited in Kim et al. 2004: 40). Lee did not identify specific films in his critique, but one might point to the KOFIC delegated art film *Hilarious Mourning* (*Ogu*, 2003, Yi Yun-t'aek, ROK), a drama/comedy about a shaman. *Hilarious Mourning* was very different from the cinema of disturbance screened by Baekdudaegan in the first year of the Dongsung Cinematheque in terms of style and theme. It was equally at odds with films screened in the Cinecube that year, for example, the representation of Kurds during the Iran–Iraq conflict in *Blackboards* (*Takhté siah*, 2000, Samira Makhmalbaf, Iran/Italy/Japan), or Inuit filmmaker Zacharias Zunuk's portrayal of indigenous communities in Canada, *Atanarjuat: The Fast Runner* (2001, Canada). Lee felt the obligation to screen films contrary to his programming style corroded the Cinecube's relationship with its regular audience.

An issue lay with KOFIC's system of determining art film status for Korean movies. The policy called for a committee chosen by KOFIC to decide what constituted an art film that theatres could show. Some exhibitors criticised the committee's determinations of what was and what was not art claiming they used arbitrary designations in their decision-making process. Officials often struggled to identify 'high-level, well-made works of art', simply because, according to the stipulations, commercial success automatically disqualified movies from art film status (Kim et al. 2004: 40). What was the basis of these criticisms? How did the KOFIC committee determine art film, and what principles governed their decisions?

KOFIC's regulations stated that specialist film status wasn't automatically awarded; in fact, producers, importers, distributors, or exhibitors had to apply for official art film recognition.[13] Film company representatives submitted copies of the movie and script for appraisal to a seven-person committee run by KOFIC, including a film professor, critic, director and producer who each served a one-year term. The committee sat four times annually. If the committee rejected an application, the film's representatives had one month to appeal the decision. The criteria for selection stressed three areas:

1. The quality of the film (*wansŏngdo*)
2. The level of the film's creative, experimental and artistic contribution (*ch'angŭisŏng, silhŏmjŏk mit yesuljŏk konghŏn*)
3. The film's level of cultural and artistic contribution (*munhwa/yesuljŏk kiyŏ*) and its performance (*silchŏk*).

(Kim et al. 2004: 37)

Exhibitors found these definitions problematic because of their inflexibility when South Korean film output was rapidly developing. The first issue was a limited set of standards that evaluated all movies, whether vintage, recent, Korean or foreign. Second, the criteria stressed the aesthetic merits of a motion picture without reference to the subject matter examined or the works of specific directors associated with art cinema. The specifications included none of the criteria that Todd Berliner argues as essential for determining art movies in addition to its narrative, stylistic and thematic practices; for example, the film's method of distribution, release, exhibition and source of finance (Berliner 2018: 68). There was only a single reference to a criterion outside the text: 'performance' (*silchŏk*), indicating box office outcome. Overall, KOFIC provided a set of standards for selecting art films that relied almost exclusively on form and style.[14]

The problematic definitions led to some arbitrary decisions; for example, exhibitors widely criticised the committee for judging films like *A Good Lawyer's Wife* and *Memories of Murder* (*Sarinŭi ch'uŏk*, 2003, Bong Joon-ho, ROK) not to be art films because of their commercial success (Kim et al. 2004: 37).[15] The committee's decision to reject *Memories of Murder* reflects what David Andrews describes as art cinema's 'most consistent myth' that art opposes commerce. Art film was understood by the committee in oppositional terms – as a clear and equivocal truth – as a rival to 'an audience-driven Hollywood cinema' (Andrews 2013: 3). Yet here were Korean films like *Memories of Murder* breaking down these distinctions and showing that the prescription for determining art film status required adaptation to a fast-developing context. Another issue critiqued by art houses at the project's initiation was that since the status of a new film's box office performance could only be determined post-screening, it was challenging to plan programmes for the year (Kim et al. 2004: 37). The committee's periodic evaluations meant cinemas screened movies without knowing whether KOFIC would grant them art film recognition, thus creating enormous uncertainty for exhibitors (Kim et al. 2004: 37).

A final problem concerned the nationwide circulation of art movies. Regional cinemas like the Kwangju Theatre faced severe challenges with art film distribution which significantly impacted their economic performance. Unlike the theatres run by importer distributors such as the Cinecube, the Kwangju Theatre relied on distribution companies for its films. The Kwangju Theatre showed a mixed programme of commercial cinema and foreign and Korean art films. The Kwangju Theatre complained film distributors often excluded art cinema from their operation because of a perceived lack of profitability. They also only allowed the theatre to screen potentially lucrative commercial films after other local first-run multiplexes had exhibited them, meaning smaller audiences and a considerable loss of revenue (Kim et al. 2004: 44).

These criticisms of KOFIC's Art Plus project raise several issues related to official understandings of art films and the character of art houses. The initial project employed criteria for selecting art films that were incapable of accounting for developments in Korean cinema and elsewhere. Kim Mi-hyŏn's report points out that while there had been a 'relatively clear' distinction between art film and general commercial film ten years earlier, this distinction was complicated by an influx of foreign art imports and developments within Korean cinema (Kim et al. 2004: 16; Berry 2002: 10; Berliner 2018: 54). Exhibitors and programmers, like Lee Kwang-mo, believed that they should be the ones to determine what should be screened in their cinema and that their audiences were the best judges of an exhibitor's programming decisions.

A second related problem was the commercial and artistic character of specialist cinemas. The architects of the initial Art Plus network project had a notion of film exhibition that was considered ossified by the authors of the 2004 report. This is evident by their assessment that art houses were run by 'small importers who mainly imported foreign films with a high level of artistry, but which were uncertain prospects at the box office in Korea' (Kim et al. 2004: 16). KOFIC was evidently referring to Cinecube or Hypertheque Nada in this assessment. Yet Lee Kwang-mo and Kim Nan-suk did much more than import foreign films; they organised educational events, libraries and archives, and worked hard to establish identities for their cinemas to survive in a swiftly changing market. KOFIC administrators showed little recognition that art houses required a specific character to attract regulars; they saw theatres as places to defend Korean-made films.

A final issue with the Art Plus network project was that KOFIC had aimed for a nationwide patchwork of art houses, yet they appear to have misunderstood the significant exhibition and distribution challenges that provincial theatres like the Kwangju Theatre faced. Most importantly, administrators had not considered a handicap impacting their art house protection policy. Namely, in return for official protection, would administrators not feel entitled to a say over the programming schedules of those very theatres that had benefited from state largesse? The problem of official intrusion into scheduling had soured relations between administrators and Lee's Dongsung Cinematheque in 1997, and the same problem re-emerged in 2004. These were some of the principal issues facing the Art Plus network of art houses that KOFIC proposed to address in 2004.

Next Plus: resolving the problems of quotas, definitions and circulation

In tackling the issues raised by the theatres, KOFIC's 2004 report (Kim et al. 2004) proposed improvements to the Art Plus network of art houses, renaming their initiative 'Next Plus' to reflect these changes. The most significant recommendation was the reduction of the screen quota. Specialist films now had to be shown for 60 per cent of the year, or 219 days, and Korean art movies for seventy of those days (down from 106 days).[16] The proposed quota reduction attempted to alleviate the pressure on cinema owners to show re-runs and engage in financially unsustainable programming that alienated regular customers (Kim et al. 2004: 10–12).

Another way the authors of the KOFIC report attempted to improve state support was by clarifying the definitions of films that art houses showed. First, the report broadened the definition by introducing an expanded category list:

1. Domestic and foreign works of outstanding work value, art films
2. Domestic non-mainstream, low-budget commercial films that failed to get a screening opportunity
3. Works contributing to film art that win critical support regardless of the production scale
4. Classic films and films worth re-screening because of their cinematic value
5. Non-mainstream genres such as documentaries and animation

6. Unusual independent film employing a new film style and innovative techniques
   7. Other films of new nationality or type that have not been introduced domestically.

   (Kim et al. 2004: 8)

Administrators attempted to draw up suitable criteria to satisfy all interests when Korean film was rapidly changing. Among those interests were art house managers seeking autonomy over programming and financial stability. For example, item 3 of the list above responded to criticisms of KOFIC's rejection of successful but critically acclaimed films like *Memories of Murder* for art status. Items 1, 3, 6 and 7 also addressed the concerns of theatre managers by significantly expanding the criteria used to select suitable movies beyond a sole focus on film style. Item 2 responded to the lack of screening opportunities allocated to low-budget but critically acclaimed films highlighted by the Waranago Incident. Item 5 addressed the growing interest in festivals showcasing animation and documentaries. Administrators needed to balance two forces – screening time had to be guaranteed for a wide variety of Korean films, while specialist art houses had to remain viable business ventures. The authors of the 2004 Next Plus report made it clear that the initial plan had over-emphasised screening time for Korean film at the expense of commercial sustainability for art houses. Another proposed improvement was expanding the support network for art houses outside the capital. This would include a distribution system that linked the circulation of films in the provinces with the capital, preventing the kind of blockages the Kwangju Theatre faced because it relied on distributors reluctant to deal in art film (Kim et al. 2004: 8).

The 2004 Next Plus project proposals influenced the subsequent direction of policy towards non-commercial film. In 2008, the proposed reduction in quota became law (through changes to the Promotion of Film and Video Contents Act), officially reducing the amount of time Korean films had to play. The notion of 'diversity' and many of the film descriptors in the 2004 Next Plus report helped frame subsequent film policies. KOFIC created a new classification of 'diversity film specialist theatres' (*Tayangsŏng yŏnghwa chŏnyonggwan*) in addition to art film specialist theatres,[17] and these theatres showed: art, animation, documentary and independent movies.[18] The 2008 stipulations also included descriptions designed to prevent the repetition of Waranago-type incidents and controversies over the art status of films (like *Memories of Murder*) by featuring clearer guidance over the release methods of specific movies.[19]

The Next Plus proposals facilitated an expansion of art houses and improved relations with exhibitors. The year after the report was published, Lee Kwang-mo's Cinecube re-joined the network of KOFIC-supported cinemas. Within two years, the number of independent cinemas involved in the network had risen from four to nine in the capital and six to seven theatres in the provinces (KOFIC 2012). This small increase suggests that the proposed changes had improved art house managers' confidence in KOFIC's support policies. The administrators had also resolved the potential embarrassment of losing the participation of well-known art house exhibitors like Lee Kwang-mo.

Many of the changes proposed in the 2004 Next Plus report formed the basis of the strategy to balance commercial and specialist film within Korean cinema. For roughly a decade after 2004, KOFIC included specialist theatres as part of an attempt to maintain diversity in Korean cinema. This was a shifting cinematic context in which CGV and Lotte expanded into the art film sector. In 2013, the number of multiplex-run dedicated art film screens had expanded to nineteen countrywide (Son Chin-a 2014). As a result of these changes, from 2006, KOFIC began to include multiplex screens in their annual assessments of the size of the specialist film sector, which caused considerable controversy, as we see below.

The art and independent film sector expanded until 2009–11, a high point in KOFIC's direct theatrical support. The number of specialist film theatres within the Next Plus network reached thirty-five in 2009 (KOFIC 2012: 238–9, see Table 6.1). Total audience numbers for art houses also increased steadily between 2004 and 2011, and seat occupancy rates climbed to the highest levels seen in the sector over the same period.[20] In 2009, over 10 million Koreans watched the 162 films designated as art or independent, accounting for almost 7 per cent of all movies viewed. More than 9 per cent of all films watched in the capital were art/independent films (KOFIC 2019: 286–7). By 2010, KOFIC designated almost 190 films as art/independent, a sign of the success of the Next Plus policy.

A new decade, old problems and a decline in the administrator/exhibitor relationship

However, the new decade saw the emergence of some older challenges that had dogged the art film exhibition sector in the 1990s, namely bureaucratic interference in programming, as well as poor economic performance, and these issues led to a worsening of exhibitor/administrator interactions. A serious deterioration in the relationship occurred mid-decade in the context of successive years of poor regional art house economic performance.[21] The 2010s reversed the previous growth in art/independent film audiences reflecting the boom/bust pattern that characterised art film exhibition at the end of the 1990s. Audience numbers for specialist movies in the capital and regions halved by 2011, and by 2013, they had halved again (KOFIC 2019: 286). The number of art houses fell in 2010 and 2011 (KOFIC 2012: 241). Most worryingly for KOFIC, of the audiences attending art houses between 2010 and 2011, the majority watched foreign, not Korean art films (KOFIC 2012: 240).[22] KOFIC subsidised individual art houses to the tune of $45,000–$71,000 per theatre (Hwang 2017: 75), yet fewer people were viewing Korean specialist films. In KOFIC's eyes, their art house subsidy strategy failed to support domestic movies sufficiently, and their plans required modifications to balance the industry.

Between 2014 and 2015, KOFIC radically changed how it attempted to administer cinematic diversity by cutting direct theatrical support, a move that particularly impacted provincial art houses. Under the previous system, twenty-five regional cinemas with auditoriums not exceeding 200 seats received KOFIC support consisting of free online promotion and operating costs subsidies amounting to 6–10 per cent of total ticket sales (Sŏng 2014). KOFIC also gave individual theatres considerable autonomy over programming (Yi 2015).[23]

Arguing it was no longer willing to subsidise failing art houses attracting few customers, KOFIC declared it was changing the system to support specific art and independent films (Sŏng 2014; Sŏng Ha-hun 2015). KOFIC proposed selecting twenty-six motion pictures under the scheme and providing thirty art houses with subsidies when they showed one of these films on a set day (Sŏng Ha-hun 2015). Some representatives

Table 6.1 The number of art (and independent film) theatres in Korea (2005–13)

Year	2005	2006	2007	2008	2009	2010	2011	2012	2013
Art houses	10	18	25	30	35	29	26	25	25
Independent film theatres	0	0	1	1	1	3	3	4	4
Total	10	18	26	31	36	32	29	29	29

Source: KOFIC 2014: 232.

of art house organisations were furious, pointing out that KOFIC's new system would cut assistance to struggling independent theatres while offering support to multiplexes. The loss of direct subsidies threatened the existence of established theatres like the Taegu Dongsung Art Hall and the Taejŏn Art Cinema. Journalists claimed this shift represented the end of diversity in Korean film and the total dominance of cinema exhibition and distribution by big business (multiplex) interests (Sŏng 2014). Other representatives were furious at the lack of consultation on the proposals (Yi 2015).[24] KOFIC's changes to the funding support system also fuelled intense media speculation that the state was essentially using its regulatory bodies to suppress artistic freedom. The government could use KOFIC to filter out movies deemed antagonistic to official policies by only supporting specific films. Journalists cited the documentary about the 2014 Sewol ferry disaster: *The Truth Shall Not Sink with Sewol* (Daibingbel; Yi Sang-ho, An Hae-ryong, 2014, ROK) as an example of the type of film which the authorities would censor since it criticised the Park Geun-hye administration's response to the disaster (Sŏng Ha-hun 2015). Another example was the 2013 documentary *Project Cheonan Ship* (Ch'ŏnanham pŭrojektŭ, 2013, Paek Sŭng-u), which cast doubts on official claims that the North Korean Navy sunk the vessel in a torpedo attack. The documentary elicited the anger of the conservative press, the Ministry of Defence and bereaved families who filed a failed injunction to ban the film's release (Park 2013). By preventing screening opportunities for controversial films while policing the programming of theatres, journalists argued the state was punishing film producers and exhibitors and reinvigorating military dictatorship-era censorship (Sŏng Ha-hun 2015).

A further deterioration in relations between exhibitors and administrators came with the 2016 blacklist scandal. In October 2016, a member of the Korean National Assembly, To Chong-hwan, exposed a secret blacklist of close to 10,000 people suspected of left-wing activities and opposing the government's policies. Further disclosures revealed that the Lee Myung-bak and Park Geun-hye administrations maintained the blacklists (Kim 2018: 85). In 2018, the incoming chairman of KOFIC, O Sŏk-gŭn, publicly apologised for KOFIC's role in denying public funding to individuals on the blacklist from 2009 onwards (Kil 2018). Amongst those refused funding were filmmakers, actors and screenwriters, but also art film distributors and exhibitors considered 'progressive' because they screened work dealing with themes deemed 'unsuitable' by the government like the Sewol Ferry disaster, national security laws and sexual minorities (Kil 2018). Included were renowned directors like Lee Chang-dong, Park Chan-wook and Bong Joon-ho (Chung and Diffrient 2021: 20). The 2016 exposés corroborated what many within the cultural industry had suspected since at least 2014: that the Lee and Park administrations actively discriminated against individuals, institutions and projects deemed unworthy of support – including art houses (Kim 2018: 88).

As with the 2014–15 cuts to art house support, revelations about the blacklist led many critics to re-evaluate the state sponsorship of cinema (Kim 2018: 85–8). In the eyes of some journalists and commentators on film, KOFIC had turned from an enlightened and generous benefactor of art house to a virtual villain in a few short years. Yet as Kim Ju Oak argues, the Lee and Park administrations had placed state officials in a difficult position. In most cases, administrators were forced, against their better judgement, to connive in the government's exclusion of artists and projects (Kim 2018: 86). KOFIC were essentially powerless to resist the orders of governments determined to intervene in theatrical exhibition for political purposes. In the years that followed the revelations, KOFIC did much to distance itself from the blacklist scandal, openly acknowledging its unwilling connivance in the political suppression instead of covering it up.[25] The criticisms deeply impacted KOFIC's sense of purpose since an organisation dedicated to promoting artistic freedom conspired in a government strategy to stifle it.[26] One unfortunate hangover of the scandal, however, is that some within art film exhibition feel that the legacy is ongoing, as this provincial art house exhibitor revealed in December 2021 on condition of anonymity:

> Exhibitor: The official reason for us losing the (KOFIC) subsidy was that upon re-evaluation, we had failed to meet their criteria for support, but then (in 2016) we found out we had been blacklisted because we showed the film *Project Cheonan Ship*. From that moment onwards, everything got more difficult for us financially.
> Interviewer: Do you receive KOFIC support in 2021?
> Exhibitor: We still receive funding from KOFIC, but since the blacklist scandal, things have become more difficult with the local authorities. They cut our support and put it into other cultural events.

This exhibitor acknowledged that they no longer faced discrimination from KOFIC but from other local officials who sympathised with the aims of the conservative administrations and continued to underfund art houses because of the type of film they showed. The poor economic performance of art houses, especially in the provinces and the political interference exemplified by the blacklist scandal soured relationships between art houses and KOFIC. In several respects, however, the disintegration of relations resulted from longer-term underlying problems facing the art film sector.

Several issues hamstrung the KOFIC Art Plus and Next Plus networks from the outset, impacting the sustainability of art houses. First, KOFIC set unrealistic targets for their desired expansion. The Next Plus network report aimed to establish a countrywide network of almost a hundred art film and specialist screens by 2007, but by 2012 there were twenty-nine, and by 2020, there were still only seventy-one (Kim et al. 2004: 5–12; KOFIC 2012: 242; see Table 6.1).[27] The desire to establish a large-scale countrywide network of art houses created difficulties for goal fulfilment, particularly in the regions which were less densely populated and lacked the extensive transport connections of the capital. By increasing the number of provincial theatres for films that had only a limited demand in the first place, policymakers stood a greater chance of spreading a thin audience even more finely.[28]

The desire for countrywide expansion necessitated the controversial involvement of multiplex screens in the Next Plus network. CGV, Lotte and Megabox opened operations dedicated to exhibiting art, independent and classic films, and KOFIC began to include multiplex screens in their statistics primarily because of the network's slow expansion. The participation of big chains must have seemed like a pragmatic response by KOFIC to achieving their desired aim of providing screening time for Korean films that struggled to thrive in the distribution and exhibition network. However, this approach impacted the face validity of the entire project. By including multiplex screens to account for their ambitious expansion, KOFIC invited accusations that they were betraying the principles of diversity they had set out to protect in the first place.

A third issue that impacted the sustainability of the specialist film sector was the lumping of art, independent and other types of film together when they meant different things to audiences. One former art house manager expressed doubts:

> My experience concludes that art and independent films are watched by distinctly different audiences, although there is crossover ... both types of film have different aesthetics and values, and Korean audiences' cultural consumption patterns and tastes for these two types of film are not the same. Therefore, if one intended to fund these movies, the independent film support system and the art film support system should have been established separately. (Anon., art film exhibitor, December 2020)

For this manager, independent film, with its roots in 1980s activism and art film, with its origins in 1990s cinephilia, appealed to distinct audiences. The crux of the criticism was rooted in an old problem. The danger was that by KOFIC attempting to dictate programming from above, theatres lost their specific character and shed their audiences. Of course, for the administrators of KOFIC, justifying support for a unified and larger non-commercial film sector may have been easier than providing subsidies for two smaller sectors. However, these observations revealed a significant divergence between exhibitors and KOFIC over strategies. The main problem was not so much one of intention, since KOFIC funded specialist cinema, but as the media reports above indicate, the issue was in the implementation:

> Rarely had (KOFIC) administrators ever worked at the frontline in exhibition, dealing with audiences day-in, day-out, seeing what it is like, and if they had such people, they disregarded their opinions, and they certainly didn't listen to us ... it is the old Korean problem with bureaucracy ... only the official committee members and the KOFIC chair's opinions count. (Anon., December 2020)[29]

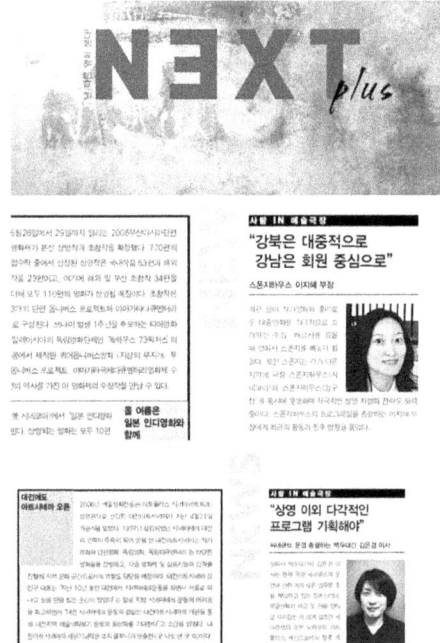

Figure 6.1 Features from early editions of KOFIC's art sector publication *Next Plus* (2 and 3) showing features dedicated to art film exhibitors at the Sponge House and Cinecube (courtesy: KOFIC; *Cine 21*).

In addition to these problems, another issue that impacted KOFIC support of the sector and led directly to the removal of direct subsidies for art houses was a deep-seated ambivalence towards funding exhibition spaces. KOFIC plans and reports indicated unresolved tensions within official attitudes towards art houses. Should officials help produce and distribute specialist films to support the film sector, or should they subsidise exhibition? This ambivalence was evident in the implementation of the 2004 Next Plus proposals. While 2004 *Next Plus* authors acknowledged the contribution of exhibitors and exhibition spaces to the overall experience of art film audiences (Kim et al. 2004: 16), this recognition did not shift attitudes amongst administrators for long, and official thinking turned against the value of the exhibition space in popularising art film. Evidence for this shift in attitudes was apparent in changes to *Next Plus*, KOFIC's fortnightly flagship magazine for their sponsorship of the art sector. The earlier issues all led with features highlighting the work of art film exhibitors entitled '*Saram in Yesulkŭkchang*' (People in art cinema). The first issue featured an interview with Kim Nan-suk (then) at the Dongsung Art Centre (KOFIC 2006), and the second an interview with the general manager of operations and Baekdudaegan representative Kim Ŭn-Yŏng (Chŏng Han-sŏk 2006; see Figure 6.1).[30] These leading articles celebrated the activities of exhibitors, the theatres, the programming strategies and spaces in the audiences' experience and the marketing of art film. However, within two years of the launch of *Next Plus*, KOFIC dropped the features on exhibitors, and the magazine's content focused entirely on the discussion of art film and directors. The 2015 cessation of direct support for art houses in favour of art films was not a sudden reversal of opinion; influential voices within KOFIC felt uncomfortable supporting spaces over films from the outset.

The increasing insecurity felt by art houses in the second half of the decade as a result of KOFIC's shifting attitudes created a need for other support networks. In 2017, fourteen small exhibitors in Seoul and the provinces founded the National Association of Art Houses (Chŏn'guk yesulyŏnghwagwan hyŏphoe, NAAC) to represent their interests in times of adversity. The NAAC joins the Korean Association of Cinematheques (Han'guksinemat'ek'ŭhyŏbŭihoe), a group representing fifteen members countrywide. The NAAC was initially founded to oppose the blacklisting of films deemed subversive by the Park Geun-hye administration. After Park's impeachment and the revelations about the associated scandal, the NAAC defended the interests of smaller theatres in their negotiations with KOFIC and during downturns in the market like the one that impacted the sector in 2020–1 (Kim Kyŏng-ae 2020).

The 2020 global COVID-19 pandemic and renewed support

Despite significant historical differences, the third decade of the new millennium brought closer cooperation between KOFIC administrators and exhibitors from a source that few would have predicted – a global pandemic. In early 2020, Korean cinemas faced their greatest existential threat in a generation. Restrictions imposed by the government designed to prevent the spread of the COVID-19 virus forced the closure of cinema auditoriums nationwide. Korean theatre managers relied on government handouts to survive as box office revenues dried up completely. Even after the government removed the strictest restrictions aimed at combatting the different strains of the virus, theatres were required to cap audience numbers and enforce bans on eating within auditoriums, severely denting incomes (Song 2022). Of course, measures aimed at preventing the spread of the virus didn't just impact art houses. Large multiplex chains also saw their 2020 revenues drop roughly 70 per cent compared to 2019.[31] Many distributors deliberately delayed the release of new films with high-earning potential until the government removed audience-capping measures (Frater 2021). In addition, the market share of Korean films, which had stood at 50 per cent in the pre-pandemic era, dropped to 30 per cent in 2021, the lowest figure in almost three decades. Between late 2021 and early 2022, representatives of Korean cinema, including powerful multiplex firms, warned of potential collapse if the government did not remove restrictive measures and provide financial support to the entire domestic film industry (Song 2022; Frater 2021).[32]

Faced with pressure from influential voices within the industry, KOFIC could easily have cut off support entirely to a small but costly art film sector to divert vital funds to the maintenance of commercial film. However, KOFIC persisted in its subsidy policy for art houses providing evidence it had not given up on the protection of specialist theatres to preserve balance. The reason may lie in the continued pressure KOFIC faced to safeguard diversity. Evidence of this can be seen from a perusal of KOFIC's *Korean Cinema* reports (the official evaluation of the industry's performance) throughout the new millennium's second decade. Scholars, journalists, film fans and politicians continued to warn of the perils of a Korean film industry too weighted toward producing, distributing and exhibiting commercially oriented genre film (see Shim 2011: 222; Lee Sang-yong 2015: 7–8; Paquet 2018: 14). Maintaining balance remained a goal despite the economic challenges posed by the pandemic, and art houses still had an important function within the sector.[33]

KOFIC's 2022 announcement of support attests to the important overall place of art houses within the fabric of South Korean cinema. KOFIC announced sponsorship for twenty-three theatres – two as 'vintage movie cinemas' and the rest as art houses. Theatres were provided with annual subsidies of between $31,000 and $83,000, depending on need. Significantly, the sponsorship report also reveals a greater understanding by KOFIC of the value of cultural spaces to the entire cinematic experience. The authors explain they based their evaluations upon 'the excellence of the programming schedule, the role of the theatre as a local cultural space', and the ability of exhibitors to create 'artistic identities' for theatres (KOFIC 2022a). How can we account for this apparent shift in attitudes towards the value of theatrical space? A clue lies in the report, which states the support aimed to preserve the 'communal culture' brought by the experience of viewing film in art houses, and that was jeopardised by the virus (KOFIC 2022a). Unlike previous threats to art film exhibition, the pandemic's greatest impact was not on film but auditoriums. Films were still being produced, and many were being shown via subscription-based streaming services like Netflix. The COVID-19 pandemic and the measures introduced to combat it pushed the centrality of space to the top of the judges' agenda because it was a cultural space that was under attack.

Conclusion

In the context of a rapidly evolving cinematic environment in which new millennium domestic motion pictures captured 50 per cent of the market, the Waranago Incident highlighted the problem of limited screening opportunities for non-mainstream film. The controversy that arose led to calls from movie fans, journalists, scholars and critics for fundamental changes to how Waranago-type films were exhibited. The one organisation that could facilitate this transformation was KOFIC, which has played a central and fundamental 'caretaker' role within Korean cinema since it has acted as both 'industry regulator and film financier' (Kil 2018; Parc and Messerlin 2021: 231). As part of this process of providing screening opportunities for non-mainstream film, from 2000 onwards, KOFIC introduced the Art Plus and then the Next Plus projects. The plans subsidised exhibition spaces to guarantee screening windows for domestic art movies. They aimed to shape a new diversified cinematic industry. The policy also signalled a change from an emphasis on defending domestic film to maintaining diversity within Korean cinema. KOFIC recognised an important task for art houses in this framework: they could provide access to different types of film, such as art, independent, animation and documentary. Invoking the spirit of 1990s cinephilia that had fuelled the original boom in art film and created the *Sacrifice* Incident, administrators believed that exhibition spaces could help shape a diversified industry. This role for art houses within Korean film represents an important legacy of the cinephilia and rise of the new film viewing spaces in the late and post-dictatorship period.

There were, however, significant problems with KOFIC's plans from the outset. This is unsurprising given the logistical challenges of establishing an ambitious nationwide network of art houses. KOFIC modified some of the more unrealistic prescriptions in the original 2004 plan that hindered the commercial viability of theatres and interfered with programming. The resultant Next Plus network of speciality theatres brought a period in which art houses and art film flourished in South Korea. The success was followed by a decade that strained the sector and the relationship between KOFIC administrators and exhibitors. KOFIC never fully resolved the issue of maintaining sustainable art houses outside the capital. Many officials were ambivalent about subsidising theatrical spaces to support art film, preferring a direct film support system. Media discourses have presented the 2015 policy shift of direct film support and the 2016 revelations about KOFIC complicity in blacklisting exhibitors as an underhand means of re-introducing state intrusion into artistic freedom. These events led to a general deterioration in relations between officials and theatre operators, which appear to have been repaired by the 2020–1 COVID-19 pandemic – a crisis that impacted the entire cinematic industry. It was exhibition that was threatened, since theatrical spaces became subject to continued government restrictions in the battle to prevent virus outbreaks. Despite demands on its finite resources from the rest of the industry, KOFIC's 2022 support for art houses illustrated their commitment to specialist film, and their report also acknowledged the vitality of space to the cinematic experience. This is official recognition of the importance of space to the cinematic experience and bodes well for the future of art house/state relationships.

Notes

1. The discussants included *Please Take Care of my Cat* producer O Ki-min, KOFIC committee member and *The Waikiki Brothers* producer Yi Ŭn, the CEO of Cinema Service (production company) and head of the committee of KOFIC's Film Distribution Improvement Committee (*Cine 21* 2001).
2. See also *Cine 21* editor An Cheong Sook (An Chŏng-suk) (2001: 6–11) who expressed identical concerns to Lee (An 2001: 10).
3. See Park (2015: 104) for more on this discussion.
4. The term *tayangsŏng* dominates KOFIC discussion of the art film sector (see Kim et al. 2004: 15, 18, 61, 118–20, 141–3, 181–97).
5. Often international marriages between Korean men in rural areas and women from the People's Republic of China, Vietnam and the Philippines; see Chung and Diffrient (2015: 220).
6. Sohn (2012: 32) argues that diversity has a double significance for cinephiles as both a 'cultural ideal' and a defence of choice. I think it is the latter significance that KOFIC administrators gave the term.
7. Berry (2002: 7) calls this a 'full service cinema'.
8. For example, the aforementioned influential film academics and journalists like An Chŏng-suk, Kim Young-jin, Sim Yŏng-sŏp, Chŏn Ch'an-il, many of whom frequently contribute to the annual *Korean Cinema* reports.
9. The Korean film industry achieves 'national' goals and promotes Korea's cultural brand abroad by achieving successes at international film festivals (Howard 2008: 96). Howard argues that there is a national imperative associated with the attempts to provide a balance within the industry to support the screening of low-budget films like *Take Care of My Cat*, short films, documentary or animation (Howard 2008: 96). He argues Korean films earmarked for support often have patriotic themes and that programming is not aimed to promote diversity but dedicated to Korean animation while foreign animation is barred from distribution (Howard 2008: 99; Parc 2017: 628).
10. See, for example, Lee Yong-kwan (2000) who feted the re-emergence of New Wave auteurs.
11. For further discussion of the importance of a diversified industry, see Jackson (2022).
12. The Kwangju Theatre was also forced to show re-runs of Korean art films to satisfy the quota and receive subsidies (Kim et al 2004: 44).
13. This is why *Motel Cactus* (Motel Sŏnginjang, 1997, Park Ki-yŏng, ROK), never received official art film status despite being art film in style.
14. We are not privy to the discussions amongst committee members and how they guided one another to formulating decisions on individual films.

15. The committee reversed the decision regarding *A Good Lawyer's Wife* upon appeal (Kim et al. 2004: 37).
16. See Kukkabŏmnyŏngbosent'ŏ (2020) (in Korean; Howard 2008: 96).
17. The 2008 legal revisions governing 'specialist' films provide an extremely truncated summation of the 2004 KOFIC report recommendations including animations, youth, short (*sohyŏng/ tanp'yŏng*) films, and KOFIC-recognised art and independent films (KOFIC 2019: 288; Howard 2008: 96). See Kukkabŏmnyŏngbosent'ŏ (2020).
18. The basis of the 2004 Next Plus criteria for the type of film that could be exhibited at art houses can be found in KOFIC's 2019 standards for recognising independent and art films. Item 1 in the 2004 Next Plus network criteria corresponds to Article 6.1 in the 2019 KOFIC list, while item 7 corresponds to Article 6.3. The 2019 standards included more extensive descriptions of these seven criteria reflecting changes in film which occurred during the intervening fifteen years. For example, KOFIC clarified diversity in cinema as: 'Works that show the lives of individuals, groups, societies and countries rarely screened in Korea, contributing to the continuous exchange and free circulation of ideas and the expansion of cultural diversity' and 'Works of a country with a national market share of less than 1 per cent based on a three-year average prior to deliberation' (KOFIC 2019: 288).
19. The regulations stipulate specialist theatres can screen: 'Movies with a market share of less than 2 per cent' and films will be excluded from specialist status if they receive a wide release (defined as more than 10 per cent of the total screens nationwide; KOFIC 2019: 288).
20. Audience numbers for art houses increased from 220,000 in 2004 to 840,000 in 2010 and to a record of 910,000 in 2011. Seat occupancy in 2011 was 12.9 per cent, down 0.3 per cent from 13.2 per cent in 2010 (KOFIC 2012: 236).
21. Sohn (2012, 2022) argues that indications of these colder ties appeared between 2009 and 2010 when KOFIC tried to replace the managing committee of the Seoul Art Cinema with a new one by holding a public contest (Yi 2010; Sohn 2012: 155). Journalists and art house exhibitors saw this as a blatant attempt by the Lee Myung-bak government at political interference in film exhibition. The idea was that KOFIC would vet applications and exclude all those deemed to be politically antagonistic to the Lee government. Exhibitors boycotted the contest and film fans protested political interference (see Sohn 2012: 152–6).
22. Audience numbers for Korean art films fell from 257,480 in 2010 to 206,372 in 2011, but numbers watching foreign art films rose from 3.19 million to 5.16 million (KOFIC 2012: 240).
23. Yi (2015) claims that cinemas had autonomy over programming, while Howard (2008: 98) argues theatres' choices were regulated by KOFIC.
24. As a concession to the opposition to their proposals, KOFIC agreed to support forty-eight films, which meant more art house support (Yi 2015).
25. Its current website features open discussion of the scandal (KOFIC 2022b).
26. Evidence of this can be seen in KOFIC's announcement that it was considering withdrawing from film financing entirely (Kil 2018).
27. The original report called for forty art houses by 2007, the Next Plus report revised the figure up.

28. KOFIC's target of the mass spread of cinemas dedicated to niche markets is at odds with the notion of the function of a specialist cinema. Hanson argues specialist films enjoy 'limited releases' targeted at 'niche markets', because of their appeal (Hanson 2007: 183).
29. Other exhibitors informed me they didn't apply to receive KOFIC support because of the paperwork they would have taken on to justify their spending (Anon., April 2022).
30. See for example editions one through to ten and compare with editions from number fifty onwards and which are available on KOFIC's website.
31. See Statisa (2021).
32. During the 2020 COVID-19 pandemic, the NAAC supported independent art houses, particularly outside Seoul, where the cultural infrastructure is less developed (Sŏ 2020). In 2020, the NAAC launched a Save Our Cinema campaign mobilising film and television stars to campaign for the survival of art houses (Sŏ 2020). Stars who joined the campaign included Ch'oe Hŭi-sŏ. It is also significant that KOFIC supported the Save our Cinema campaign, a testament to the organisation's recognition of the role of art houses in the industry and perhaps a positive sign for future cooperation between administrators and exhibitors. KOFIC supported the project by heavily subsidising the prices of admissions (author interview with Kim Sŏng-uk, April 2022).
33. KOFIC's subsidies were not able to protect all theatres during the pandemic (Sŏ 2020). One example is the Taegu Dongsung Art Hall, which between 2020 and 2021 survived on an annual support package of US$50,000, with $41,000 directly sent by KOFIC and the rest from Taegu municipal authorities (Park 2021). Yun Sang-jin*, the chief programmer for the Taegu Dongsung Art Hall, pointed out that even with this support the theatre struggled. Before the pandemic, the theatre would sell around a hundred tickets a day, but after the removal of lockdown restrictions they only saw a daily average of twenty customers. An additional challenge faced by the theatre was space. When the Taegu Dongsung Art Hall building owners decided to turn the auditorium over to other uses at the end of December 2021, the theatre's owners found themselves homeless (Kwŏn 2021). The local authority was unwilling to intervene to help the art house survive. While some municipalities had bought buildings for independent art houses to use or rented them space, Taegu prioritised auditoriums for high-prestige cultural or international events like the performing arts or opera (personal correspondence, December 2021). Regional governments had more important priorities than catering for local audience tastes and overlooked art houses.

Chapter 7

Maintaining art houses in the new millennium

In a 2014 article entitled 'The Reason for the Revolt of the Small Cinemas', the *Han'guk Kyŏngje Maegŏjin* (Magazine of the Korean economy) reported an upsurge in the number of customers attending art film theatres. The article stated that when 83.5 per cent of all cinemas in Korea were multiplexes, small independent movie theatres – especially those catering to art film – enjoyed a 'dramatic' resurgence (Yi Hyŏn-ju 2014). The article focused on the performance of the Cinecube – a theatre that Lee Kwang-mo had established but which was under new management.[1] Despite the change, Cinecube audiences were on the rise – increasing by 40 per cent in 2011 and then by 18 per cent in 2012, eventually achieving annual attendances of around 260,000, recalling the pioneering days of the 1990s Dongsung Cinematheque (Yi Hyŏn-ju 2014). Fast forward six years to May 2020, an article in the *Han'gyŏrye* newspaper entitled 'Please Save us … A Dying Independent Art house' reported on a new campaign to save art houses threatened with bankruptcy. The article dealt with the thirty-five-seater DRFA (Digital Remastering Film Archive) 365 art house run by film director and screenwriter Jonathan Yu on the small island of Tonggŏmdo, close to Inch'ŏn.[2] The cinema flourished after opening in 2016, but the 2020 state-enforced closure of cinemas to stop the spread of COVID-19 threatened its continued existence (Sŏ 2020).

These two articles are valuable points of departure for this final chapter because they illustrate that despite the increased availability of art film via the Internet and multiplex art chains, independent art houses have continued to generate media attention and form a small but vital part of South Korean cinema. The art exhibition sector is sustained by regular customers. However, it is also subject to fluctuations in interest, which can lead to periods of boom and bust, making the sector susceptible to changes in the cinematic environment. The articles invoke the memory of Baekdudaegan's Dongsung Cinematheque, revealing a persistent feature characterising much media reflection about art houses – nostalgia.

Discussion of contemporary Korean art film exhibition is frequently framed by a reference to the cinephilia boom that helped produce it in the first place. It is as if this grounding provides art houses with solidity in their historical foundations they cannot find in the economic sphere.

This chapter investigates two legacies of the late and post-dictatorship cinephilia and art film boom: first, the physical presence of independent art houses in the cinematic landscape; and second, the memorialisation of the *fin-de-siècle* cinephilia in historical and media narratives. I examine the contemporary nature of Korean art film viewing, focusing on audiences and their motivations for attending art houses during the first two decades of the new millennium. I investigate how exhibitors draw spectators during a period when theatrical exhibition faces greater competition from online viewing. Economic insecurity during the late 1990s and the early 2000s led to the loss of cinemas like the Core Art Hall and Hypertheque Nada (see Table 7.1). However, surviving theatres such as the Seoul Art Cinema, Art House Momo and the DRFA 365 maintain their clientele by continuing the practices of pioneering videotheques and art houses and by creating critical links to the earlier period of Korean cinephilia. I examine media reports, the marketing presentation of exhibitors and the opinions and memories of audiences to account for the sustainability of contemporary art houses.[3] I conclude by considering a final legacy of the 1980s–90s cinephilia boom: its presence in critical and academic memory. I analyse current reflections on the value and meaning of the 1990s cinephilia boom and its function in an ongoing discussion about diversity and balance in the Korean film industry.

Attracting art house audiences in a transformed cinematic environment

In most respects, the demographic of the average art house patron did not shift significantly between the late 1990s and 2020. A 2003 KOFIC survey reported that 64 per cent of art film audiences were young women from middle-class backgrounds with significant disposable income to spend on leisure activities,[4] and we see similar patterns of art house attendance in 2020 in both the capital and provinces (Kim et al. 2004: 76). Nowadays, the average art film spectator is a female white-collar worker with an above-average salary.[5] Many are educators in tertiary or secondary education or homemakers with disposable income. One noticeable change is a rise in the average age of the audiences between the

1980s and 2020. Before 1994, the average age was twenty-seven, whereas my 2020 survey found that the typical audience member was in their mid-to-late thirties.[6] Overall, exhibitors reported older, more loyal and mainly female patrons at their theatres.[7]

This older clientele continues to attend art houses in a changed cinematic context. Virtually all the film magazines which promoted art film, publicised art houses and served as a nexus for the emergent cinephile community in South Korea have disappeared. *Kino* closed in 2003, *Film 2.0* in 2008, while *Road Show*, the Korean *Premiere and Screen* all ceased production in 2011. *Movie Week* shut in 2013, and only *Cine 21* still exists (Kang 2013). Declining advertising revenues and readerships due to a preference for film-dedicated Internet portals killed the printed magazines, and their demise negatively impacted the art film sector. Independent art house exhibitors with a limited marketing budget lost important media allies like *Kino*, which championed art house screenings, festivals and events through their special print features. Andrew Tudor argues that the 1990s disappearance of the print review by professional film critics represented the loss of a crucial 'institution of consecration' for art films and the theatres that showed them (2006: 135).[8] This was true of the demise of Korean film print media since the online transition of critics led to an undermining of criticism and art house attendances declined (Hwang 2017: 87).

Another change came in the 2000s, with the increased availability of art film via the Internet and new exhibition platforms. South Korea developed its broadband Internet technology faster than elsewhere in East Asia, and rapid download speeds made online piracy a particular problem (Paquet 2009: 110). In addition to piracy, over-the-top (OTT) media service platforms like Netflix have allowed viewers to stream movies directly into their laptops or digital television sets. The increased popularity of OTT delivered through an efficient broadband system enabling viewers to rapidly download films has resulted in the greater accessibility of art films (Hwang 2017: 87); furthermore, with the advent of OTT, movies could be viewed anywhere – at home, at work, in transit via mobile phones, laptops or PCs. In the 2020s, many of the locations of sociality began to move from public spaces like auditoriums and foyers to the more private online domains of social media. Socialising, mingling and exchanging film information happens online, instead of face to face as in the past. Overall, this is what Shane Denson and Julia Leyda (2016: 1–4) argue has become a 'post-cinema' environment, in which new 'interactive, networked, miniaturised mobile, social . . . convergent'

Table 7.1 Art houses included in Chapter 7

Theatre	Location (# indicates outside Seoul)	Years
Art House Momo	Ewha Women's University	2008– (Baekdudaegan)
Cinecode Sonjae	Chongno (Sogyŏkdong)	2008–15
Cinecube	Kwanghwamun	2000–10 (Baekdudaegan) 2011– (Taekwang Media)
Cinehouse	Kangnam (Nonhyŏndong)	1987–2002
Cinematheque KOFA (Korean Film Archives)	Mapo	2008–
Core Art Hall	Chongo	1989–2004
Dongsung Cinematheque	Hyehwadong	1995–2003 1995–7 (run by Baekdudaegan)
DRFA 365	Tonggŏmdo, Inch'ŏn #	2016–
Hypertheque Nada	Hyehwadong	2000–22
Lumiere	Kangnam (Nonhyŏngdong)	1992–2008
Seoul Art Cinema	Chongno, Kwanghwamun	2002–
Taegu Dongsung Art Hall	Taegu (North Kyŏngsang Province) #	2004–21
Tûsup Art Cinema	Nowŏndong	2016–

Source: Hwang 2017: 5–7; KOFIC 2012.

digital networks exist alongside multiplexes and provide radically altered conditions of viewing in terms of the rapidity of access to a diversity of film. Given the challenges of this changing media environment and art film's easier availability, art houses require specific programming and spatial strategies to retain this audience.

Exclusivity of experience

Art houses have held onto regular customers in an era of online film availability by creating distinctive programmes of films unavailable elsewhere. The Seoul Art Cinema exemplifies this strategy, showing a mixture of recent international and domestic features, festival films, and retrospectives. Over one month (December 2021) for example, the Seoul Art Cinema showed sixteen films, of which four were new Korean releases shown at international film festivals, while the rest were international titles from Japan (six), Taiwan (four) and one each from France, Sweden, US, Australia and Spain. The programme included a season of Ozu Yasujirō pictures and another dedicated to 1980s and 1990s Taiwanese cinema. New releases were shown along with older pictures dealing with similar themes; so, *Coming to You* (Nŏegye kanŭn kil, 2021, Byun Gyu-ri, ROK), a documentary covering LGBTQ issues in South Korea, was shown alongside a film that pioneered the discussion of homosexuality in post-Franco Spain: *A Man called Autumn Flower* (Un hombre llamado flor de otoño, 1978, Pedro Olea, Spain). The cinema stimulated event-like interest amongst fans by linking LGBTQ films, organising the Ozu and Taiwanese film seasons, and creating original combinations of films that could only be seen on the big screen at that time.[9] The Hypertheque Nada pioneered the exclusive experience approach used by the Seoul Art Cinema in the early 2000s when they screened 'movies that multiplexes wouldn't show' (author interview with Kim Nan-suk, May 2020). The Hypertheque Nada specialised in Japanese art films such as Takeshi Kitano's *Kids Return* (1996, Japan) when they were still relatively rare in Korea (Kim et al. 2004: 56; author interview with Kim Nan-suk, May 2020). The DRFA 365 shows a mixture of rare 1960s and 1970s classics and more recent European art films.[10] Yu deliberately seeks out films that have either never been released, are challenging to locate on streaming services, or have been overlooked by critics and cinema audiences (personal correspondence, Jonathan Yu, September 2020).[11]

According to Yu, the death of serious film magazines has left a gap in the market, which he has attempted to fill with his programming. Many of Yu's regular mature clientele have less faith in the plethora of information on the Internet. Classic films hold a particular challenge for curators like Yu because of what Peter Bosma describes as the necessity to 'bridge the gap of undervaluation caused by prejudices'. They often require more interpretative effort because the quality is not 'immediately obvious and recognizable' (Bosma 2015: 94). Yu said he felt it was his function to choose classic foreign films and help situate them for audiences to facilitate appreciation. In an era when the print critic is dead, he has taken on the role of expert and appeals to an older clientele that once relied on print media for recommendations.

Not only does Yu market classic films, but his marketing strategies also stress the superior experience offered by his screenings. According to Yu, the primary reason for the poor reception of classic foreign films in Korea, especially amongst downloadable movies on the Internet, is the poor level of the translated subtitles. 'No Korean institution educates movie translators, and most decent translators today focus on Marvel and blockbuster films. The current infrastructure is too weak to provide the accuracy of translation art films require' (personal correspondence, Jonathan Yu, September 2020). Hence, Yu arranges for high-quality translations of all the classic foreign films exhibited at the DRFA 365. In his curation of classics with improved subtitling, Yu offers an experience unavailable in other cinemas or on the Internet. As a result, the DRFA 365 and the Seoul Art Cinema, like the Hypertheque Nada in the early 2000s, have succeeded in drawing regular customers by providing a distinct viewing experience.

It is not only through programming that exhibitors create a sense of exclusivity. Most art houses continue to offer the kind of pre- and post-screening educational activities pioneered in the videotheques to incentivise membership and encourage audiences to attend theatres instead of consuming film online. The Art House Momo Film School offers audiences information sessions on movies (Baekdudaegan 2016). The DRFA 365 includes a screenwriting school for members interested in scenario creation. The Seoul Art Cinema features regular masterclasses

Figure 7.1 Ticket to screening of *Green Fish* and post-film talk with Lee Chang-dong (author's image).

with prominent Korean filmmakers like Lee Chang-dong discussing their works (Figure 7.1). The educational and cultural activities help intellectualise and consecrate the cinema's film programme as highbrow. The Art House Momo and Seoul Art Cinema also promote their function as institutions of cinematic restoration. Baekdudaegan (2016) advertising stresses its goal to exhibit film and build a collection of 1000 classics of world cinema. As of 2016, Art House Momo had acquired 170 of these films, which are regularly exchanged with festival organisations. Thus, one clear strategy of art houses is the promotion of their position within broader systems of cinematic exchange and understanding. Educational engagement of audiences is central to the art house mission, and each theatre offers subtly distinct experiences.

Theatres carefully promote their geographical location as part of the totality of the experiences they offer. For example, the DRFA 365's marketing stresses its coastal location on a rural island, so 'after watching a movie, people walk along the seafront outside the theatre to talk about the film they saw' (Sŏ 2020; Figure 7.2). The advertising positions the theatre as a place of reflection and enlightenment rather than diversion.

Figure 7.2 Location of DRFA 365 (courtesy Jonathan Yu, author's image).

The physical location of the Art House Momo also features heavily in the publicity materials promoting the theatre. Pamphlets claim the cinema was the first movie theatre located on a university campus – at Ewha Women's University (Baekdudaegan 2016; Figure 7.3). This strategic siting helps validate the numerous educational activities at the theatre. The location also directly links the cinema to academic institutions that have historically played an essential role in consecrating film as art (Baumann 2007: 66–9). Ewha was home to pioneering film clubs like Kaidu, and this university link also provides the Art House Momo with additional cultural capital thanks to the historical role of colleges and their students in developing Korean democracy.[12] The theatre's promotional materials claim ties to the university while distancing the Art House Momo from sponsorship by the KB (Kungmin ŭnhaeng) Bank (the theatre is also called the 'Ewha KB Cinema'). The deliberate disassociation of Baekdudaegan from KB Bank sponsorship is a disavowal of commercial interests. The Art House Momo's location on the Ewha campus provides symbolic capital to a cinema trying to acquire the host institution's academic and cultural values and political associations.

In addition to geographical location, theatres also present their internal space as a vital part of the cinematic experience. Art houses have developed their theatres with restaurants and cafes, but also facilities with cinematic

Figure 7.3 The Ewha Women's University campus centre in which the Art House Momo is housed (courtesy Lee Kwang-mo).

themes that encourage cultural consumption.[13] The Seoul Art Cinema has cinema-related books on directors such as Derek Jarman available in the lobby for customers to browse (see Figure 7.4). Cinecube's head of marketing argues that this strategy encourages customer engagement in the spaces adjacent to the movie itself: 'staying in the space makes it feel as if you are participating in art' (Yi Hyŏn-ju 2014). The siting of restaurants and other amenities in cinemas is also a pragmatic business strategy for cinemas that cannot survive from ticket sales alone. The DRFA 365 offers lunch, coffee and screenings in one package. The Tŭsup cinema is a multi-use art space (*pokhapmunhwasisŏl*) consisting of two film auditoriums, a cafe/bar, art gallery, live music venue, study spaces, library and bookshop.[14]

Theatres create and market cultural activities to provide their customers with what Baekdudaegan claims is a 'new lifestyle through film' (Paek 2009). Art houses have historically used the same strategies to generate a sense of intimacy between viewers. Even today, current cinemas create a clublike environment for patrons and promote a feeling of cultural exclusivity by serving food and drinks perceived as exotic or tasteful.[15] Exhibitors subtly appeal to customers' sense of status, taste and prestige

Figure 7.4 Film books and posters in the Seoul Art Cinema foyer (author's image).

to promote themselves. In the Korea of the new millennium, art houses market sophistication through art or education-related activities and consumption of food and space, rather than the promise of excitement, thrills and action offered by multiplex hoardings.¹⁶

Other theatres have also involved viewers more vigorously by involving them in designing the space itself. The Hypertheque Nada created a slogan when it opened – 'By me, for me, my only cinema' (*Nae ŭihan, narŭl wihan, namanŭi kŭkchang*) – to make audiences feel personally linked to the site. The theatre allowed audiences to select the lineup for a festival of their favourite films (Kim Yŏng-ch'ang 2001). They introduced an annual competition where viewers voted to name seats in the auditorium after cultural icons. Following the historic 2000 summit between Seoul and Pyongyang, the cinema had seats named after South and North Korean leaders Kim Dae Jung, and Kim Jong Il arranged next to one another (Paek 2011). The theatre challenged traditional hierarchies of spatial design by inviting audience investment into it. One final point is worth mentioning about the creation of internal spaces. In the mid-1990s, art house managers often rented or adapted spaces not specifically constructed for film exhibition. From the 2000s onwards, theatres have often had more autonomy and customised interiors to suit the needs of their audiences (Hwang 2017: 83). Internal space design is another way in which cinemas have appealed to the lifestyles of audiences and made a unique cinematic experience for their regulars.

Establishing historical and temporal links

Art houses reach an increasingly older clientele by establishing associations with their past and appealing to a sense of nostalgia for an earlier and 'better' age of cinematic production and consumption. Baekdudaegan's publicity materials deliberately accentuate their extensive history and tradition of educational instruction dating back to their control of the Dongsung Cinematheque (Baekdudaegan 2016). The Art House Momo's motto is: 'To a Place stranger than paradise … ' referencing the Jim Jarmusch movie that opened the Dongsung Cinematheque (Figure 7.5). The Seoul Art Cinema's publicity materials stress the theatre's lineage back to the longest-lived and most prominent of the videotheques from which it developed, the Munhwahakkyo Seoul. The Taegu Dongsung Art Hall's name refers directly to Lee Kwang-mo's pioneering 1995 cinema.

Figure 7.5 The Art House Momo box office (courtesy Lee Kwang-mo).

Over the years, many art houses have competed with multiplexes, online viewing and each other by offering a more authentic link to the cinematic past. They highlight these connections through their educational activities or associations with pioneering art film exhibitors. The establishment of these links to specific cultural moments in time also indicates that art houses recognise the importance of nostalgic consumption for audiences. This explains the loyalty of older audiences and why regulars of the Art House Momo are former customers of Baekdudaegan-run cinemas like the Cinecube and the Dongsung Cinematheque (personal correspondence, Lee Kwang-mo, December 2020).

Other cinemas, which do not stress their connections to post-dictatorship Korean cinephilia, express links back to a superior cinematic past in alternative ways. Jonathan Yu reported in 2020 that the DRFA 365 primarily drew people in their forties who were passionate about older art films (Sŏ 2020). Hence, the current marketing of the DRFA 365 celebrates movies from classic 1960s periods of European cinema. These films are shown alongside more recent award-winning motion pictures and classical music concerts to increase the programme's cultural value.[17] The cinema's marketing links its activities and programming to a shared past, invoking that history to situate the cinema's ethos and attract audiences from a specific demographic group. Art houses appeal

Figure 7.6 Film posters in the hallway of the Seoul Art Cinema (author's image).

to audience nostalgia that suggests an authenticity of experience and also captures the spirit of cultural renewal, which enlivened past cycles of film consumption (Figure 7.6). This is the same nostalgia that Susan Sontag appealed to in her epiphany for European and western film; the difference here in the case of current-day Korean art houses is that most employ references to a national cinematic past.

Many Korean independent art houses successfully draw a regular clientele through programming, the effective use of space, educational activities and their use of nostalgia as a marketing tool. However, from the early 2000s on, multiplex specialist theatres have been using many of the same strategies to expand their profiles in the art film sector.

Creating art house spaces in multiplexes

In 2004, CGV opened the Indy Film Theatre (Indiyŏnghwagwan) in three locations around the capital. In 2007, CGV then created a new brand of cinemas called Movie Collage (*Mubi kkollajyu*) devoted to screening 'diversity' films or those movies that stressed the 'complexities of life rather than the light entertainment of commercial film' (Son Chin-a 2014). By 2008, Lotte had opened an auditorium dedicated to art film in Ilsan, a satellite town of Seoul (KOFIC 2012: 237–9), and in 2014, CGV expanded its operations through its new brand CGV Art House (Son Chin-a 2014). Jane Harbord (2002: 9) calls the art house and multiplex the most polarised of cinema's contemporary institutions and film cultures, yet she also contends that '(m)utual influence and cross-referencing, co-existence and appropriation subvert any definitive sense of boundary' between them (Harbord 2002: 39). We see a similar phenomenon in the growth of the relationship between Korean art houses and multiplex cinemas. From 2004 onwards, multiplex companies like CGV attempted to create distinctive institutional identities for their theatres using the strategies of independent art houses. In 2011, Movie Collage launched an audience curator programme and developed a radio show providing commentary on films and dedicated to the discussion of 'serious' movies (Son Chin-a 2014). In 2013, CGV Art House devised an on-demand theatrical system that involved audiences in creating the screening schedule. The firm surveyed theatregoers about which films they would like to see and screened the selected movie a fortnight later (Chi 2015). In introducing such innovations, the multiplex-run specialist art houses have narrowed the gap with independent theatres and attracted their audiences.[18] They were also creating identifiably distinct theatrical experiences for customers to lure them away from online movie viewing.

The creation of separate formal spaces in multiplexes like the Indy Film Theatre, Movie Collage, or CGV Art House has increased pressure on independent art houses. Between 2002 and 2005, independent cinemas made up 100 per cent of the officially recognised theatres specialising in art film. By 2009 there were equal numbers of independent and multiplex screens, and by the 2020s, the number of multiplex screens devoted to art film exceeded the number of independent cinema screens (KOFIC 2012: 237). Multiplex art film exhibitors realise that the way to attract repeat customers is to use the strategy of independent art houses and create an identifiable and distinct institutional identity through programming, activities, the physical space of exhibition and promotional materials.[19] This is how art film exhibitors see their role and have marketed themselves. But, to what extent do the exhibitors' opinions align with those of the art house users themselves, and what does this consumption tell us about the character of contemporary art film exhibition?

Consuming art houses

What is clear from my 2020 survey responses is that art house regulars are loyal to a specific venue's capacity to provide a cultural experience unavailable elsewhere. Virtually all regulars recall their initial experience of attending art houses as a kind of epiphany – so different was it from what was provided in other theatres. 'I was shocked when I went to an art house for the first time; I didn't know cinema could be like that', claims one regular of the Hypertheque Nada between 2004 and 2011. For this reason, most respondents associate their initial visit to a theatre with a director or the name of the film they saw at that time: one user was drawn to the Core Art Hall by Wim Wenders's *Wings of Desire*. Regulars often remember who they went with as well as the film that first drew them. These memories and associations are so clearly recalled because they were moments of change, and conversion, after which first-timers became avid attendees.

Regular art house attendees also indicate that geographical location and the internal physical layout and amenities add to their sense of an exclusive cinematic experience (Figure 7.7). The symbolic associations of the theatres' geographical position are vitally important for the new millennium regulars of the Hypertheque Nada. Taehangno's links to traditional theatrical performances and dance helped consecrate the cinema as a location for artistic consumption.[20] Former Hypertheque Nada patrons describe their attraction to the 'unrivalled charm of the space'.[21] One fan recalled a 2010 visit:

> The film (the documentary *El Sistema* (Maria Stodtmeier, Paul Smaczny, 2009, Germany) was boring, and from what I remember, the other people who accompanied me fell asleep during the film. What stood out most was the appearance of the place; when they opened up the curtains, the light just came in, and we could see the kimchi pots outside. It was really beautiful. Art film fans saw it as an oasis. (Extreme Movie 2015)

Other users of art film cinemas put their attendance down to the cinematic environment rather than the movies shown. Journalist Sŏng Ji-yŏn wrote in 2015 of her disappointment with the closure of the Cinecode Sonjae cinema, recalling that she saw the theatre as

> a haven, and as time went on, I got used to it being my place of refuge. Some films I saw were so strange I thought: 'what the hell was that about?' and some were so boring I dozed off. But I remember some came close to being the best I've ever seen. Cinecode Sonjae was the best classroom to comfort and teach me about different kinds of films from around the world.

For fans who have come of age since the 2000s, art houses serve a variety of functions: as a 'classroom', 'refuge', 'haven', 'oasis', but what comes across consistently in their responses is that they often enjoy the actual space and the facilities within it as much if not more than the specific films.

The sociality of cinematic experience is a standout recollection of art house regulars since the 1990s. In particular, audiences note the principal differences in viewing culture in art houses compared with other cinemas.[22] One Cinecube viewer (2019–20: 22)[23] notes: 'Unlike noisy commercial movie theatres, I like the museum-like silence.' Another client of the Hypertheque Nada (2005–9: 29) recalls: 'It was a *punwigi* (atmosphere) created by cinema-loving audiences; for example, we stayed in our seats until the end of the movie credits, which were accepted as part of the movie.'

Punwigi is a word that frequently features in the recollections of art house attendees. This silent and reverent viewing quality is a defining characteristic of the art house social site and one which generates a shift in emphasis in the viewing experience, as one Cinecube customer (2010–20: 60) reveals:

Figure 7.7 The Cinecube auditorium (courtesy Lee Kwang-mo).

> It was an atmosphere in which you could focus on the movie and not on the other people around you. We developed a sense of connection with the film . . . we felt immersed in art film (. . .) Only those who have experienced it can understand it.

Not only does the silent, serious and studious mood result in a transformed view of the film, but it also encourages greater respect for fellow-audience members, as one Hypertheque Nada (2004–11: 29) attendee recalls:

> there was a culture of appreciation for the producers. I liked the quiet and unique space and the atmosphere of the audience . . . It was a refreshing and pleasant shock. I felt a sense of respect for both the filmmaker and the audience.

Over the past two decades, the dedicated manner in which the audience views pictures has been a consistent attraction for art house attendees (in addition to the actual films). In his exploration of cinema spectatorship, Julian Hanich (2014) distinguishes between different viewing modes in auditoriums. Central to his argument are notions of 'we-intention', 'joint attention', and 'joint action' (Hanich 2014: 344). Hanich argues that cinema audiences generally share a common goal – a 'we-intention' to view film jointly rather than alone. The joint attention of cinema viewers refers to their shared goal of focusing on the movie. 'Joint action' is the ability of individual spectators to attune their behaviour to other viewers and their focus on the film (Hanich 2014: 346–8). We see an intense 'we intention', 'joint attention' and 'joint action' amongst Korean art house audiences. The focused concentration of spectators heightens solidarity. The net result of a combination of an aligned we-intention and joint action is a collective sense of camaraderie and unity amongst audiences shaped by this experience within the auditorium space.[24] Viewers willingly embrace the ascetic viewing culture which Lee Kwang-mo established at the Dongsung Cinematheque in the mid-1990s, defined by films that played until the final credit, the absence of snacks, advertising trailers, mobile phones and distracting chatter. Another result of this disciplined audience behaviour in the auditorium is a sense of mutual respect. During performances, audiences respect the film and each other, a vital part of social consumption. Viewers have to consume in a group to have their reverent consumption acknowledged. Dudley Andrew (2002 [1986], 18) has observed that cinephilia's ritualistic, communal aspects resemble churchgoing practices, and his observation is apt, considering many art house users describe their initial experience as a kind of awakening. The epiphany for most viewers is the culture that shapes audiences' behaviour and stands in contrast to spectator engagement at other cinemas. Overall, far more than the films themselves, the audiences, without exception, recall what drew them and continues to draw them to art houses is the specific atmosphere created within the exhibition sites. In particular, audiences value viewing habits and routinised spectatorship structures, which encourage a sense of solidarity.

A lifestyle of opposition

Another constant and ongoing feature of late and post-dictatorship cinephilia is the sense of opposition imbued in audiences' consumption of cinema. When asked about the value of art houses and why they go to them, many users revealed a vague opposition to what they perceive as mainstream commercial film culture. Art house survey respondents have a definite awareness of their transformed auditorium experience compared to an inferior one they believe is found in other cinemas. If this other space is identified, it is called an 'ordinary' (*ilban*) or 'largescale' (*taehyŏng*) movie theatre – where audiences engage in more distracting practices and less focused viewing.[25] Cinecube regulars reported in 2014 that all parts of their experience – the programming, space and cultural activity – were unlike what multiplexes offered (Yi Hyŏn-ju 2014). For journalist and Cinecode Sonjae attendee Sŏng Ji-yŏn, the opposition arises from the type of films cinemas show. While 'heavyweight' Hollywood-style blockbusters dominate mainstream commercial box offices, the Cinecode Sonjae offered her 'refreshing' cinematic experiences. The motion pictures represented by mainstream cinemas were predictable, while art film cinema provided novelty (Sŏng Ji-yŏn 2015). All art house users define art cinemas as signifying everything other theatres do not.

In newspaper reports marking the closure of art houses, this sense of opposition to multiplexes often becomes more pronounced (see Nam 2011). Throughout the early 2000s, an increasing number of art houses went out of business due to a combination of crippling rental costs and lower audience numbers. The Core Art Hall ceased operations in 2004 when the building's owners decided the theatre could only cope with the rental expenditures by moving out of film exhibition (Yi 2004). The Lumiere had operated continuously since 1992 in the expensive district of Kangnam and closed in 2008 (Chŏng Yu-mi 2008). The Chongno-based

Cinecode Sonje shut in 2015 with large debts (Yonhap 2015). Perhaps the most notable theatre to stop operating during this period was the Hypertheque Nada. This art house had been the first to receive KOFIC support under the Art Plus cinema network policy in 2002 (KOFIC 2012: 236), but dramatic falls in sales left the cinema dangerously exposed financially. The cinema had once boasted 10,000 regular paid-up members, but this had dropped to just 300 by 2011 (Paek 2011).[26] The cinema's attempts to create revenue through its restaurant did not stave off the inevitable closure, and it ceased trading in July 2011.

The disappearance of the Hypertheque Nada provoked profound media criticisms of multiplexes. A *Kyŏnghyang Sinmun* article from 2011 provides us with an account of the cinema's final post-screening discussion between fans, film critic Chŏng Sŏng-il and theatre manager Kim Nan-suk about what had gone wrong, who was to blame, and what was lost. Even though a prime reason for the closure of many independents had been higher rental costs and competition from online viewing, Chŏng Sŏng-il used the occasion to attack multiplexes. Chŏng argued that the shutting of the Hypertheque Nada and other independent art houses made the cinematic culture of Korea far more anonymous and uninspiring: 'each (Seoul art house) had its own distinct, characteristic atmosphere. Multiplexes have turned that atmosphere into a wasteland' (cited in Paek 2011). Like other art house users, Chŏng invoked the notion of 'opposition' – but this time in far more militant terms. Chŏng asserted art houses were engaged in a mortal cultural war against mainstream cinema represented by multiplexes: '(The Hypertheque) Nada was a line of defence. If one line of defence breaks, the line will be pushed further inward' (Paek 2011). For critics like Chŏng, consumption at art houses is more than just seeing a film: it is a statement of political affiliation and a symbolic act of resistance against the mainstream culture represented by multiplexes. For many like Chŏng, there appear to be two distinct sides involved in a Manichean struggle, with no room for compromise. At the discussion, Chŏng claimed he felt great camaraderie with those he thought were on the same side – other art film theatre users, stating: 'I met many movie comrades (*yŏnghwa tongji*) at the Hypertheque Nada, but I never considered those I watched movies with at Megabox and CGV to be my comrades' (Paek 2011). This sense of camaraderie among like-minded people was a defining characteristic of cinephiles during the mid-to-late 1990s. Just as film magazines like *Kino* helped created a community of cinephiles (Hong 2018), Chŏng Sŏng-il sensed a similar bond with other spectators at the Hypertheque Nada. The theatre was a centre, a focal point for a community of people united in their difference from users of mainstream cinemas.

It is curious, then that despite the depth of feeling about the central place of this cinematic culture, these sentiments did not always translate into action. One film fan attending the Hypertheque Nada's final screening exclaimed: 'Although I'm a member, I didn't come that often. However, every time I passed the cinema, I thought "that's my cinema," and now, because it's shutting, I think I'm going to start crying' (Paek 2011). Theatres like the Hypertheque and the Cinecode Sonjae closed their doors at least partly because of declining sales, but the closures reveal a paradox, namely why fans stopped coming when the cinema was such an essential factor of self-identification.

Media reports as well as my survey results indicate that many of those who attended art house did so because they regarded them to be both different and better than cinematic experiences offered elsewhere. Other art house customers also considered their cinematic consumption as indicative of their own cultural identity. One Core Art Hall client (2000–4: 55) indicated that his art house attendance made him feel 'internally superior'. Of course, he would need another film culture to feel superior to, distinct from and socially elevated above. Art house regulars have a clear notion of what constitutes this other space but seldom articulate or identify it. Jane Harbord summarises this feature of art houses succinctly:

> art house cinema functions through a notion of independence, implicit to its identity is that which it is independent of. Thus, inscribed in its own programme is the dialectic of mainstream, monopolised filmic culture and a tradition separate from and acting against its definition of film. This dialectic suggests that the mainstream is homogeneous, coherent and consistent in its production of a film culture. (Harbord 2002: 44)

Couched within this notion of an 'independent art house' sector are the aesthetic and inherent political affinities. This is especially true of an art house 'system of distribution characterised by its independence from mass cultural dissemination' and therefore nominally opposed to capitalist monopolistic practices (Harbord 2002: 43). Art house clientele like Chŏng Sŏng-il have a strong sense of what they support and dislike. What is curious is that Chŏng made his statements when the distinction between the multiplex and independent art house was breaking down, thanks to the creation of spaces like CGV Art House. Yet he connected his perception of difference to his cultural identity, thus accounting for his loyalty to art houses.

Roughly a quarter of my survey respondents reported enjoying art films in specialist multiplex theatres like CGV Art House.[27] At the same time, several of them shared the same kind of hostility towards multiplexes that Chŏng expressed. My respondents largely blamed the loss of independent art on the popularity of CGV, Lotte and Megabox theatres. This raises the question of why some viewers attend multiplexes, despite their animosity towards them. Some claimed they attended multiplex-run art cinemas out of convenience because there were no independent art houses nearby. However, viewers reported enjoying the same communal viewing atmosphere at CGV Art House as at independent cinemas. Thus, the attraction of social cinematic consumption is a vital draw of art film fans to theatres, whether they are multiplex chain theatres or independent.

Implications of sociality and spaces for audiences

What is clear from the above discussion is that internal and external spaces have always been vital to the cinematic experience for many art house audiences since the theatre represented more than an auditorium and screen. Art houses are places to be immersed in film and film spectatorship culture. Exhibitors in the new millennium have understood the importance of spatial aspects to the audience experience, and they have adapted their activities and exhibition sites to facilitate the intense consumption of cinemagoers. However, evidence of the popularity of art houses amongst exhibitors and audiences contradicts one principle central to KOFIC policy until the COVID-19 pandemic: namely, that art house consumers privileged programming over the venue (see the previous chapter). One consistent finding of media and survey investigations into the popularity of independent art houses is that success is not determined by programming alone. The choice of films first brought audiences to cinemas, but spatial experiences have kept them returning. The fans value the differences, and the exhibitors also understand the importance of each theatre's individual personality to cinemagoers.[28]

In the light of the specific manner of cinematic consumption, one final point should be made about how current art house users themselves recognise their chosen pastime activity and its place within the cultural fabric of Korea. With their opposition to other forms of cinemagoing, their solidarity with fellow spectators and intense auditorium experience, current art house users resemble a subculture. In his analysis of 1970s British youth fashions, Dick Hebdige argues that subcultures are 'cultures of conspicuous consumption', in which members perform 'distinctive rituals of consumption' to reveal their specific identity and mark themselves and their subculture off from 'more orthodox cultural formations' (1979: 101–3). Contemporary art house devotees share this desire for wider social recognition of their cultural consumption as exclusive and distinct from other pastimes.

Remembering the 1990s art film boom and cinephilia

The responses of fans and critics like Chŏng Sŏng-il show that they regard the demise of the Hypertheque Nada as the end of a period of cultural renewal that had played a transformative role in their lives. Media reports generally date the start of this era to 1995, when *The Sacrifice* became a success in Seoul and the magazines *Kino* and *Cine 21* began production. Many journalists and academics also see the Dongsung Cinematheque as the standard-bearer of the cinematic legacy of the late 1990s. The invocation of the 1990s cinephilia boom is featured in articles about the closures of prominent art houses like the Hypertheque Nada, and discussions over the current state of the industry (see Kim Ŭn-hyŏng 2006; Na et al. 2008; Yi Tae-hyŏn 2009; Yi Hyŏn-ju 2014; Kim and Lee 2022: 214). In this final section, I examine how and why film historians, critics, scholars, journalists and fans have memorialised 1990s cinephilia. There are two salient features of these memorialisation discourses – the first being the indistinct characterisation of the 1990s art film boom and the second its use as a channel to critique the current state of Korean cinema.

The art film boom as cultural regeneration

The 1990s art film boom and period of cinephilia are commonly recalled as part of a vital moment of renewal in Korea's cultural history (see Na 2013; Ch'oe 2015; Yi Hyŏn-ju 2014). Journalists, cinema historians and filmmakers have attempted to explain the significance of 1990s art film consumption in several ways. First, scholars have associated cinephilia with the emergence of innovative directors like Bong Joon-ho, Park Chan-wook, Ryu Seung-wan (Ryu Sŭng-wan) and Kim Jee-woon (Kim Chi-un), who created boundary-pushing film popularising Korean cinema domestically and internationally.[29] Critic Jung Ji-youn (Chŏng Chi-yŏn) has argued that the late 1990s 'renaissance' for Korean cinema was 'propelled by the creativity, dynamic quality and diverse experimental spirit of young cinephiles who appeared *en masse* during this time'. For Jung (2008: 16–17), the liberating atmosphere created by the cinephilia boom led to the emergence of this innovative generation of commercial auteurs who breathed 'new life into Korean cinema'. They produced some of the most critically acclaimed and biggest box office successes in Korean cinematic history (Jung 2008: 9; Paquet 2009: 66–7).

Kim Young-jin (2019: 8) has suggested a more direct link between the art film boom and the emergence of these ground-breaking filmmakers, who he calls the 'children of cinema' because of their formative experiences in art houses at the height of the cinephilia:

> Underlying the Korean film renaissance in the 2000s is the story of young movie buffs who actively embraced art films during this (late 1990s) period, becoming professional filmmakers. Park Chan-wook made a living by writing movie reviews during this period, and directors such as Bong Joon-ho and Ryu Seung-wan also travelled to art houses to build their knowledge of film culture. In the Dongsung Cinematheque and art movie theatres, they learned knowledge not taught in film school. This was similar to what happened in the Cinémathèque Française in the 1950s. (Personal correspondence, Kim Young-jin, June 2020)

These directors immersed themselves in the cinema-going atmosphere of the boom, interacting directly with art houses and the film media of the time, all of which helped develop their artistic vision (see also Paquet 2009: 66–7).

Filmmaker and former minister of culture in the Roh Moo-hyun administration, Lee Chang-dong pointed out a vital three-way link between the emergence of directors prepared to make more avant-garde cinema, art houses, and the lucrative 1990s video market (Kim Young-jin 2007: 78). Chaebols such as Samsung and Daewoo funded formally challenging films on contentious topics, which faced potential box office failure because they knew they could recoup their investment from ancillary video sales.[30] Filmmakers also made risk-taking films, confident their movies wouldn't go straight to video but would screen at smaller independent theatres, which attracted adventurous audiences, thereby guaranteeing exhibition in Korea before going on the international festival circuit (Hwang 2017: 55–6).

Common to most accounts by film critics, scholars and historians is an indistinct characterisation of what constituted this 'boom'. There is little attempt to define the nature of the period of cinephilia – whether it represented an increased interest in cinema in general or a greater desire for art film. Cinephilia is identified as a radically different pattern of consumption from what came before and what followed. This was a moment of adventurous spectatorship and innovative exhibition practices followed by extreme cinematic creativity and transformation. For critics, scholars and historians like Kim Young-jin and Jung Ji-youn, the cause-and-effect narrative is appealing because the historical memory of the 1990s art film boom was useful to them as a tool for demanding structural change in Korean cinema.

The 1990s art film boom: a historical mirror to criticise the present

The decades that followed the cinephilia boom have ushered in a period of success for Korean cinema. Apart from 2007–8, which saw a temporary decline in fortune, domestic film consistently outperformed Hollywood movies at the box office, cinema attendances rose and exports of Korean film increased exponentially (Shim 2011: 214).[31] In the context of this phenomenal success, some critics regard the post-dictatorship cinephilia boom as a period against which to critique the direction of the industry during its twenty-first-century expansion. Jung Ji-youn argued that the 2007–8 decline in attendances for Korean film was partly due to the lack of 'cinematic diversity', which had emerged during the cinephilia of the late 1990s (Jung 2008: 9; see also Park 2014: 93). For Lee Chang-dong, writing in 2007, the 'artistic vitality of the late 1990s' had disappeared, and 'creative young' filmmakers like Hong Sang-soo and Kim Ki-duk were no longer emerging. Systemic problems, including the collapse of the video market, made companies less willing to take risks with innovative filmmaking (cited in Kim Young-jin 2007: 76). Coupled with this, according to Lee, the monopolisation of the box office by commercial genre movies meant that domestic cinemagoers had become less tolerant of watching 'ambiguous films'. In the early 2000s, audiences used to 'respect and pay attention' to such films (cited in Kim Young-jin 2007: 12).

Following *Parasite*'s 2019 international critical and commercial success, Kim Young-jin wrote that the structure of Korean cinema is less forgiving of failure than before – even for talented directors. Kim pointed out that Bong Joon-ho's debut feature-length film *A Higher Animal* (Barking Dogs Don't Bite; *P'ŭllaendŏsŭŭi kae*, 2000, Bong Joon-ho, ROK, 57,469) had been a commercial flop, but Bong had managed to follow up with the successful *Memories of Murder*. The industry in 2019 no longer tolerated such failures (Kim Young-jin 2019: 8–9).

Kim argued another problem was that domestic audiences had changed from the 1990s period of cinephilia. Fewer viewers were watching the type of films that required 'a high degree of concentration (because they were) watching movies on computers and mobile phones (rather than) at theatres'. With fewer opportunities for experimenting, Kim claimed it was unlikely that ground-breaking and boundary-pushing filmmakers like Bong Joon-ho or Park Chan-wook would emerge again (personal correspondence, Kim Young-jin, June 2020). These critics argued that in a system in which box office success is paramount, the current production, exhibition and distribution system had conditioned audiences to be less tolerant of boundary-pushing films.[32] As a result, the late 1990s creative energy is no longer apparent.

The memory of 1990s cinephilia and its connections with the emergence of notable Korean directors provides grounds for influential critics to attack an industry for placing too much weight on commercial success. Of course, the irony is that while these critics look back on the 1990s period as one of artistic creativity, it was also a time when the industry faced significant commercial challenges. Between 1995 and 1998, just 20–25 per cent of films seen in cinemas were Korean-made. Domestic consumption of Korean movies doubled from 1999 onwards (KOFIC 2005: 26).[33] In his *History in Three Keys*, Paul Cohen distinguishes between three ways of knowing the past – as event, experience and myth. For Cohen, a 'dynamic interaction is set up between present and past, in which the past is continually being reshaped, either consciously or unconsciously, in accordance with the diverse and shifting preoccupations of people in the present' (Cohen 1997, xii). Through the elision of the financial fragility of the mid-to-late 1990s, critics have constructed a simplified narrative of the impact of the 1990s expansion of art film consumption that provides 'symbolic representations designed less to elucidate the ... past than to draw energy from it ...' (Cohen 1997, xiii). The evocation of this period of 1990s cinephilia is important in terms of its use in a struggle over the current direction of the Korean film industry.

Much media discussion of Korean art film exhibition (like the two articles that started this chapter) evokes what Thomas Elsaesser calls a 'crisis of memory'; a central feature of 'cinephilia of whatever form' that ties practitioners to a distant cinematic past (Elsaesser 2005a: 40). It is the 'impossibility of experience in the present, and the need to always be conscious of several temporalities' (Elsaesser 2005a: 40). Cinephilia, in other words, is directly linked to nostalgia, a constant sense of loss, and part of its experience is resisting the present to regain what has been lost. Critics like Kim Young-jin, who invoke the cinephilia of the 1990s to critique the later development of Korean film, actively participated in this moment of cinematic history. The cinephilia of the 1990s faded, but its impact is felt many years later.

Conclusion

Given the transformed post-cinema context in Korea with the entrance of powerful multiplex chains into the art film market, and the proliferation of online viewing opportunities – one would be tempted to conclude that the survival of small, independent art houses showing films aimed at a niche market is nothing short of miraculous. Independent art houses managed to survive for several reasons. Through the combination of space, activities and programming, theatres established institutional identities that differentiated their services from what was on offer online or from competitors. Art cinemas have drawn generously from the blueprints laid down by film clubs, videotheques and pioneering art houses decades before. Art houses have used nostalgia as a big draw for viewers, and exhibitors have marketed their association with late and post-dictatorship cinephilia to provide a sense of distinction to the experience they offer. Art house regulars are also drawn to theatres by the sociality of viewing – an audience's collective sense of solidarity and mutual recognition. Until the 2020 COVID-19 pandemic, KOFIC did not appreciate the significant connections of individual cinemas with their clientele. They saw the maintenance of a network of art houses primarily as a way of providing screening opportunities for Korean speciality films. Yet the evidence collected in this chapter suggests that far more than the films themselves, it is the distinct experience offered within the space that has drawn and continues to draw audiences.

With multiplex firms adopting the spatial strategies of independent art houses, not all theatres managed to retain their long-term regular audiences, and several well-known art houses ended up closing. What emerged from the discussion surrounding the closure of the Hypertheque Nada, in particular, was that cinemagoers partly conceptualised their use of independent film theatres in opposition to what they perceived to be mainstream commercial cinematic culture represented by multiplexes. They associated their cultural identity with art houses suggesting a particularly intense relationship with the theatrical space.

Vital connections exist between cinephilia's 1980s–90s boom and contemporary art filmmaking and exhibition. Exhibitors have used this period as inspiration for their programmes and as tools to recruit and market their theatres. Critics of the current successful commercial film sector have also evoked nostalgia for 1990s cinephilia and the cinematic creativity it unleashed to argue for a greater rebalancing of the Korean film industry in much the same way Sontag used the classical period of European art cinema to critique 1990s genre film. The cultural energy of the 1980s and 1990s period of cinematic regeneration still serves to inspire more than two decades after the flames of Korean cinephilia were extinguished.

Notes

1. After a contract dispute with Baekdudaegan, Taekwang Media took over operations in 2009 – a change that had proved unpopular with art cinema fans since Taekwang Media is the cultural arm of the chemical and textile manufacturer Taekwang Industries (and owners of Heungkuk Life Insurance which hosts the cinema; Paek 2009).
2. This island is close to Inch'ŏn International Airport, serving Seoul.
3. The audience data in this section is based on the responses of my 2020 survey on art film consumption (see Appendix 3).
4. Three-quarters of audiences had between 27 and 45 US dollars (in 2003) to spend on leisure, when a cinema ticket cost around $7 (Kim et al. 2004: 76).
5. In my 2020 art house memories survey, 56 per cent of respondents were women and 50 per cent of respondents reported receiving monthly salaries of approximately $4,000, at a time when the average earning for a worker was around $2,800 per month for men and $1,734 per month for women (see Statista 2020). A

quarter replied they worked in offices, while 40 per cent described themselves as freelancers, approximately one in ten were homemakers. See Park (2008); Appendix 3.

6. The 2003 KOFIC survey (Kim et al. 2004) reported that 87 per cent of art film audiences were under thirty. The Taegu Dongsung Art Hall programmer Yun Sang-jin* reported that most of his audiences in the pre-Covid 19 era were students and women in their thirties and forties (personal correspondence, Yun Sang-jin*, December 2021).
7. Of fifty-three art film fans in my survey, almost half were between the ages of forty and seventy (see Yi 2013; Yi Hyŏn-ju 2014). Most 1990s Dongsung Cinematheque repeat customers were in their mid-twenties, and 2000s Cinecube regulars were in their late thirties, but since 2010, Art House Momo Theatre attendees are in their fifties (personal correspondence, Lee Kwang-mo, June and December 2020). Of the 100,000 who have signed up to receive news and updates about Art House Momo events, Lee reported that the majority are regulars (personal correspondence, Lee Kwang-mo, December 2020).
8. The collapse of printed film journalism and professional critics has left a gap that has been filled by a variety of online literature ranging from viewer ratings to film-related blogs, reviews and academic essays on movies and directors (see Hwang 2017: 85).
9. Taegu's Dongsung Art Hall and the Korean Film Archive's own official Cinematheque also maintained a diverse schedule featuring both international and domestic, independent, and classic films grouped according to themes (see KOFA 2021). The full programme for the Seoul Art Cinema in December 2021 included: *The Power of the Dog* (2021, Jane Campion, US/Aus); *A Room in Town* (Une Chambre en ville, 1982, Jacques Demy, France); *Coming to You* (2021, Byun Gyuri, ROK); *An Autumn Flower* (*A Man called Autumn Flower*/ Un hombre llamado flor de otoño, 1978, Pedro Olea, Spain); *Late Autumn* (*Akibiyori*, 1960, Yasujirō Ozu, Japan); *Early Summer* (*Bakushū*, 1951, Yasujirō Ozu, Japan); *About Endlessness* (Om det oändliga, 2019, Roy Andersson, Sweden); *A One and a Two* (Yi Yi, 2000, Edward Yang, Taiwan); *The Young Man* (Chŏlmŭn namja, 1994, Pae Ch'ang-ho, ROK).
10. *Il Viaggio* (1974, Vittorio de Sica, Italy) and *Bridge to the Sun* (1961, Etienne Périer, US/France) were some examples of films shown in June 2020.
11. The Cinecube screens films dealing with serious, real-life issues like ageing, death, parenthood and family relationships for more mature audiences, for example (Yi Hyŏn-ju 2014). In 2014, this included *A Late Quartet* (2012, Yaron Zilberman, US, 110,000 tickets sold). The Baekdudaegan-run Art House Momo has continued the tradition established by Lee Kwang-mo at the Dongsung Cinematheque, specialising in European art film (Chi Yong-jin 2015).
12. See Lee 2006: 111; on 17 May 1980, the day before the Kwangju Uprising, student leaders coordinating protests against the Chun Doo Hwan administration convened a meeting on Ewha University's campus. This meeting was raided by the police who thwarted the continued nationwide spread of demonstrations by arresting student leaders.
13. The Cinecode Sonjae had an art gallery.

14. The Hypertheque Nada was well-known for its restaurant and the attractive views from the auditorium onto landscaped gardens (Kim et al. 2004: 49; Kim Yŏng-ch'ang 2001; Extreme Movie 2015).
15. This has been a traditional commercial strategy of art houses. Wilinsky (2001: 198) reports that early US art houses sold freshly brewed coffee in foyers, and O'Brien (2018: 79) observes that in the UK, one 1960s London art house had a Swiss chef serving 'continental specialities'.
16. The Korean Film Archive provides such an experience featuring coffee shops, free access to film viewing and a museum.
17. See DRFA 2021, for example.
18. Approximately 20 per cent of my respondents replied they regularly attended multiplex-run art houses and previously attended independent art cinemas (Appendix 3).
19. Multiplex specialist cinemas had an advantage over competitors since they could customise spaces to suit the activities they held there (Hwang 2017: 83).
20. Two users of the Dongsung Cinematheque and Hypertheque Nada between 2005 and 2009 claimed the cinema's proximity to other performance arts was a major draw.
21. Ch'oe Mi-jin* (Dongsung Cinematheque, 2005–9), Kim Min-ji* (Hypertheque Nada 2004–11).
22. Sohn (2012: 11) also notices a similar focused attention ethic amongst 2005–8 cinephiles in her study.
23. 2019–22 indicates years regularly attended, and 22, indicates the age at the time of the survey.
24. A few respondents claimed they enjoyed watching the films and found the Dongsung Cinematheque's atmosphere too 'rigid' (*ttakttakhae*) for their tastes, but they were a minority.
25. Respondents referred to the art house space as an 'alternative' (*taean*) space or small theatre (*sokŭkjang*).
26. The Hypertheque Nada ran a similar membership scheme to other art houses, which guaranteed entry to popular screenings (author interview with Kim Nan-suk, May 2020).
27. Some had attended independent art houses previously, and some had only attended multiplex-run specialist theatres.
28. Evidence that exhibitors are aware of the impact of institutional identity in attracting an audience can be seen in the 2014 comments of Ch'oe Nak-yong, the then vice-president of Baekdudaegan. Ch'oe asserted that the principal characteristic of a successful art house 'is that once you take a step into it you become loyal . . . the secret to survival in the midst of the storm is to retain your character and your stance [on art film] . . . ' (cited in Yi Hyŏn-ju 2014).
29. Ryu Seung-wan directed *Veteran* (2015, ROK) which gained 13.4 million admissions and Kim Ji-woon directed *The Quiet Family* (Choyonghan kajok, 1998, ROK) and *The Good, the Bad, the Weird* (Choŭn nom, nappŭn nom, isanghan nom, 2008, ROK).
30. Samsung provided funding for *To the Starry Island* (*Kŭ some kagosipta*, 1993, Park Kwang-su, ROK, 147: 310 admissions), *To You From Me* (*Nŏ ege narŭl ponenŭnda*, 1994, Jang Sun-woo, ROK 380,000), *A Single Spark* and *A Petal*. Samsung also

financed *Three Friends*, while capital investment fund Ilshin Investment financed *Christmas in August* (Cho 2006: 193–4, 199–200), and Mirae Asset invested in Jang Sun-woo's *Lies* (Choi 2010: 173).

31. As of March 2020, all 100 of the biggest domestically produced Korean box office hits were released between 1999 and 2020. Eighty-six of these appeared between 2007 and 2020; source: KOBIS (2020).
32. See Parc and Messerlin (2021: 193–6) for analysis of the debate over the screen monopoly and commercial genre domination and its impact upon Korean film.
33. The number of films produced domestically doubled in 1999 in comparison to previous years, and Korean motion pictures accounted for 40 per cent of all tickets sold (KOFIC 2005: 26).

Conclusion

This book's analysis of the late and post-dictatorship cinephilia boom and the growth of art film exhibition in Korea has raised interrelated historical questions. One is how we can conceptualise a particular historical moment, its legacy and the feelings, aspirations and activities of a group of people who made that specific time worthy of recall. Another question is how we can best or most accurately represent historically those characters and the spaces and cultures they created. The postmodern critique of Rankean historical discourses contends that historical studies are not facts written down, but accounts of events historians distort to create a coherent narrative (Black and Macraild 2007: 156–7). Curiously, the events that make up the late and post-dictatorship blossoming of art film exhibition lend themselves to historical (one might say even cinematic or dramatic) narrativisation. The story of this cinephilia features characters whose desires and determination initiated an intense mode of cinematic consumption in new exhibition spaces that briefly became front-page news in Korea. It includes pivotal events that attracted this media attention and drew many young people to art film. These key episodes were impacted by socioeconomic shifts, political developments and the forces of contingency. Finally, the story features a distinct beginning, middle and end; it charts a rise and a fall and leaves a significant legacy in present-day South Korean cinema. I end this history of the 1990s Korean art film boom by returning to the events, characters, trajectory and significance of this historical narrative and the cinematic cultures that emerged.

A central question of this book is why this cinephilia and art film consumption emerged in the late and post-dictatorship period. In his study of the emergence of European and world cinema in the 1960s, *Revolution,* Peter Cowie (2004) identifies a 'desire for' and a 'reaction against' – factors that motivated young cinephiles to transform film exhibition and production practices. An 'overriding sense that film was a medium that knew no artistic limitations' characterised the period and served as a single unifying feature for many young filmmakers and cinephiles worldwide (Cowie 2004, xii). Cowie argues this 'overriding sense' was a feeling common to young people in different countries at the same moment and which went on to shape global filmmaking and film consumption in the years that followed. In late-dictatorship and post-1987 Korea, young cinephiles shared an 'overriding sense' of the power of film, film production and exhibition spaces as powerful agents of social, political and cultural change. The unifying feature linking these young Koreans was a longing for liberated cultural consumption. These cinephiles focused on obtaining, watching and discussing films freely, seeking an experience of cinematic culture without limitations. Ultimately their craving for new film experiences contributed to the blossoming of cinephilia and art film consumption in late and post-dictatorship South Korea. These desires drove non-theatrical art exhibition growth in European cultural centres, film clubs and videotheques, which became important places for unrestricted cinematic viewing in a de-authoritarianising society. These desires shaped the DIY culture of videotheques and early art houses by encouraging self-education and active participation in spaces dedicated to film.

A reaction against established cinematic practices accompanied the yearning of Korean cinephiles for freer cinematic consumption. Continued censorship led to widespread mistrust of state control over cinema. Cinephiles bypassed much of what they associated with the *chedogwŏn* – the institutions linked to the state, military and chaebols. They regarded the established, state-regulated avenues of cinematic exhibition and distribution found in Ch'ungmuro with suspicion. Accordingly, small groups of cinephiles sought alternative means of experiencing cinema; some joined clubs to both view and learn how to produce films. They created venues to collect and exchange cinema-related resources. Thirty years of military rule gave rise to a system that made importing art or classic cinema a major challenge in South Korea. So cinephiles smuggled and pirated film, while pioneering exhibitors travelled abroad to source, import, distribute and exhibit movies. These trailblazers brought films that no one would have thought could be successfully shown in Korea to eager audiences. In a few short years, these desires, coupled with a sense of political opposition, helped transform many peoples' viewing practices and the conceptualisation of cinema. They regarded their activities as nothing less than a cultural revolution of their creation.

Reaction against the cinematic status quo and desire for unrestricted cultural consumption motivated 1990s Korean film fans, but the cultural and economic context of late and post-dictatorship Korea facilitated the rise of cinephilia. Persistent weaknesses in exhibition practices helped drive audiences away from first-run theatres and led some to seek alternative ways of watching and discussing film. Other significant developments in politics, technology and the media environment provided the context in which this cinephilia could thrive. From the late 1970s onwards, screenings of art films at European cultural centres offered new opportunities for young people to immerse themselves in cinematic culture. Between the late 1970s and the late 1980s, regulatory changes contributed to the emergence of small theatres, paving the way for 1990s art houses. Relaxed rules on group activities on university campuses in the mid-1980s facilitated the formation of student cinema groups dedicated to film study. The liberalisation of import restrictions on foreign film opened the door for a more diversified supply of overseas motion pictures. The rapid growth of the video market provided a convenient and low-cost method to circulate and exhibit art films. The establishment of satellite TV channels allowed cinephiles to illegally copy unreleased movies from Japanese broadcasters to screen at film clubs and videotheques.

All narratives need central pivotal events, clear-cut incidents that anchor moments of change in the public imagination. This story of post-dictatorship cinephilia and art film exhibition had several of these points. The *Bluebird* Incident encapsulated for a generation of film activists the persuasive political potential of film, not just in terms of its content but also in its exhibition and distribution. The 2001 Waranago Incident demonstrated the economic vulnerability of non-commercial domestic film, and the policy changes KOFIC implemented because of this case provided an essential role for art houses within the industry. However, the *Sacrifice* Incident in 1995 shaped the period's historical memorialisation more than any other single event. It announced the surge of interest in art film and the rise of a new cinephilia. The movie's popularity at Seoul screenings and on video created a nationwide media sensation and served as a vital catalyst for the rapid expansion of art film in Korea. Its popularity demonstrated what had been thought unlikely in Korea – art film could reach a large audience.

Vital emerging structures and relationships facilitated the spread of cinephilia, creating a transformed media environment. In mid-1990s Korea, cinema magazines like *Cine 21* and *Kino*, as well as national dailies, carried special features publicising the films and activities of the Dongsung Cinematheque and other art houses. This new media coverage helped foster a sense of community amongst cinephiles. The specialist film magazines championed the new exhibitors' innovations, shared the cinephiles' interests and embraced their sense of discovery. The success of *The Sacrifice* was not inevitable; existing exhibition and distribution structures opposed the film's screening. Lee Kwang-mo's media connections and promotional nous explain how his programming of 'disturbance' drew significant audience numbers. Publicity and media coverage helped transform the significance of viewing art cinema. This exposure made a type of film that had previously attracted few in Korea appealing to many during this brief period. As a result, Korean cinephilia entered a wider public domain.

This new film media was a vital part of a complex network of institutional and personal relationships that constituted the development of the post-dictatorship cinephilia, the establishment of systematic art film exhibition and the expansion of art houses. These relationships were particularly evident in the academic links with early art film exhibition. University scholars contributed reviews and critical essays to the media and played a vital role in the educational activities of the videotheques and art houses. Audiences, journalists, film critics and academics unified in their educational zeal. These groups celebrated changes to accepted practices in exhibition, distribution and production. *Kino* didn't just report cinema: it taught, campaigned and proselytised. Its mission (like the videotheques and art houses) was to change audiences. The collective involvement of film magazines, newspapers and academics helped publicise and valorise art film consumption and cinephilia. Most significantly, these institutional interconnections did not dissipate at the end of the 1990s but filtered into the expanding Korean film industry, impacting its development.

The exhibition spaces of the film clubs, cinematheques and art houses outlined in this history are worthy of discussion now because of the cinematic cultures that developed within them. This period produced a diversity of exhibition venues which, in terms of programme, space and atmosphere, were subtly different. However, a particular set of behaviours remained common. Critics, academics, exhibitors and audiences established a healthy pattern of borrowing and developing ideas about cinema. This cross-pollination of ideas occurred because of the impetus of the period – what many have alluded to as the 'spirit of the times', the *zeitgeist* where cultural, social and political influences helped shape common activities and attitudes amongst cinephiles. The film fans adopted autodidacticism, independence and defiance from the *minjung* movement and applied these behaviours to a new cultural frontline. Historians have made much of a significant division between those late-dictatorship cinephiles who embraced film as art and those who saw cinema as a political tool. Yet even those participants like Lee Kwang-mo and *Kino* journalists who most proactively embraced art cinema characterised their philosophy of cinema within the confines of this radical spirit of upheaval. Their desires for cinematic renewal were influenced by the movement's political urgency and stood in opposition to the values they associated with the *chedogwŏn*.

Another characteristic of the culture created in this period was the urgency with which cinephiles demanded transformation. Their desire for cinematic knowledge had the fervour of a revolutionary upheaval. This impatience for consumption resulted in the trend to pirate, smuggle and self-source visual materials. The point was the consumption of material now, not later. The 'historic compression' of the period can be characterised by *Kino*'s cramming of thirty years of European and North American film theory and cultural theory into two pages of a monthly magazine. The cinephiles were anxious for access and knowledge and constructed cinematic cultures dedicated to their findings.

Given their rejection of values associated with the *chedogwŏn*, an essential contradiction of the post-dictatorship cinephilic culture is its embrace of commercialism. The commercial growth of art film exhibition is part and parcel of the cinematic cultures between the late 1980s and the 2020s. The expansion of art houses and even videotheques took place in an environment where exhibitors competed to sell a product. A large audience turnout was evidence of a popular screening programme, but it was also lucrative, and exhibitors relished the publicity as much as the profits. In the late 1980s and early 1990s, some theatres experimented with mixed-programming strategies consisting of festival winners, European films alongside titillating dramas and mainstream Hollywood genre movies as a pragmatic way to survive in a competitive environment. Pioneering art houses differentiated their product from competitors by creating unique institutional identities through specialised programming, educational activities and spatial organisation. The Core Art Hall gained a reputation for programming the latest European film festival award-winners and developed an institutional identity differing from competitors through its systematic approach to art movies. Baekdudaegan's Dongsung Cinematheque programmed a darker, more challenging collection of classic and less well-known contemporary art films, fostering cinema as a high-level cultural and educational activity.

This history of spatial culture has focused on a multitude of exhibition venues, which were subject to the interaction of economic forces and shifting cultural tastes. In addition to activism, one additional factor linked these geographically and temporally distinct exhibition sites. Audiences and exhibitors in these early theatres adopted a mode of cinematic consumption that embraced a celluloid past to construct a cultural present and a cinematic future. Cinephiles saw nostalgic cinematic consumption as essential to the cultural reconstruction of a domestic industry. This nostalgic consumption necessitated the spatial configuration of art film exhibition sites with their academic interventions, libraries and study groups. In the new millennium, art house cultures are also shaped by nostalgia not just for films from cinema's past but also for sites from Korean cinephilia's history. Prominent contemporary art cinemas accentuate their lineage back to the cinephilia boom to stress the authenticity of the experience they offer.

A vital question to our understanding of audiences' interactions within and with these diverse exhibition spaces concerns the allure of art cinema. Schedules of film clubs, videotheques and early art houses included road movies, banned and censored pictures, classical Hollywood, cult films, American independents, and cinema from all corners of the globe. Young Korean cinephiles from the 1980s onwards embraced diversity many years before the notion became an organising principle for state cultural policy. However, more than other types of picture, European and particularly French art film dominated their programmes. Art movies drew young Koreans for diverse reasons. They were consecrated by the university academics who lectured at exhibition venues, by budding directors as part of the informal self-instruction programmes, and by journalists and critics in the film press. European art cinema offered respectability for cinematic consumption in a fluid social and economic context where young people had greater leisure spending capacity. European films provided young students with their closest contact with foreign cultures when overseas travel was restricted. Films became an instructional tool for world knowledge in the pre-Internet era. More than anything else, the allure of art film lay in its symbolic use value to young cinephiles in a late and post-dictatorship period. Many of these decades-old art films had lost, as Kim Soyoung argued, any political significance they had once contained, but young Koreans embraced the oppositional associations of European cinema, and its perceived differences from Hollywood releases. Cinephile audiences were determined to experience a culture blocked off to them by the authorities for so long. The films of Bertolucci, Antonioni, Bergman, Godard and Polanski required understanding, interpretation and explanation to be truly appreciated. Thus, art film fit perfectly with cinephiles' autonomous and autodidactic tendencies and their sense of a non-conformist identity. Cinephiles pitted what they saw as their culture, learning, free expression and progress against the ignorance and narrow-mindedness of the dictatorship. Acquiring, exhibiting and appreciating art films put late and post-dictatorship audiences in direct opposition to the authorities, and this is why cinephiles consumed art film with such fervour.

A wide diversity of characters and motivations drove the events of this history. Art film consumption and cinephilia of the late 1980s and 1990s proved a socially and culturally expansive space for many young women. Female fans consumed art film in a rigidly hierarchical social environment. Art film viewing was an acceptable intellectual activity to peers, thanks to its associations with alterity and to society because of its refined European cultural connotations. Women also played prominent roles in art film exhibition by leading the establishment of the videotheque movement and Korea's film festivals. Videotheques were newly created spaces that lacked the strictly designated hierarchies of other cinematic institutions. Cinephilia, exhibition and exhibition culture gave women a productive outlet in film that they did not enjoy in other parts of the industry in this period.

The cinephilia of many participants was firmly rooted in their creative desires. Kim Nan-suk, Lee Kwang-mo, Yi Ŏn-gyŏng and Son Chu-yŏn are all examples of Koreans whose interest was primarily directed toward the production of film rather than its exhibition or distribution. The avid consumption, exhibition and circulation of movies by fans dominating the cultural centres, film clubs, videotheques and art houses were a means to an end. Exhibition, in particular, represented an entry point to film production within a system in flux but which still offered few opportunities, especially for women. The newly developed film venues provided an accessible education in cinema, although many participants never progressed beyond film consumption or exhibition.

Rise and fall historical narratives often require the identification of a single cause – a central villain, structural defect, or event that led to a decline. This is complicated by the events of 1997–8 and after. The art film sector became marked by inconsistency, with art film consumption falling one year only to rise the next. The late 1990s signalled the end of a high point of art house attendance, but not its end. What declined most was the prominence of art film exhibition in the public imagination and the sense of community that unified cinephiles. The period following the end of the Asian financial crisis saw the creation of a buzz around domestic film, and audience tastes shifted with the result that the performance of European art films became more unpredictable for theatres. Underlying tensions contributed to cinephilia's decline during this period of economic instability. Some critics attacked politically unengaged art house programming, while others condemned the intellectual one-upmanship between cinephiles and their predilection for foreign film over domestic works. These tensions were off-putting to some cinephiles, while others simply drifted away from art house attendance.

For Cowie, the 1960s New Waves of world film left an indelible mark on cinematic form, institutional structures, and the development of academic film studies. The late and post-dictatorship era of Korean cinephilia and art film exhibition left a physical, institutional and cultural legacy within Korean film. The continued presence of Korean art houses in the cinematic infrastructure is one vestige of the era. The 2021 KOFIC statistics revealed over 140 specialist cinema screens in South Korea dedicated to art, independent, or other forms of non-mainstream film. Art houses have responded to the challenges created by a transformed media environment in which online platforms have expanded the availability of previously obscure movies. Today's art houses offer distinct cinematic experiences unavailable online by creating cultural spaces that appeal to a sense of nostalgia, the organisation of film-related activities and programming. While many regulars attend independent art houses, multiplex corporations run most of the screens dedicated to art, independent and non-mainstream films. The success of multiplex giants can be explained partly by their wholesale adoption of the characteristic spatial and programming strategies of their smaller competitors. The exclusivity and sociality of the spatial experience are common to multiplex and independent art houses. Participants believe this mode of film consumption is participatory and communal and thus very distinct from viewing experiences in other theatres.

This art film boom also left a lasting institutional legacy. In the wake of the Waranago Incident and the challenging new millennium economic context, the recently reformed KOFIC proposed an essential role for art houses in protecting domestic art film. Accordingly, KOFIC established a country-wide project that subsidised art houses to guarantee screening opportunities for niche films. KOFIC intended its project to form a small but significant part of a successful Korean film industry supporting both commercial mainstream film and specialist cinematic production. This multi-sector industry achieves valuable state goals of producing commercially profitable films and attracting international recognition for Korean cinematic output, but it also nurtures talent and provides an expression outlet for different communities within Korean society. Despite significant and often controversial changes to funding methods, art houses are still tasked with guaranteeing screening windows to niche films within a diversified cinematic industry.

Another legacy of the 1980s to 1990s cinephilia is its memorialisation in academic and media discourses. For one group of critics, the current successful commercial bent of Korean film is not adequately balanced. It, therefore, betrays the function and value of a post-1987 cinema that emerged from the challenge of Hollywood. For this constituency, the legacy of this period of cinephilic creativity has a particular symbolic use-value. Events like *The Sacrifice* represented cultural renewal within conservative, suspicious and resistant cinematic institutions. Thirty years on, their memory is still invoked by journalists, academics and filmmakers calling for the rehabilitation of what they see as a cinematic industry grown fat on the profit of formulaic commercial big sellers. The discourse of this small but influential group of intellectuals echoes the 1996 concerns of Susan Sontag over commercial cinematic output in the 1990s. Much as Sontag did, they mourn the passing of a cinephilic age that they shared, helped construct, and feel has been too easily forgotten.

An essential link between cinephilia and the present cinematic industry is the prevalence of human networks. We see a significant crossover of personnel between the 1980s–90s art film scene and cinephilia boom and the new millennium Korean film industry. Many of those actively involved in the cinephilia of the 1980s and 1990s as consumers and exhibitors of cultural centres, college film clubs, videotheques and art houses became film journalists, KOFIC administrators, festival organisers, academics, filmmakers and producers. People who fostered their love for film in the cauldron of late and post-dictatorship cinephilia are today responsible for exhibition, distribution, production and management of a highly diversified industry. These networks constituted a brief moment – the 'historic compression' – where influential people came together to produce, exhibit, distribute and discuss film and helped shape an industry during a period of growth. They remain human links to a moment of creative cinematic energy.

Another vital connection to the success of South Korean film lies in the influence of this period of cinephilia in helping to shape the tastes of domestic audiences. Much is made in academic and media discourses about the relative sophistication of Korean domestic audiences and its ability to accept genre-bending and boundary-pushing experimentation. According to industry observers, this is why Hollywood companies select the Korean market as a test bed for their films before releasing them elsewhere (Kim 2022). Tony Rayns (1998) and other scholars observed the emergence of such an audience from the late 1990s onwards (see Kim and Lee 2022: 214; Parc and Messerlin 2021: 232). This audience consumed a diverse range of cinema with a fervour that impressed the British critic but disappointed him by rejecting their own creative filmmakers. It is noticeable that this same audience went from rejection to a full embrace of many domestic auteurs in a few short years. The new film media made public the cinematic cultures of cinephiles, art houses and emerging international film festivals. This media attention did much to consecrate a diverse range of cinema and prime a domestic audience that would go on to embrace the new millennium output of Korean cinema.

In the development of late and post-dictatorship Korean cinephilia, we see some curious contradictions formed by contingency and shifts in the trajectory that forced people to compromise ideological stances. These reversals illustrate wider political and cultural changes within Korean film and Korea itself. One reversal is the relationship between art film exhibitors and state officials administrating the industry in the thirty years after 1987. The state authorities and college and videotheque cinematic groups regarded one another with mutual suspicion. The early consumers of art film sought ways to escape officially sanctioned forms of cinematic exhibition, and the authorities occasionally clamped down on these groups. By the early 2000s, art houses and state administrators enjoyed a symbiotic relationship facilitating each other's interests. The state turned from controller and oppressor to benefactor. The arrival of governments hostile to the public funding of diversity challenged KOFIC/art house relationships and for a time, brought back the spectre of authoritarianism and the fragility of the post-1987 cultural liberation era. In her analysis of art film exhibition in the UK, Jane Harbord (2002: 10) argues that 'cultural production oscillates between the official art of state patronage, a bohemian rejection of such official practice, and culture as commerce'. The Korean art house responses to state sponsorship were influenced by the experience of the movement years. Art film exhibition, consumption and its related cinephilia were born in struggle in Korea. The administrator-exhibitor relationship is therefore (in part) defined by pre-existing structures, which encourage mutual suspicions. This relationship has developed, broken down, fractured and healed. Ultimately, it has survived despite the odds, offering a model of state support of the art sector for other countries to emulate.

With the fluctuating relationship between exhibitors, audiences and state administrators, we see another reversal in the sense of opposition that accompanied art film consumption. One crucial element of the dynamism of Korean cinephilia and its associated art film exhibition derives from a notion of resistance against the military regime. This alterity was a key component of the fuel that drove cinephilia in these early non-theatrical exhibition spaces. Within art houses, art film consumers expressed these rebellious notions through a sense of opposition – one that altered considerably over thirty years of development. Opposition to the state through consumption characterised early art film exhibition. However, later art house clientele saw their association with independent art movie theatres as expressions of a cultural identity that opposed the values represented by multiplexes. Of course, in constructing a cultural self, art film consumers and exhibitors often conflated their struggle against adversaries such as the dictatorship, Hollywood, the USA, the *chedogwŏn*, Ch'ungmuro with the multiplexes. Another irony is that the identities of the adversaries in opposition to which these notions of resistance were constructed were themselves in constant flux. This is true of the multiplex chains, which eventually adopted many spatial strategies of independent art houses, becoming part of the complex network of art film institutions. However ambiguous and ill-defined these understandings of resistance, opposition, or alterity appear, these notions have become central to how art house users and exhibitors see their cultural identity and role in Korean cinema.

References

Ahn, SooJeong. 2012. *The Pusan International Film Festival: South Korean Cinema and Globalization*. TransAsia Screen Cultures. Hong Kong: Hong Kong University Press.
Allen, C., Robert. 1990. 'From Exhibition to Reception: Reflections on the Audience in Film History.' *Screen* 31 (4) (Winter): 347–56.
Allen, C., Robert. 2006. 'The Place of Space in Film Historiography.' *TMG Journal for Media History* 9, no. 2: 15–27.
Allen, C., Robert. 2011. 'Reimagining the History of the Experience of Cinema in a Post-Moviegoing Age.' In *Explorations in New Cinema History: Approaches and Case Studies*, edited by Richard Maltby, Daniel Biltereyst and Philippe Meers, 41–57. Oxford: Blackwell.
An, Cheong Sook. (An Chŏng-suk). 2001. 'Introduction: Korean Cinema at a Crossroads.' *Korean Cinema 2001*: 6–12. Seoul: KOFIC.
An Chŏng-suk. 1995. 'Yesulyŏnghwa chŏnyongkwan naedal sipiril munyŏnda' (Next month an art film only cinema is opening its doors). *Han'gyŏrye*, 7 October.
An Chŏng-suk. 1996. 'Kungnaedanp'yŏng net sangyŏng' (Four screenings of domestic short films). *Han'gyŏrye*, 20 April.
Andrew, Dudley. 2002 (1986). 'Film and Society: Public Rituals and Private Space.' In *Exhibition, the Film Reader*, edited by Ina Rae Hark, 161–71. London: Routledge
Andrews, David. 2013. *Theorizing Art Cinemas: Foreign, Cult, Avant-Garde and Beyond*. Austin: University of Texas Press.
Baekdudaegan. 1996. 'Yesuryŏnghwajŏnyonggwan tonsungssinemat'aek 1chunyŏn kinyŏm paeksŏ' (White paper on the first year of operation of the art film speciality theatre Dongsung Cinematheque). Seoul: Baekdudaegan.
Baekdudaegan. 1998. *Arŭmdaun sijŏl – podo charyo* (*Spring in My Hometown* – Press Release). 21 November. Seoul: Baekdudaegan.
Baekdudaegan. 2016. 'Yŏnghwasa Paekdudaegan' (Baekdudaegan film company). Accessed 24 March, 2020. http://arthousemomo.co.kr/pages/about_company.php.
Barthes, Roland. 1975. 'En Sortant du Cinema' (On leaving cinemas). *Communications* 23: 104–7.
Baumann, Shyon. 2007. *Hollywood Highbrow: From Entertainment to Art*. Princeton: Princeton University Press.

Berliner, Todd. 2018. 'Legally Independent: The Exhibition of Independent Art Films.' *Historical Journal of Film, Radio and Television* 38, no. 1: 54–72.

Berry, Chris. 2002. 'Full Service Cinema: The South Korean Cinema Success Story (So far).' In *Texts and Context of Korean Cinema: Crossing Borders*, edited by Young-Key Kim-Renaud, R. Richard Grinker, and Kirk W. Larsen, 7–16. Washington DC: George Washington University, Sigur Center Asia Paper 17.

Betz, Mark. 2009. *Beyond the Subtitle: Remapping European Art Cinema*. Minneapolis: University of Minnesota Press.

BIFF Archive. N.d. http://www.biff.kr/eng/html/archive/arc_history01_01.asp.

Black, Jeremy and Donald M. Macraild. *Studying History*. London: Palgrave.

Bordwell, David. 1986. *Narration in the Fiction Film*. London: Routledge.

Bosma, Peter. 2015. *Film Programming: Curating for Cinemas, Festivals, Archives*. New York: Wallflower Press, Columbia University Press.

Bourdieu, Pierre. 1980. 'The Production of Belief: Contribution to an Economy of Symbolic Goods.' *Media, Culture and Society* 2: 261–93.

Bourdieu, Pierre. 1984. *Distinction: A Social Critique of the Judgement of Taste*. Translated by Richard Nice. Cambridge: Harvard University Press.

Cardinal, Roger. 1986. 'Pausing over Peripheral Detail.' *Framework* 30 (January): 112–30.

Chi Yong-jin. 2015. 'Kihoek. Ta katchi tolja yesulyŏnghwagwan han pak'wi' (Going out. Let's all do the rounds of the art houses). *Chungang Ilbo*, 11 June. Accessed 29 April 2022. https://www.joongang.co.kr/article/18047919.

Ch'oe Chi-ung. 2015. 'Tongsung sinemat'aekŭi kŏlchaktŭl' (Posters from Dongsung Cinematheque). *Korean Movie Data Base*.

Cho, Joon-hyeong. 2006. 'Korean Film Industry and its Policy: 1980–1997.' In *A History of Korean Cinema*, edited by KOFIC, 150–210. Seoul: KOFIC.

Cho Sŏn-hŭi. 1993. 'Sŭk' ŭrink'wŏt'ae molligo sae chakp'um pin'gonhagot'60nyŏndae myŏnghwaoch'ouochŏlbak'an chaesangyŏng'ŏ' (A hurriedly imposed screen quota ... inferior new releases and a desperate rescreening of 1960's classic *Early Rain*). *Han'gyŏrye*, 21 August.

Cho Sŏn-hŭi. 1994. 'Yŏnghwa charyo chŏnmunjŏm 'k'anŭ' munyŏrŏ' ('Cannes' a specialist exposition for film materials opens). *Han'gyŏrye*, 17 June.

Cho Yu-bin. 2020. 'Ŭngdaphara 1990 i2020machŏ hŭndŭrŏtda' (*Reply 1990*, has even shaken 2020). *Sisa Journal*, 20 August. Accessed 15 June 2021. http://www.sisajournal.com/news/articleView.html?idxno=203705.

Choi, Jinhee. 2010. *The South Korean Film Renaissance: Local Hitmakers, Global Provocateurs*. Middletown, CT: Wesleyan University Press.

Chŏn Hyo-jun. 2020. 'Sesang'iŭi kŭkchanggaebongsa' (A guide to film releases). Blog, accessed 12 June 2022. https://blog.naver.com/merenguero.

Chon, Woohyung. 2022. 'Beyond the International Film Festival: Contact Zoons for the Agnostics and Solidarity.' In *Korean Film and Festivals: Global Transcultural Flows*, edited by Hyunseon Lee, 81–97. London: Routledge.

Chŏng Hye-yŏn. 2008. 'Han'gugyŏngwabangmulgwan chŏnsip'um kijŭng illei 22) <yŏngsangjiptan> ch'angganho' (The Korean Film Museum exhibit donation relay 22: the first issue of *Film Collective*). *Cine 21*, 28 January. Accessed 9 April, 2022. http://www.cine21.com/news/view/?mag_id=50009.

Chŏng Chae-suk. 1996. 'Sesangen irŏn kamdok iron yŏnghwado itda: 'Ssinae isibil' 'Baekdudaegan' onŭl put'ŏ 'mijiŭi myŏnggamdokjŏn' ... 'Leningŭradŭ' tŭk yukp'yŏn' (In this world are there these kinds of directors and these kinds of films? *Cine 21*, Baekdudaegan from today [starts] a season of 'unknown auteurs' [featuring] *Leningrad Cowboys Go America* and six other films). *Han'gyŏrye*, 18 May.

Chŏng Han-sŏk. 2006. '"Sangyŏng ioe tagakchŏgin p'ŭrogŭraem kihoekhaeya." Ssinek'yubŭ unyŏng ch'onggwarhanŭn Paektudaegan Kim Ŭnyŏng isa. Saram in yesulgŭkchang.' ("You have to plan a variety of activities in addition to screening films." Kim Ŭn-yŏng, Baekdudaegan director, who oversees operations at Cinecube. People in Art Houses.) *Next Plus 2*, 27 April: 3.

Chŏng Yu-mi. 2008. 'Kangnam ruimierŭ kŭkjang'i isipo il p'yegwan' (Kangnam's Lumiere Cinema closed). *Max Movie*, 27 August. Accessed 26 March, 2020.

Chung, Hye Seung. 2012. *Kim Ki-duk*. Urbana: University of Illinois Press.

Chung, Hye Seung and David Scott Diffrient. 2015. *Movie Migrations: Transnational Genre Flows and South Korean Cinema*. New Brunswick, NJ. Rutgers University Press.

Chung, Hye Seung and David Scott Diffrient. 2021. 'The Rise of Rights-Advocacy Cinema in Postauthoritarian South Korea.' In *Movie Minorities: Transnational Rights Advocacy and South Korean Cinema*, edited by Hye Seung Chung and David Scott Diffrient, 19–37. New Brunswick, Rutgers University Press.

Chungang Ilbo. 1986. 'Ŭisikhwayŏngwa, ch'ujŏkchosa' (A Police investigation of consciousness raising movies). 11 November. Accessed 9 April 2022. https://www.joongang.co.kr/article/2074092#home.

Chungang Ilbo. 1997. 'Usu tanp'yŏnyŏngwa chŏnggisangyŏng-tongsungsinemat'ek' (Regular screenings of outstanding short films at the Dongsung Cinematheque). 7 January. Accessed 15 April 2022. https://www.joongang.co.kr/article/3380627#home.

Cine 21. 2001. 'Mainŏ ligŭ ŏbsŭmyŏn han'gukyŏnghwa miraeŏbda' (If there is no minor league within the industry then Korean film has no future). *Cine 21*, 16 November.

Cine 21. 2003. 'Yŏngwabip'yŏng kyeganjapchi 'yŏngwaŏnŏ' pokkan' (The Reprinting of the theoretical movie journal *Film Language*). *Cine 21*, 23 July. Accessed 18 January 2022. http://m.cine21.com/news/view/?mag_id=20033.

Cohen, Paul. 1997. *History in Three Keys: The Boxers as Event, Experience, and Myth*. New York: Columbia University Press.

Cowie, Peter. 2004. *Revolution! The Explosion of World Cinema in the 60s*. London: Faber and Faber.

Cumings, Bruce. 1997. *Korea's Place in the Sun: A Modern History*. New York: W. W. Norton.

Czach, Liz. 2010. 'Cinephilia, Stars, and Film Festivals.' *Cinema Journal* (Winter) 49, no. 2: 139–45.

De Luca, Tiago and Nuno Barradas Jorge. 2016. 'Introduction: From Slow Cinema to Slow Cinemas.' In *Slow Cinema*, edited by Tiago De Luca and Nuno Barradas Jorge, 1–25. Edinburgh: Edinburgh University Press.

Denson, Shane and Julia Leyda, eds. 2016. *Post-Cinema: Theorizing 21st-Century Film*. Falmer: Reframe Books.

De Valck, Marijke and Malte Hagener. 2005. 'Down with Cinephilia? Long Live Cinephilia? And Other Videosyncratic Pleasures.' In *Cinephilia: Movies, Love and Memory*, edited by Marijke de Valck and Malte Hagener, 11–24. Amsterdam: Amsterdam University Press.

Desser, David. 2005. 'Hong Kong Film and the New Cinephilia.' In *Hong Kong Connections: Transnational Imagination in Action Cinema*, edited by Meaghan Morris et al., 205–21. Hong Kong: Hong Kong University Press.

Dong-a Ilbo. 1997. 'Kamsangago punsŏkhago t'oronhago yŏngwabip'yŏng 'mania'ŭi kongganŭro' (Let's go to the space where cinephiles analyse, evaluate and discuss movies). 5 November.

DRFA 365. 2021. Official website. Accessed 19 December 2021. http://www.drfa.co.kr/.

Eckert, Carter J., Ki-Baik Lee, Young Ick Lew, Michael Robinson and Edward W. Wagner. 1991. *Korea Old and New: A History*. Cambridge: Harvard University Press.

Eisner, John, and Roger Cardinal, eds. 1994. *The Cultures of Collecting*. London: Reaktion Books.

Elsaesser, Thomas. 2005a. 'Cinephilia or the Uses of Disenchantment.' In *Cinephilia: Movies, Love and Memory*, edited by Marijke de Valck and Malte Hagener, 27–44. Amsterdam: Amsterdam University Press.

Elsaesser, Thomas. 2005b. 'Film Festival Networks: The New Topographies of Cinema in Europe.'In *European Cinema: Face to Face with Hollywood*, edited by Thomas Elsaesser, 82–107. Amsterdam: Amsterdam University Press.

Extreme Movie. 2015. 'Yŏnghwa suda' (Chat about movies). Blog, 10 November. Accessed 2 May 2021. https://extmovie.com/movietalk/9062855.

Fee, Annie. N.d. 'Women's Cinephilia.' In *Cinephilia*, edited by Annie Fee. Oxford Bibliographies. Accessed 16 June 2021. https://www.oxfordbibliographies.com/view/document/obo-9780199791286/obo-9780199791286-0278.xml#obo-9780199791286-0278-div1-0009.

Frater, Patrick. 2021. 'Korea's Movie Industry Warns of Collapse as Covid Restrictions Return.' *Variety*. 16 December. Accessed 13 April 2022. https://variety.com/2021/film/asia/korea-movie-theatres-covid-spiderman-1235135844/.

FX Top (2022). Accessed 18 March 2022. https://fxtop.com/en/historical-exchange-rates.php

Gateward, Frances. 2007. *Seoul Searching: Culture and Identity in Contemporary Korean Cinema*. New York: SUNY University Press.

Gerstner, David A. and Janet Staiger. 2003. *Authorship and Film*. New York: Routledge.

Gillis, Alex. 2011. *A Killing Art: The Untold Story of Taekwondo*. Toronto: ECW Press.

Hagener, Malte. 2007. *Moving Forward, Looking Back: the European Avant-garde and the Invention of Film Culture, 1919–1939*. Amsterdam: Amsterdam University Press.

Hanich, Julian. 2014. 'Watching a Film with Others: Towards a Theory of Collective Spectatorship.' *Screen* 55, no. 3 (Autumn): 338–59.

Han'gyŏrye. 1990. 'Yŏnghwa Chŏnmun'gongbubang Saenggyŏtta' (A specialist film study centre has been set up). 27 June.

Hanson, Stuart. 2007. *From Silent Screen to Multi-screen: A History of Cinema Exhibition in Britain since 1896*. Manchester: Manchester University Press.

Harbord, Janet. 2002. *Film Cultures*. London: Sage Publications.

Hebdige, Dick. 1979. *Subculture: the Meaning of Style*. London: Routledge.

Hillier, Jim, ed. 1986. *Cahiers du Cinéma. 1960–1968: New Wave, New Cinema, Reevaluating Hollywood*. Cambridge: Harvard University Press.

Hŏ Mun-yŏng, Cho Chong-guk. 1998. 'Han'guk yŏnghwa, tto tarŭn ŏndŏkŭl palgyŏnhada. (South Korean film, yet another hill appears). *Cine 21*, 17 November.

Hong Chŏng-gyun. 2018. '*Kino*, uri naraŭi sangsangjŏk kongdongch'e' (*Kino*, An Imagined Community for South Korean Cinephiles, an interview with Korean Language and Literature Visiting Professor Yi Yŏng-jae). *Sŏngdae Sinmun*, 11 November.

Howard, Chris. 2008. 'Contemporary South Korean Cinema: "National Conjunction" and "Diversity."' In *East Asian Cinemas: Exploring Transnational Connections on Film*, edited by Leon Hunt and Leung Wing-Fai, 88–102. London: I. B. Tauris.

Huh, Moonyoung (Hŏ Mun-yŏng). 2007. *Hong Sangsoo*. Korean Film Directors Series, Seoul: KOFIC.

Hwang, Ha-yŏp. 2017. 'Kungnae yesul yŏnghwagwanŭi yŏksachŏk hyŏngsŏng kwajŏngkwa munhwachŏk t'ŭksŏng: Seoul chiyŏkŭl chungsimŭro' (The Historical Formation and Cultural Characteristics of Korean Art Film Theatre - focusing on the Seoul Area). Unpublished MA dissertation, Yonsei University, Seoul.

Im In-t'aek. 2006. 'P'rangsŭ munhwawŏn . . . munhwa haebangkuija, Pak Chŏng-hŭi sidaeŭi sŭlp'ŭn ket'o' (The French Cultural Institute. a zone of liberated culture, a sad ghetto during the Park Chung Hee era). *Han'gyŏrye*, 18 January. Accessed 22 May 2020. http://www.hani.co.kr/arti/culture/culture_general/96163.html.

Jacobowitz, Florence and Richard Lippe. 2008. 'The Art House Film.' *Cineaction* 75: 1

Jackson, Andrew David. 2020. 'Jürgen Hinzpeter and Foreign Correspondents in the 1980 Kwangju Uprising.' *International Journal of Asian Studies* 17: 19–37.

Jackson, Andrew David. 2022. 'South Korean Film: Commercial Success, Full Service Cinema and the Crisis-Consciousness.' In *Routledge Handbook of Contemporary South Korea*, edited by Sojin Lim and Niki J. P. Alsford, 209–22. London: Routledge.

James, David and Kyung Hyun Kim. 2002. *Im Kwon-Taek: The Making of a Korean National Cinema*. Detroit: Wayne State University Press.

Jung Ji-youn. 2008. *Korean Film Directors: Bong Joon-ho*. Seoul: KOFIC.

Kang Sŏng-nyul. 2013. 'Ch'ŏnman kwan'gaek han'guk yŏnghwa p'yŏngnon chapjinŭn hanappun' (There is only a single film criticism magazine left for ten million Korean film viewers). *Maeil Sinmun*, 28 March.

Kang, So-won. 2006. 'Korean Cinema in the 1980s.' In *A History of Korean Cinema*, edited by KOFIC, 46–100. Seoul: KOFIC.

Keathley, Christian. 2005. *Cinephilia and History, or The Wind in the Trees*. Bloomington: Indiana University Press.

Kil, Sonia. 2018. 'Korean Film Council Apology Reveals Devastating Extent of Blacklist Policy.' *Variety*, 5 April. Accessed 26 June 2021. https://variety.com/2018/film/asia/korean-film-council-apology-reveals-extent-of-blacklist-policy-1202744674/.

Kim Han-sang. 2007. 'Han'gukesŏŭ 'yesulyŏnghwa' tamnon'gwa sijang, kwan'gekŭi hyŏngsŏngkwajŏng' ('Art cinema' discourse in Korea, and the formation of a market and audience). Unpublished MA dissertation, Seoul National University.

Kim, Hong-joon and Hyunseon Lee. 2022. 'Film Festivals and the South Korean Film Industry: Kim Hong-joon in Interview with Hyunseon Lee.' In *Korean Film and Festivals: Global Transcultural Flows*, edited by Hyunseon Lee, 197–217. London: Routledge.

Kim, Hyae-joon. 2007. 'Changes in the Korean Film Industry after Direct Distribution.' In *Korean Cinema: From Origins to Renaissance*, edited by Kim Mee-hyun, 325–6. Seoul: Communication Books.

Kim Hye-ri 2001. 'Ch'arari kŭkjangŭl pillija' (It would be better to rent a cinema). *Cine 21*, 12 November. Accessed 6 May 2020. http://www.Cine21.com/news/view/?mag_id=5210.

Kim, Hyung-a and Clark W. Sorensen. 2011. 'Introduction.' In *Reassessing the Park Chung Hee Era, 1961–1979: Development, Political Thought, Democracy and Cultural Interest*, edited by Hyung-a Kim and Clark W. Sorensen, 3–16. Seattle: University of Washington Press.

Kim, Ji-soo. 2020. '*Parasite* to Give Much-needed Boost to Korean Cinema.' *The Korea Times*, 25 February. Accessed 23 April 2022. https://www.koreatimes.co.kr/www/art/2020/04/398_284031.html.

Kim, Ju Oak. 2018. 'Korea's Blacklist Scandal: Governmentality, Culture and Creativity.' *Culture, Theory and Critique* 59, no. 2: 81–93.

Kim Kyŏng-ae. 2020. '"Tŭlkkodyŏngwasang kongnosang." Chŏn'gugyesuryŏngwagw anhyŏphoe.' ("Wildflower Film Award" The National Association of Art Houses).' *Han'gyŏrye*, 12 May. Accessed 5 June 2022. https://www.hani.co.kr/arti/culture/movie/944686.html.

Kim, Kyung Hyun. 2002. 'Korean Cinema and Im Kwon-Taek: An Overview.' In *Im Kwon-Taek: The Making of a Korean National Cinema*, edited by David E. James and Kyung Hyun Kim, 19–47, Detroit: Wayne State University Press.

Kim, Kyung Hyun. 2004. *The Remasculinization of Korean Cinema*. Durham, NC: Duke University Press.

Kim, Kyung Hyun. 2011. *Virtual Hallyu: Korean Cinema of the Global Era*. Durham, NC: Duke University Press.

Kim, Kyung Hyun. 2020. 'K-Pop.' In *InfoKorea: An Essential Guide For Educators*, edited by the Understanding Korea Project, 76–93. Sŏngnam, Academy of Korean Studies.

Kim, Mee-hyun (Kim Mi-hyŏn). 2007. 'Trends in the Structure of the Korean Film Industry.' In *Korean Cinema: From Origins to Renaissance*, edited by Kim Mee-hyun, 413–9. Seoul: Communication Books.

Kim Mi-hyŏn, Kim Nan-suk, Song Kyu-bong, Kim Hyŏn-su and Ryu Hyŏng-jin. 2004. *Yesul yŏnghwagwan chiwŏnchŏngch'aek yŏn'gu* (A study of policy towards supporting specialist art houses). Seoul: KOFIC.

Kim, Millim. 2011. 'The Role of the Government in Cultural Industry: Some Observations from Korea's Experience.' *Keio Communication Review* 33: 163–82.

Kim Seung-Kuk. 2000. 'Changing Lifestyles and Consumption Patterns of the South Korean Middle Class and New Generations.' In *Consumption in Asia: Lifestyle and Identities*, edited by Beng Huat Chua, 61–81. London: Routledge.

Kim Soyoung (So-yŏng). 1996. 'Sinep'iliawa nekŭrop'illia' (Cinephilia and necrophilia). *Munhwagwasahoe* 9, no. 3:1051–69.

Kim, Soyoung. 2005. '"Cine-mania" or Cinephilia: Film Festivals and the Identity Question.' In *New Korean Cinema*, edited by Chi-Yun Shin and Julian Stringer, 79–95. Edinburgh: Edinburgh University Press.

Kim Sang-man. 2006. 'Kŭttae, kŭ yŏngwajapchidŭl' (That time, and those film magazines). *Mijiŏ onŭl* (Media Today), 24 May. Accessed 16 April 2022. http://www.mediatoday.co.kr/news/articleView.html?idxno=46765.

Kim, Sunah. 2007a. 'Jangsangotmae and the Struggle to Screen *Night before the Strike*.' In *Korean Cinema: From Origins to Renaissance*, edited by Kim Mee Hyun, 331–2. Seoul: Communication Books.

Kim, Sunah. 2007b. 'Art Film Exhibition: From Videotheques to Art Film Theaters.' In *Korean Cinema: From Origins to Renaissance*, edited by Kim Mee Hyun, 345–6. Seoul: Communication Books.

Kim Ŭn-hyŏng. 2006. 'Yesul.dongipyŏnghwagwan 10nyŏn ch'imch'eggŭt 'hŭimangch'atgi' (Finding Hope at the end of a 10-year period of stagnation in arts and independent cinemas). *Han'gyŏrye*, 7 April.

Kim Yŏng-ch'ang. 2001. 'Kaegwan iljunyŏn majun haip'ŏt'aek nada kŭkjang' (The Hypertheque Nada Cinema is one year old). *Max Movie*, 25 August. Accessed 2 May 2020. https://news.maxmovie.com/1257/.

Kim, Young-jin. 2007. *Korean Film Directors: Lee Chang-dong*. Seoul: KOFIC.

Kim, Young-jin. 2019. 'A Review of Korean Cinema in 2019: The Enormous Success of Parasite, and the Shadow of Polarization.' In *Korean Film Report 2019*, edited by KOFIC, 8–15. Busan: KOFIC.

Kim Yu-rim. 2022. 'Halliudŭ yŏnghwa, chŏn segye ch'oech'o' Han'guksŏ kaebonghanŭn iyu' (The reason why Hollywood releases movies in South Korea first). *Money S* (Daum Media), 18 January. Accessed 24 January 2022. https://movie.v.daum.net/v/20220118134841395.

KMPPC (Yŏnghwajinhŭngkongsa). 1988. *Han'gukyŏnghwayŏn'gam 1988* (Korean film yearbook 1988). Seoul: Tongmyŏnch'ulp'ansa.

KMPPC. 1989. *Han'gukyŏnghwayŏn'gam 1989*. Seoul: Tongmyŏnch'ulp'ansa.

KMPPC. 1990. *Han'gukyŏnghwayŏn'gam 1990*. Seoul: Tongmyŏnch'ulp'ansa.

KMPPC. 1991. *Han'gukyŏnghwayŏn'gam 1991*. Seoul: Saehanchŏngp'ansa.

KMPPC. 1992. *Han'gukyŏnghwayŏn'gam 1992*. Seoul: Chŏngmunsa.

KMPPC. 1993. *Han'gukyŏnghwayŏn'gam 1993*. Seoul: Chŏngmunsa.

KMPPC. 1994. *Han'gukyŏnghwayŏn'gam 1994*. Seoul: Saehanchŏngp'ansa.

KMPPC. 1996. *Han'gukyŏnghwayŏn'gam 1996*. Seoul: Chipmundang.

KMPPC. 1997. *Han'gukyŏnghwayŏn'gam 1997*. Seoul: Chipmundang.

KMPPC. 1998. *Han'gukyŏnghwayŏn'gam 1998*. Seoul: Chipmundang.

KMPPC. 1999. *Han'gukyŏnghwayŏn'gam 1999*. Seoul: Chipmundang.

KOFA. 2021. *KOFA Cinematheque*. Accessed 19 June 2021. https://www.koreafilm.or.kr/cinematheque/search#none.

KOBIS. 2020. Official website. Accessed 19 June 2020. https://www.kobis.or.kr/kobis/business/stat/offc/findYearlyBoxOfficeList.do.

KOFIC (Yŏnghwajinhŭngwiwŏnhoe). 2000. *Han'gukyŏnghwayŏn'gam 2000*. Seoul: Chipmundang.

KOFIC. 2005. 'Korean Film Industry for the Last 10 Years.' *Korean Film Industry Guide 2005*. Seoul: KOFIC/Lee Choong-jik.

KOFIC. 2006. 'Chagŭn Yŏnghwadŭrŭi hŏbŭrŭl mandŭlgo sipda' (I want to make a hub for small films). *Next Plus* 1, 12 April.

KOFIC. 2012. *Han'guk yŏnghwa yŏn'gam 2012 nyŏn top'an*. Seoul: Communication Books.

KOFIC. 2014. *Han'guk yŏnghwa yŏn'gam 2014 nyŏn top'an*. Pusan: Sanzini Books.

KOFIC. 2019. *Han'guk yŏnghwa yŏn'gam 2019 nyŏn top'an*. Pusan: Sanzini Books.

KOFIC. 2021. *Han'guk yŏnghwa yŏn'gam 2021 nyŏn top'an*. Pusan: Sanzini Books.

KOFIC. 2022a. '2022 nyŏnyesulyŏnghwajŏnyonggwan unyŏngjiwŏn saŏp simsagyŏlgwa kongji' (Announcement of the outcome of the annual review of the operational support plan for art houses). 11 March. Accessed 13 May 2022. https://www.kofic.or.kr/kofic/business/prom/promotionBoardDetail.do?seqNo=13334.

KOFIC. 2022b. 'Yŏngwhajinhŭngwiwŏnhoe pŭllaengisŭt'ŭ t'ŭkpyŏrwiwŏnhoe charyoshil' (KOFIC blacklist select committee archives). Accessed 11 April 2022. https://www.kofic.or.kr/kofic/business/board/selectBoardList.do?boardNumber=381.

Kuhn, Annette. 2002. *An Everyday Magic: Cinema and Cultural Memory*. London: Bloomsbury.

Kukkabŏmnyŏngbosent'ŏ. 2020. (National legal statistical information centre): http://www.law.go.kr/ (in Korean). Accessed 8 May 2020. http://www.law.go.kr/%EB%B2%95%EB%A0%B9/%EC%98%81%ED%99%94%EB%B0%8F%EB%B9%84%EB%94%94%EC%98%A4%EB%AC%BC%EC%9D%98%EC%A7%84%ED%9D%A5EC%97%90%EA%B4%80%ED%95%9C%EB%B2%95%EB%A5%A0.

Kwon Seung-Ho and Joseph Kim. 2013. 'From Censorship to Active Support: The Korean State and Korea's Cultural Industries.' *The Economic and Labour Relations Review* 24, no. 4: 517–32.

Kwŏn So-yŏng. 2021. 'Taegu yesulyŏngwajŏnyonggŭkchang Tongsŏngat'ŭhol naenyŏnbut'ŏjamjŏng hyugwan' (From next year onwards, the Taegu art film specialist theatre Dongsung Art Hall will be temporarily closing). *Nok'ŏt nyusŭ*, 12 November. Accessed 24 December 2021. https://www.nocutnews.co.kr/news/5656358.

Kyŏnghyang Sinmun. 1995. 'Tongsang sinemat'aek hugyŏnin mochip' (Search for financial backers for the Dongsung Cinematheque). 12 December.

Lee, Hyunseon, ed. 2022. *Korean Film and Festivals: Global Transcultural Flows*. London: Routledge.

Lee, Sangjoon. 2018. 'The South Korean Film Industry.' Lecture delivered at Melbourne Metropolitan Korean Studies Seminar Series, Monash University, 10 May.

Lee, Sang-yong. 2015. 'Overview of Korean Film Industry in 2015.' In *Korean Cinema 2015*, edited by KOFIC, 5–16. Pusan: Sanzini Books.

Lee, Sun-Hwa and Ahn Min-hwa. 2003. 'The Kim Ki-young Revival: An Interview with Chung Sung-ill.' *The House of Kim Ki-young*. Accessed 30 April 2021. https://web.archive.org/web/20031209005842/http://www.asianfilms.org/korea/kky/KKY/What-Saw/CSIINT.htm.

Lee, Namhee. 2006. 'The South Korean Student Movement: *Undongkwŏn* as a Counterpublic Sphere.' In *Korean Society: Civil Society, Democracy and the State*, edited by Charles K. Armstrong, 96–121. London: Routledge.

Lee Woo-suk. 2006. 'The Subculture of Second-run Theaters.' In *A History of Korean Cinema: From 1970s through 1990s*, edited by Kim Mee-hyun, 256–8. Korean Film Archive, Seoul: Universe and People.

Lee, Hyang-jin. 2000. *Contemporary Korean Cinema*. Manchester: Manchester University Press.

Lee, Kee-hyeung. 2007. 'Looking Back at the Cultural Politics of Youth Culture in South Korea in the 1990s: On the "New Generation" Phenomenon and the Emergence of Cultural Studies.' *Korea Journal of Communication Studies* 15, no. 4 (November): 47–79.

Lee Yeon-ho. 2007. 'The 3S Policy and Erotic Films.' *Korean Cinema: From Origins to Renaissance*, edited by Kim Mee Hyun, 277–9. Seoul: Communication Books.

Lee, Yong-kwan. 2000. '"Nouvelle Renaissance" of Korean Cinema.' Introduction to *Korean Cinema 2000*, edited by KOFIC, 10–21. Seoul: KOFIC.

McHugh, Kathleen and Nancy Abelmann, eds. 2005. *South Korean Golden Age Melodrama, Gender, Genre, and National Cinema*. Detroit: Wayne State University Press.

Maliangkay, Roald. 2014. 'The Popularity of Individualism: The Seo Taiji Phenomenon in the 1990s.' In *The Korean Popular Culture Reader*, edited by Kyung Hyun Kim and Yougmin Choe, 296–313. Durham, NC: Duke University Press.

Maliangkay, Roald. 2022. *Pictori, Korean Media Library*. Australian National University Korean Studies. Accessed 8 April 2022. https://pictori.anu.edu.au/tags/%EA%B7%B9%EC%9E%A5-%EA%B0%84%ED%8C%90.

Massey, Doreen. 1994. *Space, Place and Gender*. Minneapolis: University of Minnesota Press.

MBC. 1995. 'MBC Njujŭ Tudei' (MBC News today). *MBC* (Munhwa broadcasting company). 10 November. Accessed 9 April 2022. https://www.youtube.com/watch?v=MvIWvU8v0hY.

Min, Eunjung, Jinsook Joo and Han Ju Kwak. 2003. *Korean film, History, Resistance and Democratic Imagination*. Westport: Praeger.

Mobrand, Erik. 2019. *Top-Down Democracy in South Korea*. Seattle: University of Washington Press.

Mohedas, Sonia Duenas. 2022. 'The Evolution of South Korean Cinema in the Festival Network.' In *Korean Film and Festivals: Global Transcultural Flows*, edited by Hyunseon Lee, 41–59. London: Routledge.

Mun Chae-ch'ŏl. 2011. 'Yŏnghwajajŏng kyŏnghŏmyangsikŭrosŏ han'gung shinep'ire taehan yŏn'gur 50nyŏndaeesŏ 70nyŏndaekkajirŭl chungshimŭro' (A study of the cinematic experiences of Korean cinephiles, between the 1950s and 1970s). *Yŏnghwayŏn'gu* 47: 113–38.

Na Che-gi, Kang Hŭi-wŏn, Kang Yu-jin. 2008. 'K'ŏbŏŭ sŭt'ori. Yesulyŏnghwa chŏnyonggwan 'saekdarŭm kamdong chaemi sangyŏngchung' (Cover Story: screening what is uniquely moving and interesting). *Han'guk Ilbo*, 5 December. Accessed 18 May 2020. https://www.hankookilbo.com/News/Read/200812050459940535.

Na Che-gi. 2013. 'Yesulyŏnghwa pulmojie myomok simgo k'iun "Paekdudaegan."' (Baekdudaegan which planted and grew the seeds on an infertile ground). *Han'guk Ilbo*, 12 September. Accessed 12 May 2020. https://www.hankookilbo.com/News/Read/201309121213081978.

Nam, In-young. 2007. 'Korean Women Directors.' In *Korean Cinema: From Origins to Renaissance*, edited by Kim Mee Hyun, 161–8. Seoul: Communication Books.

Nam Ŭn-ju. 2011. 'Choman'gan tashi mannayo – kaegwan 11nyŏn mane tongsungdong yesulyŏnghwa chŏnyonggwan haep'ŏt'aeknada' (We'll meet again – the art house Hyperthèque Nada is leaving Dongsungdong after eleven years). *Cine 21*, 27 June.

Neale, Steve. 1981. 'Art Cinema as Institution.' *Screen* 22, no. 1: 11–39.

Neale, Steve. 2013. 'Hollywood Blockbusters: Historical Dimensions.' In *Movie Blockbusters*, edited by Julian Stringer, 47–61. London: Routledge.

O'Brien, Margaret. 2018. 'The Rise of Art Cinema in Postwar Film Culture: The Exhibition, Distribution and Reception of Foreign Language Films in Britain 1945–1968.' Unpublished PhD dissertation, Birkbeck College, University of London.

O Sang-hwan. 2000. '20 segi kŏlchak, kusip nyŏndae hwachechak' (Twentieth-century masterpieces and much talked about films of the 1990s). *Oh My News*, 18 December. Accessed 24 March 2000. http://star.ohmynews.com/NWS_Web/OhmyStar/at_pg_m.aspx?CNTN_CD=A0000027708#cb.

Paek Sŭng-ch'ang. 2011. 'Hyp'ŏt'aek nada' majimak sangyŏng ... yesulyŏnghwaŭi mek'a mun datda' (The last screening at the Hypertheque Nada ... the Mecca for art film is closing). *Kyŏnghyang Sinmum*, 3 July. Accessed 2 May 2020. http://news.khan.co.kr/kh_news/khan_art_view.html?art_id=201107032100595.

Paek, Hal-lyang. 2009. 'Yŏnghwasa Paekdudaegani Kwanghwamunŭi myŏngso ssinaek'yubŭ ddŏnanda' (The film company Baekdudaegan is leaving its well-known location at the Cinecube in Kwanghwamun). Blog. Accessed 25 March 2020. http://blog.naver.com/PostView.nhn?blogId=100clooney&logNo=10067285443&parentCategoryNo=&categoryNo=2&viewDate=&isShowPopularPosts=false&from=postView.

Paquet, Darcy. 2001. 'Going to the Movies in Korea.' Accessed 12 July 2020. http://koreanfilm.org/movies.html.

Paquet, Darcy. 2009. *New Korean Cinema: Breaking the Waves.* London: Wallflower Press.

Paquet, Darcy. 2016. 'Review of Korean Films: A Year to Remember.' In *Korean Cinema 2016*, edited by KOFIC, 7–14. Pusan: KOFIC.

Paquet, Darcy. 2018. 'Review of Korean Films: A Year of Surprises.' In *Korean Cinema 2018*, edited by KOFIC, 7–14. Pusan: KOFIC.

Parc, Jimmyn. 2017. 'The Effects of Protection in Cultural Industries: the Case of the Korean Film Policies.' *International Journal of Cultural Policy*. 23, no. 5: 618–63.

Parc, Jimmyn and Patrick A. Messerlin. 2021. *The Untold Story of the Korean Film Industry: A Global Business and Economic Perspective*. Switzerland: Palgrave Springer.

Park A-na. 2014. 'From Caligari to Cinephile: 1990nyŏndae yesuryŏnghwa tamnon B(kŭp) yŏnghwa kamsŏng karojirŭgi' (From Caligari to Cinephile: embracing art film discourses and love for B-movies). *Yŏnghwa Yesul Yŏn'gu* 25: 57–96.

Park Chae-hyŏng. 2021. 'Tongsŏngat'ŭhol'chonp'yegallimgil..chiwŏnch'aek maryŏnhaeya' (The Dongsung Art Hall is at a crossroads and a support package must be prepared). *MBC News* (Taegu), 4 October. Accessed 24 December 2021. https://dgmbc.com/article/kjDDCtyODbpUdyqtxE?fbclid=IwAR1WMkgNUUFnpWeOZ3hIhPsyrEwwGrbvMRxa5vXk4qAknRmFYcX6TUnfuw8.

Park Kyŏng-man. 2013. 'Yŏnghwa ch'ŏnanham chŏn'gung kaebongt'tchinshirŭn mwŏlkka' (The movie 'Cheonan' opens nationwide, but what is the true story?) *Han'gyŏrye*, 5 September. Accessed 3 January 2022. https://www.hani.co.kr/arti/culture/movie/602387.html.

Park Mi-yŏng. 2008. 'Ilbonindiyŏnghwa suyongŭl t'onghae pon han'guk yosŏnggwan'gaegŭi munhwajŏngch'esŏng – (chu)sŭp'onjient'iŭi p'aendŏmmunhwarŭl chungsimŭro (A study of the cultural identity of Korean female audiences who consume Japanese independent film – focussing on fans at the Sponge House). Unpublished MA dissertation, Chungang University.

Park, Nohchool. 2008. 'A Cultural Interpretation of the South Korean Independent Cinema Movement, 1975–2004.' Unpublished PhD dissertation, University of Kansas.

Park, Nohchool. 2009. 'The New Waves at the Margin: a Historical Overview of South Korean Cinema Movements 1975–84.' *Journal of Japanese and Korean Cinema* 1, no. 1: 45–63.

Park, Seung Hyun. 2002. 'Film Censorship and Political Legitimation in South Korea: 1987–1992.' *Cinema Journal* 42, no. 1: 120–38.

Park, Young-a. 2015. *Unexpected Alliances: Independent Filmmakers, the State, and the Film Industry in Post-authoritarian South Korea*. Stanford, CA: Stanford University Press.

Parkinson, David. 2013. 'Andrei Tarkovsky's *The Sacrifice* – To Sleep, Perchance to Dream?'. *Movie Mail*, 27 July. Accessed 20 April 2022. https://web.archive.org/web/20131213233740/http://www.moviemail.com/blog/foreign-classics/1623-Andrei-Tarkovsky-s-The-Sacrifice-To-Sleep-Perchance-to-Dream/.

Pulver, Andrew. 2019. 'Bong Joon-ho's Parasite Wins Palme d'Or at Cannes Film Festival.' *The Guardian*, 26 May. Accessed 23 April 2020. https://www.theguardian.com/film/2019/may/25/bong-joon-hos-parasite-wins-palme-dor-at-cannes-film-festival.

Pyŏn Hŭi-jun. 2019. 'Chongno k'oat'ŭhol & Chonggakk'oaat'ŭhol & Chonggak p'ianogil pesŭk'illabinsŭ' (Chongno Core Art Hall & Chonggak Core Art Hall & Chonggak Piano Street Baskin Robins). Blog, 23 April. Accessed 5 May 2022. https://m.blog.naver.com/takeda7777/221520325744.

Rayns, Tony. 1998. 'Cinephile Nation.' *Sight and Sound* 8, no. 1: 24–7.

Richard, Jacques. 2005. *Henri Langlois: Phantom of the Cinematheque* (Le fantôme d'Henri Langlois, Jacques Richard, 2005, France).

Robinson, Michael. 2005. 'Contemporary Cultural Production in South Korea: Vanishing Meta-Narratives of Nation.' In *New Korean Cinema*, edited by Chi-Yun Shin and Julian Stringer, 15–31. Edinburgh: Edinburgh University Press.

Robinson, Michael. 2007. *Korea's Twentieth Century Odyssey: A Short History*. Honolulu: Hawai'i University Press.

Shackleton, Liz. 2010. 'Global Stars attend 15th Pusan International Film Festival.' *Screen Daily*, 8 October. Accessed 25 November 2021. https://www.screendaily.com/global-stars-attend-15th-pusan-international-film-festival/5019164.article.

Shim, Doo-bo. 2011. 'Whither the Korean Film Industry?'. *Acta Koreana* 14, no. 1 (June): 213–27.

Shin, Kang-ho. 2007a. 'Small-scale Theater Culture and the Popularisation of Videos.' In *Korean Cinema: From Origins to Renaissance*, edited by Kim Mee Hyun, 306–7. Seoul: Communication Books.

Shin, Kang-ho. 2007b. 'The Cultural Center Generation and the Growth of Film Buff Culture.' In *Korean Cinema: From Origins to Renaissance*, edited by Kim Mee Hyun, 258–60. Seoul: Communication Books.

Shin, Kang-ho. 2007c. 'In Search of New and Alternative Cinema.' In *Korean Cinema: From Origins to Renaissance*, edited by Kim Mee Hyun, 295–300. Seoul: Communication Books.

Shin, Kang-ho. 2007d. 'Globalization: Awards at International Film Festivals.' In *Korean Cinema: From Origins to Renaissance*, edited by Kim Mee Hyun, 295–7. Seoul: Communication Books.

Shin, Jeeyoung. 2005. 'Globalisation and New Korean Cinema.' In *New Korean Cinema*, edited by Chi-Yun Shin and Julian Stringer, 51–63. Edinburgh: Edinburgh University Press.

Shin, Chi-Yun and Julian Stringer. 2005. *New Korean Cinema*. Edinburgh: Edinburgh University Press.
Shin, Chi-yun and Julian Stringer. 2007. 'Storming the Big Screen: The *Shiri* Syndrome.' In *Seoul Searching: Culture and Identity in Contemporary Korean Cinema*, edited by Frances Gateward, 55–73. Albany, NY: State University of New York Press.
Shoji, Kaori. 2017. 'As it Approaches 50, Iwanami Hall Remains Vital to Cinema Lovers.' *The Japan Times*, 4 May. Last accessed 27 March 2020. https://www.japantimes.co.jp/culture/2017/05/04/films/approaches-50-iwanami-hall-remains-vital-cinema-lovers/#.Xn1g1Igza70.
Sight and Sound. 2022. British Film Organisation. Accessed 6 May 2022. https://www2.bfi.org.uk/news-opinion/sight-sound-magazine/advertise-sight-sound-magazine#:~:text=Dating%20back%20to%201932%2C%20it's,love%20film%20and%20film%20culture.
Sŏ Chŏng-min 2020. 'Pudi chigyŏ chuseyo ... maegbak kkŏjŏ kanŭn tongnipyesulyŏnghwagwan' (Please protect me ... an independent art house whose pulse is fading). *Han'gyŏrye*, 21 May. Accessed 30 June 2020. http://www.hani.co.kr/arti/culture/culture_general/945797.html.
Sohn, Jie-ae. 1997. 'Korean Student Group Shrinks after Protest Deaths.' CNN, 13 July. Accessed 12 May 2022. http://edition.cnn.com/WORLD/9707/13/korea.students/.
Sohn, Jung Yeon. 2012. '24 Frames a Second: The Cosmopolitan Cinephilia of South Korean College Students.' Unpublished PhD dissertation, University of Illinois at Urbana-Champaign.
Sohn, Jung Yeon Josie. 2022. *Campus Cinephilia in Neoliberal South Korea: A Different Kind of Fun*. Cham, Switzerland: Palgrave/Springer.
Son Chin-a. 2014. 'M+kihoek ... 'mubikkollaju' 2. Yi Wŏn-jae pŭrogŭraemŏ 'tayangsŏnghwarŭl poda ch'in'gŭnhage' ('M+ Planning ... Movie Collage 2. Programmer Yi Wŏn-jae: 'making diversity films more friendly'). *Maeil Kyŏngje*, 20 October.
Son, Min-ho. 2014. 'After Travel Rules Relaxed, Koreans Took to the Skies.' *JoongAng Daily*, 14 January. Accessed 27 March 2020. http://koreajoongangdaily.joins.com/news/article/article.aspx?aid=29834452.
Sŏng Ha-hun. 2014. 'Ŭiji innŭn yesulyŏnghwagwan taesin taegiŏp mŏltip'ŭleksŭrani' (You're telling me it's a large multiplex instead of willing art house). *Oh My News*, 8 December. Accessed 14 April 2022. http://star.ohmynews.com/NWS_Web/OhmyStar/at_pg.aspx?CNTN_CD=A0002033360.
Sŏng Ha-hun. 2015. 'Yŏngjinwiga hŏrakhan yŏnghwaman? Chiwŏnin'ga, kŏmyŏlin'ga' (Only Movies Allowed by KOFIC? Is this support or is it censorship?). *Oh My News*, 30 January.
Sŏng Ha-hun 2020a. 'Bong Joon-hoŭi sŏngjang ... yŏgil ppaenok'o iyagi hagin ŏryŏpta. (Han'gukyŏnghwaundong 40nyŏn- 6: chakŭnyŏnghwa undongŭi chungshime sŏttŏn yŏnghwamadanguriwa yŏnghwagonggan1895. It's hard to discuss the development of Bong Joon-ho without considering this. The Korean Film Movement after 40 years, no. 6. Yŏnghwamadanguri and Yŏnghwagonggan1895 which stood at the vanguard of the short film movement.) *Oh My Star*, 25 February. Accessed 23 December 2021. http://star.ohmynews.com/NWS_Web/OhmyStar/at_pg.aspx?CNTN_CD=A0002614326.

Sŏng Ha-hun. 2020b. 'Yŏngjang ŏmnŭn p'illŭm kangt'are hangŭihaja yŏnhaengt'tshinemat'ek'ŭŭi sunan (han'gukyŏnghwaundong 40nyŏn shinemat'ek'ŭ tajin yŏnghwagonggan1895-ssiangssie-munhwahakkyo Seoul. Arrested after protesting the confiscation of films during raids conducted without warrants: The ordeal of the Videotheques. The Korean Film Movement after 40 years, no. 18 Yŏnghwagonggan1895, SA-Sé, Munhwahakkyo Seoul that laid the foundations of videotheques). *Oh My News*, 13 November. Accessed 23 December 2021. https://news.nate.com/view/20201012n38603.

Sŏng Ha-hun. 2020c. '"Yŏjadŭlkkiri moyŏsŭni," kŭ mare punnohaekko tokhaejŏtta. (Han'gugyŏngwaundong 40nyŏn_17) Yŏsŏngyŏngsangjiptan parit'oro sijaktoen yŏsŏngyŏngwaundong' ('It's just a bunch of women', hearing those words made me both angry and stronger. The Korean Film Movement after 40 years, no. 17) The Women's film movement which started with the women film making collective Parit'ŏ). *Oh My Star*, 17 September. Accessed 7 April 2022. http://star.ohmynews.com/NWS_Web/OhmyStar/at_pg.aspx?CNTN_CD=A0002649825.

Sŏng Ha-hun. 2020d. '"Yŏngwa mandŭrŏttago taegongbunsillo" kwŏllyŏgŭi t'anabi sijaktwaetta' (Han'gugyŏngwaundong 40nyŏn 9) ch'ŏngnyŏn yŏngwain kusoksik'in 'P'arangsae sagŏn'kwat'aehagyŏngwayŏnhap kyŏlsŏng' (We heard that you made a film . . . . this was when the suppression of the authorities began. The Korean Film Movement after 40 years, no. 9. The formation of the University Film Collective and the '*Bluebird* Incident.') *Oh My Star*, 9 April. Accessed 7 April 2022. http://star.ohmynews.com/NWS_Web/OhmyStar/at_pg.aspx?CNTN_CD=A0002629766.

Sŏng Ji-yŏn. 2015. 'Yesulkŭjang Ssinaek'odŭ sŏnjaerŭl ttŏnabomyŏ' (The art film theatre Cinecode Sonjae is leaving). *The Fact*, 12 November. Accessed 10 May 2020. http://news.tf.co.kr/read/entertain/1602028.htm.

Song Chun. 1997. '"Shinema chiok" moranaenŭn chŏlmŭn kŭkchang' (The young theatre driving out 'cinema hell'). *Sisa Journal*, 13 November. Accessed 9 April 2022. https://www.sisajournal.com/news/articleView.html?idxno=115319.

Song Seun-hyun. 2022. 'Korean Theatre Association Urges Government Aid Amid Covid-19.' *Korea Herald*, 25 January. Accessed 13 April 2022. http://www.koreaherald.com/view.php?ud=20220125000785.

Sontag, Susan. 1996. 'The Decay of Cinema.' *New York Times Magazine*, 25 February. Accessed 29 May 2020. https://www.nytimes.com/1996/02/25/magazine/the-decay-of-cinema.html.

Sorensen, Clark. W. 2011. 'Rural Modernization under the Park Regime in the 1960s.' In *Reassessing the Park Chung Hee Era, 1961–1979: Development, Political Thought, Democracy and Cultural Interest*, edited by Hyung-a Kim and Clark W. Sorensen, 145–66. Seattle: University of Washington Press.

Standish, Isolde. 1994. 'Korean Cinema and the New Realism: Text and Context.' In *Colonialism and Nationalism in Asian Cinema*, edited by Wimal Dissanayake, 65–89. Bloomington: Indiana University Press.

Statista. 2020. 'South Korean Average Annual Salaries.' Accessed 21 December 2020. https://www.statista.com/statistics/557759/south-korea-average-annual-wage/#:~:text=The%20average%20monthly%20income%20in,50%20to%2059%20years%20old.

Statista. 2021. 'Cinema Attendances in South Korea.' Accessed 19 June 2021. https://www.statista.com/topics/5764/cinemas-in-south-korea/#dossierKeyfigures.

Tudor, Andrew. 2006. 'The Rise and Fall of the Art (House) Movie.' In *The Sociology of Art: Ways of Seeing*, edited by David Inglis and John Hughson, 125–38. London: Palgrave.

Twomey, John E. (2002 [1956]). 'Some Considerations on the Rise of the Art-Film Theater (1956).' In *Moviegoing in America*, edited by Gregory A. Waller, 259–62. Oxford: Blackwell.

Wilinsky, Barbara. 1996. '"A Thinly Disguised Art Veneer Covering a Filthy Sex Picture": Discourses on Art Houses in the 1950s.' *Film History* 8, no. 2: 143–58.

Wilinsky, Barbara. 2001. *Sure Seaters: The Emergence of Art House Cinema*. Minneapolis: University of Minnesota Press.

Wimmer, Leila. 2014. 'Modernity, Femininity and Hollywood Fashions: Women's Cinephilia in 1930s French Fan Magazines.' *Film, Fashion and Consumption* 3, no. 1: 61–76.

Yecies, Brian. 2007. 'Parleying Culture against Trade: Hollywood's Affairs with Korea's Screen Quotas.' *Korea Observer* 38, no. 1 (Spring): 1–32.

Yecies, Brian and Aegyung Shim. 2016. *The Changing Face of Korean Cinema: 1960 to 2015*. London: Routledge.

Yi Chu-hyŏn. 2019. 'Seoulkukjeyŏsŏngch'angjakjibdan parit'ŏ, parit'ŏ samsip chunyŏnŭi ŭimirŭl malhada' (Seoul International Women's Festival. Discussing the significance of the women's filmmaking collective Parit'ŏ 30 years after its formation). *Cine 21*, 18 August. Accessed 27 December 2021. http://m.cine21.com/news/view/?mag_id=93851.

Yi Hu-gyŏng. 2013. 'Kŭ tŭrŭn ŏjjihayŏ Kwanghwamune moyŏ yŏnghwarŭl pogye twoeŏtna – Ssinek'yubŭŭi sallimggun t'ikaesŭtŭe kwanhan ŭnmilhan pogosŏ' (Why on earth do they come to Kwanghwamun to watch a movie? – a private report on the housewives and characters that make up the clientele at the Cinecube). *Cine 21*, 10 March.

Yi Hye-in. 2015. 'Chach'e sŏnjŏng chakp'um sangyŏnggwanman chiwŏn' Yŏngjinwi yesulyŏnghwasaŏp ilbang kanghaeng' (Only Movie Theatres it selects are Supported' ... KOFIC unilaterally Enforces Art Film Business). *Kyŏnghyang Sinmun*, 22 July. https://m.khan.co.kr/view.html?art_id=201507222134505.

Yi Hyŏn-ju. 2014. 'Special Report: Chagŭn yŏnghwagwanŭi iyu inŭn pallan' (Special Report: The reason for the revolt of the small cinemas). *Han'guk Kyŏngje Maegŏjin*, 14 March. Accessed 4 May 2020. http://magazine.hankyung.com/apps/news?popup=0&nid=0&nkey=2014031300953000111&mode=sub_view.

Yi Kang-yun. 1997. 'Yesulyŏnghwagwan 1ho "Tongsŭng sinemat'aek"' (The first officially designated art house, Dongsung Cinematheque). *Munhwa Ilbo*, 16 April.

Yi Kyu-ch'ang. 2004. 'K'oa atŭ hol p'yegwan 'suikŭn kwoench'ananŭnde . . .' (The closure of the Core Art Hall: 'The profits were ok but . . .'). *Star News*, 18 November.

Yi Nam. 1996. 'Yesulyŏnghwa chŏnyongkwan kŭrŏndaero sŏnggong- "Tongsung sinemat'aek" kaegwan ilnyŏn p'yŏngga' (An evaluation of the success of the first year of the dedicated art film cinema Dongsung Cinematheque) *Chungang Ilbo*, 19 November.

Yi Nam. 1997. 'Tongsung sinemat'aek sangyŏng yŏnghwa "yesulyŏnghwa" injŏng nollanildŭt' (Possible controversy over what constitutes an art film at the Dongsung Cinematheque). *Chungang Ilbo*, 11 March. Accessed 7 June 2020. https://news.joins.com/article/3420409.

Yi Sŏng-uk. 1996a. 'Kwan'gaekdongwŏn sŏnggong, munhwahwaldong silp'ae' (We succeeded in getting audiences in, but our cultural activities disappointed). *Han'gyŏrye*, 16 November.

Yi Sŏng-uk. 1996b. 'Yesulyŏnghwa chŏnyongkwan sŏsŏhi bburi.' (The dedicated art-house film cinema is gradually establishing its roots). *Han'gyŏrae*, 16 November.

Yi Sŏn-ju (Lee Sun Joo). 2014. 'Saeroun yŏnghwa ilgiŭi chaean hokŭn pip'anjŏk sinaep'iliaŭi hyŏngsŏng. 1990 nyŏndae Han'guk yŏnghwaesŏ Munhwahakkyo Sŏulŭi hwaldongdŭl' (Towards a new reading of film or the formation of a critical cinephilia, focusing on the activities of Seoul Cultural School within 1990s Korean film culture). *Yŏnghwa Yŏngu* 3: 223–52.

Yi Sŏn-ju. 2017. 'Yŏngwa(*Kino*)ŭi sidae–yŏngwajapchi <k'ino>wa 1990nyŏndae 'pip'anjŏk sinep'illia'ŭi munhwajŏngch'i' (The age of film – the film magazine *kino* and 1990s cultural politics and critical cinephilia). *Taejungsŏsayŏn'gu* 23, no. 3: 415–52.

Yi Tae-hyŏn. 2001. 'Kaegwan 1 chunyŏn mannŭn 'ssinaek'ubŭ Kwanghwamun' 'yesulyŏnghwagwan' charijabatda.' (Celebrating the first anniversary of its opening, the Cinecube Kwanghwamun has really found its place). *Han'guk Ilbo*, 8 November.

Yi Tae-hyŏn. 2009. 'Paekdudaegan Yi Kwang-mo.' *Han'guk Ilbo*, 13 August. Accessed 2 May 2020. https://www.hankookilbo.com/News/Read/200908132314563421.

Yi Yŏng-jin. 2010. 'Ch'oe Chŏng-un: kwan'gaegŭi ttŭkwa hamkkye ujik'age kanda. Sinemat'ek'ŭ chŏnyonggwan kongmo kŏbuhan sŏurat'ŭsinema ch'oejŏngun taepyo' (I go along with what the audience wants and try to be honest. Ch'oe Chŏng-un, managing director of Seoul Art Cinema who refused to participate in the call for a designated specialist cinematheque). *Cine 21*, 5 March. Accessed 10 April 2022. http://www.cine21.com/news/view/?mag_id=59930.

Yi Yŏng-hun. 1998. 'Sinsadonge kojŏn yŏnghwa chŏnmum 'ojŭ' naedal kaegwan' (Next month a classic film specialist cinema "Oz" opens in Sinsadong). *Han'guk Kyŏngje*, 10 December. Accessed 6 May 2020. https://www.hankyung.com/life/article/1998121000551.

Yi Yŏng-jae. 1998. 'Arŭmdaun sijŏl - naŭi saldŏn kohyangŭn' ('Beautiful season [Spring in My Hometown] – in the town where I lived). *Kino* (November): 174–81.

Yonhap. 2015. 'Kungnae ch'ŏt yesulyŏnghwajŏnyonggwan, ssinaek'odŭ sŏnjae taŭm tal p'yegwan' (The first domestic art film specialist cinema, CineCode Sonje is closing next month). *Yonhap News*, 28 October. Accessed 10 May 2020. https://www.youtube.com/watch?v=CZkYgAF76Z8.

Yu, Gina (Yu Chi-na). 2007a. 'The Beginning of Hollywood Direct Distribution and Resistance.' In *Korean Cinema: From Origins to Renaissance*, edited by Kim Mee Hyun, 303–6. Seoul: Communication Books.

Yu, Gina. 2007b. 'Defend the Screen Quota System!' In *Korean Cinema: From Origins to Renaissance*, edited by Kim Mee Hyun, 346–9. Seoul: Communication Books.

Yu Mi-na appa. 2015. 'Eiriŏn 2 tugaji pŏjŏnŭro tŭ kt'emhaettŏn kŭkchanggaebongsi yŏngwak'adŭ' (Two versions of *Aliens 2* movie cards). Blog, 27 September. Accessed 1 May 2022. https://m.blog.naver.com/PostView.naver?isHttpsRedirect=true&blogId=2wan2&logNo=220492955019.

Appendix 1

Exhibition schedules of Core Art Hall (1990–3) and Lumiere theatre (1993)
 Source: KMPPC 1991: 104–30; KMPPC 1993: 120–64; KMPPC 1994: 97–100: 111–54; Cho 1993; Chŏn 2020.
 Fr: France, ROK: South Korea, Ch: China, HK: Hong Kong.

Core Art Hall exhibition schedule, 1990–3

		1990		
Theatre	Movie	Length of run		Attendance
		From	To	
Core Art Hall Auditorium 1	*My Nights Are More Beautiful Than Your Days* (Mes Nuits sont plus belles que vos jours; Andrzej Zulawski, 1989, Fr)	1/26-	2/9	8,941
	Private Lessons 2 (?)	3/10	3/23	7,947
	The Unbearable Lightness of Being (Philip Kaufman, 1988, US)	4/14		4,500
	All That Falls Has Wings (Ch'urakhanŭn kŏsŭn nalgaega itta, Chang Kil-su, 1990, ROK)	4/28		3,500
	Blood and Sand (Sangre y arena, Javier Elorrieta, 1989, US/Spain)	6/9		4,200
	Cyrano de Bergerac (Jean-Paul Rappeneau, 1990, Fr)	7/14		3,700
	Mosquito Coast (Peter Weir, 1986, US)	8/11	8/24	4,411
	Elvira Madigan (Bo Widerberg, 1967, Sweden)	8/25		2,200

	Papillon (Franklin J. Schaffner, 1973, US/Fr)	9/29	10/19	12,625
	Deep Night in Capri 2 (Appuntamento in Nero, Antonio Bonifacio, 1990, Italy/Germany)	11/3	11/5	1,572
	The Woman Who Walks On Water (Mulwirŭl kŏdnŭn yŏja, Park Ch'ŏl-su, 1990, ROK)	11/17		1,400
	Ghost (Jerry Zucker, 1990, US)	11/24		15,000
Auditorium 2	*The Officer with a Rose* (Dejan Šorak, 1987, Croatia)	7/28	8/10	2,790
	Cinema Paradiso (Giuseppe Tornatore, 1988, Italy)	8/25	9/28	24,990
	Wild Orchid (Zalman King, 1989, US)	9/29		2,900
	Ju Dou (Zhang Yimou, Yang Fengliang, 1990, Ch)	10/20		2,500
	Papillon (Franklin J. Schaffner, 1973, US/Fr)	10/20	10/29	4,030
	Deep Night in Capri 2	11/6	11/16	2,789
	Total filmgoers for the year			110,950

1992				
Core Art Hall Auditorium 1	*The Little Mermaid* (Ron Clements, John Musker, 1989, US)	91/12/21	92/2/7	53,726
	In Bed with Madonna (Alek Keshishian, 1991, US)	1/25	2/14	13,665
	Henry V (Kenneth Branagh, 1989, UK)	2/15	21	2,307
	The Lover on the Bicycle (Chajŏngŏŭl t'ago on yŏin, Yŏn T'aewan, 1992, ROK)	2/29	3/20	863
	Curly Sue (John Hughes, 1991, US)	3/21	4/24	41,795
	The Return of Martin Guerre (Le Retour de Martin Guerre, Daniel Vigne, 1982, Fr)	4/25	5/8	5,967
	Deceived (Damian Harris, 1991, US)	5/9	29	6,254
	Delicatessen (Jean-Pierre Jeunet, Marc Caro, 1991, Fr)	5/30	7/10	52,077
	Indochine (Régis Wargnier, 1992, Fr)	7/11	9/25	96,761
	Life on a String (Biān zŏu biān chàng, Chen Kaige, 1991, Ch)	9/5	24	11,776
	The Umbrellas of Cherbourg (Les Parapluies de Cherbourg, Jacques Demy, 1964, Fr)	9/26	11/6	25,467

Auditorium 2	*Valmont* (Miloš Forman, 1989, US/Fr)	11/21	12/11	14,566
	The Little Mermaid (Ron Clements, John Musker, 1989, US)	91/12/21		70,586
Auditorium 3	*Purple Noon* (Plein Soleil, René Clément, 1960, Fr)	9/26	10/30	11,074
	Jeux Interdits (Forbidden Games, René Clément, 1952, Fr)	9/26	10/30	21,174
	Sorrow, Like a Withdrawn Dagger, Left my Heart (Kasŭme todnŭn k'allo sŭlp'umŭl chalgo, Hong Ki-sŏn, 1992, ROK)	11/7	20	1,845
	All the Mornings of the World (Tous les Matins du Monde, Alain Corneau, 1991, Fr)	11/21	12/11	11,800
	Total			437,691

1993

Core Art Hall Auditorium 1	*Fried Green Tomatoes* (Jon Avnet, 1991, US)	92/12/12	93/1/31	55,000
	Time of the Gypsies (Dom za vešanje, Emir Kusturica, 1988, Yugoslavia)	2/6	3/12	35,305
	The Blue in You (Kŭ taeanŭi pŭllu, Yi Hyŏn-sŭng, 1992, ROK)	2/13	3/5	5,500
	Last of the Mohicans (Michael Mann, 1992, US)	3/6	12	
	Jacob's Ladder (Adrian Lyne, 1990, US)	3/13/	4/9	31,608
	Howard's End (James Ivory, 1992, UK, Japan, US)	4/10	5/27	43,569
	Wings of Desire (Der Himmel über Berlin, Wim Wenders, 1987, West Germany, Fr)	5/15	6/4	19,738
	Savage Nights (Les Nuits Fauves, Cyril Collard, 1992, Fr)	6/5	7/16	39,676
	The Visitors (Les Visiteurs, Jean-Marie Poiré, 1993, Fr)	7/3		27,635
	Mediterraneo (Gabriele Salvatores, 1991, Italy)	7/31	9/24	63,562
	The End of a Short Trip (JJalbŭn yŏhaengŭi ggŭt, Yu Kŏn-jo, 1992, ROK).	9/11	24	287
	The Piano (Jane Campion, 1993, New Zealand, Australia, Fr)	9/25	12/23	16,9714
	Two Men in Town (Deux Hommes dans la Ville, Jean-Jacques Tarbes, 1973, Fr)	11/13	12/3	6,050

Auditorium 2	*Farewell my Concubine* (Bà Wáng Bié Jī, Chen Kaige, 1993, Ch/HK)	12/24	31	17,309
	Raise the Red Lantern (Dà Hóng Dēnglong Gāogāo Guà, Zhang Yimou, 1991, Ch, HK, Taiwan)	1/1	12	8,729
	Our Twisted Hero (Uridŭl ŭi ilkŭrŏjin yŏngung, Park Jong-won, 1992, ROK)	3/27		3,500
	Made in America (Richard Benjamin, 1993, US)	7/17	30	6,056
	Deux (Claude Zidi, 1989, Fr)	8/14	27	7,309
	Blind Side (Geoff Murphy, 1993, US)	8/28	9/10	5,733
	Early Rain (Ch'ou, Chŏng Chin-u, 1966, ROK)	9/4		950
	Cinema Paradiso (Giuseppe Tornatore, 1988, Italy)	12/4		9,500
	Total			525,580

Lumiere exhibition schedule, 1993

Lumiere	*Fried Green Tomatoes* (Jon Avnet, 1991, US)	1/1	21	925
	Taxi Blues (Taksi-Blyuz, Pavel Lungin, 1990, Russia)	1/22	2/5	767
	Fried Green Tomatoes	2/4		3,980
	Alive (Frank Marshall, 1993, US)	5/15		1,550
	Like Water for Chocolate (Como Agua Para Chocolate, Alfonso Arau, 1992, Mexico)	6/5	18	705
	The Raffle (La Rifa, Francesco Laudadio, 1991, Italy)	6/12	25	706
	The Gunrunner (Nardo Castillo, 1989, US)	6/26	7/1	390
	Love at First Sight (Liebe auf dem ersten block, Rudolf Thome, 1991, Germany)	7/17	8/5	1,422
	Prague (Ian Sellar, 1992, UK)	8/7	9/2	921
	The End of a Short Trip (Jjalbŭn yŏhaengŭi kkŭt, Yu Kŏn-jo, 1992, ROK)	9/7	11	93

Film			
Crush (Alison Maclean, 1992, New Zealand)	10/16	22	82
Cinema Paradiso (Giuseppe Tornatore, 1988, Italy)	11/20	12/31	6,473
Madame Bovary (Claude Chabrol, 1991, Fr)	12/24	1/21	1,033
Time of the Gypsies (Dom za vešanje, Emir Kusturica, 1988, Yugoslavia)	2/20		625
Raising Cain (Brian De Palma, 1992, US)	4/17	30	1,391
Howard's End (James Ivory, 1992, UK, Japan, US)	5/15		735
Dragon: The Bruce Lee Story (Rob Cohen, 1993, US)	6/26	7/1	696
An Abyss of Freedom (En Afgrund Af Frihed, Peter Eszterhas, 1989, Denmark)	7/3	8	45
Warlock: The Armageddon (Anthony Hickox, 1993, US)	7/10	15	561
Indecent Proposal (Adrian Lyne, 1993, US)	7/17		660
Blown Away (Brenton Spencer, 1993, US)	8/14	26	284
Farewell my Concubine (Bà Wáng Bié Jī, Chen kaige, 1993, Ch/HK)	12/24	31	2,247
Folks (Ted Kotcheff, 1992, US)	92/12/25	1/20	422
Sweet Emma Dear Böbe (Édes Emma, drága Böbe- vázlatok, aktok, István Szabó, 1992, Hungary)	1/22	2/19	3,030
The Blue in You (Kŭ taeanŭi pŭllu, Yi Hyŏn-sŭng, 1992, ROK)	2/20		560
Swordsmen in Double Flag Town (Shuāngqízhèn dāokè, He Ping, 1991, Ch)	3/13	19	120
Midnight Heat (Sunset Heat, John Nicolella, 1992, US)	3/27	4/2	334
Raise the Red Lantern (Dà Hóng Dēnglong Gāogāo Guà, Zhang Yimou, 1991, Ch, HK, Taiwan)	4/10	23	231
Interceptor (Michael Cohn, 1992, US)	4/24	30	29
Max and Jeremie (*Max et Jérémie*, Claire Devers, 1992, Fr)	5/1	14	5

The Return of Casanova (Le Retour de Casanova, Édouard Niermans, 1992, Fr)	5/28	6/4	255
The Nutt House (Adam Rifkin, 1992, US)	6/19	7/1	1,148
The 101st Proposition (Paekhanbŏnjjae p' ŭrop'ojŭ, O Sŏk-gŭn, 1993, ROK)	7/17		365
Cop and a Half (Henry Winkler, 1993, US).	8/7	12	237
Total			33,027

Appendix 2

Screenings of domestic and foreign films compared at four Seoul theatres, 1993–9

Sources: KMPPC 1994: 97–100, 111–54; KMPPC 1996: 107–11, 123–77; KMPPC 1998: 103–7, 121–87; KMPPC 1999: 106–8, 115–88; Chŏn 2020.

The Core Art Hall

Year	Total Korean films	Total films	Korean film audience nos	Total audience nos	Average audiences/film	Korean films as percentage	Korean film audiences as percentage
1993	3	21	10,237	**525,580**	2,047	14%	2%
1995	2	22	17,038	**499,704**	8,519	9%	3.4%
1997	5	23	12,262	**485,881**	2,452	21%	2.5%
1998	1	33	22,240	**308,365**	9,340	3%	7%

Lumiere

Year	Total Korean films	Total films	Korean film audience nos	Total audience nos	Average audiences/film	Korean films as percentage of total	Korean film audiences as percentage
1993	3	33	1,018	**33,027**	339	9%	3%
1995	2	23	508	**50,019**	254	8%	1%
1997	12	65	20,786	**141,676**	1,732	18%	14%
1998	7	52	24,250	**148,461**	2,855	13%	16%

Dongsung Art Centre (including the Dongsung Cinematheque)

Year	Total Korean films	Total films	Korean film audience nos	Total audience nos	Average audiences/ film	Korean films as percentage	Korean film audiences as percentage
1993	1	10	3,011	**208,954**	3,011	10%	14%
1995	2	39	16,604	**424,414**	8,302	5%	39%
1997	8	29	84,200	**346,162**	10,525	27%	24%
1998	9	41	79,127	**298,927**	7,290	22%	26%

Cinehouse

Year	Total Korean films	Total films	Korean film audience nos	Total audience nos	Average audiences/ film	Korean films as percentage	Korean film audiences as percentage
1993	8	99	38,594	**993,858**	4,824	8%	4%
1995	6	81	69,239	**866,828**	11,540	7%	8%
1997	25	96	134,032	**1,074,186**	11,189	26%	12%
1998	20	104	123,940	**960,788**	9,238	19%	13%

Appendix 3

Film survey

The book's analysis is partially based on an online survey titled 'Memories of Art Film and Art Houses' I conducted between December 2020 and May 2021, in which I sought out regular or former art film fans in South Korea and enquired about their memories and experiences of watching art film theatrically. Fifty-three respondents were asked in Korean about how they first gained an interest in art film and where they watched art film most regularly. They were also asked about their most memorable experiences while watching art film, whether they maintained an interest in art film consumption, and how they related to and interacted with specific exhibition spaces.

The aim of the survey was to gain insights into the experiences and memories of regular art film viewers within specific sites of exhibition and explore how these spaces helped create a film culture that impacted audience perceptions of cinema.

Link **to Translation of questions**
Link **to summary of results (in Korean)**

Index

Allen, Robert C., 6, 12
anti-Americanism, 18, 32, 36; see also
    minjung
art film, 1–10, 14–16, 24–5, 32, 38, 41,
    48, 63, 73, 81–2, 97–101, 109, 113,
    126, 135, 143–5, 149, 151, 167,
    176–7, 197, 200, 212
    boom in the US/UK, 117
    cinephilia, 22
    declines in consumption, 153–6,
        160–6, 168–70, 182, 188, 236
    definition/understandings, 1, 16–20,
        86–7, 150–1, 178, 180, 182–5
    early screenings in 1980s, 85–7,
        87–90, 231
    eroticism, 94
    European films, 17, 93–4, 204, 234
    festivals, 18, 139–42
    film as art vs film as activism *see*
        cinephilia
    importation and distribution,
        98–100, 114–17, 136–8, 155, 181,
        184, 186, 190, 231
    Korean art films, 150, 155, 161, 182
    Korean audiences, 201, 210
    Korean women's consumption,
        104–8, 201
    mixed programming strategy, 89
    motivations for watching, 70–1
    multiplexes, 187, 212, 219
    nostalgia in art film, 209–11, 234
    opposition, 18, 216–8, 238–9
    state protection, 151–2, 176–84,
        187–95, 238–9
    videotheque screenings, 70–1
Art House Momo (cinema), 201
    audiences, 210
    institutional identity, 205–7
art houses, 1–6, 24–5, 32, 102, 113,
    116, 175
    art halls and early development, 85–9
    audiences, 104–6, 135, 201–3,
        213–24
    business model, 98, 136–9, 166–8,
        203–11, 233
    COVID-19 challenge, 194–5
    criticisms, 164–6
    declining audiences, 153–70, 181,
        188
    definition, 19–20
    educational role, 122, 164, 203–6,
        230
    European films, 70
    influence of film clubs, cultural
        centres and videotheques, 54–5, 59,
        77–9, 81–2
    in US and UK, 117, 127
    independent vs multiplex, 200,
        211–13, 216–19, 239
    institutional identity, 12–13, 17, 54,
        96, 139, 151, 161, 170, 212, 224,
        230, 233
    link to Korean festivals, 139–44,
        160–1

link to print media, 122–3, 139–44, 232, 238
nostalgia, 209–11, 220–2, 224
outside Seoul, 138–9, 185
programming, 13, 90, 128, 161–2, 182, 185–6, 189–90, 204–5, 234
significance in Korea, 7–10, 124, 141–3, 178–80, 196, 201, 220–4, 236–8
small theatres law, 48–9, 231
space, 11–12, 98, 206–9, 213–16, 225, 232
tensions with state, 150–3, 181–5, 187–94, 196
women (spectators and exhibitors), 104–6, 107, 109–10
see also Core Art Hall, Dongsung Cinematheque, Hoam Art Hall, Hypertheque Nada
Art Plus (cinema network), 180–5, 217
aims, 180, 196
problems, 181–2, 184–5, 191
Asian Financial Crisis, 9, 24, 149, 153, 154, 156, 167, 169, 236
atmosphere (*punwigi*), 80, 98, 134, 135, 214–17, 219, 227n, 232

Baekdudaegan, 78, 135, 142, 144, 166, 193,
business structure, 136–8
end of Dongsung cinematheque, 152–3
formation and aims, 114–17, 206–8
role in Dongsung Cinematheque, 124–32
see also Art House Momo, Cinecube
Baumann, Shyon, 10, 11, 122
blacklist scandal, 189–91
Bluebird Incident, 60–1, 63, 80, 231
Bong Joon-ho (director), 79, 157, 190, 221, 223
links to 1990s cinephilia, 160
Bosma, Peter, 11, 127–8, 131, 204
Bourdieu, Pierre, 10–11, 94, 129, 133
Byun Young-joo (director), 62, 118, 165, 180

Cahiers du Cinéma (journal), 80, 107, 119–20
Cannes Film Festival, 18, 70, 88, 100, 114, 115, 118
censorship, 36–9, 42, 48, 55, 60, 63, 71, 76, 128, 137, 152, 156, 189, 230
1996 repeal of censorship, 63, 189
CGV (multiplex), 155–6, 168, 217–19
opening of art houses, 187, 191, 211, 212,
chaebol, 40, 44
involvement in film, 50, 117, 155
links to dictatorship, 34
sponsorship of arts, 87
see also CJ, Daewoo, Lotte, Samsung
Changsan'gonmae (filmmaking group), 62–3, 67, 118
chedogwŏn chinip (sell out), 163
chedogwŏn, 43, 67, 75, 80, 82, 104, 108, 112n, 133, 163, 165, 230, 233, 239
definition, 35
Chŏn Ch'an-il (critic), 78, 123
Chŏng Sŏng-il (critic), 3, 16, 55, 59, 70, 217–18, 220
Chongno (Seoul), 45, 66, 92, 97, 100, 106, 216
Chun Doo Hwan, 31, 49, 50, 158
Chungang Ilbo, 116, 136, 150, 151, 165
Chung Ji-young (director), 43, 59
Ch'ungmuro, 42–3, 80, 82, 107, 230 239
Cine-Club *see* cultural centres
Cinecode Sonjae (cinema), 213, 216, 218
Cinecube (cinema), 167–8, 170, 200
audiences, 200, 210, 216
institutional identity, 214, 216
state support, 181–2, 187
Cinehouse (cinema), 91–2, 95–7, 126, 161–2
cinema of disturbance, 128, 151, 170, 182

Cinémathèque Française, 80, 134–5, 221
Cinephilia, 1–10, 12, 15–16, 24–5, 62, 85, 143, 149, 176, 210, 216, 229–39
    academia and learning, 74–6, 130–6, 232
    art films, 70–1, 235
    decline, 149, 163–6
    definition, 1, 21–4
    DIY spirit/DIY culture, 74, 77, 82, 109, 230
    film magazines, 119–22, 202, 231–2
    Korean cinephilia, 101–10, 230
    Korean women, 104–7, 235
    legacy, 142–4, 236–7, 238
    nostalgia (memory of Korean cinephilia), 167, 196, 201, 220–5, 234, 237
    productive character, 79, 106, 235
    rebellious character, 22, 65, 77, 231, 239
    tension between 'art' and 'activism', 58, 108–9, 164–6, 134, 231, 238–9
Cine 21 (magazine), 70, 73, 74, 202, 220
    criticisms of state policy, 175, 180
    establishment and aims, 119–21
    role in promoting cinephilia, 122–3, 231
circles (*tongari*) *see* film clubs
CJ (Chaebol), 155
classic films, 76, 94, 180, 185, 191, 204
Core Art Hall, 49, 59, 96, 103–8, 109, 115, 116, 122, 130, 133, 143, 151, 154
    audiences, 105, 213, 218
    decline, 162, 169, 201, 216
    establishment, model and success, 97–101, 138–9
    programming, 90, 95, 233
    women, 105
COVID-19, 24, 194–5, 200, 219, 224
critics (film), 7, 8, 17–18, 20, 42, 55, 117, 144, 150, 190, 195, 204, 217, 220
    declining influence, 202
    influence on policy, 176–7, 179, 220, 223–5
    links to 1990s cinephilia, 55, 59, 67, 74, 81
    nostalgia, 220, 223–5, 237
    role in developing cinephilia, 123, 130, 144, 232–4
cultural blockade, 36–8, 54, 73, 81
cultural capital, 10, 11, 72, 77, 102, 109, 159, 207
cultural centres (European), 24, 54–9, 74, 81, 85, 87
    audiences, 67, 75, 106
    French Cultural Centre, 55–8, 64, 70, 105, 107
    German Cultural Centre, 55, 64, 77, 97, 106
    links to 1990s cinephilia and festivals, 142, 166, 230–1, 235, 237
    problems, 58, 70
cultural identity, 10, 102, 123, 218–19, 225, 239
curfew, 49

Daewoo, 50, 117, 221
de-authoritarianisation, 36, 39, 51
'The Decay of Cinema' *see* Sontag
dictatorship (1961–87), 3, 31–8, 42, 55, 56, 57, 61, 71, 75, 88, 94, 97, 134, 235, 239; *see also minjung* and cultural blockade
diversity, 143, 153, 158, 222, 234
    film policy, 177–9, 186–9, 191, 194, 196, 201, 238
    programming strategy, 100, 128, 211
DIY culture *see* cinephilia
Dong-a Ilbo, 122, 135
Dongsung Cinematheque, 1–2, 14, 59, 77, 139, 161, 167, 169, 185, 200, 209, 220, 232, 234
    audiences, 104, 215
    decline, 149–53, 163–4
    education, 131–3
    establishment, 122, 124–7, 134–5
    festivals, 142
    financial structure, 136–7
    programming, 125–9, 144

DRFA 365 (cinema), 201
audiences, 210
institutional identity, 204–6, 208

East-West Cinema club *see* cultural centres
Eight Point Declaration, 31, 34
Elsaesser, Thomas, 18, 21–2, 224
'event' status, 72, 88
Ewha Women's University, 59, 62–3, 203, 207

'festival fever', 6, 139, 142; *see also* film festivals
film as activism *see* cinephilia
film as art *see* cinephilia
film clubs (university), 8, 59–70, 117
activism, 60–1, 62–4
activities, 64–6
formation, 59
links with cinephilia, 67–8
film festivals, 5, 6, 17, 43, 204, 235,
BIFF, 113, 139–41
cultural capital, 102
JIFF, 140–1
Korean international film festivals, 139–41
links to art film, 17, 142
links to 1990s cinephilia, 78, 123, 142–3, 162, 179, 238
Montreal International Film Festival, 158
overseas film festivals, 86, 100, 157–9
SIWFF, 106–7
videotheques, 71
women's film festivals, 106, 140
first-run theatres, 49, 87, 93–4, 231
Forbidden Games (film), 56

Godard, Jean-Luc, 17, 56, 80, 127, 134, 142, 162, 235

Han'gyŏrye, 37, 100, 101, 117, 138, 151, 200
Cine 21, 119, 122
'historic compression', 80, 233, 238

Hoam Art Hall, 87–9, 92, 96, 98, 109, 133
Hollywood films, 48, 57, 71, 92–3, 97, 100, 108, 114, 137, 141, 162, 222, 234
influence on Korean film, 216
opening of Korean market and opposition, 7–8, 41–4, 134, 159, 178–9, 237–9
vs art film, 17–19, 21, 86–7, 90, 114, 235
Hong Ki-sŏn (director), 61–2, 67
Hong Sang-soo (director), 157, 158, 169, 222
Hyehwadong (Seoul), 69, 80, 203
Hypertheque Nada (cinema), 63, 107, 181, 184
closure, 201, 213, 217–18, 220, 225
establishment, 166–7, 170
institutional identity, 204–5, 209, 213–5
programming, 204

imports of art film *see* Dongsung Cinematheque financial structure
independent film, 5, 8, 76, 81, 160, 178–9, 186–9, 192, 225
definition, 20–1
Indy Film Theatre (multiplex), 211–12
institution, 10–11, 17, 21, 34, 232, 239
definition, 4–5
see also art houses
institutional identity *see* Art Houses
Italian Neo-realism, 69–70
Iwanami Hall (Tokyo), 97

Jang Sun-woo (director), 43, 67, 157
June Uprising, 31–2, 59, 61
Jung Ji-youn (academic, critic), 221–2

Kaidu (filmmaking group), 62, 207
Kang Kyoung Lae (academic), 15, 51, 71–5
Kangnam (Seoul), 91, 92, 99, 107, 162, 216
Kersten, Father Kevin, 64–6

Kim Dae Jung, 34, 36, 179, 209
Kim Dong-won (director), 20, 43
Kim Hong-jun (scholar), 7, 55–6, 135
Kim Ki-duk (director), 157, 158, 182, 222
Kim Ki-yŏng (director), 161
Kim Nan-suk (exhibitor, distributor), 14, 63–6, 81, 103, 107–8, 116, 120–1, 139, 181, 184, 193, 204, 217, 235
Kim Sŏng-uk (exhibitor), 3, 14, 69–70, 77, 104
Kim Young-jin, (critic, academic), 15, 51, 68, 70, 72, 77, 97, 124, 128, 121–2, 223–4
Kim Young Sam, 24, 34–5, 50
Kino (magazine), 75, 119
  celebration of Korean cinema, 160
  closure, 202
  criticisms, 164–5
  links to cinephilia, 120–3, 217, 220, 231
  mission and character, 107, 120, 165, 232–3
KOFIC (KMPCC until 1999), 5, 16, 21, 78, 87, 161
  blacklist scandal, 189–90
  COVID-19 challenge, 194–5
  establishment of Art Plus/Next Plus, 175–87, 191–3, 217, 237–8
  links with 1990s cinephilia, 78, 123
  multiplexes, 191
  support for space, 191–3, 196–7, 219
Korean Academy of Film Arts, 134
Korean Cinema (publication), 179, 194
Korean National University of the Arts, 123, 134
kwangjang, 111n, 124, 130, 131, 132, 145n, 152, 165
Kwangju Theatre, 181, 184–6
Kwangju Uprising, 24, 32–4, 38, 57, 59, 61, 63, 65
Kyŏnghyang Sinmun, 61, 130, 132, 217

Lee Chang-dong (director), 3, 157, 162, 190, 206, 221–2
Lee Hee-seung (academic), 15, 58, 63–7, 81, 88, 93, 95, 97, 105, 107

Lee Kwang-mo (exhibitor, distributor, director), 3, 8, 14, 48, 70, 78, 96, 114–39, 144, 151, 181–2, 184, 187, 200, 215, 233, 235
Lotte (multiplex), 155, 168
  opening of art houses, 187, 191, 212, 219
Lumiere (cinema), 92, 97, 98, 100, 107, 116, 122, 126
  closure, 216
  programming, 92–5, 143, 161–2

Massey, Doreen, 12, 106
mainstream films *see* Hollywood
Megabox (multiplex), 168, 191, 217, 219
mini-theatres (Japan), 19
Ministry of Culture and Sports, 149
minjung (people's) movement, 20, 32–8, 43, 57–8, 67, 77, 93, 101–2, 103, 119, 129, 134, 179
  links to Korean filmmaking, 43, 61
  links to 1990s cinephilia, 114, 133, 166, 233
mixed programming, 89–98, 107, 126, 161, 233
Motion Picture Law, 52n, 86, 110n; *see also* Screen Quota
Movie Collage (multiplex), 211–12
multiculturalism, 177–8
multiplexes, 3, 25, 45, 91, 143, 168, 175, 184, 189, 203, 204, 210, 225
  connections to 1990s cinephilia, 79
  opposition, 216–9, 225, 239
  popularity, 155–6, 180, 200
  threat to art houses, 168–9, 210–12
Munhwahakkyo Seoul (videotheque), 14, 68–71, 73, 75, 78, 209
The Murmuring (film), 118, 180

NAAC (National Association of Art Houses), 193
New Generation (*sinsedae*), 40
New Wave (Korean), 43, 59, 67, 107, 143, 157, 159
New Wave (Nouvelle Vague), 55, 70, 71, 80, 107, 134

Next Plus (cinema network), 196
  aims, 181, 185–7
  problems, 191–3
The Night Before the Strike (film), 63
1988 Olympics, 31, 85, 140
noraebang, 39, 44–5
Nordpolitik, 86
Nostalgia (film), 1, 115, 126, 128, 167
nostalgia *see* art film; art houses; cinephilia; critics

OTT, 202

Parasite (film), 6, 25, 223
Parit'ŏ (film club), 62, 106, 165
Park Chan-wook (director), 67, 130, 176, 221, 223
  links to cinephilia, 67
Park Chung Hee, 32, 55
Park Geun-hye, 189, 193
Park Kwang-su (director), 43, 67, 157
platform release, 27n, 71
pornography, 42, 67
Post-cinema, 202, 224
Premiere (magazine), 119, 202
programmers and programming, 19, 78, 123, 184, 26n, 71, 115, 125–9, 144, 151–3, 156, 163, 170, 182, 184–6, 195, 203–5, 212, 219, 224, 232, 236
  cinema of disturbance, 128, 151, 170, 182, 232
  conflict over programming, 151, 182–3, 187, 189, 192, 196
  vs schedulers, 11, 13
  see also mixed programming
Project Cheonan Ship (film), 189–90
punwigi see atmosphere
Pyŏn Chae-ran (director, academic), 61–2, 67

Rayns, Tony (critic), 141, 143–4, 238
Renaissance (cinema), 91
rituals (of moviegoing), 13, 21, 220
Roadshow (magazine), 70, 119, 123
rock cafes, 39, 67, 95
Roh Moo-hyun, 221

Roh Tae Woo, 31, 34–5, 37, 50, 85
Rome Open City (film), 69, 117–18

The Sacrifice (film), 137, 144
  The Sacrifice Incident, 113–18, 130, 145, 180, 196, 220, 231–2
  video release, 117–18
samizdat, 33, 77
Samsung, 50, 87, 221
Sanggyedong Olympic (film), 20, 65
SA-Sé (videotheque), 68, 71, 73, 76, 78–9, 107
Screen Quota System (SQS), 8, 41
Seo Taiji and Boys, 39
Seoul Art Cinema, 3, 14, 69, 78, 201, 208
  institutional identity, 203–6
Seoul Film Collective (film club), 59–61, 63, 67
Seoul National University, 59
Sewol ferry disaster, 189
Shiri (film), 156–7, 159, 163, 169, 176–7
Sight and Sound (magazine), 71, 119, 120
Sim Yŏng-sŏp (critic), 123
'slippage', 23
slogan (of cinemas), 83n, 90, 129, 209
small theatres (policy), 49, 231
sociality of moviegoing, 13, 103–4, 202, 214–6, 219, 224, 236
Sogang University, 59
  Communication Centre, 64–5
Son Chu-yŏn (exhibitor, producer), 71, 76, 78, 106, 235
Sontag, Susan, 1–2, 16, 21, 101, 103, 211, 225, 237
specialist art film theatre, 124, 149–51; *see also* Dongsung Cinematheque
specialist film, 153
  definition, 178, 181, 187, 191, 196, 232
spectatorship, 57, 102, 109, 135, 215, 219, 222
spirit of the times (*sidaejŏngsin*), 3, 166
Spring in My Hometown (film), 14, 114, 156–7, 161, 167

Stranger than Paradise (film), 127, 128, 136, 209
subculture, 220
subtitles, 136
  problems, 48, 58, 65–6, 69, 77, 132, 205

The Taegu Dongsung Art Hall, 15, 189, 199n
Taehangno (Seoul), 1, 92, 213
taste, 1, 11–12, 18, 23, 102, 130, 143–4, 234, 236
television, 22, 37, 44–5, 50, 66, 69, 77, 81, 137, 202
386 (democratic) generation, 36, 39–40, 129
3-S policy, 42
tojejedo (master-apprentice system), 42
Truffaut, Francois, 22, 80, 108
The Tusŭp (cinema), 208

undongkwŏn see minjung
University Film Collective (film club), 61–2

video/VCR/VCD, 22, 33, 44–5, 50, 65, 76–7, 103
  video stores, 44, 117
videotheques, 24, 54, 68–82, 85, 103, 139, 141–2
  audiences, 103–4, 230
  connection with success of Korean cinema, 79–80
  education and training, 72–4, 122–3, 232
  festivals, 70–2
  formation, 68
  illegal activities, 76–7, 231
  links with cinephilia, 166, 201, 209, 224
  problems and decline, 78, 97, 100, 102, 109, 114, 145, 163–4
  programming, 70
  women, 106

Waranago Incident, 119, 175–8, 180, 186, 195, 231, 237
'well-made', 87

Yallasang, 59–60, 67, 124
Yi Hyo-in (critic), 60, 67, 78
Yi Ŏn-gyŏng (exhibitor, filmmaker), 68–70, 74, 78, 82, 106, 235
  foundation of videotheques, 68
Yi Yŏng-jae (critic, academic), 122, 123
Yim Soon-rye, 157, 177; *see also* Waranago
Yŏnghwagonggan 1895 (videotheque), 68–71, 72, 74, 76, 78–9, 80, 106–7
  links to success of Korean film, 79
Yŏnghwamadang'uri (film club), 59–60
Yŏnghwaŏnŏ (journal), 74
Yonsei University, 59, 61
Yu, Jonathan (exhibitor, director), 15, 200, 204–6, 210

EU representative:
Easy Access System Europe
Mustamäe tee 50, 10621 Tallinn, Estonia
Gpsr.requests@easproject.com

www.ingramcontent.com/pod-product-compliance
Lightning Source LLC
Chambersburg PA
CBHW050210240426
43671CB00013B/2284